Mark Schmitt
British White Trash

Culture & Theory | Volume 154

Mark Schmitt is a postdoctoral Stuart Hall Fellow at TU Dortmund University, where he teaches British Cultural Studies. His research interests include British and Irish literature and film, cultural theory as well as discourses of social and racial abjection.

Mark Schmitt

British White Trash

Figurations of Tainted Whiteness in the Novels of Irvine Welsh, Niall Griffiths and John King

[transcript]

This book was accepted as an inaugural dissertation at the Faculty of Philology at Ruhr-University Bochum in 2016.

The completion of the manuscript was funded with a grant by the FAZIT Foundation (FAZIT Stiftung).

Bibliographic information published by the Deutsche Nationalbibliothek

The Deutsche Nationalbibliothek lists this publication in the Deutsche Nationalbibliografie; detailed bibliographic data are available in the Internet at http://dnb.d-nb.de

Cover layout: Maria Arndt, Bielefeld
Cover illustration: Jonathan Schöps / photocase.de
Typeset by Michael Rauscher, Bielefeld
Printed by Majuskel Medienproduktion GmbH, Wetzlar
Print-ISBN 978-3-8376-4101-1
PDF-ISBN 978-3-8394-4101-5

Contents

Acknowledgements

This book is a slightly revised version of my doctoral thesis submitted at the Faculty of Philology at Ruhr-University Bochum. I am indebted to a number of people without whom the present book would not be the same. First, I would like to thank my supervisors Anette Pankratz and Sarah Heinz for their support and encouragement throughout the years of writing. Their academic advice and feedback as well as their help during critical phases and beyond the call of duty have been invaluable.

This book took shape during my employments at the English Departments at the University of Mannheim and TU Dortmund and was significantly influenced by their respective intellectual and academic environments. I would like to thank my colleagues in Mannheim and Dortmund for their support and for providing an inspiring working atmosphere. In particular, I would like to thank the Dortmund team of British Cultural Studies for having my back during the final months of writing: Julia Becker, Marie Hologa, Christian Lenz, Sophia Möllers, Cyprian Piskurek and Gerold Sedlmayr. I would like to thank Ariane de Waal, Johannes Fehrle, Kai Fischer, Evangelia Kindinger, Igor Krstić and Solvejg Nitzke for patiently and competently commenting on my drafts, for suggestions, inspiring in-depth discussions and for their friendship.

Conferences, colloquia and workshops in Bochum, Leuven, Leeds, London, Mannheim and Maynooth offered the opportunity to present and discuss the results of my research. I am particularly indebted to John Brannigan, Shona Hunter and Clive James Nwonka for sharing their expertise and offering crucial suggestions during these occasions. I would also like to thank Niall Griffiths for providing me with material in the final phase of writing as well as for his kindness and intellectual generosity.

During my time as a B.A. and M.A. student at the Departments for English and Comparative Literature at Ruhr-University Bochum, I was lucky to meet instructors whose guidance proved to be instrumental in my decision to move forward with my ideas for a doctoral research project. For their support and mentorship, I would like to express my gratitude to Uwe Lindemann, Monika Schmitz-Emans and Claus-Ulrich Viol.

I would like to thank the FAZIT Foundation for supporting my work with a transitional grant during the final stages of writing. I am grateful to Kristie Kachler for the thorough copy-editing (I am solely responsible for all mistakes you might still find in the present book).

Beyond academia, my heartfelt thanks go to my friends who have met both my fits of euphoria as well as bouts of self-doubt and moaning throughout the years with equal patience and empathy: Vilim Brezina, Christof Danielsmayer, Valentin Gube, Celia and Neil Hickey, Marcel de Oliveira, Anika Simon and Andreas Warneke.

Finally, I would like to express my immense gratitude to my family for their unconditional support on all levels: Gabi, Paul-Gerhard and Miriam Schmitt.

Introduction

Whiteness and the C Word

In January 2009, almost a decade after it had commissioned the Parekh Report on the "future of multi-ethnic Britain", the Runnymede Trust published a collection of analyses with the provocative title *Who Cares about the White Working Class?* This question might at the time have prompted the instinctive answer: not too many. As the Runnymede Trust's vice-chair, Kate Gavron, anticipates in her foreword, such a question might surprise readers for a number of reasons. Most importantly, for an organisation which has dedicated its work and its resources to "promot[ing] a successful multi-ethnic Britain by addressing issues of racial equality and discrimination against minority communities" to put their focus on "the grievances of a part of the white majority is not an obvious development" (Gavron 2009: 2). In addition, in a supposedly post-class and post-industrial time, the mere mention of the working class must for many British people seem to be oddly out of touch with contemporary society. In fact, in September 2008, only a few months before the publication of the Runnymede Trust's study, Harriet Harman, then deputy leader of the Labour Party, caused media outrage by mentioning "the c word", as the *Telegraph* contemptuously put it, in an advance script for a talk about the social and economic factors influencing an individual's life chances in contemporary Britain to be held at the Trade Union Conference (Pollard 2008). "The class war is over – do tell Labour", proclaimed the *Telegraph*, and in a knee-jerk reaction to the backlash in public discourse, she eventually skipped the contentious term in her actual talk (Pollard 2008, Sveinsson 2009b: 3). Yet, despite media backlash and criticism of Harman's allegedly anachronistic focus on class, which, as the *Telegraph* venomously commented, supposedly echoed the concerns of "Old Labour" (Pollard 2008), other policymakers have also called attention to class as a decisive factor of social inequality. Similarly, class is increasingly being regarded in its intersections with race and other identity factors such as gender and age in public discourse.

Even before the discourse on the white working class escalated when historian David Starkey reacted to the English riots in August 2011 with the comment that "black gangster culture" was to blame and that the "whites have become black" *(BBC Newsnight)*, speaking about class in Britain had conspicuously retreated to a vocabulary of racialisation. This was most prominently documented in BBC Two's *The White Season*, which aired in early 2008 with the aim "to shine the spotlight on the white working-class in Britain today" *(The White Season)*. Featuring films which examined the origins of xenophobia and cultural alienation amongst the white working class, starting with Enoch Powell's "Rivers of Blood" speech in 1968 and moving on to the growing popularity of the British National Party in the early 2000s, *The White Season*, however, also acknowledged the growing hostility towards the white working class, expressed, as the programme announcement states, in a conspicuous choice of slurs: "As 'white trash' and 'chav' become commonplace insults, the films explore the complex mix of feelings that lead some people to feel under siege and that their very sense of self is being brought into question" *(The White Season)*. *Chav*, a uniquely British term "ordinarily directed towards the white poor" and "[bodying] forth a whiteness polluted by poverty and contaminated by territorial proximity to poor black and migrant populations" (Tyler 2013: 188), emerged in the early 2000s, even though its precise origin is still a matter of debate. Imogen Tyler situates the emergence of the term at "around 2002" (2013: 154). In 2004, the *Oxford English Dictionary* named *chav* the "buzzword of the year" (Tyler 2013: 163), and a drastic increase in the use of the term in British newspapers can be detected around the year 2005, which corresponds with a decline in the use of the term *underclass* during the same period (see Hayward and Yar 2006: 10). Writing in 2008, Imogen Tyler detects the emergence of "a new vocabulary of social class" in Britain in "the last three years" (17) and claims 2004 to be the peak of the press's fascination with the term (21).[1]

The emergence of the *chav* as well as situations of social crisis such as the 2011 English riots have brought issues of class and its intersection with

1 | For further discussion of the etymology of *chav*, see Haywood and Yar 2006: 16; Jones 2011: 7-9.

race back to attention. This is not only evidenced by the wealth of sociological inquiry into the riots and their conditions themselves (see, for instance, Briggs 2011, Tyler 2013: 179–206, Liebig 2014a and 2014b) and by a newly emerging general interest in processes of social abjection (see Tyler 2008, 2013; Nayak 2003, 2009), but also by a return to class issues in British literary studies, as was prominently evidenced in the conference entitled "Whatever Happened to the Working Class? Rediscovering Class Consciousness in Contemporary Literature", held in London in September 2015. Similarly, this new awareness of class in literary studies is present in the recent research on poverty and precarity in contemporary literature which regards the "new poverty" in Britain as a subject of transdisciplinary poverty studies and acknowledges its "[entanglement] with a new discussion about class" and the "neoliberal economy" (Korte/Zipp 2014: 2; see also Korte/Regard 2014a and 2014b). The present book explores contemporary British literature's negotiation of whiteness, class and social abjection to contribute to this emerging area of research, which is situated at the intersection of cultural studies and sociology, class and race studies and literary studies.

The parallels between the British concept of the chavs (or, as they had earlier been called, Charver Kids) and the American concept of white trash have been noted by Anoop Nayak, who compares the shared imagery of abject bodies signifying lower race and class status: "Popular discourses constructed Charvers as a retarded race with deep voices, hunched statures and aggressive, unpredictable attitudes. As a symbol of lower-class urban decline, the Charvers embodied the fears of a community: effectively they are Britain's equivalent to 'white trash'" (2003: 97).[2] The use of the American term *white trash* in a British context, however, appears conspicuous at first glance. Even if one is more prepared than the *Telegraph* and other media outlets or politicians to acknowledge the persistence of class (and the working class in particular) as an important and decisive cultural and economic category in contemporary Britain, one is still left to wonder why the term *white trash* could possibly have adapted in a British cultural context. Did this term – along with related terms and synonyms like *cracker, hick,* and *hillbilly* – not, after all, emerge within a particular set of race and class relations – and not least a system of racial oppression – that is unique to the United States and to its history of slavery as it specifically took shape in the South?

2 | For a further comparison of the terms *white trash* and *chavs*, see Tyler 2008: 25.

In fact, "poor white trash", in its original usage, emerged "[b]y the 1830s" as a new term "for socially downcast whites" in the British colonies of Virginia and North Carolina after it had become commonplace among the colonial authorities and elites to "[deplore] the habits and morals of socially outcast whites" throughout the 1700s (Wray 2006: 22). The "crackers", as they were then called, upset the authorities with their lawlessness, and throughout the eighteenth and early nineteenth centuries the notion of "poor white trash" developed symbolically along the lines of the languages of race and class: "What is striking about reading historical documents of the period then is the similar way in which poor whites, Indians, and blacks are described – as immoral, lazy, and dirty" (Wray 2006: 23). Throughout the twentieth century and especially towards the end of it, the usage of *white trash* as an insult shifted in meaning. While it initially implied a form of whiteness that was "the lowest of the low because socially and economically they have sunk so far that they might as well be black" (Penley 2004: 310) within the racial hierarchy of the South, the phrase is now used predominantly by those people (and especially whites) who want to distinguish themselves from the nation's racist past – that is, the phrase now "conjures images of poor, ignorant, racist whites: trailer park and wife beaters, too many kids and not enough government cheese" (Wray 2006: 1). The connotations of backwardness and degeneracy remain, but they have semantically shifted according to the changes in what one might call with Paul Gilroy (2004) and Vron Ware (2001) the "raciology" of the United States.

The semantic ambivalence is symptomatic of the history of the term (and this, as the research on the term *chav* shows, is one of the structural similarities *white trash* shares with its contemporary British equivalent, *chav*). As the major American studies (Wray 2006 and Hartigan Jr. 2005) on the concept show, researchers struggle with the exact location of its origin as well as with the precise semantic and social context within which it was first used. But even if the term offers "little reliable information about the objective social structures of the times", it is "exemplary of a specific type of symbolic boundary" (Wray 2006: 23) and provides a "vast reservoir of signification" (Hartigan Jr. 2005: 16). Thus, to come back to the question regarding the peculiar cultural transfer of the concept of white trash, it is not necessarily surprising that the term has entered British discourses, for, as John Hartigan Jr. writes, the concept has even within the United States adapted to "complex, mutable social settings"

(2005: 17). Instead, it is far more complicated to answer the question when exactly and why it has entered British usage. But even more importantly, one has to pay attention not only to the term *white trash* itself, for, as the American context shows, the idea signified by the phrase can change over time – and as the emergence of *chav* at the beginning of the twenty-first century shows, British culture has developed its own synonyms and equivalents which, however, point towards a similar semantics of race and class as well as the boundaries and delineations around and within them.

I consider this development as indicative of the fundamentally problematic complexity of current race and class relations in Great Britain. In order to name the conspicuous intersection of race and class that is expressed in concepts like white trash and the chavs, I have chosen to use the term *tainted whiteness* which I adapt from Anoop Nayak (2003: 85). *Tainted whiteness* on the one hand aptly reflects the same "differential meanings of white trash – what it is because of what it is not, a regular down-home version of honey and ashes, the raw and the cooked" (Penley 2004: 309) or, as Matt Wray puts it, "[s]plit the phrase in two and read the meanings against each other: *white* and *trash*. Slowly, the term reveals itself as an expression of fundamental tensions and deep structural antinomies: between the sacred and the profane, purity and impurity, morality and immorality, cleanliness and dirt" (2006: 2). On the other hand, however, *tainted whiteness*, more than the conceptually static if ambivalent dichotomy of "white" (i.e., cleanliness) and "trash" (i.e., dirt), emphasises the processual character of *becoming* rather than *being* trash or tainted. It implies that something is being done to whiteness, that whiteness in itself is not a quality essential to a body or one's behaviour or status, but something which is continually being qualified and produced as a flexible cultural position which is relational and dependent on a number of factors. In paying analytical and theoretical attention to such processes and how they are negotiated in contemporary literature, my thesis is dedicated and indebted to the continuously growing discipline of Critical Whiteness Studies, as I will explain in more detail below.

As a contribution to a text- and, more precisely, literature-centred cultural studies, this thesis combines the theories of Critical Whiteness Studies and the sociology of class with the methodology of literary analysis in order to trace tainted whiteness and its various guises in contemporary British literature. Such a methodologically complex and interdisciplinary approach is necessary in order to do justice to the overlaps and reciprocal relations between the various spheres and discourses that produce classed and raced subject positions. Thus, I take my cue from approaches that operate from a position of intersectionality[3] by contending identities and subject positions cannot be studied by isolating identity categories and privileging one over the other (such as race or gender over class or vice versa), in my analysis of class and whiteness in literary texts. It is my contention that narrative literary texts reflect, negotiate and take part in producing subject positions and identities by acknowledging their complex and sometimes aporetic intersections. An approach to literary analysis which pays attention to such complexities, however, requires a similarly multidimensional theoretical and methodological framework which, as I contend with Korte and Zipp (2014), is in its nature necessarily a transdisciplinary one. As my analyses in this thesis will demonstrate, a literary studies approach which intends to inquire into these intersections must pay minute attention to the various discourses with which literary texts intersect and how they effect, potentially deconstruct and are shaped as cultural products by these discourses. In that, I consider the present study as a cultural materialist[4] reading of literature in the vein of Alan Sinfield's

3 | For an account of the development of intersectionality as the study of multidimensional forms of identity formation and their oppression, see Nash 2008 and Levine-Rasky 2013. There has been much debate about what groups and identities should be the focus of intersectionality theory. While the approach emerged from black feminism and is often limited to the study of multiple forms of oppression (and thus focuses on marginalised groups exclusively), I contend with Cynthia Levine-Rasky that the approach may also be "adapted to conceptualize domination for different groups of white peoples" (2013: 89) and that "steps must be made toward integrating an analysis of whiteness and power" (2013: 105) to account for the "relational positionality" and multidirectional workings of dominance and oppression (2013: 106). In short, intersectionality also needs to account for how different identity vectors constitute privileged and dominant positions (and their relational fluidity), rather than focusing on the oppressed groups alone.

4 | "Cultural materialists investigate the historical conditions in which textual representations are produced, circulated and received. They engage with questions about the relations between dominant and subordinate cultures, the implications of racism, sexism and homophobia, the scope of subaltern resistance, and the modes through which the system tends to accommodate or repel diverse kinds of dissidence. In this approach, the terms 'art' and 'literature' [...] are neither spontaneous nor innocent. They are bestowed by the gatekeepers of the cultural

historicising account of *Literature, Politics and Culture in Postwar Britain* (1997/2004).

This transdisciplinary and cultural materialist approach to literary texts also requires me to carefully situate my research within the field of Critical Whiteness Studies, which, despite having emerged in the late 1980s and therefore being a relatively young research area, bears its own particular intricacies. More precisely, two major points have to be qualified before I provide a brief outline of this thesis. First, the particular relationship of Critical Whiteness Studies as a predominantly US-American discipline to the European-British context of my research must be considered, and secondly, Critical Whiteness studies have to be related to literature, that is, the subject of my research, and the methodologies of literary studies that I employ.

Critical Whiteness Studies and the European-British Context

Fairly early in the development of Critical Whiteness Studies, the difficulties and challenges of transposing the discipline's methodological and theoretical framework from the American context onto the European and, more specifically, British one have been identified.[5] For my thesis, I predominantly take my cue from two explorations of this problem from the beginning of the 2000s: Gabriele Griffin and Rosi Braidotti's essay "Whiteness and European Situatedness" (2002) and Vron Ware's "Perfidious Albion" (2001). Griffin and Braidotti consider Critical Whiteness

apparatus, and should be understood as strategies for conferring authority upon certain representations, and hence upon certain viewpoints" (Sinfield 2004: xxiv).

5 | Given that the field of Critical Whiteness Studies is still permanently evolving, providing a research overview with the claim of being up to date provides a considerable challenge. For a concise overview of the most recent developments, main strands and waves of Critical Whiteness Studies, with a special focus on Europe and the Republic of Ireland, see Heinz 2013; for a comprehensive tentative bibliography of Critical Whiteness Studies across different disciplines until the year 2006, including literary and cultural studies, see the online document *Towards a Bibliography of Critical Whiteness Studies*, edited by the Center on Democracy in a Multiracial Society at the University of Illinois (2006).

Studies and its roots in black American feminism, which brought forth the race-specific differences within what had formerly been constructed as a "universal sisterhood and equality of oppressedness" (2002: 222). This newly raised awareness for intra-group differences, which in this case was the larger group of women for whom different racial backgrounds entailed different experiences of patriarchal oppression, is adapted by Griffin and Braidotti for examining the differentialities in thinking whiteness on a broader scale – that is, an international and intercontinental one. The "spectre of whiteness and its racialized and racializing meanings" (Griffin and Braidotti 2002: 221) has different implications in Europe and Britain than it has in the United States. Although they experienced a "happy embrace" in Europe, Critical Whiteness Studies were at first still conducted in Europe with a predominantly American focus because the

> specificity of the whiteness debate [...] as it was conducted in the first half of the 1990s, enabled Europeans to participate in it without in some respects needing to engage with the whiteness issues that were pertinent to their own actual race-political situation. [...]. The colour casting of the debate, its specificity in analysing a black-white dynamic, spoke to a certain set of race relations and racialized positions but left unacknowledged those racialized positions which could not be drawn in such stark terms, where the issues were not 'black' and 'white' as seemingly suggested by the debate. (Griffin and Braidotti 2002: 225)

That is, European researchers' embrace of the debate was a deflection since "when we deal with issues of race we find it easier to contemplate them as they occur elsewhere than as they come to the surface within Europe itself" (Griffin and Braidotti 2002: 226). Thus, Griffin and Braidotti argue that it is necessary to examine the ontological and epistemological bases for racism in European countries by looking at the continent's history of scientific racism as it emerged in the nineteenth and early twentieth century.

This necessitates the critical rethinking of the perceived biological ontology of whiteness as a mere matter of skin colour. Most prominently, Griffin and Braidotti argue, the Holocaust committed by Nazi Germany had historically shown that even while the Germans imagined themselves as Aryans who were "validated in their superiority biologically by their skin colour, 'white'", whiteness "in and of itself was not a sufficient or determining factor, for if it had been why send communists, homosexuals, gypsies and Ashkenazi Jews to the gas chambers?" (2002: 226). Whiteness as a mere biological factor becomes thus insufficient as a concept and must be rethought, including a thorough deconstruction and reconceptualisation of 'race' as a biological fact:

> the black-and-white dynamic, whilst offering a symbolic opportunity to analyse power relations determined by biological markers, leaves untouched the whole issue of diversity among groups seemingly of one colour, the intra-group differences that account for many of the most serious racial and ethnicized conflicts in Europe. (Griffin and Braidotti 2002: 227)

Moreover, a biological approach to race "leaves untouched the extent to which biology is culture, and must be read as such" (Griffin and Braidotti 2002: 227). This is one of the premises guiding my study of tainted whiteness in the British context, for it is not necessarily the case that the figurations of tainted whiteness presented in the literary texts I examine relate to biology or the notion of 'race' as an ontologically given fact. Rather, they exhibit the cultural mechanisms – the semiotic practices, performances, contexts and qualifying factors – which determine whiteness and non-whiteness[6] as cultural positions which might rely on the symbolism of skin colour, but are not confined to it. In fact, the very notion of white trash or tainted whiteness – the idea that whiteness as the property of an individual or group can be corrupted by certain factors – is the test case for conceptions of whiteness as something that is ontologically stable. Contrary to these conceptions, whiteness seems to be constantly in motion, or, as Sarah Heinz argues, in the process of becoming (2013: 3)[7], and thus,

6 | Throughout this study, I will occasionally use the term *non-white*. I share Richard Dyer's reluctance to do so since "[t]his is problematic because of its negativity, as if people who are not white only have identity by virtue of what they are not" (1997: 11). However, I will use this term within certain contexts in order to specifically make visible, distinguish and highlight particular forms of whiteness and its often normative and hegemonic character.

7 | It is important, however, to not consider "becoming" as synonymous with "fluid and contingent" in the sense that Steve Garner has criticised as one of the "pitfalls" of Whiteness Studies. In such extreme approaches, "[t]he element of cultural choice is emphasised to the exclusion of the material (or structural) parameters on people's agency, to give the idea of people opting in and out of

if examined critically, tainted whiteness enables the denaturalisation of whiteness as a "location of structural advantage, of race privilege" and as a "set of cultural practices that are usually unmarked and unnamed" (Frankenberg 1993: 1).

The systematic destabilisation of a presumed ontology of whiteness ties in with Vron Ware's suggestion to conceive of whiteness as an "interconnected global system" (2001: 184). Ware proposes the analogy of pollution in order to approach whiteness:

> The image of pollution is more suitable because it is a product of the destructive and exploitative nature of industrial capitalism; it may be produced in one place, but its effects are not containable by cultural or political borders. It is possible to organize against the causes and effect of pollution on local, national, and international levels; but unless there is concerted effort from producers, consumers, governments and law enforcers, the measures taken will have minimal impact on the environmental devastation that is taking place day by day. (2001: 184)

Ware's approach to whiteness as a global system which takes into consideration the persistent power of the nation as a category of political and ideological organisation corresponds to Griffin and Braidotti's argument that European whiteness studies have to take into consideration the "conflation between ethnicity, culture and national identity" (2002: 229).

While Griffin and Braidotti perceive the "critical deconstruction of *whiteness*" in a "historical correlation" with "the crisis of postmodernity, exemplified in the crisis of European identity [and] the decline of the European nation-state" (2002: 233), Ware similarly emphasises the particular tensions between British national identity and the national-cultural identities of Britain's composite nations, England, Wales and Scotland, in the postcolonial and post-imperial era (see 2001: 185–186): "[W]hiteness

---

racial identification. Here 'race' as a social identity becomes so de-essentialised that the approach undermines its relevance by over-emphasising context and fluidity" (Garner 2007: 9). In heeding Garner's call for avoiding this pitfall, I maintain the view that even if "race" is a culturally and socially constructed category, its symbolic power still has an effect on how people are able to live their identities. Equally, as I will show throughout my analyses, it is seldom (if ever) possible for people to design their racial identities, white or otherwise, at will and independently from the symbolic parameters of the culture they inhabit.

is synonymous with Englishness, forthcoming as a hidden normative code that determines who is in or out on the basis of birth *and* complexion" (2001: 193). However, as Ware argues, "the content of Englishness, like whiteness itself, appears to be of a volatile nature, easily evaporating when put under pressure" (2001: 192). Especially during the post-imperial era, and with the processes of Welsh, Northern Irish and Scottish devolution challenging previous understandings of British and English national identity, a recourse to the human body as the 'natural' site of national (conflated with racial) identity becomes prominent (see Ware 2001: 190). This crisis of national identity is further complicated by the shifting notion of Britain as a multicultural, postcolonial nation which, nevertheless, still struggles with its former identity as a world-dominating empire which employed the category of whiteness as a tool for coming to terms with intra-group distinction. And this, as Ware argues, necessitates an approach to British whiteness which is "slightly different" to the critical examination of whiteness in the United States – that is, an approach "that examines the fluidity of [whiteness's] naturalizing power in relation to internal differences of class rather than 'race'" (2001: 191).

Ware specifically alludes to the "racialization" of the "indigenous urban working class" who were "rendered subhuman by their inferior economic and social status" (2001: 191). Ware argues that there is a decisive difference between American whiteness scholarship, which predominantly sets out to show that whiteness, rather than a merely racial category, is also an "economic, political, and social category in the United States" (2001: 191), and the British situation, where the relationship between whiteness as race and whiteness as socio-economic category has since the emergence of the "race-thinkers" of the nineteenth century presented itself in a reversed way. In other words, while race and whiteness have socio-economic effects in the United States, class and socio-economic situation were subsequently expressed and justified in processes of racialisation. While this argument is in line with much of the socio-historical research on whiteness and the British working class that I will elaborate on in chapter I, I would add to Ware's argument that figurations of tainted whiteness on both sides of the Atlantic show the inconsistencies in the constructions of race and class in the United States as well as the United Kingdom. That is, following Ware's call for an "unmaking" of whiteness, the concept of white trash implicitly bears the potential to undo and rethink the "naturalizing power" of whiteness, and as my literary analyses will show, the novels by Irvine Welsh,

Niall Griffiths and John King can be read as literary interrogations of this possibility. They especially do so by incorporating transnational allusions to the American context into their depictions of British society as well as to the particular intra-national intricacies that Ware mentions as a challenge to British and English conceptions of whiteness. In their engagement with the devolutionary struggles, the three authors present a decidedly "sub-British" (Gardiner 2004) perspective which challenges hegemonic cultural views of the nation and its raciology.

However, the question remains why the figure of white trash, evoked as a "commonplace insult" *(The White Season)* and as an object of literary representation, arises at a particular moment in Britain. Given the selection of primary texts for this thesis, one can roughly locate the emergence of a British awareness of the term *white trash* as starting with Irvine Welsh's *Trainspotting* in 1993 (arguably the first British literary text to explicitly make use of this "curious phrase" [Wray 2006: 1]), which coincided with the phrase's rise in popularity in the media after the identification of the racist white murderers of black teenager Stephen Lawrence.[8] I examine seven novels by three authors published between the years 1993 and 2001 – that is, during the period shortly before "chav" was named a buzzword by the *OED* and, even more importantly, during a time of crucial political changes within the United Kingdom, with New Labour ending a seventeen-year phase of Conservative governments in 1997 and promoting a new phase of British multiculturalism in an attempt to give "the idea of Britishness a well-earned makeover" (Ware 2001: 194).

Tainted Whiteness, Class, Neoliberalism

The question of why the literary texts I examine in this thesis turn towards forms of tainted whiteness and are particularly interested in intersections of whiteness and class in contemporary Britain must be answered with regard to this particular socio-political moment in British history – a moment which Stuart Hall, Doreen Massey and Michael Rustin have described as the development of the alliance of Thatcherism and Rea-

8 | As I will argue in chapter I, the Lawrence case and its aftermath in the 1990s and early 2000s marks a crucial development in British culture's relation to race and whiteness.

ganism in the 1980s into the transatlantic neoliberalism of the 1990s and 2000s in their *Kilburn Manifesto* (2013a). If neoliberalism as a specific development of capitalism within the last thirty years possesses, as Hall, Massey and Rustin argue (2013b: 5–8), a particularly global dimension that impacts race and class relations, then figures of abjection like white trash or the chav are not merely local or regional manifestations but are, as I would argue, embedded in and produced by broader transnational conditions. By arguing in this way, I heed Vron Ware's call for examining whiteness as an "interconnected global system" which "requires the technologies of satellite as well as microscope" (2001: 185). The contributors to the *Kilburn Manifesto* operate in a similar fashion by examining the impact of contemporary neoliberalism on the intersectional categories of race, class, age and gender, with a particular focus on the role of whiteness in upholding power imbalances and systems of domination globally and in Britain.

In their contribution to the *Manifesto*, Sally Davison and George Shire examine the function of whiteness and race for the neoliberal economy. They argue that while "theories of the market, neoliberal or otherwise, are not themselves racialised [...], the functioning of the contemporary global economy is deeply embedded in the histories and practices of racism" (2013: 4). This is as much due to the history of British imperialism and colonialism as it is to the need to sustain neoliberal hegemony through "racialised forms of common sense" (Davison and Shire 2013: 5). Thus,

> [r]acialised thinking is [...] closely related to another stalwart of neoliberal common sense – meritocracy. The idea that those who are at the top are there because of merit necessarily implies that those who are under-represented lack merit in some way. (And the corollary is that lack of success must be linked to a failure to work hard, or to personal flaws such as laziness, criminality or parasitism.) (Davison and Shire 2013: 6)

Conspicuously, however, race, nation and whiteness are not necessarily explicitly articulated but are "submerged just beneath the surface" in order to evade class differences in favour of "an alliance between the wealthy and a working class addressed in national rather than class terms" (Davison/Shire 2013: 5). Racialisation is therefore the mode through which privilege is naturalised in order to defer attention from the persistence of class differences.[9]

As I would argue, this takes place in a transatlantic environment which is shaped by the simultaneously developed ideology of post-raciality, or what Steve Garner has called the "neoliberal postracial state" (2016: 34).[10] Drawing on a series of lectures given by Stuart Hall in 1989, Keith Feldman argues that post-racial ideology is the means by which neoliberalism has attempted to evade the "frank racial nationalism" (2015: 4) of the Thatcherite and Reaganite political culture of the 1980s in favour of a "neoliberal subject of recognition" who transcends the colour line, which is abandoned in favour of the logic of individual merit: "In staging such transcendence, the debts to materialist anti-racism are tidily paid off, and a neoliberal subject of recognition is presumed to move into a post-racial free market untethered by the world-ordering operations of racial capitalism" (2015: 7). However – and here, the discourse of post-raciality can be connected to the disavowal of class with which I started out this introduction – processes of racialisation remain in force and actually "[intensify] under the sign of the post-racial" as "the redistribution of subalternity, expendability and disposability" demonstrate (Feldman 2015: 19). Phenomena of such a redistribution are, according to Feldman, movements like Occupy, but I would argue that the phenomenon of the 2011 English riots is another paradigmatic example of this redistribution.

9 | Steve Garner (2016) provides a useful definition of racialisation, which I will follow here. He proposes that, rather than considering "race" as merely a social construct, racialisation allows for the examination of the way discourse can produce certain groups based on the perception of certain physical characteristics which are loaded with meaning – racialisation is thus "incessantly amalgamating bodies with putative characteristics" (Garner 2016: 5). Thus, racialisation is a historicising "way of understanding how, and under what conditions groups are 'made'" (Garner 2016: 6).

10 | As Garner argues, "[t]he 'neolioberal postracial state' (NPS) is a loose model designed here to capture a transition period historically located in the space where official anti-racism […] – now divorced from the struggles that brought it about as a discourse and set of practices in the late 1960s and 1970s – co-exist with very powerful forces channelling 'race' and racism from the public into the private domains" (2016: 46).

This becomes especially evident in the strange shift of attention from the actual event that triggered the initial riot in Tottenham – the shooting of Mark Duggan by police, the ensuing protests against improper police conduct and racially biased police activity – to the following copycat riots spreading across several major English cities throughout the days following the shooting. Especially the conservative press and politicians were eager to declare the riots an unruly, yet unpolitical, uprising of the "underclass" irrespective of their racial and class background (see Liebig 2014 a and 2014b, Tyler 2013). The refusal to consider the riots political unrest expressed by subjects who have experienced systemic racial and class inequality, and the insistence on instead framing the riots as the escalation of a subaltern group of people responsible for their own economic situation, is symptomatic of the same post-racial and post-class ideology that shapes the abject figures of tainted whiteness depicted in the novels I examine in this thesis.

(Tainted) Whiteness in Contemporary British Literature

By subjecting the texts by Welsh, Griffiths and King to close readings regarding their engagement with tainted whiteness, and especially by paying attention to their allusions to transatlantic phenomena, be it by making use of the American terminology of tainted whiteness, intertextual references to American literary texts engaging with white trash or other allusions, this thesis will contribute to the interdisciplinary study of whiteness, its intersections with class and its representations. I am thus especially indebted to the current sociological research on social abjection and its figurations in contemporary neoliberal Britain led by Imogen Tyler (2008, 2013). While Tyler examines a number of discourses and pays particular attention to representations in the media and political debate, a comprehensive study on the role of literature and its potential to represent and interrogate figurations of abjection has not yet been produced. Similarly, a systematic study of literary representations of white trash, and especially of British white trash, has not yet been done. By combining sociological approaches with the methods of literary analysis, I hope to contribute to these fields of research.

By employing the concept of "figuration", I once more connect my thesis to the research methods of Imogen Tyler and other sociologists. John Hartigan Jr., who has used the concept of figuration for his sociological and ethnographic research on white trash in Detroit, argues that "the value of figures as an analytical concept [...] is in directing our view to the representational dynamics involved with invoking collective forms of identity without reductively asserting that these collectives are 'real' or 'unreal' in an empirical sense" (2005: 18). Thus, the concept of figuration acknowledges the various spheres and discourses which form what Barbara Korte and Georg Zipp, following Charles Taylor, call the "social imaginary" (2014: 2). In employing this concept, it can be made sure that no sphere or discourse is privileged over the other in terms of its epistemological validity. That is, fictions and narratives (literary, filmic or otherwise) contribute as much as any other discourse or social and cultural practice to the way people or certain individuals are perceived and, in the particular case of white trash, figured as socially abject. While Tyler and Hartigan Jr. use the concept in their sociological studies, Korte and Zipp make a claim for the concept of figuration in the study of literary narratives on poverty. Their argument that "[l]iterary treatments of poverty call for a whole box of analytical tools: some from literary studies, others from the theorisation of poverty in cultural and social studies" holds equally true for the purposes of my study of tainted whiteness (Korte and Zipp 2014: 12).

With Korte and Zipp, I contend that "literary texts mould images and imaginations of the world through their specific textual elements and structures" and that a "figurations approach [...] will thus have to address levels of presentation that concern individual texts as well as their extratextual relations" (2014: 12). Korte and Zipp list a number of aspects which are central to the analysis of literary texts in terms of a figurations approach, two of which I would like to point out as equally central to my own discussion of narrative texts in the following analyses, which are the modes and perspectivation (i.e., the narrating and focalising agents) (2014: 13). These two are especially central to the analysis of whiteness and race in literature, because when analysing the representation or figuration of race, it is important to pay as much attention to what is left unsaid as to what is being said or shown.

As Toni Morrison (1992) and Rebecca Aanerud (1997) have remarked in what can thus far be regarded as the two most fundamental treatments of whiteness in literature, narrative texts are often complicit in the naturalisation of whiteness as a hegemonic identity position. Thus, they contribute to what Richard Dyer has identified as "[t]he invisibility of whiteness as a racial position in white (which is to say dominant) discourse": "Whites are everywhere in representation. Yet precisely because of this and their placing as norm they seem not to be represented to themselves *as* whites" (1997: 3). Similarly, whiteness is usually normatively invisible in literary texts. As Morrison says about a character in Ernest Hemingway's novel *To Have and Have Not* (1937): "Eddy is white, and we know he is because nobody says so" (Morrison 1992: 72).

In contemporary British literature, a prime example of this invisible whiteness can be found in the character of Henry Perowne in Ian McEwan's *Saturday* (2005). While the reader gets a thorough impression of the material and cultural capital of this successful neurosurgeon, living in the affluent suburbs of London, his racial identity is never mentioned – which is, of course, hardly surprising, as the novel does not on the surface seem to deal with racial issues per se. However, the elision of Perowne and his family's upper-middle-class whiteness becomes peculiar when judged in comparison to the way other characters are racially marked. The first such case is Baxter, a street thug who follows Perowne home after an argument and who threatens Perowne's family with his gang in tow. Baxter is described by the novel's heterodiegetic (and therefore more or less seemingly neutral and observant) narrator with Perowne as focaliser:

> He's a fidgety, small-faced young man with thick eyebrows and dark brown hair razored close to the skull. The mouth is set bulbously, with the smoothly shaved shadow of a strong beard adding to the effect of a muzzle. The general simian air is compounded by sloping shoulders, and the built-up trapezoids suggest time in the gym. (*Sat* 87–88)

As Lars Eckstein writes in his polemic about the novel: "I cannot remember reading another novel in recent years in which class division, here between Baxter and the Perownes, was so starkly exposed, and in which moral agency was almost exclusively reserved for the cultured and affluent elite" (2011: 8). Indeed, class division is not named explicitly, but it is in the above-quoted passage inferred through the description of Baxter's physique which, with its attention to unattractive and "simian" (i. e., barely human) features, renders Baxter in a racialised way. Baxter appears as racially inferior to Perowne and thus shares some features of the prototypical white trash figure.

More interestingly, one of Perwone's patients is almost described as a complimentary piece to Baxter. Andrea Chapman, a "fourteen-year-old Nigerian girl" who had come to England two years before, is described as a "problem patient": "Something in her that village life in rural north Nigeria kept buttoned down was released once she started at her local Brixton comprehensive. She took to the music, the clothes, the talk, the values – the street" (*Sat* 10–11). In this description, politically conservative notions of black urban gang culture are evoked and render the black African girl through the description of her behaviour and attitude as belonging to the urban "underclass". That is, while the white lower-class character is raced, the black girl is classed through the description of her attitude. Even more conspicuous, then, is the transformation that Andrea undergoes after her successful surgery. At the end of the novel, Perowne watches her sitting on the ward

> [w]ith her fine dark skin, her round and lovely face, and the thick crêpe bandage that he wound round her head yesterday afternoon, she has a dignified, sepulchral look. An African queen. [...]. He's intrigued. Her change in manner, her communicative warmth, the abandonment of the hard street talk, can't simply be down to her medication, or tiredness. The area he was operating in, the vermis, has no bearing on emotional function. (*Sat* 259)

Perowne's observation that her change in behaviour is not due to neurology (and therefore biology) but to something he as a doctor and scientist cannot explain makes her racialisation even more problematic. As she lets him know, she is "going to be a doctor. [...]. A neurosurgeon" just like him (*Sat* 260). Therefore, it is implied that her change in behaviour from a 'bad' (i. e., urban and from "the street") to a 'good' black girl – an "African queen", as the exoticising description has it, – must have been triggered by being surrounded by educated professionals who inspired her aspirations. That is, white male professionals have affected the Nigerian girl's classed behaviour, and the description "African queen" might as well be read as a synonym for "noble savage". Heeding Rebecca Aanerud's call for "[r]eading whiteness into texts [...] that are not overtly about race" as "an essential step toward disrupting whiteness as the unchallenged racial norm" (1997: 43), McEwan's novel can thus be read as a text which leaves whiteness, and more precisely male upper-middle-class whiteness, as the unmarked norm which can only be read as a distinct type through the presence of tainted whites like Baxter and exotic blacks like Andrea. This exemplary reading of a text which is by now widely regarded as part of the contemporary canon of British literature is, as I intended to show, an illustration of the critical and analytical potential that resides in the interconnection of literary analysis and Critical Whiteness Studies. Such a critical reading can then serve the "project of 'making whiteness strange'" (Dyer 1997: 4).

In that respect, the novels that the corpus of my study is comprised of can be regarded as a counterproject to novels like *Saturday* and their representation of what Niall Griffiths has in a statement on his poetics called the "white, male, middle-class Oxbridge-inflected monotone" of much of British literature (2014).[11] Irvine Welsh, Niall Griffiths and John King's texts belong to what Nicola Allen has referred to as the "novel of marginality" (2008): "[T]he novel of marginality, and specifically, the taxonomies of the misfit protagonist, [...] and the grotesque form, all represent means of exposing the very specific gaps in the ideology of liberal humanism" (17). Within the context of my thesis, whiteness can be regarded as a particular aspect of the ideology that is denaturalised in such novels, and their white trash characters can be identified as prototypical "misfit protagonists". In the texts that I will discuss in the following chapters, these socially marginalised "misfit protagonists" come to the narrative centre, and their abject, tainted whiteness becomes a hypervisible one that is opposed to and has repercussions for the post-racial unmarked whiteness in texts such as McEwan's *Saturday*.

The novels of Welsh, Griffiths and King that form the corpus of my study prove to be paradigmatic examples of a literature that challenges traditional notions of "English Literature" from within. What makes the three writers' work unique is their scepticism towards normative narratives of (Anglo-)British nationhood. In the devolutionary context, Irvine Welsh and Niall Griffiths are of particular interest because they challenge what it means to be British – and what it means to write as a British author – from the Scottish and Welsh fringe of Britain. For the English context,

11 | I should like to thank Niall Griffiths for providing me with the manuscript of his inaugural lecture delivered for his appointment as Professor of Creative Writing at the University of Wolverhampton in 2014.

John King similarly challenges such notions from within the centre of the Anglo-British hegemonic cultural formation. All three authors are united by particular formal literary features which undermine a sense of normative writing. Their texts employ distinct modes of demotic writing, representing regional dialects and sociolects. The most prominent feature with respect to discussions of tainted whiteness, however, is the three writers' emphasis on matters of class and race. What makes their texts stand out is that they are the first ones to explicitly use the concept of white trash and its synonyms and connotations in a British context. A comparative study of the three writers that focuses on the intersection of whiteness and class within the British context can thus contribute to an enhanced understanding of a literary and cultural moment (the 1990s and early 2000s) which is marked by an evasion of class and was dominated, as David Stubbs has argued, by a sense of a seemingly "happy, central, sunlit upland of post-political inclusivity" (2016: 8) epitomised by Blair's New Labour victory and "Cool Britannia".[12] The three authors' books challenge such notions from different positions within the United Kingdom itself and choose a similar set of subject matters, motifs and formal-stylistic patterns to establish this counternarrative. Most clearly, they employ figurations of tainted whiteness in a unique way to work through these complex issues.

Chapter Overview

The first chapter is designed as an introduction to the theoretical foundations of my thesis. I return to the issues of class discourse in contemporary Britain and its intersections with race. In order to illustrate the configuration of British class and whiteness, I consider two exemplary cases as hallmark in recent British history: the Stephen Lawrence murder case of 1993 and the media's coverage of the event, which, as I argue, echoes processes of racialisation from the nineteenth century. The connection to nineteenth-century race thinking is established as a major notional precursor to contemporary figurations of British tainted whiteness. The 2011 English riots and the media's reaction to them in the light of the figure

12 | Ironically, however, Stubbs remarks that it was Irvine Welsh's bleak *Trainspotting* of all books that Danny Boyle's film adaptation managed to turn "into one of the feelgood films of the year [1996]!" (2016: 29).

of the chav serve as a second example of the emergence of narratives of tainted whiteness in mainstream discourse. Based on these examples, I then develop the theoretical and methodological tools required for the analysis of narratives of tainted whiteness. By drawing on the sociological research by John Hartigan Jr., Beverly Skeggs and Imogen Tyler as well as on the work of Gilles Deleuze and Félix Guattari, I introduce the concepts of figuration and inscription before I illustrate the different sites of figurations and inscriptions of race and class. In the final section of chapter I, I elaborate on literature as one major site of such figurations and inscriptions with a particular emphasis on the relationship between whiteness and British national identity.

Chapters II, III and IV are devoted to authors Irvine Welsh, Niall Griffiths and John King respectively. Each chapter starts out with an introduction which situates my analyses within the current state of research on the respective authors. Each novel is subjected to a close reading with particular attention to their peculiarities in terms of formal presentation, narrative situation and focalisation as well as main themes and motifs in relation to the subject of my thesis. Chapter II regards Irvine Welsh's early novels *Trainspotting* (1993), *Marabou Stork Nightmares* (1995) and *Filth* (1998) with a particular emphasis on their depictions of tainted whiteness in the context of the Thatcher and immediate post-Thatcher years and Scottish devolution. I put particular emphasis on the representation of grotesque bodies and their implications for figurations of tainted whiteness.

In my analysis of Niall Griffiths's novels *Grits* (2000) and *Sheepshagger* (2001), I pay particular attention to the context of Welsh culture and devolution as well as to the corresponding concept of post-Britishness, especially in comparison to Irvine Welsh's Scottish novels. I consider the novels' plurality of voices and their poetics of the grotesque in their relation to the idea of a post-British community and its repercussions on figurations of race and class. In my analysis of *Sheepshagger*, I take into consideration its major American intertext, Cormac McCarthy's Southern Gothic novel *Child of God* (1973). I argue that *Sheepshagger* demonstrates the influence of American figurations of white trash (such as the main character of McCarthy's novel) on contemporary British figurations of tainted whiteness, and I consider Griffiths's text as a play on the pastoral narrative under the auspices of a postcolonial Wales.

While my analyses of Welsh and Griffiths's novels focus on the significance of the "sub-British" contexts of Welsh and Scottish devolution (that is, the British nations beyond Anglocentric culture), I consider John King's novels *The Football Factory* (1996) and *White Trash* (2001) as narratives which denaturalise the hegemonic centre of the United Kingdom, England, by engaging with forms of marginalised working-class whiteness (chapter IV). In the first part of this chapter, I examine the interrogation of white male Anglo-Saxon identity in the post-imperial age through the figure of the football hooligan in King's debut novel. I conclude my thesis with a reading of King's *White Trash* as a novel about neoliberal surveillance and ways of policing the underclass and as an adaptation of what Gael Sweeney (1997) calls the "American White Trash Aesthetic".

I What Happened to the British (White) Working Class?

Theoretical and Methodological Framework

The Disappearance and Return of Class

Despite several attempts during the last decades of British political history to assert the contrary, the issue of class has anything but vanished from British social life – and in fact, the very rebuttal of the alleged disappearance of class as a central category within contemporary British culture has itself almost become an academic cliché. Thus, whereas in the 1990s, researchers in cultural studies and sociology were faced with the argument that "class doesn't sell" (Skeggs 1997: 7) and had a hard time convincing their readership of the ongoing importance of class just while John Major and, subsequently, Tony Blair famously pronounced a "classless society" purely based on merit or the end of the class war, recent years have seen an upsurge in academic interest in class as is testified by, among others, the publication of recent volumes by Taylor (2010), Jones (2011), Tyler (2013) and Biressi and Nunn (2013), the latter stating that "[i]ndeed, if anything, the last few years, and especially those following the global financial crisis, have seen social class, in all of its guises, return to the centre of cultural, political and media agendas" (18).[1]

My claim is that class – especially in its raced guises – has anything but vanished and was a decisive factor even in the 1990s. What is more, these recent manifestations of clas are shaped by even older constructions of the intersection of class and ethnicity as well as by a transnational connection with American notions of class and racialisation. Throughout this chapter

1 | For a detailed argument on the discursive "death of class" and its resurgence in other guises, see Tyler 2013: 155-159.

I will develop a conception of raced and classed subject positions as the product of, among others, figurations that are constituted not only by the socioeconomic realities of class but also by the figurative representations (Tyler 2008, Castañeda 2002) of identity categories, with literature being one of the many sites of emergence of such figurations. On these grounds, I understand class with Biressi and Nunn (2013) as "an ongoing social process experienced throughout our lifetime trajectories" that, although "formed through material conditions and economic (in)securities and [...] shaped by early disadvantage or natal privilege and the uneven distribution of life chances and opportunities which these conditions create", is also significantly dependent on cultural signifying processes that "[work] to classify, label and formulate class judgments" (1). Thus, Biressi and Nunn state that "classed subjects are shaped by the classed judgments of others and by prevailing political and popular discourses which often work to privilege, protect or normalise particular lifestyles, conducts and values" (2013: 1). In light of the debates on intersectionality, one could qualify this observation by adding the decisive factor of a circulatory movement in the figuration of classed subjects – that is, it is at times hard to define a hierarchy or clear origin of classed images, as figurations of class are condensed forms nourished by various discourses. Thus, "class is not a given but is in continual production" (Skeggs 2004: 3). In that context,

> culture articulates, frames, organises and produces stories about social class, class difference and its various attachments. These attachments include those explicitly connected to economic conditions and the material life (consumption, social mobility, social exclusions, work and leisure) and those linked to the interior life (hope, pride, shame, aspiration, fear and resentment), although it will be immediately obvious that these necessarily overlap. (Biressi and Nunn 2013: 1)

The conspicuous "evasion of class" (Driscoll 2009) in academic, but also in political and literary discourses throughout much of the 1990s and early 2000s must be considered within this context of overlapping cultural articulations of class.

As Beverly Skeggs argues, "[to] abandon class as a theoretical tool does not mean that it does not exist anymore; only that some theorists do not value it" (1997: 6). Writing from the standpoint of feminist gender analysis, Skeggs claims that "the retreat from class has occurred across a range of academic sites; as a result, the category is either ignored or declared redundant" (1997: 6), and other identity categories such as gender are isolated from the aspect of class. However, as she claims: "Class inequality exists beyond its theoretical representation" (Skeggs 1997: 6). Likewise, at around the same time, John Westergaard (1995) criticises "the analytical myopia involved in talk which takes 'gender, race and class' as conceptually parallel dimensions of inequality; and which goes on then to pose gender and race as forces, today, towards displacement of class" (147). Westergaard goes on to argue for the importance of class as a category that despite the many proclamations of its "demise" (1995: 113) potentially reinforces supposedly more pressing inequalities of race and gender – an argument that has been tackled in more depth by proponents of intersectional approaches: "Class inequality remains potent in itself: and just so also in constituting one prime structure through which the distinct inequalities of gender and ethnicity are articulated" (1995: 147). Westergaard's argument might have been slightly unfashionable at the time of its publication, a time that, as he critically observes, saw class to be "re-declared dead or dying in all social significance" (1995: 114), but regarded in the light of today's re-emergence of class discourse in conjunction with intersectional approaches, it proves to be telling of the discursive developments around the issue of class in Britain at the close of the twentieth century that form the subject of my study and that likewise anticipate related issues like the emergence of the term *chav* and the English riots of August 2011. In retrospect, it seems that the diminishing of class-centred research in favour of a focus on other, supposedly more "pressing" identity categories in the 1990s has recently evolved into a reconsideration of previous analytical isolations of single identity categories as well as into a growing scepticism towards the tempting rhetoric of classlessness.

In the light of such reconsiderations, Westergaard's slightly reticent formulation of the "displacement of class" (1995: 147) by other identity categories does not properly account for the actual historical, political and discursive processes precipitating this shift. Why, after all, would a fundamental category such as class, historically acknowledged as one of the major determiners of outcomes in Western societies, suddenly disappear and be supplanted by other categories such as race? Paul Gilroy provides an explanatory and analytical model for the discursive shift from class to race in 1980s Britain by focusing on the constructions of the black British population in the aftermath of the riots in 1981 and 1985 that were significant for the strengthening focus on race: "The riots of 1981 and 1985 are remembered as somehow racial events. Given that a minority – between 29 per cent and 33 per cent – of those arrested in 1981 were 'non-white' it is essential to ask how this memory has been constructed?" (2002: 26). Gilroy argues that this "racialisation" of the riots and outbursts by different groups in early 1980s Britain's climate of social unrest in the context of a struggling national economy is symptomatic of the way the "form of the state structures the form of political struggle" (2002: 29) and particularly of a "racialization of British political life" (2002: 22). And for 1980s Britain, the Britain of Thatcher, this means that political rhetoric and systems of representation subsume different figures of dissent under one label: "This synchronization and unification can also be fostered by a political language which defines all those who challenge the dominant order as a common, natural enemy. Miners and blacks discover that they share being labelled 'the enemy within'" (2002: 29). For Gilroy, British racism in the 1980s is thus also a matter of class. However,

> [all] this is not merely a more complex way of saying that the discourses of powerless and dispossessed groups will tend to resonate for one another. This is certainly true and the depth of support for the miners' struggle in the black communities bears it out. I am suggesting that these heterogenous struggles somehow encompass class and are in the process of moving beyond the challenge to the mode of production which defines class politics. [...]. New types of class relations are being shaped and reproduced in the novel economic conditions we inhabit. The scale of these changes, which can be glimpsed through the pertinence of a populist politics of 'race' and nation, is such that it calls the vocabulary and analytic frameworks of class analysis into question. It emphasizes the fact that class is not something given in economic antagonisms which can be expressed straightforwardly in political formations. It no longer has a monopoly of the political stage, if indeed it ever had one. (2002: 29–30)

Gilroy thus emphasises that rather than proclaiming the disappearance of class, the historical continuity and singularity of class as an analytical category must be called into question and subjected to methodological and theoretical reconsiderations in order to acknowledge the "contingent and necessarily indeterminate affair" that class is (2002: 30). Nevertheless, Gilroy warns that "[the] processes of 'race' and class formation are not identical. The former is not reducible to the latter even where they become mutually entangled" (2002: 38). In reading Gilroy, two major reasons for this can be identified which are of central importance for my study of representations of tainted whiteness in Britain. The first is that British racism since the 1980s (and I consider this racism as the fertile ground for the emergence of stereotypes of tainted whiteness) cannot be decoded in mere hierarchical terms that are implied in previous notions of class struggle or older forms of racism inspired by the colonialist enterprise: "Today's British racism, anchored in national decline rather than imperial expansion overseas, does not necessarily proceed through readily apparent notions of superiority and inferiority. The order of racial power relations has become more subtle and elusive than that" (2002: 38).

Thus, although class issues significantly contribute to contemporary forms of racism, the latter cannot be explained by merely substituting the structures of race relations with those of class. It is therefore not possible to apply traditional Marxist modes of social analysis to the intersections of class and race. Such intersections rather demand a more complex rethinking of power structures in society, classes, race, and the ways the two are lived. In the latter respect, Gilroy supports Stuart Hall's observation from the early 1980s that in contemporary (meaning post-Winter of Discontent) Britain, race is "the modality in which class is lived" (2002: 23, quoting Hall 1980). The second reason, which has important implications for the study of representations of race, is to be found in the semantic basis of the term *race*: "The very emptiness of racial signifiers, the sense in which 'race' is meaningless, contains a warning that its political vitality and volatility may increase as the practices and ideologies which comprise it become less stable and more contradictory" (Gilroy 2002: 38). This implies that race can become a multidimensional signifier – or complex of signifiers – that may be applied to rework and resignify other forms of identity and difference which historically might have origins previously not attached to issues of race at all. Gilroy's subsequent analyses in *There Ain't No Black in the Union Jack* (1987/2002) indicate that within the British context, race has come to signify a bundle of concepts that can be traced back to shifting notions of "nation", thus taking shape in different arenas relevant for the ideologem of "nation". Thus, race must be understood as a signifier that is easily adaptable to different contexts. In other words, it is a signifier which might be used to fill ideological gaps.[2]

2 | In that, race as a signifier is unique, for it is precisely because of its scientific invalidity (i. e., it is not grounded in biological facts) that race becomes a floating

While Gilroy's study remains a central reference point when it comes to identifying and analysing the complex and drastic shifts within British political culture and its conceptions of race, class and national belonging after 1979, a new wave of class analysis taking up concepts of intersectionality and an awareness for the contingency of class (and race) can be detected at the beginning of the twenty-first century.

What has emerged, then, during the first decade of the twenty-first century, is a renewed awareness of the remaining influence of class in the formation of identities and subjectivities combined with an awareness of the need for intersectional analyses, as Yvette Taylor points out in her collection tellingly titled *Classed Intersections*:

> Class investigation is returning to sociological agendas [...]. Examination of class as produced through combined social, cultural and economic processes, serves to reject a straightforward situation and polarisation between 'old' 'objectivist' approaches, seeking to precisely name, measure and define class, and 'new' class analysis models, which map the lived, subjective experience of class, where 'the economic' and 'the cultural' combine. (2010: 3)

What is at the core of what Taylor calls "new class research" (2010: 2) is, firstly, the realisation that "class is also made, known and (re)produced through gender, sexuality and race" (2010: 2) – an awareness that is shared by many researchers in the field of Critical Whiteness Studies and that finds in the phenomenon of white trash one of its prime objects of study since it presents a test case for many of the theoretical assumptions of this field of study. Secondly, a new analytic interest in class also represents a refined sense for the multidimensional processes that bring class into existence. While previous analyses of class can be said to have primarily focused on material economic conditions that create class, a resurging interest in class acknowledges the theoretical and methodological heritage of the Birmingham school of cultural studies. That is, the signifying practices that produce class in the symbolic-cultural dimension are coming into focus. Thus, while material and economic circumstances are undoubtedly a major factor in forming the grounds for classed identities, it is nonethe-

---

and adaptable signifier. In comparison, class might also be tied to symbolic practices and different frames of articulation, but it can always be traced back to economic and material constituting factors.

less the symbolic and discursive realms in which class is perpetuated and, ultimately, *cultivated*. This necessitates the analysis of literary texts and other forms of cultural-symbolic production with a focus on the formations and functions of intersectionally classed and raced identities.

In this chapter, I will argue that the discursive evasion of class especially in the last two decades of the twentieth century concurs with a renewed racialisation of class identity, the discursive and conceptual origins of which can be traced back to nineteenth-century conceptions of class (and race) as well as to transnational connections and reciprocities with American discourses. The novels that this thesis deals with will subsequently be considered as texts that reflect, interrogate and partly prefigure the developments of class discourse in the 1990s and early 2000s. Thus, as I will show in my analyses, the novels by Welsh, Griffiths and King stand oddly opposed to what Lawrence Driscoll (2009) has called the "evasion of class" in contemporary British literature – a claim that I will engage with in more detail towards the end of this chapter.

For a sketch of the socio-cultural context within which the primary texts gain and simultaneously produce their discursive meaning, I will here focus on two landmarks in recent British history that prove to be significant with respect to the racialisation of class and the construction of white, classed subjects. In a first step, I consider the murder of Stephen Lawrence and the discourse surrounding the white suspects in the 1990s as a landmark that is significant for the context the novels speak to. I will then look at the way the English riots of August 2011 were conceived of as the culmination of social conflicts in the first decade of the twenty-first century and how they have been interpreted in public discourses in terms of class and ethnicity. The riots are closely linked to the chav figure, which had come to prominence throughout the previous decade and can in turn be considered the product of earlier discourses and developments in which class and ethnicity intersect in the 1990s.

In order to make sense of these two landmarks, I will refer to Biressi and Nunn's description of class as the product of cultural articulation, framing and storytelling. These practices play an important part in what Imogen Tyler describes as "representational struggles" and "figurative forms":

> Social classifications are complex political formations that are generated and characterised by representational struggles. Indeed, all processes of social clas-

sification, including gender, race, and sexuality, are mediated. It is my contention that these representational struggles are often played out within highly condensed figurative forms. [...] I use the term 'figure' to describe the ways in which at different historical and cultural moments specific social 'types' become overdetermined and are publicly imagined (are figured) in excessive, distorted, and caricatured ways. It is my contention that the emergence of these figures is always expressive of an underlying social crisis or anxiety: these figures are mobilised in ways that attribute superior forms of social capital to the subject positions and social groups they are implicitly or explicitly differentiated from. (Tyler 2008: 18)

Considering the definitions by Biressi and Nunn and Tyler, it can be concluded that class is a process-related identity position. Class is not only produced by economic structures but also by "class names"[3] and is thus always the effect of the "practices and [the] process of making" (Tyler 2013: 155).

Chris Haylett's research (2001) on poverty and whiteness in Britain in the early 2000s provides significant and, at the time of its publication, pioneering insight into the way processes of racialisation became a significant practice of "making" class.[4] She argues that:

The poststructuralist turn did not so much represent a wilful rejection of class matters, as an opening up of the discursive terrain to other identity positions and cross-cutting axes of identity, and importantly other ways of conceptualising and talking about identity per se [...]. However, as it happens, class matters have been less apparent within those new 'ways of doing' identity in social science [...]. (Haylett 2001: 353)

---

3 | Tyler draws on Jacques Rancière here by arguing that class is "*a struggle over names*" (2013: 154, emphasis in orig.).

4 | In a recent study, Satnam Virdee sketches a history of racialised British working-class identity that pays attention to the way the working class assumed throughout the nineteenth and twentieth centuries a sense of British national identity, especially in opposition to immigrants (including Irish Catholics, Jews, Asians and Caribbeans): "Subjectively, they too began to embrace a British national identity constructed in opposition to the racialized other [...]. The idea of the nation operated as a power container, limiting the political imagination of even most of those who were representatives of the exploited and the oppressed" (2014: 5).

In her analysis, Haylett focuses on how "cross-cutting axes of identity" – an expression that conveys the notion of intersectionality – have come to produce the poor working-class white as a particularly problematic subject that plays out precisely at the cultural moment that succeeded a shift in British post-war class relations:

> In the contemporary period, the racialised production of the white working-class poor can be understood as part of the production of the modern social, as a stage in a powerful discourse of modernisation. Its end product, envisaged as modern subjects for a modern nation, is meant to fit the cultural economy of late capitalism and leave behind its postwar counterpart. (2001: 353)

The newly emerging figurations of the poor working-class white as a subject position must be considered within the context of an "English identity in crisis" (Haylett 2001: 356). This crisis was caused by shifts in economics and class relations and the devolutionary process in Scotland, Wales and Northern Ireland – a process that "has instigated questions about the shape of English representative democracy and of English identity per se, with 'Englishness' standing for white British identities" (Haylett 2001: 356). This white Englishness, Haylett argues, needed reinventing itself "for a modern national imaginary – multicultural, postimperial Britain" (2001: 356). The white working class, and especially its poorer segments, the "underclass", were seen as standing outside of this new national order:

> During the early 1990s the idea of a British 'underclass' emerged through a dominant motif of degeneration. Characterised by a stamp of difference and division from the rest of us - middle class and respectable working class - this group was cast as a national aberration but also a warning sign of national decline. 'Underclass' works as a discourse of familial disorder and dysfunction; of dangerous masculinities and dependent femininities; of antisocial behaviour; of moral and ecological decay. [...]. The dominant meanings of 'underclass' are based on inextricable, causal relations between class, culture, and poverty. Those relations are seen to produce people who are outside/beyond/beneath the nation. Their meaning is racialised in historical origin, referring to working-class groups outside of British imperial society as uncivilised, dangerous, a 'race apart.' (Haylett 2001: 358)

I will take up the notion of the working class as a "race apart" and its historical origin in the class system of Victorian Britain in the following sections that sketch the genealogy of the notion of British tainted whiteness. In the following, I will show how in contemporary British culture, class identities – and particularly lower-class positions – have recently become determined by racial components. The discourses that developed around the figure of the chav and the medial construction of the suspects in the Stephen Lawrence murder case can be considered as landmarks in the emergence of British concept of white trash.

Being Too White? The Murder of Stephen Lawrence

The murder of the teenage, black, London-based student Stephen Lawrence by a group of young whites on 22 April 1993 sparked a public uproar and a renewed debate about racism in the United Kingdom, centring around what according to an eyewitness were the only words uttered during that unprovoked attack: "What, what, nigger?" (McLaughlin 2005: 166). According to Collins (2004) and McLaughlin (2005), the media – and the conservative press in the form of the *Daily Mail* in particular – addressed the subject with a focus on the white suspects' class background. Michael Collins argues that the media treatment of the suspects is representative of increased stereotyping of the British working class since the 1980s:

> It was not their colour – or at least not just their colour – but their class, that assisted in this stereotyping. Suzanne Moore was one of a number to write of the 'white trash' suspects.[5] In the USA, the term had previously been described by

5 | In a column about Owen Jones's book *Chavs. The Demonzation of the Working Class* in 2011, Suzanne Moore commented on Collins's accusations by defending her use of the term *white trash* by writing: "Michael Collins wrote *The Likes of Us: A Biography of the White Working Class* in 2004. He had a go at me in it, as I have described the killers of Stephen Lawrence as 'white trash'. I stand by that absolutely. In fact, one of my all-time heroes, Roseanne Barr, once described herself as America's greatest nightmare – 'white trash with money' – and much of what Jones describes – the turning of the lower orders into subhumans – is not confined to the UK." However, she also treads on Starkeyan discursive territory by speaking in the same article about the alleged convergence of "black" and white working-class cultures and their language as caricatured in the character Lauren Cooper from *The Catherine Tate Show*: "part of Lauren's diatribe was actually about chavs and

film director John Waters as the last racist phrase that you can get away with. Yet it refers both to colour and to class. This became apparent when references to the illiteracy of the men - the spelling and grammar within their handwritten press release - and to their lack of education - "they didn't have an 'O' level between them" - were cited as though further evidence of guilt. Meanwhile much was made of the fact that their mothers were neither nonsmokers nor natural blondes. It wasn't simply the suspects, their families, that were on trial but the neighbourhoods in which the tragedy was played out. [...]. The moral panic that ensued, around racism and white working-class youths, had echoes of the past - from the 'hooliganism' of the 1890s, to the cosh boys and Teddy boys of the 1950s and the 'mugging' phenomenon first documented in the 1970s. (2004: 7-8)

While Collins's historical argument about a recurring stereotyping of working-class (sub)cultures highlights the class dimension in the press coverage on the murder case, Eugene McLaughlin focuses on the processes of "racialised framing" (2005: 166) of the suspects in the mass media. What interests me the most here are the spatialising strategies that McLaughlin highlights in his analysis of the *Daily Mail*'s coverage of the case. McLaughlin describes how the newspaper articles in the months after the murder drew the picture of "natural born racists" who were the product of their surroundings, the working-class council estates of Eltham – the "racist badlands of South London" or the "heart of darkness" (2005: 172).[6] Strikingly, the use of words semantically evokes not only the poor South of the United States, home to America's white trash, with the murderers being described as behaving "like some deep south lynch mob" (McLaughlin 2005: 177), but similarly draws on imperialist images of "dark Africa". The racialised framing of the lower classes at the end of the twentieth century thus spans back to discursive strategies of the nineteenth century when the urban metropolis was imagined as providing

pikeys. Her accent is heavy patois. This is now the London accent. The fact is our 'racist' white working class sound mostly black" (Moore 2011 n. p.).

6 | As Imogen Tyler demonstrates, spatialisation and the production of "territorial stigma" is an intricate part in figuring and framing the underclass in contemporary Britain. Most prominently, this can be seen in the council estates (Tyler 2013: 159-163). I will elaborate on the significance of the council estate as a topos of white trash in my analyses of Irvine Welsh's *Marabou Stork Nightmares* (chapter II.2) and Niall Griffiths's *Grits* (chapter III.1).

separate spaces for the unruly degenerate poor in analogy to the impenetrable uncivilised jungles of Africa:

> In the last decades of the nineteenth century, the urban crowd became a recurring fetish for ruling-class fears of social unrest and underclass militancy. Lurking in the resplendent metropolis, the crowd embodied a 'savage' and dangerous underclass waiting to spring upon the propertied classes. As the embodiment of deviant agency, the crowd became the metonymic symbol of the unemployed and unruly poor; who were associated with criminals and the insane; who were in turn associated with children; who were associated with 'primitives' and the realm of empire. (McClintock 1995: 118–119)

Anne McClintock's dissection of metonymic relations between the poor and the "primitives" in nineteenth-century Britain finds its echoes in contemporary concepts of race and class. This conceptualisation becomes more nuanced in terms of constructions of whiteness as a racial marker: "In the last decades of the nineteenth century, the term 'race' was used in shifting and unstable ways, sometimes as synonymous with 'species,' sometimes with 'culture,' sometimes with 'nation,' sometimes to denote biological ethnicity or sub-groups within national groupings: the English 'race' compared, say, with the 'Irish' race" (McClintock 1995: 52). Thus, it seems not to be too far-fetched to consider the representation of the white lower-class suspects in the Lawrence murder case within the historically broader discursive context of fashioning the poor as not only a separate class but a "race apart" (Marriott 1999: 82) that peaked during nineteenth-century British imperialism and can likewise be detected at around the same time in representations of poor whites in the rural South of the United States.

The Stephen Lawrence case saw the term *white trash* finally entering *British* debates on racism and social problem cases alongside a spatialised national imaginary resembling the imaginary topographies not only of imperialist Britain but also of *America* at the turn to the twentieth century. Taking into account the emergence of the figure of the chav as a scapegoat and stereotype in Britain at the beginning twenty-first century, one can identify a discourse that construes identities based on what McClintock calls a "three-dimensional graph of comparison" that shows "minute shadings of difference in which social hierarchies of race, class and gender [overlap] each other" (1995: 54). This connection between identity categories, which can also be described in terms of intersectional theory, works within a biopolitical[7] *dispositif* of race and class emerging in the nineteenth century and taking different shapes throughout the course of the twentieth and early twenty-first centuries. Within the formation of this *dispositif*, the three major identity categories of race, class and gender can be said to intersectionally constitute each other, as Anne McClintock explains:

> Race, gender and class are not distinct realms of experience, existing in splendid isolation from each other; nor can they be simply yoked together retrospectively like armatures of Lego. Rather, they come into existence in and through relation to each other - if in contradictory and conflictual ways. In this sense, gender, race and class can be called articulated categories. [...]. Race is not simply a question of skin color but also a question of labor power, cross-hatched by gender. [...] I do not mean to imply that these domains are reducible to, or identical with, each other; instead, they exist in intimate, reciprocal and contradictory relations. [...]. The invention of race in the urban metropoles [...] became central not only to the self-definition of the middle class but also to the policing of the 'dangerous classes': the working class, the Irish, Jews, prostitutes, feminists, gays and lesbians, criminals, the militant crowd and so on. (1995: 5)

However, no matter how tempting it is to draw a historical line that directly connects the racialised imperialist discourses of the nineteenth century with the two examples of the discursive construction of lower-class whites responsible for the murder of a young black man in the early 1990s and of the lower-class white thugs inspired (or tainted) by black urban gang culture in the 2000s, such a direct analogy poses its methodological and conceptual problems.

7 | Throughout this thesis, I use the term *biopolitical* as Michel Foucault defined it, that is, as "the attempt, starting from the eighteenth century, to rationalize the problems posed to governmental practice by phenomena characteristic of a set of living beings forming a population: health, hygiene, birthrate, life expectancy, race" which is "inseparable from the framework of political rationality" (2008: 317).

Becoming Black: The 2011 English Riots

In terms of the repressed issues of class and its intersection with race, the English riots of 6–10 August 2011 prove to be a test case. As Imogen Tyler recapitulates, the riots can be considered "the largest and most pervasive scenes of civil unrest in recent British history" (2013: 179). Originally ignited by quickly escalating protests following a fatal case of police brutality in Tottenham, the riots spread across the country and gained a more complex political dimension, although ironically this is precisely what many politicians and media comments were denying at the time. In her analysis of the representations of the riots, Imogen Tyler demonstrates how the denial of the riots' political components is symptomatic for the tackling of class issues in British culture of the last decades, which has been increasingly dominated by the employment of the concept of the "underclass" as a "conceptual and perceptual frame" (2013: 182). If nothing else, the public debates attempting to make sense of the events revealed a deep-seated racism in at least some segments of the public. The by-now infamous statement of historian David Starkey on *BBC Newsnight* on 13 August that "a substantial section of the chavs [...] have become black" clearly epitomises such sentiments:

> The whites have become black. A particular sort of violent, destructive, nihilistic gangster culture has become the fashion. And black and white [...] operate in this language together, [...], which is this Jamaican patois that has been intruded [sic] in England, and this is why so many of us have this sense of literally a foreign country [...]. It is about black culture [...] it is not skin colour, it is culture. *(BBC Newsnight)*[8]

His conspicuous choice of words and the confusing emphasis on "cultural" matters[9] exemplify the way different identity categories intersectionally

8 | Transcribed from the *Newsnight* programme, retrieved from bbc.co.uk. For large parts of transcription of Starkey's comments, see also Tyler 2013: 188.

9 | Starkey's comments can thus be situated within what Ali Rattansi has called "new racisms" which superficially seem to shift attention from 'traditional' racial images to the different cultures and ways of life. "Cultural racism" is one strand of these "new racisms" which, despite their rhetoric efforts to overcome the concept of race, nonetheless employ racialising strategies of signification (2007: 93-106).

overlap and signify each other. What is more, Starkey did not shy away from citing Enoch Powell's "Rivers of Blood" speech (1968). He claimed that, to some extent, the riots proved Powell to be right in his predictions (Starkey 2011). Starkey's conjuring of a permanent threat of cultural and (despite his assurance that his argument is "not about skin colour") ethnic decline, echoed by Prime Minister David Cameron's talk of a "slow-motion moral collapse" in his public reaction on 15 August (Cameron 2011), are typical of recent discourse about the so-called underclass.

Although seemingly alluding to and acknowledging the persistence of class-related matters, the concept of the underclass is conspicuous since, as Tyler argues, it is actually symptomatic of the *denial* of class as a deciding factor of one's position in society and a defining structural principle. After all, what makes people belong to the "underclass" is in fact their alleged inability and unwillingness to actively strive for a proper economic position in society: "It is because the underclass are imagined as a *race* and not as a class that poverty and disadvantage can be conceived as not economic or even properly political issues, but as a *hereditary condition, a disease*" (Tyler 2013: 188; emphasis in orig.).

Here, it is important to note that the British conception of the underclass as it came to prominence in the 1980s was significantly influenced by American political scientist Charles Murray, who proved to be influential in his comparative analysis of the British underclass and the American ghettoes[10] and thus "was an important link in the debate on both sides of the Atlantic" (Welshman 2006: 181). In order to fathom the relevance of the notion of the underclass for contemporary Britain and the significance of the riots, Murray's emphasis on the behavioural and 'cultural' components of the underclass, is noteworthy: "When I use the term 'underclass' I am indeed focusing on a certain type of poor person defined not by his condition, e.g. long-term unemployment, but by *his deplorable behaviour* in response to that condition, e.g. *unwilling* to take jobs that are available to him" (Murray 1990: 68, qtd. in Welshman 2006: 164, my emphasis). While Murray and his followers mainly argued that poor people's behaviour was predominantly influenced by the given social structures of the

10 | For a thorough comparison of the "underclass" discourse in the United States and in Britain as well as for a detailed summary of Murray's arguments and their influence on the British popular press and politics, see Welshman 2006: 127-181. See also Hayward and Yar 2006.

welfare state and consequently proposed the abolishment of welfare (see Welshman 2006: 167), the component of race and heredity, according to Welshman, was not as prominent in Britain as it was in America: "the debate in the United States was much more 'racialised', with the place of black families playing a much more central role" (2006: 181). However, while this may be true for the historical focus of Welshman's account on the 1980s, this observation has to be revised in light of subsequent developments in the "underclass" discourse and particularly after the 2011 riots that made Britain's racialised class discourse plainly visible.[11]

In the more recent development of the underclass discourse since the early 2000s, the figure of the chav has gained prominence, as I have outlined in the introduction. Anoop Nayak's ethnographic study of young white people in Northeast England, *Race, Place and Globalization* (2003), offers a detailed account of the so-called Charver Kids, a subculture in Tyneside whose name can now be considered to be the prototype of the contemporary term *chav*:

> The term '*Charver*' has many inflections, though its origin remains uncertain. One reading emphasizes that the term has Romany connections associated with travellers. Another suggests the word is derived from a hybrid combination of the allegedly archetypal lower-class names Sharon and Trevor (i. e. Shar/vor). In one case white youth elaborated on the term *Charver* to shout 'Charwallah' (a term that refers to Indian tea-servants) at another white student, thus providing the phrase with the additional derogatory value of a lower race and class status. Others still have suggested that regional variations of this phrase exist in other areas beyond the North East (e. g. Chavvy in the South of England) and can be compared with Liverpool 'Scallies' or Hull's 'Fila youth'. (Nayak 2003: 82)

Nayak shows the ubiquity of a social semantics that is based on the intersection of race and class prevalent in contemporary Britain: "*Charver* is defined across a shared discourse of lower working-class origins. *Charvers* were portrayed as a sullied urban 'underclass', and, for a variety of reasons, have become subject to a racialized discourse that constructs them as urban primitives" (Nayak 2003: 82). Thus, the emergence of the chav as

11 | In fact, a closer look at the British underclass discourse reveals a sometimes more explicitly pronounced, sometimes latent form of racialisation, as will become evident throughout this chapter.

a figure at the intersection of race and class is produced by a variety of discourses that have gained significance at the beginning of the twenty-first century but are in their historicity the amalgamation, convergence and culmination of a multifaceted set of pre-existing discursive formations and socio-cultural semiotic systems. Neither did the chav come out of the blue nor is he/she merely the product of fleeting contemporary sentiments, a fashion of the day. Rather, the chav is for our time another landmark in a longstanding history of racialised class discourse that did not just begin within the last decade but has been developing and adapting to given socio-political situations at least since the nineteenth century. This discourse was informed by discursive transcultural interrelations with the United States at the turn of the twentieth century, and it peaked, as I have shown in relation to the debate on the underclass, in the 1980s. The use of the term *white trash* on both sides of the Atlantic is one major expression of this mutual understanding of precarious intersections of race and class.[12] Thus, as Tyler notes, the chav not only "conjures up debates from the 1980s and 90s about the rise of a socially excluded 'underclass'", but also embodies "in a condensed form a series of older stereotypes of the white poor" (2008: 21) and most prominently echoes "Victorian and Edwardian accounts of the dangerous, immoral, and libidinal lower classes" (2008: 22, see also Tyler 2013: 163). Likewise, Hayward and Yar notice "a striking similarity" between the media discourse about the chavs and

12 | Given its subject matter, this thesis focuses on the British and, to some extent, the American, context (see my article on the construction of the American South as a space of the racial other in Schmitt 2010). However, a point could be made about similar intersectional scapegoats of race and class in other Western cultures as well. While it is close at hand to consider the neighbouring Irish context in that regard (which, with the terms *skanger* [see Emig 2008] and *knacker* has its own stigmatypes for poor whites – also see Share 2005: 182 and 278 for etymologies of these terms), similar processes of what Imogen Tyler appropriately calls social abjection can also be found in contemporary France (for a comparative study of race/class marginality concentrating on US ghettoes and the French banlieues, see Wacquant 2008) and, increasingly, in Germany (for an analysis of comparable normativising discourses of crisis around welfare scroungers and immigrants fuelled by a new right, see Link 2013), to name but a few examples.

> the type of language used to describe the so-called 'Great Unwashed' of Victorian England [...]. Moreover, just as was the case in the 19th century, when terms such as 'moral wretch', 'degenerate poor', 'depraved nomad', and 'savage outcast' all ultimately came to be incorporated under the umbrella term 'dangerous class', the word 'chav' is increasingly acting as a ubiquitous structural category - a soft semantic target for those keen to rebadge the underprivileged and socially excluded among us as a new form of feckless underclass. (Hayward and Yar 2006: 17)

In that sense, the English riots represent a contemporary echo of urban unrest among the lower classes in the nineteenth-century British metropoles that fuelled what Anne McClintock terms the "fetish image of the crowd as degenerate" (1995: 119). This escalated in an increasing collective middle- and upper-class anxiety regarding civil unrest, mass strikes, anarchist uprisings and the Trafalgar Square riots in the 1880s and 1890s (McClintock 1995: 119). What connects the nineteenth-century British image of the poor, American white trash and the contemporary chav debate is the notion of a "contaminated whiteness" (Tyler 2008: 26) or "tainted whiteness" (Nayak 2003: 85) – a whiteness defined and qualified as inferior by poverty. While nineteenth-century notions of degeneracy gained their significance and their discursive repertoire from the enterprise of imperialism, as Anne McClintock demonstrates in *Imperial Leather* (1995), the contemporary variant is in a similar way fuelled by the fear of an influx of "black" culture, as is evident in David Starkey's statements. This fear, however, simultaneously unfolds within a more liberal discourse of multiculturalism, as the Stephen Lawrence case in the 1990s demonstrates. Here, the accused poor whites were deemed in the popular press as backwards in terms of cultural and political progress – they bore the remaining shame of racism still present in a society that would like to fashion itself as 'postcolonial' and 'post-racist' (see McLaughlin 2005: 172, Collins 2004: 7–8, 233).

It should become clear from the two examples from recent British history that the intersections of race (and, more specifically, whiteness) and class represented by the racist "white trash" murderers and those represented by "the chavs" have been constructed and valued with differing purposes. In the Stephen Lawrence case, the figure of white trash is employed to signify a part of the population that still refuses to acknowledge the changes of a postcolonial, multiethnic society – a group of people who represent the old racist Britain that is supposed to have been overcome. But the chav and the 2011 rioter are figures which represent another form of "bad" whiteness: those parts of the population who, according to commentators like David Starkey, have merged with a "black" gangster culture that in turn represents the racist vision of a multiculturalism gone too far.[13]

Although in both cases, whiteness and lower-class status are a negative deviation from a perceived majority of normative types of person whose race and class are more or less invisible, the two examples show the strong ambivalences with which the concepts of race and class are fraught. While, as I have shown above, the concept of class has been made invisible rhetorically, race has undergone comparable conceptual and discursive changes and has, at times, been subjected to similar eradicatory attempts that would erase histories of oppression, separation and violence along its lines. Yet, as Brian Niro states in his introduction to the term: "All the inverted commas in the world will not amend the fact that the word race is alive and well" (2003: 2). In tracing the history of the term's use in Western cultures back to its etymological roots, its conceptualisation during the Enlightenment and its later employment, which peaked in the nineteenth and twentieth centuries, Niro points out that the concept of race has always been an imprecise one (see 2003: 181). Despite various recent attempts at erasing the term or at going "colour-blind", the concept still has a hold in contemporary Western cultures, not least due to its historical persistence and the fact that it "is not always where we think it may be" (2003: 3). Thus, not unlike the declaration of classless societies, which will not undo economic and material conditions of existence no matter from which academic, ideological or political direction the declaration is uttered, an evasion of race will not bring along the abolishment of the very material effects the concept still has for many people. After all, as Niro argues, there is a "difference between the academic in his/her ivory tower, who speculates that race is an arbitrary cultural construction, and the black man on the pavement with a policeman's boot over his neck" (2003: 183).

13 | A similar ambivalence can be detected in the development of white trash as a concept and figure in the United States from the nineteenth century until today: while *white trash* used to denote the poor whites from the rural South within the racist framework of pre-Civil War America, *white trash* now embodies the ideologically backwards leftovers as a scapegoat figure in a supposedly "post-racist" society.

In that respect, it is necessary to examine the symbolic systems that influence and sustain the material effects of racism and boundary creation. The emergence of the white trash/chav figure in recent British culture can be read as a boundary figure (Wray 2006) that is to a considerable degree shaped by a symbolic repertoire which goes back to the nineteenth century in both the United Kingdom and the United States. As I will argue throughout the following section, the complex conditions of such figures must be studied by taking into consideration different sites and discourses of emergence. In particular, it must be examined how certain images and conceptions of bodies are figured as socially abject and thereby assume a symbolic status which exceeds the material. Conceiving of such processes in terms of figuration and inscription provides the apt methodology which can trace the emergence of figures of social abjection across different and intersecting social signifying systems, including literature. Taking Imogen Tyler's figurative approach (2008, 2013) and Beverley Skeggs's (2004) concept of performativity and inscription as a framework to analyse such concepts as white trash accounts for the intersectional dimension of subject identities as well as for the discursive plurality and multidimensionality of identity formations. The figurative approach allows for a multimodal analysis of the functions and effects of cultural production (such as literary texts) on the social imaginary. In line with the "new" class research, it also focuses not only on the material and economic conditions of class identities, but considers the intersections of other factors. Thus, an exchange between such approaches, which derive predominantly from the disciplines of sociology and cultural studies (Tyler and Skeggs), can be productively combined with a cultural materialist conception of literature (see Brannigan 1998, Sinfield 2004) that considers literary production as embedded in the signifying processes that interrelate with the material conditions of a society. This approach to literary texts further contributes to a thorough understanding of the correlations of symbolic and material boundaries (see Wray 2006) that shape raced and classed identities.

Figurations and Inscriptions of Race and Class

In his analysis of the lives of poor whites in Detroit, John Hartigan Jr. argues for a figurative approach in sociological studies that draws inspiration from literary studies and approaches and approaches intrarace identity categories as tropic constructions that manifest themselves in a variety of cultural sites. Hartigan Jr. proposes using the concept of the figure rather than of the stereotype in order to avoid the limiting dichotomy of Self and Other that is implied by the latter and which might be useful on individual levels (see 2005: 13) but which does not account for the particulars of intrarace categories like white trash. After all, the concept of white trash is essentially characterised by the fact that it "first appears as a form of otherness", while "its most troubling aspect is its dimension of sameness" (2005: 60). The methodological advantage of thinking white trash as a form of figuration thus resides in the fact that

> figures call attention to the way people come to consider their identities in relation to potent images that circulate within a culture. Figuration is a drastic improvement over stereotype in that it captures the active way people subjected to certain debasing images are able to inhabit them in complex ways that involve critique and elaboration. (Hartigan Jr. 2005: 16)

An analysis of racialised subject positions such as white trash must therefore take into consideration the "figural play of images in the lives of racial subjects" in order to account for "the vast reservoir of signification that animate a figure like white trash [...] in its common usage" (Hartigan Jr. 2005: 16) and the way such a figure results from the dissemination across "complex, mutable social settings" (Hartigan Jr. 2005: 17). Hartigan Jr.'s approach is of considerable value for bridging the gap between sociological approaches to the lived and experienced reality of white trash and other classed and raced figures on the one hand and, on the other, cultural and literary studies approaches to the representational and symbolic level of such phenomena.

A similar methodological approach can be found in Imogen Tyler's analyses of social abjection that can likewise be applied to the study of literary representations of social phenomena and the potentially reciprocal relation between different social and cultural sites. Tyler's figurative method, first outlined in her article on "chav mums" (2008) and further developed and applied to a variety of subjects in her recent book *Revolting Subjects* (2013), can thus be integrated into a cultural materialist approach to literature that connects the latter to sociological subjects and approaches. For a literary analysis that wants to concern itself with the relationship between a text's modes of aesthetic representation and what it actually represents (actual social matters, groups of people, politics, etc.), such an approach offers the necessary tool to adequately describe a text's situatedness within the cultural and social conditions from which it emerges. It avoids the risk of reducing not only the text to a mere illustration of sociological findings and theories but also one's own literary analysis to a scholarly approach that is merely secondary and commentarial to sociological approaches.

Tyler's figurative method, very much in line with an increased awareness of recent class sociology for the function of cultural signifying processes contributing to forming classed identities, arises from the need to bridge the gap between the material and semiotic factors contributing to the emergence of a figure such as the chav in the recent British cultural imaginary:

> This approach refuses any binary distinction between the material and the semiotic, signs and signifying practices are understood as having material effects that shape the appearance of and our experience of others. [...] we should understand mediation not only as representational (in a more structuralist sense) but as a constitutive and generative process. [...] it is through *the repetition of a figure across different media* that specific figures acquire accreted form and accrue affective value in ways that have significant social and political impact. [...] it is only when a range of different media forms and practices *coalesce* that these overdetermined figures materialise. [...]. [...] social class is often represented through caricatured figures – the toff, the yuppie, the public school boy, the suburban wife, the flat-capped working man, the gypsy, the chav – figures that are often communicated in highly emotive ways. (Tyler 2008: 18–19)

The "representational struggle" that is at the heart of formations and classifications of identity such as class, race and sexuality is thus

> often played out within highly condensed figurative forms. [...] I use the term 'figure' to describe the ways in which at different historical and cultural moments specific social 'types' become over determined and are publicly imagined (are figured) in excessive, distorted, and caricatured ways. (Tyler 2008: 18)

Tyler notes that her approach to figurations and specifically her emphasis on resolving the binary distinction between the semiotic and the material is derived from Isabel Castañeda's use of the concept in her study *Figurations: Childs, Bodies, Worlds* (2002). Castañeda distinguishes her use of the term from common literary uses in the sense of a more one-directional relation between a signifier and its signified in representational terms:

> My use of this term turns on a relation between the semiotic and the material: figuration entails simultaneously semiotic and material practices. This concept of figuration makes it possible to describe in detail the process by which a concept or entity is given particular form – how it is figured – in ways that speak to the making of worlds. [...]. A figure [...] is the simultaneously material and semiotic effect of specific practices. Understood as figures, furthermore, particular categories of existence can also be considered in terms of their uses – what they 'body forth' in turn. (Castañeda 2002: 3)

Hence, what is at the core of this use of the concept of figuration is the way symbolising practices have material effects and vice versa. The focus thus is, broadly speaking, communicative practices (see Tyler 2013: 10) which can here be understood as a variety of forms of mediation or signification. While Tyler in her analysis of "the chavs" and other abject populations primarily focuses on mass media and broadsheet newspapers, literature must similarly be understood as being a communicative subsystem taking part in these processes. What my subsequent analyses will be concerned with, then, is to trace the way figurations of white trash, or, to stick to Tyler and Haylett's concepts, abject whiteness, take shape in literary texts and how they evoke, cite and, most importantly, renegotiate previously existing figurations.

Doubtlessly, one can conclude that this approach to communicative practices and their resulting figurations is indebted to Foucauldian discourse analysis as well as to a concept of performativity deriving from the works of Judith Butler – a conceptual and theoretical basis that I will return to in more detail later, and which can also be found at the base of Beverley Skeggs's approach to thinking classed identities as the effects of symbolic processes that can be described as forms of inscription. Thus, rather than just being something that is materially lived, class is something which is being made under certain conditions and possibilities that are beyond the active influence of those who will be subsumed under any given class label (Skeggs 2004: 2). Skeggs's concept of inscription helps to refine the notion of figurations and how they come into existence: while, quite similar to Tyler, Skeggs is concerned with processes of condensation (2004: 1), her methodology offers insight into the actual relation between the symbolic and the material that converges in certain classed (or raced, gendered…) figurations. This becomes clear in the example with which she starts out her study *Class, Self, Culture* (2004) – the case of black coolness (2004: 1–6). Skeggs argues that "what we learn to recognize as categorizations of race and class are not just classification or social positions but an amalgam of features of a culture that are read onto our bodies as personal dispositions – which themselves have been generated through systems of inscriptions in the first place" (2004: 1). Referring to the example of black working-class male coolness given in a study by Manthia Diawara, Skeggs shows how in popular American culture, certain forms of blackness – held to be cool not least by a white audience – are attached, or inscribed (on)to certain bodies. Drawing on Diawara, Skeggs cites the example of Quentin Tarantino's *Pulp Fiction* (1994), in which the black actor Samuel L. Jackson embodies a form of black coolness – he "*is* cool" in an essentialised way while his white acting partner John Travolta "acts 'black cool'" in some scenes of the film (2004: 1):

> The black male character appears not to be acting; he just *is*. Hence, black dispositions are culturally essentialized and made authentic. This is an example of a symbolic economy where the inscription and marking of characteristics onto certain bodies condenses a whole complex cultural history. Some bodies can be expanded rather than condensed. At the same time they become a resource for others. (2004: 1)

Skeggs is thus concerned with questions of social and spatial mobility attached to differently marked bodies; while, to stick with her example, a black man might be restricted to an essentialising conception of racialised "coolness" which keeps him in place and "[excludes him] symbolically from performing 'whiteness'" (2004: 1), a white man might performatively adapt this coolness in order to expand his options of mobility. While I do think that this particular example bears its inherent problems,[14] the

14 | For one, the confusion of character and actor in the passage quoted above is a conceptual fallacy not to be ignored since the status of any supposed "essentialism" in a film that lives off its exposed artificiality and 'actedness' is questionable; using the juxtaposition of a black and a white actor confused with their roles further bears problems if transposed onto other examples stretching beyond the realm of the fictional.

overall argument can productively be applied in analysing figurations of tainted whiteness. Vicky Pollard, played by actor Matt Lucas in the show *Little Britain* (2003–2005), is an example of an actor with a privileged class background who slips into the role of a member of the marginal class of the chavs and white trash. Tyler analyses Vicky Pollard as one of the major figurations of the chavs' abject and caricatured class status:

> During the airing of *Little Britain* barely a day went by without the use of the name or an image of Vicky Pollard in a newspaper story about the feckless, violent underclass. This figure moved relentlessly through public culture on a wave of mockery, contempt and disgust. Social media and the feedback loops offered by the message boards of online newspapers are a critical part of this process in that they enable publics to shape and craft the chav as a knowable figure. (Tyler 2013: 165)

If one considers the figure of Vicky Pollard as a case of inscription as class-making, Vicky can be interpreted as a body that is marked as abject and grotesque (she is obese, sexually excessive, has bad eating habits and poor taste in fashion, her talking is excessive and "wrong", etc.). Vicky's body, marked as classed by being the condensed embodied citation of established class markers, functions as an essentialising embodiment of class – that is, she in turn offers the blueprint for recognising the bodies of other populations categorised as the "feckless underclass" as marked and symbolically meaningful. This process can only be successful, however, by the mutual intersection of accompanying identity categories:

> Class cannot be made alone, without all the other classifications that accompany it. […] We need to think how bodies are being inscribed simultaneously by different symbolic systems; how inscription attributes difference and how we learn to interpret bodies through the different perspectives to which we have access. These different systems of inscription and interpretation may operate both in simultaneity and contradiction. This enables us to explore how some people can use the classifications and characteristics of race, class or femininity as a resource whilst others cannot because they are positioned *as* them. (Skeggs 2004: 3)

The latter point is particularly important for the making of Vicky Pollard as a recognisable figure of class disgust since she becomes meaningful in terms of class through, to name but one example, the overdetermination of her grotesque femininity, characterised by her sexual excess and overall inappropriate, comically exaggerated public behaviour. Thus, her class is marked by her femininity and vice versa.[15] This process of marking is continued on another superordinate level when working-class and underclass bodies are considered within a national context.

Drawing on Ghassan Hage's study *White Nation* (1998), Skeggs argues that "whiteness becomes the mark of national belonging" (2004: 19) through spatialisation and bodily inscription. The nation relies on its own "metaphorical space", the "inscription of the nation onto the body" by making whiteness the signifier of nationhood, and "the national perspective that marks some bodies as more valuable than others" (Skeggs: 2004: 19). Skeggs's emphasis on the relation between inscription and sign implied by Gilles Deleuze and Félix Guattari's concept of inscription (2009) should be noted: "It is important not to confuse the process of inscription with the sign itself – which is the product of inscription [...]" (2004: 13). Thus, a white body becomes a sign when this whiteness is invested in a process of inscription through other factors of marking such as class, gender, etc. National belonging on the basis of race relies on the mutual work of creating a centre of "real belonging" from which non-national bodies can be excluded, or constructed as "an *object of spatial exclusion*" (Skeggs: 2004: 19, emphasis in orig.) that deviates from the embodiment of "the right characteristics and dispositions" that rely on processes of essentialisation (Skeggs: 2004: 19). Coming back to Vicky Pollard, it can be said that she becomes such an object of spatial exclusion from the national centre because she is essentially constructed as deviant through her grotesquely "wrong" femininity. Thus, while her whiteness might have been inscribed onto her body as a marker of national belonging, her whiteness now becomes filled with a different meaning because her body is at the same time marked by her "inappropriate" gender as well as by her unruly behaviour, her way of talking (her accent significantly marking her speech), etc. Thus, the inferiorisation of whiteness through a classed and deficiently gendered body inherent in the figure of Vicky Pollard can be read as a form of British white trash since the latter concept, according to Skeggs "encompasses perfectly the association of the working-class with

15 | Skeggs names Anne McClintock's study *Imperial Leather* as a case in point for the intersections of race, class and gender in the making and inscribing of identities (see Skeggs 2004: 4).

disgust and waste – it racializes the working-class so that distance can be drawn from other forms of whiteness" (2004: 103).[16]

While Skeggs does not explicitly refer to white trash in a British context, she nonetheless employs the term and its connotations as a case in point for similar processes of inscribing race and class onto bodies in contexts beyond the United States, and she thus confirms the tendency previously outlined by my recapitulation of the research on the chav phenomenon that the term *white trash* is increasingly infiltrating British discourses on classed and raced bodies both on the side of cultural production/popular discourse and academic scholarship. *White trash* thus becomes the emblem of "the long tradition of attributing dirt and danger to the working-class [...], continuing to identify the working-class with waste, excrement, sewerage, that threatens to spill over and contaminate the order of the nation" (Skeggs 2004: 104).[17] Thus, the white trash figure becomes representative of a threat to the nation, especially in times of a post-British identity crisis.

However, white trash is not the only racial figure relevant in that respect. Since the 1980s in particular, Britain saw an increased debate about forms of national belonging that were fought out on the bodies of the racially marginalised, sparked by the race riots in the early years of the decade and the 1981 Nationality Act. Increasingly, this conflict was also inscribed onto the bodies of the disintegrating working class, particularly after the Miners' Strike. Paul Gilroy, through a critique of Benedict Anderson's constructivist model of nation building, shows how race became the fundamental aspect of any thinking of the British nation. According to Gilroy, Anderson's claim that "racism is essentially antithetical to nationalism because nations are made possible in and through print languages rather than notions of biological difference and kinship" does not hold

16 | It should be noted, however, that Vicky Pollard on the one hand, being part of a sketch show and thus exposed as a staged character, comes across as an ostentatiously hyperbolic performance rather than a mimetic representation of the realities of gender, class and race, which, it might be assumed, the audience is all too aware of. Yet, on the other hand, a similar degree of ostentatiously hyperbolic and grotesque staging can also be found in, say, blackface minstrelsy, which does not make this form of staging any less racist and offensive.

17 | The observations made by Skeggs about the working class are similarly valid for what has frequently been termed the "underclass" since the 1980s, as I have shown earlier in this chapter.

true for the British nation since the "politics of 'race' in this country is fired by conceptions of national belonging and homogeneity which not only blur the distinction between 'race' and nation, but rely on that very ambiguity for their effect" (2002: 44). The nation is rendered "in terms which are simultaneously biological and cultural" (Gilroy 2002: 44), as phrases like "the Island Race" and "the Bulldog Breed" testify (Gilroy 2002: 44). The legal basis for such a conception of British nationality was provided by the modification of the previous *ius soli* in the form of the Nationality Act of 1981 (see Gilroy 2002: 44) and happened just shortly before the Falklands conflict – according to Gilroy one of many moments "at which the discourse of 'race' and nation erupted into popular politics and culture" (2002: 69) that can simultaneously be linked to increasing debates about "multi-racialism":

> The Falklands episode celebrated the cultural and spiritual continuity which could transcend 8,000 miles and call the nation to arms in defence of its own distant people. Images of the nation at war were also used to draw attention to problems in 'multi-racialism' at home. There was a rich irony discovered in the contrast between the intimacy of the 'natural' if long-distance relationship with the Falklanders and the more difficult task of relating to alien intruders who persisted in disrupting life in Britain and were not seen to be laying down their lives for the greater good. (2002: 54)

Thus, the 1980s mark an intensified struggle over questions of national belonging, represented by racial bodies and concepts of territoriality that mutually define each other. While the Falklands War can thus be interpreted as the territorial defense of the national idea, bodies and their belonging are struggled over at home. This becomes apparent in Gilroy's analysis of a poster from the Tories' election campaign in 1983, showing a young black man in a suit with the caption "Labour says he's black. Tories say he's British" (2002: 64). The poster intends to challenge conceptions of race and attempts to erase them through the category of citizenship that is supposed to be "essentially colourless, or at least colour-blind" (Gilroy 2002: 63). However, to use Skeggs's terminology, the black man depicted on the poster is not free from the inscriptions of race; they are simply translated into the language of national culture by showing the black man to be a conscious diversion of anything that is stereotypically associated with black British culture in the 1980s:

> National culture is present in the young man's clothing. Isolated and shorn of the mugger's key icons – a tea-cosy hat and the dreadlocks of Rastafari – he is redeemed by his suit, the signifier of British civilization. The image of black youth as a problem is thus contained and rendered assimilable. (Gilroy 2002: 65)

In the Thatcherite rhetoric of the campaign poster, the black man is not a "special case" but can be treated as "equal" when he subscribes to the meritocratic principles of good British citizenry: "The Conservatives believe that everyone wants to work hard and be rewarded for it. Those rewards will only come about by creating a mood of equal opportunity for everyone in Britain, regardless of their race, creed or colour" (qtd. in Gilroy 2002: 64).[18] The black body, in a discursive strategy of unmarking in terms of race or colour, thus becomes reframed as a potential equal citizen with the economic and cultural values of the Tories. The visual presentation of the young man in his "British" clothes as well as the rhetoric of the campaign text are the tools of inscription that render the black man's body a battleground of national territorialisation on which the ideological struggle between Labour Party and Tories is fought.

However, the seemingly anti-racist rhetoric betrays a more perfidious form of cultural racism that lies at the heart of this struggle over who has the primary means of defining and appropriating "the black man". What is more: "The solitary maleness of the figure is also highly significant. It avoids the hidden threat of excessive fertility which is a constant presence in the representation of black women [...]. This lone young man is incapable of swamping 'us'" (Gilroy 2002: 65). Thus, the figuration of the black British citizen employed by the Tories can be said to be inscribed intersectionally by notions of gender that in turn are mirrored in figures like the white underclass abject female Vicky Pollard: the firm British black man versus the hyperfertile and excessive black and white trash women. Thus, the emergence of the abject figure of the white underclass/white trash/chav(ette) marks one side of the continuum of racist figurations in Britain since the 1980s.[19]

18 | Quotes from the poster text taken from figure 1 in Gilroy 2002: 64.

19 | This does not mean, however, that the racism directed at people of colour equals the marginalisation of tainted whites or that those can be measured in equal terms. Yet, both are the effects of a racial worldview.

While Beverley Skeggs only briefly mentions inscription as an important concept in the work of Gilles Deleuze and Félix Guattari without further elaboration on their use of the concept (2004: 12–13), I want to expand on their notion of inscription because it is helpful to understand the full scope with which it can be used to understand the interplay of semiotic and material processes and effects of racial and class figurations. Deleuze and Guattari (2004, 2009) formulate a theory of inscription as underlying the evolution of human societies in terms of the principles of production and exchange from primitive societies to civilised and contemporary capitalist society. They define the "territorial machine" as the "first form of socius, the machine of primitive inscription, the 'megamachine' that covers a social field", while the Earth "is the surface on which the whole process of production is inscribed, on which the forces and means of labor are recorded, and the agents and the products distributed" (Deleuze/Guattari 2009: 141). However, they reject the notion that exchange and circulation are the primary driving force of social formations. Rather, they set inscription as defining the socius first and foremost: "Society is not first of all a milieu for exchange [...], but rather a socius of inscription where the essential thing is to mark and be marked. There is circulation only if inscription requires or permits it" (Deleuze/Guattari 2009: 142).

What societies have to establish first, then, is to mark out their territory onto which production, labor and ultimately exchange can take place. Primitive, precivilisatory societies are characterised by their quite literal marking of bodies (see Skeggs's discussion of Deleuze/Guattari 2004: 12–13): "The primitive territorial machine codes flows, invests organs, and marks bodies" (Deleuze/Guattari 2004: 144). The sign, the product of inscription (see Skeggs 2004: 13), is the result of a process that "makes men or their organs into the parts and wheels of the social machine" (Deleuze/Guattari 2004: 145). Deleuze and Guattari's corporeal conception of this process of inscription interprets the signs as "territorial signs that plant their flags in bodies" (2009: 145). This image of the human body within the socius as a metonymic replacement for the territorialised Earth as the basis for all social exchange and production can contribute to a more concise understanding of the inscriptive effects of race, class and gender formations in the creation of national figurations. Every figuration of a classed, raced or gendered human being can become a form of national territorialisation. Such a conception of territorialisation is crucial for understanding the nationalist ideology that incorporates certain races or classes as belonging to the nation, and hence as metonymically embodying the nation.

To return to the Tories' election campaign and to Vicky Pollard, one can say that the Tories territorialise the male black body by marking it with their flags that turn the body into a metonymic sign for the British nation, effacing its racial components. Vicky, on the contrary, is inscribed with the antithesis of the ideal white British nation; her whiteness marks her body in a form of hypervisibility that contrasts the effacement (or, to stick with Gilroy's interpretation, culturalisation) of race in the example from the 1983 election campaign.

In their follow-up collaboration *A Thousand Plateaus: Capitalism and Schizophrenia II* (1980/2004), Deleuze and Guattari refine the notion of inscription by developing their ideas around the concepts of "significance" and "subjectivation". They explicate their concepts in relation to "faciality", the generation of significant faces as forms of what one could call identity inscription with the aim of establishing figurations of norms and deviating forms. Deleuze and Guattari's concept of faciality lends itself as a conceptual complement to the ideas of figuration and inscription of classed and raced formations:

> Signifiance is never without a white wall upon which it inscribes its signs and redundancies. Subjectification is never without a black hole in which it lodges its consciousness, passion, redundancies. Since all semiotics are mixed and strata come at least in twos, it should come as no surprise that a very special mechanism is situated at their intersection. Oddly enough, it is a face: the *white wall/black hole* system. A broad face with white cheeks, a chalk face with eyes cut in for a black hole. Clown head, white clown, moon-white mime, angel of death. Holy Shroud. (2004: 186, emphasis in orig.)

Deleuze and Guattari's associative style of writing can in this case best be interpreted as being commanded by a strategy of alienation that attempts to denaturalise the perception of faces as a physiological or anatomic given that can be further read as the expression of a person's character. It is notable that they link the "white" face to other images of whiteness (angel of death, Holy Shroud), alluding to the associations of the colour white that are not only limited to whiteness as a racial trait but can, in Deleuze and Guattari's argument, always be traced back to it – that is, whiteness might conjure purity or absence, but this notion then has repercussions for common perceptions of whiteness as a racial trait.[20] This makes their conceptualisation of faciality a form of Critical Whiteness Studies that tries to unsettle normative notions of the face as a semiotically determined surface of normality.

In Deleuze and Guattari's argument, the face is part of an *"abstract machine of faciality (visagéité)"* (2004: 187, emphasis in orig.) that organises processes of "biunivocalisation, or binarisation" (2004: 196) and thus, as John Brannigan argues in his analysis of face measurement and the racialisation of the Irish in the nineteenth and twentieth centuries, it "enables individuality, conformity, and deviance" (Brannigan 2009: 115). In that respect, it is important to note that Deleuze and Guattari consider "facialisation" a process that makes individuals and groups recognisable by assigning significance to their bodies. This is not so much concerned with the actual face as such but with the way the entire body becomes facialised (i. e., becomes meaningful in terms of character, type, and belonging). However, Deleuze and Guattari do not attribute such signifying powers to the face as an anatomic actuality but to the processes of interpreting faces or other corporeal characteristics that allow for facialisation as meaningful. Thus, they state that "you don't so much have a face as slide into one" (Deleuze/Guattari 2004: 196). The face belongs to a pre-existing system of signification (or, for that matter, inscription) that does not allow for an individual face to become meaningful or expressive of the actual individual that it belongs to; rather, the face is interpreted in terms of pre-existing parameters of signification: "The abstract machine has you inscribed in its overall grid" (Deleuze/Guattari 2004: 197). The way that phrenology interpreted certain types of faces as racially significant and functioned as what Deleuze and Guattari call the "computation of normalities" (2004: 197) perfectly illustrates the way an "abstract machine" of facialisation works. Deleuze and Guattari describe this machine as a "deviance detector" that distinguishes between degrees of normality and deviance (2004: 197). In European culture, the "White Man" becomes the typical face that measures all other types of face (see Deleuze/Guattari 2004: 196).

Thus, "White Man" becomes the status quo for racism which "operates by the determination of degrees of deviance in relation to the White-Man

20 | It is noteworthy that in later Critical Whiteness Studies, especially in Richard Dyer's *White*, whiteness is analysed in relation to the idea of the "absence of colour" (Dyer 1997: 207) and as associated with death (Dyer 1997: 210).

face" (Deleuze/Guattari 2004: 197). According to Deleuze and Guattari, racism is the result of "waves of sameness" (Deleuze/Guattari 2004: 197) that interpret the system of signification providing for faciality in terms of conformity and nonconformity in relation to the White Man face. Forms of alterity can only be accepted under permitting circumstances within this system, and can only be maintained in "a given ghetto" (Deleuze/Guattari 2004: 197). Deleuze and Guattari's ideas of the "computation of normalities" and the degrees of this normality can be linked to one of the central aims of Critical Whiteness Studies – namely to make visible and dissect the ways that whiteness is imagined. As Richard Dyer states:

> whiteness generally colonises the stereotypical definition of all social categories other than those of race. To be normal, even to be normally deviant (queer, crippled), is to be white. White people in their whiteness, however, are imagined as individual and/or endlessly diverse, complex and changing. There are also gradations of whiteness: some people are whiter than others. (1997: 12)

This "representational range" is not being granted to "non-white people", as Dyer makes clear (1997: 12), and this faulty or omitting mode of racial representation (which renders whites as somehow "unraced" or racially invisible, while all others are exclusively and predominantly distinguishable through their deviance from the white norm) is, if one uses the vocabulary provided by Deleuze and Guattari, achieved and maintained through the computation of normalities and (inscribed) deviances.

A conception of the face as the product of an abstract machine of signification that is required by "*certain* social formations" (Deleuze/Guattari 2004: 200, emphasis in orig.) in order to manage and distribute social power is useful for rethinking the way figurations of class and race work within different discourses. After all, it is the role of the face as a bearer of human – that is, racial and social – typologies that Deleuze and Guattari are concerned with. Their concept of the relation between signifier and figure (or face), or subject and face respectively, further offers an important angle that helps to conceive of the function of figurations (as Imogen Tyler describes them) in discourses that mediate the social imaginaries of race and class:

> [The face] does not assume a preexistent subject or signifier; but it is subjacent to them and provides the substance necessary to them. What chooses the faces is

> not a subject [...]; it is faces that choose their subjects. What interprets the black blotch/white hole figure, or the white page/black hole, is not a signifier [...]; it is that figure which programs the signifiers. (Deleuze/Guattari 2004: 199)

This assumption, which is not dissimilar to Paul Gilroy's observation about the emptiness of racial signifiers (2002: 38), has its precursor in *Anti-Oedipus* where Deleuze and Guattari draw on Lyotard's observation about figurality: "Lyotard everywhere reverses the order of the signifier and the figure. It is not the figures that depend on the signifier and its effects, but the signifying chain that depends on the figural effects" (2009: 244). Thus, Deleuze and Guattari draw attention to a type of materialism that underlies signifying practices in the making of social formations and in the inscription of racial and class identities – a materialism that not only makes it possible to conceive of "words as things" (2009: 244), but also of figurations of race and class (and their intersections) as semiotic formations that are not necessarily contingent upon linguistic forms of signification. In other words, this rethinking of figurations helps to account for the curious way in which white trash or the chav seem to become almost self-perpetuating figures that follow their own cultural poetics irrespective of actual historical or etymological origins.

Nothing makes this clearer than the painstaking efforts of sociologists to come to terms with the actual origin of the term *chav*, whose origins at times are supposed to be found in the Romani language and at times are merely explained by way of acronyms for such expressions as "Council-Housed And Violent", "Council-Housed And Vile" or "Council-Housed Associated Vermin" (Tyler 2008: 21). Despite these efforts of analysing the semantics of the term, *chav* is best to be understood as something that "you know when you see it" – the word *chav* is determined by a figure and its assumed properties rather than a contained signifier. The same can be said about the conspicuous history of the concept of white trash, which assumed different shapes at least throughout the last three hundred years. When Brian Niro writes that "Race is a monster" that "changes shape, size, and color as the need arises" (2003: 1), it is precisely the emptiness of the signifier of race that rather lives through its figurations that he means. The monstrosity of a concept such as race (or, for that matter, class) resides precisely in the detachment of the signifier from its figurations, which, despite the signifier's emptiness, have repercussions for the way certain lives are lived and perceived. It is in this same vein that Deleuze and

Guattari write that "the face is a horror story", since it is a figuration that is not defined through a signifier (2004: 187).

Applying Matt Wray's own use of boundary theory, which assumes the interaction of symbolic and material boundaries within social power relations, can reveal the material, naturalising effects of such figurations:

> As social power operates through boundaries, it creates different kinds of social stratification and inequality corresponding to those boundaries. In the broadest sense, then, boundary theory offers exceptionally coherent ways of thinking about identity, differentiation, and inequality at multiple levels of social organization. (2006: 9)

Wray's methodological proposal could be described as a kind of Foucauldian, genealogical analysis that traces the emergence and the discursive conditions of boundary figures across different cultural sites:[21]

> Once popularized and imposed, a symbolic boundary can help establish social distinctions and justify taboos. If it gains enough social power, such a boundary may result in laws and prohibitions, such as bans against interracial sex and other forms of racial propinquity. When this occurs, the symbolic boundary has become a social boundary. [...]. However, social boundaries are not primarily symbolic or cognitive. They are embodied and materialized in our collective practices, our shared activities, and our social institutions. [...] They are artificial structures that exert structuring forces in everyday life, but they seem to be part of the natural order of things. (2006: 9-14)[22]

Wray argues that symbolic and social boundaries are primarily created through what he calls "stigmatypes". According to Wray, stigmatypes are "stigmatizing boundary terms that simultaneously denote and enact cultural and cognitive divides between in-groups and out-groups, between acceptable and unacceptable identities, between proper and improper behaviors" (2006: 23). A stigmatype like white trash thus creates "categories of status and prestige, explicitly, through labeling and naming, and implicitly, through individous comparison" (Wray 2006: 23).

21 | In his conception of symbolic boundary work and social distinction, Wray particularly draws on Pierre Bourdieu's work in *Language and Symbolic Power* (2001).

22 | Pages 10-13 in Wray 2006 reserved for figures.

In order to situate the emergence of a British variant of white trash as stigmatyping figurations, the following chapter gives a brief comparative historical overview of figurations of American white trash and the dynamics of race and lower-class identities in Britain in the nineteenth century. The aim is to define the sites on which, to return to the terminology of Deleuze and Guattari, the discourses of race and class plant their flags in bodies. Considering the function of tainted whites as abject boundary figures, I will sketch the way the tainted white body becomes a signifier of disease that not only functions individually as a demarcation between healthy and diseased human bodies, but is simultaneously a figure of territorialisation that marks the stratification of social bodies under the dispositif of hygiene.

In *Imperial Leather,* Anne McClintock provides a historical sketch of the emergence of a "poetics of degeneration" (1995: 46) that accompanied the social crises in nineteenth-century Britain, where the demarcation of boundaries between normality and degeneration became necessary in order to maintain a sense of cultural order:

> Imagining the degeneration into which humanity could fall was a necessary part of imagining the exaltation to which it could aspire. The degenerate classes, defined as departures from the normal human type, were as necessary to the self-definition of the middle class as the idea of degeneration was to the idea of progress, for the distance along the path of progress traveled by some portions of humanity could be measured only by the distance others lagged behind. Normality thus emerged as a product of deviance, and the baroque invention of clusters of degenerate types highlighted the boundaries of the normal. The poetics of degeneration was a poetics of social crisis. (1995: 46)

According to McClintock, this poetics of degeneration relied on the demarcation not only of individual human bodies but also on the transposition of these corporeal orders of normality and degeneration into the spatialised social order of Britain's cities and the colonies overseas:

> In the last decades of the century, Victorian social planners drew deeply on social Darwinism and the idea of degeneration to figure the social crises erupting relentlessly in the cities and colonies. By the end of the 1870s, Britain was foundering in severe depression, and throughout the 1880s class insurgency, feminist upheavals, the socialist revival, swelling poverty and the dearth of housing and jobs fed deepening middle class fears. [...]. The atmosphere of impending catas-

trophe gave rise to major changes in social theory, which drew on the poetics of degeneration for legitimation. (1995: 46)

Thus, the late nineteenth century sees a considerable form of social stratification that is based on bodily images, separating normal bodies from degenerate ones, healthy bodies from diseased ones, and adapting these dichotomies in "almost every nook and cranny of Victorian social life", thereby "providing the Victorian elite with the justification it needed to discipline and contain the 'dangerous classes'" (McClintock 1995: 46). The resulting "complex hierarchy of social metaphors" (McClintock 1995: 46) consequently produced a mapping of social life that ordered the British populace according to the racial model of the colonised countries, with the black "primitives" serving as a metonymy for the "unruly poor" (54, see also my previous discussion of McClintock).

These constructions of the British population according to the parameters of health and disease and the mapping of such dichotomies onto the bodies of collectives and individuals who subsequently become part of the spatial imagination of imperialist Britain is of central importance for an analysis of contemporary figurations of British white trash; it is in this form of biologist mapping that major precursors of contemporary imaginings of the racialised underclasses can be found. At the same time, these are the elements that connect British concepts of a racially filthy or degenerate underclass to American figurations of racially inferior whites in the nineteenth-century South. What is at stake in all cases is not only the stability of the empirically manifest social order of the British or American nation but also the symbolic order. Both are connected in the figurations that demarcate stable boundaries, as Matt Wray describes in relation to the South's white trash:

In conjoining such primal opposites [of the sacred and profane, purity and impurity, morality and immorality, cleanliness and dirt] into a single category, *white trash* names a kind of disturbing liminality: a monstrous, transgressive identity of mutually violating boundary terms, a dangerous threshold state of being neither one nor the other. It brings together into a single ontological category that which must be kept apart in order to establish a meaningful and stable symbolic order. (Wray 2006: 2)

Thus, "*white trash* names a people whose very existence seems to threaten the symbolic and social order. As such, the term can evoke strong emotions of contempt, anger, and disgust" (Wray 2006: 2). In the South, the white body becomes the ambivalently inscribed demarcating figure of the dichotomies of normality and degeneration, health and disease. On both sides of the dichotomies, whiteness can become meaningful in different ways. Likewise, Alastair Bonnett argues in relation to Victorian Britain that "in the nineteenth century, the notion that all Britons were white was asserted with considerably more force and conviction outside Britain than within it" (2000: 28) – far from being a self-evident trait of all Britons, whiteness was a very class-specific attribution. While within the "colonial imagination", all Europeans simultaneously could claim to be white and thus claim to bear the phenotypic markers of civilisation, Europe – and Britain – were clearly intranationally divided when it came to the designation of the privileges of whiteness (Bonnett 2000: 32).

In fact, Bonnett's analysis of nineteenth-century discourses shows that the British working classes were likewise considered a race apart from white upper-class Britons. However, while American white trash was figured in the nineteenth century as a primarily rural phenomenon, and the South specifically was held as a backward and disease-ridden region diametrically opposed to the civilised, largely urbanised and progressive North, the British national imaginary of the time considered rural areas a space of purity, while the urban centres saw increasing racial hybridisation,[23] "unclean" work and a lack of proper sanitary facilities. Bonnett quotes several publications from the late nineteenth century that draw analogies between the "dark continent" of Africa and the working-class areas and slums of the British inner city. While George Sims in *How the Poor Live* (1883) writes that there exists "a dark continent that is within easy walking distance of the General Post Office", inhabited by "wild races" (qtd. in Bonnett 2000: 33), William Booth writes about *Darkest England and the Way Out* (1890, qtd. in Bonnett 2000: 33) and, as John Marriott shows, draws "parallels between degenerated Africans living in foetid darkness and the metropolitan poor" (1999: 95).

While in the nineteenth century, the urban poor and the working class were defined "as the dark other of bourgeois whiteness" (Bonnett 2000: 36), hampered by the unhealthy and poor living conditions of the urban areas (Bonnett 2000: 38) and as "a race apart" (Marriott 1999: 82)

23 | Bonnett shows that Irish immigrants in particular, then considered to be racially other, close to the "Moors" and of darker skin, were increasingly "mixing" with inner-city Britons (2000: 35).

that was associated with the "'grotesque', 'faecal' dirt of the poor – filth, sewage, swamp, slime and putrefaction" (Marriott 1999: 84) that in turn was "colour coded" as "unambiguously black" (Marriott 1999: 85),[24] the American South and its lazy, hookworm-infested white trash posed similar concerns of bodily and national health. Bonnett and Matt Wray argue in the same vein when it comes to the process of "whitening" (Wray 2006: 132) the so-called crackers and the British working class. Both detect changes in the capitalist systems of the United States and Britain at the turn of the twentieth century. Wray argues that the campaign against the hookworm in the South took place because

> the South needed its workers, and this capitalist imperative, perhaps more than any other force, explains why the South - and not the West, which also experienced high rates of hookworm infection - was singled out for the crusade. The South was the ideal place to harness the discourses of race and nationality and to impose the middle-class cult of cleanliness and hygiene. (Wray 2006: 132)[25]

Likewise, Bonnett detects transformations in British whiteness that are linked to "imperialism's impact upon the political and economic restructuring of British capitalism", which included the introduction of "significant non-market, state-interventionist and social consensus (most importantly, populist nationalism) tendencies into British society" (2000: 39).

24 | Marriott shows the significant place that dirt had in the bourgeois imaginary of the nineteenth century: "Dirt was colour coded; it was neither brown nor grey, but unambiguously black. This was no semantic or poetic device. This synonymic association was part of a structuring process through which a complex chain of signification was established in a series of binary oppositions: dirt/filth-cleanliness; unwashed-washed; darkness/shadow-light; impure/defiled-pure; black-white; low-high. Until the 1850s much of this coding was muted; for most Victorians heretofore, race described social rather than colour distinctions. [...]. During the 1880s, however, the associations with 'black' became more direct" (1999: 85).

25 | With regard to the context of the British lower classes, it is also significant that, as Wray explains, "by insisting that these poor white victims were of pure Anglo-Saxon descent, crusaders sought to provoke sympathy where before there had been scorn and disgust" (2006: 132) - which proves Bonnett's claim that outside of Britain, it was sufficient to be of British descent for the claim to whiteness (2000: 28, 31).

This increasing tendency to shape the British workforce for a nationalist project necessitating the racially more monolithic conception of a uniformly white British people developed in line with an increased interest to care for the wellbeing of the nation's poor and the working classes, resulting from the "widespread conviction that welfare was needed in order to breed the kind of healthy and vigorous race capable of controlling an empire" (Bonnett 2000: 39) – a motivation not unlike the one that prompted the hookworm crusades in the American South.

Thus, just as individuals formerly held as poor white trash were reconceived as the victims of an epidemic that kept them from developing their full potential as white Anglo-Saxons, British state intervention and welfare (which started to develop in the early twentieth century and peaked directly after the end of the Second World War), "both fused and recuperated contradictory and potentially explosively antagonistic social forces into a national project", and thus furthered "changes within both the social boundaries of whiteness and its connotative range" (Bonnett 2000: 40). According to Bonnett, the new notion of welfare and the notion of British racial unity turned whiteness from a supremacist-elitist identity into the "identity of the ordinary; it evokes [...] the homely virtues of quietness, tidiness, cleanness and decency" (2000: 40). Within this transformed notion of (British) whiteness, however, 'black' still remained the signifier of the racially and culturally Other. This is important to bear in mind when going a few steps further than Bonnett, who in his historical account of the "becoming-white" of the British working class does not take into account the subsequent shift in the semantic dimensions of British working-class whiteness. This shift marks the white working class and its subgroup, the 'underclass' not as ordinarily (and thus invisibly) white, but as problematically white. In that respect, Chris Haylett interprets the shift towards a working-class or underclass abject whiteness within the racist semantics within which "black" is the prime signifier of the abject:

> Where 'black' is the originary signifier of the abject, as residual matter, defilement, and disorder, 'white' embodied in degenerate working-class 'others' come to share the same symbolic register [...]. Importantly, that symbolic slippage between 'black' and 'white' reveals racial difference to be a psychosocial construction rather than a biological fact, that is, it is not about skin and biology but about skin and politics. In this way, poor whites can be seen as dangerous to the symbolic order of British nationhood where hierarchies of national belonging and privilege are still natural-

ised by skin colour. This is the situation that the project of reconstructing the white working-class poor is partly addressed to, it is about the maintenance of a dominant material and symbolic order of class – 'race' – nation. (Haylett 2001: 361)

Haylett's interpretation of the semantics of whiteness, class and nationhood is thus analogous to Matt Wray's analysis of the interplay of material and symbolic boundaries. In both the United States and the United Kingdom, tainted whiteness becomes an abject signifier that negotiates the intersection of class, race and the nation. Thus, class and race can at times even become mutually expressive of each other in an almost reciprocal way, and their respective constellations represent the nation along a dichotomy of Self and Other. This dichotomy of national belonging operates through the abject signifier of blackness, which is also the qualifier for the gradations of whiteness from 'respectable' to 'abject'.

In that context, *white trash* becomes what Sara Ahmed (2004a) has called a "sticky signifier". Drawing on Judith Butler's concept of performativity, Ahmed analyses disgust and its cultural dimension as a performative semiotic process in which the symbolic and the material converge: "Disgust works performatively not only as the intensification of contact between bodies and objects, but also as a speech act. […] disgust can generate effects by 'binding' signs to bodies as a binding that 'blocks' new meanings" (2004a: 92). Ahmed's explanation of how words or concepts "stick" to material bodies helps to explain the interplay of symbolic and material boundaries that the white trash body is subjected to, and it also serves as a tool for explaining the way race and class become signs mutually expressing each other (i. e., race can become a signifying system for class and vice versa). The notion of a binding of signs to bodies that blocks new meanings also explains the conspicuous persistence of a view of the working-class body as potentially deviant – a notion which, as I have shown throughout this chapter, has been persistent from the nineteenth century well into the twenty-first. Consequently, the dimension of time has to be acknowledged in explaining their discursive power.

In her Butler-influenced approach to the performativity of "sticky" signs, Ahmed particularly emphasises the temporal and relational dimensions of such signs. Accordingly, she claims that the performative approach accounts for the way signs can develop meaning over time in that "performativity depends upon the sedimentation of the past; it reiterates what has already been said, and its power and authority depend upon how it recalls that which has already been brought into existence" (Ahmed 2004a: 92–93). Thus, "this model of performativity relates to my argument about the temporality of disgust: it both 'lags behind' the object from which it recoils, and generates the object in the very event of recoiling" (Ahmed 2004a: 93). If applied to the context of contemporary figurations of tainted whiteness and an abject working class or underclass, one can say that these contemporary figurations have such powerful discursive effects not only because they are widely and aggressively disseminated in the present moment but because they also draw on an historically established repertoire of signs. As Ahmed explains:

> A performative utterance can only 'succeed' if it repeats a coded or iterable utterance: it works precisely by citing norms and conventions that already exist. [...]. Importantly, the historicity of the performative and its role in the generation of effects cannot be separated. If the performative opens up the future, it does so precisely in the process of repeating past conventions, as to repeat something is always to open up the (structural) possibility that one will repeat something with a difference. (Ahmed 2004a: 93)

Ahmed's last point here is particularly significant for the way working-class whiteness could shift in meaning over time, and it is also of major importance for analysing literary interventions into the figuring processes described in this thesis because it is precisely the repertoire of signs associated with whiteness, class and disgust that the literary texts I will examine draw on, cite, reiterate and reshape. It is important to see the historical and discursive preconditions of the emergence of British white trash in its contemporary figurations, and this is why one has to acknowledge the complex semiotic interplay of material, symbolic and contextual factors. For, as Ahmed explains,

> to name something as disgusting [...] is performative. It relies on previous norms and conventions of speech, and it generates the object that it names (the disgusting object/event). To name something as disgusting is not to make something out of nothing. But to say something is disgusting is still to 'make something'; it generates a set of effects, *which then adhere as a disgusting object*. Indeed, the word 'disgust' is itself a sticky sign, insofar as other signs stick to it ('yuk', 'bad', 'savage'), and insofar as it sticks to some bodies and objects ('the naked savage'), rather than others. To name something as disgusting is to transfer the stickiness of

the word 'disgust' to an object, which henceforth becomes generated as the very thing that is spoken. (Ahmed 2004a: 93-94)

With Ahmed, I contend that the disgusting quality ascribed to *white trash* on a semiotic-material level relies on the disgust potential of "blackness" as a spectrum reaching into forms of "impure" whiteness as well as on what Ahmed calls the "figurability of disgust" – that is, the possibility to attribute "quality to substance" on the basis of the historical iterability of certain signs (2004a: 90). The "stickiness" of *white trash* as a signifier of disgust is what makes it so adaptable to multiple contexts. This is why, as I will show throughout this thesis, this particular sticky sign is not restricted to the spheres of race and class alone but is also of central importance for gender, sexuality and for discourses of the British national community as a whole, thus becoming meaningful in a number of subcontexts. In that, the semantic stickiness is also a product of intersectional connections between identity categories as well as of the cultural contexts within which disgust is figured.

It is precisely the range within which the figure of white trash becomes meaningful that the stickiness of disgust signifiers accounts for. To be more concrete, when looking at the literary texts by Irvine Welsh, Niall Griffiths and John King, it is striking how the depiction of tainted whiteness is related to a variety of contexts within contemporary British culture, ranging from the actual interrelation of working-class identity and whiteness to the broader contexts of Scottish and Welsh devolution and contemporary British neoliberalism. In all these contexts, tainted whiteness is evoked and interrogated as a signification of socio-cultural abjection.

Literary Figurations of Race and Class

There seems to be an analogy between the "disappearance" of class between the 1980s and early 2000s and the role of class in British literature. Nicola Allen states that "[it] seems that with regards to fiction that is predominantly discussed in academia, class can still be considered as a difficult or taboo subject" (2008: 42), and that while there might be an increased recognition of the marginal in vast areas of contemporary British literary criticism, these "marginal areas of study are moulded to fit a middle-class-centred approach, such that feminist and gay literature gained a foothold on such courses, typifying a growing acceptance of those lifestyles that had been previously marginalized but existed firmly within the middle classes [...]" (42). Allen further detects a "blurring and subsequent obscuring" of class-based categories because of an "increasing hybridization of culture" and because "the markers of working class culture were extended and appropriated by the middle classes" that in turn facilitates the increased marginalisation of the working classes "as they no longer possess a distinct voice through which to speak" (2008: 42). Allen's argument seems to imply that contemporary literature and the critical discourse about it are complicit with a process of marginalising working and lower classes. Meanwhile, the middle classes, in their appropriation of different hybridised identity markers have become an invisible normative identity formation within which there is space for potential other forms of identity, be they marked in terms of ethnicity, gender or otherwise. Such a form of a classed invisible norm resembles the claims of literary critics influenced by Critical Whiteness Studies such as Toni Morrison and Rebecca Aanerud who, largely within the context of American literature, argue that in many literary texts "whiteness as race operates as an unmarked racial category" (Aanerud 1997: 37) that emerges through the unspoken presence of whiteness in conjunction with the often explicitly marked blackness of characters.

In his 2009 study *Evading Class in Contemporary British Literature*, Lawrence Driscoll argues quite in the same vein as Nicola Allen that under the "ideological and political pressure to erase class in the period from Margaret Thatcher to Tony Blair" British literature "both articulates and silences questions of class, thereby enabling and sustaining the ideological notion of a 'classless' contemporary British literature and culture" (1). The return of class is thus "a troubling, subterranean and repressed element in contemporary literature, theory, and culture" (Driscoll 2009: 1). Driscoll argues that within a broader movement of embourgeoisement and according ideological shifts in the period "from Thatcher to Blair", in the British novel "working-class experience has been revised and rewritten during this period so as to eliminate it as an object of knowledge and power and that this rewriting of both middle- and working-class identity can be delineated and traced through the pages of the contemporary British novel" (2009: 3). However, it would be misleading to completely deny the existence of class as a topic in British literature during the last decades. In that respect, it must be questioned in what modes class is spoken nowadays. It is notable that the "recently canonized middle-class authors" whose works Driscoll subjects to "critical readings", and which he subsumes under the label of the "contemporary British novel" – namely, Martin Amis, Zadie Smith, Ian McEwan, Peter Ackroyd, Jonathan Coe, Kazuo Ishiguro, Pat Barker, Will Self and Alan Hollinghurst (2009: 1) – are in fact exclusively writers from (or who have immigrated to) and residing in England, and are thus not necessarily representative of the other British nations. Thus, a nation such as Scotland, which has spawned many contemporary authors who could be considered as contemporary writers concerned with working-class subjects, such as Irvine Welsh, James Kelman, Janice Galloway or Alan Warner, is left out of the equation.

But perhaps this flaw is even more telling of the conspicuous issue of narrating class in post-Thatcherite Britain: after all, it could be said that Englishness, very much like whiteness and middle-classedness, is an invisible norm not only within the formations that shape British national identity but also within the canon of "British" literature. In his study *Devolving English Literature*, Robert Crawford argues that the unity of "English Literature" (meaning literature from the British archipelago in English) is an "illusion" and must be critically devolved in line with the political processes of devolution within Britain. Crawford argues that the few tendencies that focus on "teasing apart the strands" of that illusory unity tend to "concentrate on groups most obviously typified as 'other' than the white English male" but that "far less attention has been paid to less immediately visible cultural differences within 'English Literature'" (2000: 3). He criticises the "academic ghettos" that emerged when scholars tended to literatures beyond the Anglocentricity of British literature (Crawford 2000: 3). In recent years, Michael Gardiner has published several studies on the devolution of "English" literature and the inherent cultural differences within the literatures of the archipelago (2004, 2012 and 2013). According to these studies, it is precisely from the national margins of the British nations that a monolithic notion of British literature and cultural representation can be challenged. Gardiner's approach is particularly useful for situating the texts by Irvine Welsh, Niall Griffiths, John King and their treatment of tainted whiteness in devolutionary contexts which, as I will argue in the following chapters, reveal "the underside of English Literature's British-imperial story" (Gardiner 2012: 111).

Such issues tie in with Chris Haylett's diagnoses of the cultural contexts within which new notions of tainted whiteness and questions of class emerge. As discussed above, Haylett understands the "white working-class poor" as "part of the production of the modern social" (2001: 353), and in connection to the British modern social, questions of devolution and the subsequent renegotiation of British, and specifically English, national identity are being raised. Such questions are once again strongly connected to notions of racialisation:

> The process of political devolution for Scotland, Northern Ireland, and Wales has instigated questions about the shape of English representative democracy and of English identity per se, with 'Englishness' standing for white British identities. The idea of an English identity 'in crisis' has promoted discussion of Englishness as a culturally and historically distinct ethnicity like any other. Now faced with the task of reinventing itself for a modern national imaginary – multicultural, postimperial Britain – Englishness has apparently become the focus of a national self-reflexivity [...]. (2001: 356)

In this context, then, Englishness and Britishness become questions of race, and national identity becomes a matter of racialisation. It is precisely within this context of national self-reflexivity in post-British times that literary interrogations of British tainted whiteness must be regarded. What this chapter has shown is that the newly emerging figures of tainted whiteness – be they called *white trash, chavs* or something else – only at first glance are exclusively related to class alone. Rather, class is but one of the decisive identity categories which have been experiencing fundamental shifts within the last decades – and these shifts are not only related to the socio-political and economic bases of class identity which have been challenged by the political changes in post-war Britain (most importantly during the years of political redefinition through Thatcher, Major and New Labour). Rather, they are all connected to a more complex (and sometimes, as the literary texts that I analyse show, paradoxical) intersectional context which constitutes contemporary identities.

Within this context, it is the "spectre of whiteness and its racialized and racializing meanings" (Griffin and Braidotti 2002: 221) that haunts the emergence of identity positions in Britain. Following such observations, the figuration of white trash in contemporary British literature can be said to embody this volatility or spectrality in an uncanny way. It represents precisely that which is problematic, undesirable and maybe even anachronistic about whiteness in post-Empire British culture – and, in its evocation of imperial modes of racialisation, it becomes the past haunting the present.

II "The trash ay Europe"

Abject Working-Class Whiteness in the Novels of Irvine Welsh

Irvine Welsh is certainly the best known and most thoroughly researched of the three authors discussed here. During the last ten years, literary criticism has caught up with the popularity of Welsh's work, resulting in several articles and, so far, two major monographs (Kelly 2005; Morace 2007), as well as an edited volume, the *Edinburgh Companion to Irvine Welsh* (Schoene 2010a). The most common current of Welsh criticism situates his writing within a renaissance of Scottish literature peaking in the 1980s and 1990s with the work of writers such as, among others, James Kelman, Duncan McLean, Janice Galloway and Alan Warner – writers whose emphasis rests on decidedly Scottish and lower-class issues and who employ innovative representative modes such as dialect writing. Consequently, criticism on Welsh has predominantly produced analyses of his work's contribution to the representation of Scottishness, with a special emphasis on a postcolonial angle. Cairns Craig's study *The Modern Scottish Novel: Narrative and the National Imagination* (1999) can in this respect be considered as the groundbreaking work of criticism. Rather than providing an extensive literature review on the current state of research on Welsh's fiction, I would like to focus on a particular angle in Welsh criticism which forms the point of departure for my own approach to his novels' representations of tainted whiteness, and which, as is my contention, has so far been often overlooked in favour of more readily available approaches. The approach I want to focus on here has been provided by Gavin Miller in a chapter of the *Edinburgh Companion to Irvine Welsh,* titled "Welsh and Identity Politics" (2010). Miller assesses and challenges a certain

> view of contemporary Scottish literature in which the value of Irvine Welsh's work is in its contribution to the cultural diversity of the Scottish canon. 'Voice' is a keyword in the jargon of this critical approach: Welsh's writing matters because it gives a voice to a subordinated social group – the urban working class – and this voice 'speaks' in Welsh's work without belittlement. The term 'voice' functions in this kind of criticism as a synecdoche for 'values', 'culture' or 'ethos'. (2010: 89)

Miller provocatively objects to such a reading by questioning whether Welsh's texts "really represent, dignify and celebrate the difference of his favoured identity group" and suggests paying more attention to the "equivocal" evidence provided by Welsh's texts (2010: 89). As he argues, "Scottish literary criticism must refuse the neoliberal invitation to regard Welsh's work as a writing that celebrates the difference of the working class" (Miller 2010: 99). In fact, he claims that

> there is [...] something quite radical that can be gleaned from Welsh's interrogation of contemporary identity politics. His writing traces sceptically the disavowed racial or genealogical essentialism, the persistence of 'blood' in such contemporary identity discourses as Scottish sectarianism, the supposed transhistorical memory of guilt and trauma, and the curious transformation of economic class into cultural identity. (Miller 2010: 98–99)

Miller rests his argument on the interpretation of exemplary aspects in some of Welsh's major works, most notably his novels *Marabou Stork Nightmares* (1995), *Glue* (2001) and *Porno* (2002), by looking at the way race and racialisation are critically assessed in Welsh's novels as a means to draw connections to other identity categories such as national or religious identity and class. What is, according to Miller, scrutinised in Welsh's novels is the tendency to consider ideas of Scottishness and working-class identity as hereditary identities which supposedly can be traced along the lines of 'bloodlines' and descent:

> Welsh's fiction represents 'blood' – descent, heredity and, more broadly, 'race' – as the usual stuff of identity, lurking within seemingly more innocent ideas such as 'memory' and 'trauma'. Even the concept of social class, as Welsh presents it, has been reworked in this way, so that a specious 'working-class identity' is passed down to the sons and daughters of the working class. (2010: 90)

Instead of taking such problematic notions of a quasi-racial descent of cultural identities for granted – something which, as Miller argues, is the inherent danger of a literary criticism which all too readily subscribes to and affirms such representations – Welsh goes a step further and hallenges such identity models.

Miller exemplifies this with a passage from *Porno*, which also fits well within the context of my analysis of figurations of white trash. In this passage, Spud Murphy, an unemployed recovering heroin addict, enters a library and, when encountering a security guard, "feels himself to be the object of a racial gaze" (Miller 2010: 92): "ah could jist sortay tell thit this boy kens what ah am: tea leaf, junky, schemie, ghetto child, third-generation bog-wog, gyppo" (*P* 145). Spud's belief that "his Irish racial identity as a 'bog-wog' (that is, as an 'Irish nigger') [...] is somehow visible to the guard, rather than the more obvious marks of his poverty and addiction" (Miller 2010: 92) – can be read ironically as what I would describe as a paranoid hypersensitivity to race, which is believed to be something inherently natural and ubiquitous while in fact it would be impossible to identify any 'racial' or 'ethnic' markers that might hint at third-generation 'Irishness'. Spud, who appears in *Trainspotting* as well as in its sequel *Porno* and the prequel *Skagboys* (2012) and is in all three novels characterised as a good-natured but unfortunate lowlife of low intelligence, here serves as a caricature of the belief in the construction of race as a "natural" and inherited mode of identity which is applicable to different cultural forms, including Irish-Scottish or working-class forms: "Even though he may not inherit his race, he claims to inherit a history of trauma that has arisen because others believe in the existence of an Irish race, and it is this cultural-cum-psychological inheritance that identifies his supposed non-biological descent group – namely, 'Irish-Scottish'" (Miller 2010: 92).

This belief in the existence of racialised identities, I would argue, is at the heart of many identity conflicts in post-British culture. Thus, it is close at hand that in Irvine Welsh's fiction the discourse of Scottish political and cultural devolution is always linked with other identity factors. Scottish national identity seems to be inseparable from questions of (working) class, gender (especially masculinity) and, most importantly, race and whiteness. In fact, the latter becomes the mode with which all the other identity categories are thought and figured. I will follow Gavin Miller's observation that Welsh's key texts present and dissect characters who try to come to terms with their conflicted identities along the vectors of Scottishness, working-classedness and masculinity in their racialised forms, but I will extend Miller's focus by paying particular attention to the centrality of whiteness and the figure of white trash in Welsh's texts as embodiments of these conflicts. As I will show, Welsh's characters cling to an imaginary that is based on what Gavin Miller calls a "quasi-racial mythology" (2010: 98), which is exposed and deconstructed by Welsh's non-linear and sometimes experimental narratives.

II.1 *Trainspotting*

Trainspotting describes the flipside of British culture from the points-of-view of several Edinburgh-based protagonists living on the margins of society – unemployed, addicted to drugs and indulging in subcultural forms of expression such as punk and football fandom, the protagonists are rejected by society and at the same time reject both the political oppression of their Scottish home country by the central government in Westminster and any norm set by the establishment. This is also reflected in the novel's 'anarchic' nonlinear narrative composition and its multiplicity of discursive voices, which in the early reception of the novel led some critics to question its status as a "proper" novel (see Matt McGuire 2010: 19, quoting Michael Brockington: It was "hard to call it a novel, more a ragged accretion of short stories"). Such questions of genre and style are symptomatic of the novel's early reception, as are questions regarding its bleak and controversial subject matter, which largely dealt with the devastating effects of unemployment, drug addiction and the spread of HIV in mid-1980s Edinburgh as well as with subcultural forms of expression attached to the social milieu most affected by these maladies. What further contributed to the perplexing effect of Welsh's prose is that it largely refuses standard written English and rather prefers the direct transcription of the sociolect and vernacular of the working-class population in the Edinburgh district of Leith, with only occasional interferences by an authorial narrator. As Matt McGuire observes with regard to Irvine Welsh's self-proclaimed anti-literary stance, "the episodic and fragmented nature of *Trainspotting* is crucial to the universe of experiences it is attempting to depict. The junkies, misfits and 'schemies' that populate the novel inhabit highly chaotic and unpredictable lives" (2010: 20).

Often interpreted as a challenge to hegemonic bourgeois forms of narrative, *Trainspotting* thus has been positioned as a countermodel to the common form of the modernist realist novel that dominated the twentieth century: "The lack of a stable narrative vantage point mirrors the experience of many characters in *Trainspotting*. Displaced to the socio-economic margins of society, their lives cannot be rendered by the cosy and predictable plots of bourgeois life. [...] *Trainspotting* deliberately subverts such hierarchical organization, with the characters themselves acting as guides within the world of the novel" (McGuire 2010: 20–21). Welsh's debut novel can thus, in Aaron Kelly's words, be described as a "decentred fiction"

(Kelly 2005: 14). Kelly has highlighted the proximity of such a writing to Mikhail Bakhtin's notion of dialogic and heteroglot uses of literary language (2005: 17–18).

This heteroglot form and Welsh's refusal to offer a text which is easy to pin down along the lines of clearly defined ideologies is what informs the novel's negotiation of social issues and notions of national identity in pre-devolution Scotland, since "Welsh repudiates the fixity of class by problematising class-bound identities and showing working-class identity not only as heterogeneous, but as profoundly troubled and contradictory" (2010: 4). The depiction of figurations of tainted whiteness must also be considered within this deliberately ambiguous context. The novel's central allusion to white trash is made in an interior monologue by one of the novel's main voices, Mark Renton, on his home district of Leith, which, in his eyes is "a place ay dispossessed white trash in a country fill ay dispossessed white trash. Some say that the Irish are the trash ay Europe. That's shite. It's the Scots. The Irish hud the bottle tae win thir country back, or at least maist ay it" (*T* 190). This statement appears striking for several reasons. First of all, Mark Renton here situates himself and his existence within a broader socio-cultural context in Great Britain. It clearly shows that he equates his situation on the microlevel (Leith) with the situation on a broader scale, as Leith's social malaise becomes metonymic for the state of Scotland and its situation within the United Kingdom in general. Some chapters before, when contemplating his sociopathic associate Frank Begbie, Renton renders Frank as representative of the larger scheme of things in the Scottish nation:

> Ah hate cunts like that. Cunts like Begbie. Cunts that are intae baseball-batting every fucker that's different; pakis, poofs, n what huv ye. Fuckin failures in a country ay failures. It's nae good blamin it oan the English fir colonising us. Ah don't hate the English. They're just wankers. We are colonised by wankers. We can't even pick a decent, vibrant, healthy culture to be colonised by. No. We're ruled by effete arseholes. What does that make us? The lowest of the fuckin low, the scum of the earth. The most wretched, servile, miserable, pathetic trash that was ever shat intae creation. Ah don't hate the English. They just git oan wi the shite thuv goat. Ah hate the Scots. (*T* 78)

This quote is one of the central parts of the novel that triggers critical discussions of its postcolonial implications with regard to the history of

Scotland's subjection to English rule.[1] As Berthold Schoene states, such moments express the novel's "celebration of cultural dislocation" and its tendency to "vociferously [militate] against its own Scottishness" (2010: 3). Thus, *Trainspotting* can be regarded as a reaction to "Scottish literature's chief preoccupations: identity, class, language and fantasy" (Schoene 2010b: 2), breaking with clear-cut definitions of Scottish national or class identities. In Welsh's novel, "Scottishness can signify cultural paralysis, rootedness and mobility, identity as well as difference" (Schoene 2010b: 2). This ambiguous revision of notions of Scottishness has been one of the focal points of criticism on Welsh so far. What becomes evident in these two quotes from Renton and what is symptomatic for the novel as a whole is that it treats the individual subject as deeply immersed in collective issues.

Several aspects are important for the context of Mark Renton's use of the phrase *white trash*. First of all, it is crucial to situate the phrase and its function with relation to two of the central dichotomies guiding the entire novel, the one being the cultural tension between Scotland and England, represented on a microlevel by the tension between working-class Leith and the commercial centres of Edinburgh, and the other being the one between health and illness. That these dichotomies are mutually entwined, and that the private and the collective form a further tension in the novel, becomes clear in the overall make-up of Mark's interior monologues. He constantly moves from the personal to the political and considers his personality, his subjective perspective and his mind and body as fatally inseparable from the systemic, the collective and the political – a fact that he constantly struggles with. It is also noteworthy that his monologues often arise from mentally and physically extreme and demanding situations – for instance, when he suffers from heroin withdrawal and is observed by his parents, all the more highlighting the connections between his personal situation and the collective-political circumstances broadly determining his own situation.

In his previously quoted monologue about the white trash of Leith, one can clearly detect the movement from the micro- to the macrolevel that is particular for the novel as a whole. In a first step, Renton compares Leith to the whole of Scotland by stating that, just like Leith, Scotland is "a

1 | For a detailed consideration of *Trainspotting* in the context of gender politics and postcolonialism in Scottish literature, see Lehner 2011.

country fill ay dispossessed white trash" (*T* 190). He then goes on to link this observation to a broader European context, drawing on common pre-Celtic Tiger images of Ireland as one of the poorest countries in Europe. Strikingly, Mark Renton here not only evokes the discourse around the Irish as an economic, postcolonial problem case within Europe until the onset of the Celtic Tiger boom. What is even more striking in his observations is that he links this to the discourse around the ambivalent racial status of the Irish. Since the Irish and their relative whiteness are a recurrent test case in Critical Race/Whiteness Studies and Irish Studies focusing on issues of race, it is remarkable that *Trainspotting*'s main focaliser and narrative instance chooses to reflect on the use of the term *white trash* for the Scots and the Irish alike.[2] As Noel Ignatiev has shown in his study *How the Irish Became White* (1995), the status of the Irish as "white", which might be seemingly self-evident due to the complexion of their skin, has in fact been challenged throughout history and has been perceived relative to socio-cultural circumstances – that is, the Irish were not able to assume the privileges associated with their skin in certain historical contexts.[3]

Thus, when Renton refers to the Irish as trash, he evokes the very racial tensions that resulted from Ireland's experience as a country colonised by the English as well as from the ethnic constellations Irish emigrants had to face in the new colonies in America. Using a stigmatype that emerged in the particular American context but which, however, was intricately shaped by the British differentiation of social groups based on class from the fifteenth to the seventeenth century, as Matt Wray argues (see 2006: 135), clearly suggests that the racial and class tensions characteristic of this stigmatype can also be found on the British Isles, and most particularly in Scotland and Ireland.

---

2 | For a comparative account of the racialisation of the Irish-Catholic and the British working class in Victorian Britain, see my discussion of Bonnett 2000 in the previous chapter.

3 | In the chapter "How the Irish Became White (Again)" in his introductory book on *Whiteness* (2007), Steve Garner, in response to Ignatiev's book, has also argued that the Irish had to continuously "renew" their status as white even up until the time of the Celtic Tiger that saw an increased rate of migrations into the Republic of Ireland and an analogous decreased rate of emigration from the Republic (120–135).

The monologue thus also links the novel and its cultural comment to another novel that was published six years previous to *Trainspotting* and comparably evokes the racial tensions of the United States and the times of African-American slavery within an Anglo-Irish and Irish-European context: in Roddy Doyle's *The Commitments* (1987), it is the member of a soul group consisting of unemployed Dubliners who states that "The Irish are the niggers of Europe, lads [...]. An' Dubliners are the niggers of Ireland [...]. An' the northside Dubliners are the niggers o' Dublin – Say it loud. I'm black an' I'm proud" (*Com* 9). Both The Commitments and Trainspotting thus demonstrate a tendency in British and Irish literature to draw on the vocabulary and symbolic components of American race relations to make their points about the difficult relationship between race, class and region in Britain and Ireland. It is, however, important to consider further aspects that inform the use of this conspicuous term within a British context. Apart from the Scottish-devolutionist context that has frequently been discussed in relation to Welsh's work (see Craig 1999, Gardiner 2004, Hologa 2016: 123–238, March 2002), it is firstly important to consider the discourse around "multiculturalism" as it was formed during the 1980s and especially after the 1981 Brixton riots – an event that can be considered as the culmination of problems related to the economic recession at that time and its effects on the non-white population of Britain – and, secondly, to consider the impact of Thatcherite politics and rhetoric with regard to the same situation and as to its strongly conservative and revisionist utilisation of notions of Britishness and empire during the Falklands crisis.

Welsh's occupation with class, race and whiteness in *Trainspotting* as well as in his subsequent novels *Marabou Stork Nightmares* and *Filth* can be considered as an interrogation of these different discourses and their complex interconnections. *Trainspotting* marks a moment in recent British history that sees the (white) British population becoming shamefully aware of its own whiteness as well as of its classedness. In this context, *white trash* demarcates a liminal figure in the process of making sense of peculiar constellations of race and class, and Welsh's own take on this figuration can be read as an examination of the "sticky signs" of classed and raced forms of abjection.

Challenges to the White Self in Multicultural Britain

In the same year *Trainspotting* was published, black teenager Stephen Lawrence was stabbed to death by a group of white youths (see chapter I). This case, happening just two months after the abduction, torture and murder of the toddler James Bulger at the hands of two ten-year-old boys,[4] deeply shook Britain not only because it was another case of seemingly unmotivated violence among adolescents, but even more so due to its racist context as I have outlined in the previous chapter. Published three months after the Lawrence murder, Welsh's novel can of course by no means be read as a direct reaction to the ensuing discussion of racist crimes committed by white working-class youths. But it is nevertheless a significant yardstick for the cultural and political context that produced and was subsequently shaped by the Lawrence murder case when it comes to the themes of race, British 1990s multiculturalism and class politics. Michael Collins, whose examination of the Lawrence case I discussed earlier, analyses the 1990s attempt to erase class as a political and cultural identity category and retraces forms of stigmatyping common in the American use of the term *white trash* in the new "demonisation of the white working-class" around the time of the Lawrence murder:

> They [the British white working class] were reputedly more obese than their equivalent throughout Europe. They loved Gucci; loathed the Euro. More important, to their pallbearers in the press they were racist, xenophobic, thick, illiterate, parochial. They survived on the distant memory of winning one world cup and two world wars, and were still tuning in to the ailing soap that is the House of Windsor. All they represent and hold dear was reportedly redundant in modern, multicultural Britain. (2004: 8)

According to his construction of this "demonisation", British white trash emerges as a scapegoat figure during a time when liberal Britain attempts to come to terms with an increasingly multicultural society that wants to overcome old racisms. Although Collins does not give a clear explanation as to why and at which historical point exactly the white British working class turned into a demonised figure, his observations regarding the stig-

4 | The James Bulger case prompted John Major's famous statement that "We should condemn more and understand less" – the phrase that lends itself as an epigraph for Welsh's *Marabou Stork Nightmares* (*MSN* n. pag.).

matyped white working class correspond to recent sociological analyses of the discourse around the "new" underclass and the chavs. Anna Biressi and Heather Nunn (2013) state that "the white working class have become the container or reservoir for a range of persistent notions of inherent, uneducated racism" (142). While Collins blames "certain white middle-class columnists of the left" (223) for this kind of stigmatyping, Biressi and Nunn hint at a more complex process when they observe that a white underclass or working class deemed to be racist "[functions] as a kind of distraction from, or masking of, the ways in which prejudice, anxiety and unwelcoming attitudes are more broadly circulated and institutionalised in politics and culture" (2013: 142). Biressi and Nunn identify the Thatcherite politics of effacing the discourse of class in the 1980s as the point of origin for the declining reputation of the working class:

> The success of the project of economic liberalism which Thatcherism helped to set in motion depended, in part, on the dissemination of certain *values* as well as practices, including those of self-improvement, individual responsibility and personal investment, as exemplified in the practice of home-ownership and the privatisation of national industries. (2013: 8)

Such a model of entrepreneurialism, individualism and potential social mobility has no need for social contracts or working-class solidarity, but at the same time it embodies all the ideals of white masculinity.[5]

However, Biressi and Nunn indicate that another important factor for the emergence of the white underclass/working class as an abject stigmatype embodying undesirable political attitudes is evident in the attributions of "black" attitudes to the revolting white youths of the 2011 English riots, making the processes underlying the stigmatyping of British white trash far more complex than Collins's blaming of the left-leaning media might suggest: "spatial and bodily tropes of proper and improper behaviour in public space were used to mark the underclass out as a rude intrusion on middle-class (often white) urban and suburban respectability" (2013: 48). Thus, what lies at the heart of the conception of a problematic white underclass is the premise "that black culture had somehow contaminated a white, probably underclass population" (2013: 48). Although Biressi and Nunn are eager to emphasise that this view is that of a minority

5 | On white masculinity and its embodiments, see Dyer 1997: 14–39.

of conservative commentators, this concept of tainted whiteness can be considered to be part of an ideological tradition that can certainly be traced back to the origins of the American white trash stigmatype.[6]

In Britian, then, the term *white trash* thus emerges as the expression of a complex and contradictory netting of different discourses and is as such an essentially paradoxical and liminal phenomenon. While its emergence is symptomatic of a troubled class consciousness and a breakdown of traditional forms of classed identities in (post-)Thatcherite society, similar observations can be made about the status of whiteness in that context. Just as the working class no longer provides for solid identity positions, whiteness in the same way has become a problematic identity. As Jason Mezey (2010) argues, Thatcherite politics stood for a reinforcement of the "transhistorical power of white British identity" (81) most clearly expressed in its recourse to imperialist self-conceptions in the rhetoric during the Falklands conflict and the Nationality Bill that defined British nationality by biology rather than by the former *ius solis* (80). Those same aspects, however, were simultaneously a cause for shame in the face of an increasingly multicultural society whose non-white members refused to surrender to increasing forms of cultural, economic and political discrimination and made themselves heard not only through the Brixton riots but also through increased participation in politics and academia.[7]

---

6 | See Gael Sweeney (2001) for a comparable argument with regard to the American context: "Poor Black and White Trash are linked together. [...]. When White Trash is said to 'act like Blacks,' in the ideology of racism that is worse than actually being Black because it constitutes a 'degradation' of the White race, and therefore the most degenerate of society: lazy and shiftless, ignorant and no-account" (147). Sweeney's argument is particularly insightful in her comments on the intersection of race in class that reveals racist discourse to bespeak an inherent classism that transcends racial boundaries and is at the same time raced: "But White Trash reveals the lie at the heart of racism: that the 'inferiority' of the Blacks is embedded racially, rather than in conditions of poverty and deprivation" (147).

7 | In his interpretation of Richard Attenborough's *Gandhi* (1982), Mezey argues that the film (which also stars a white actor in the titular role) "is instrumental in this process by showing how British characters evinced the best of England's imperial past through their recognition of Gandhi's greatness. In this way, British audiences in 1982 could simultaneously align themselves with the enlightened white figures of the film while reaffirming the transhistorical power of white British identity" (2010: 81).

It is this tainting, or "trashing", of British whiteness throughout the 1980s that also informs Mark Renton's rant about Scottish white trash when he observes of his sociopathic associate Frank Begbie that he is one among many "cunts that are intae baseball-batting every fucker that's different; pakis, poofs, n what huv ye. Fuckin failures in a country ay failures" (*T* 78). Mark's disdain and self-loathing can be interpreted as an expression of shame with regard to one's "own" people. Simultaneously, Mark and his friends find themselves challenged in their whiteness not only within the context of the marginalisation of Scotland within the British archipelago, but also in encounters with non-white members of the population. In the chapter "Victory on New Year's Day" (*T* 41-50), Stevie, who is waiting for his girlfriend Stella at the train station, is attacked by a group of football fans because he happens to wear the wrong – that is, a green – scarf and is hence taken for a "Hibby bastard" (*T* 49). Despite his attempt to avoid confrontation by claiming to be a "Borussia Munchengladbach man" rather than a "Hibby", he nonetheless gets punched in the face. His attackers then go on and "turned their attention to abusing an Asian woman and her two small children", calling her a "fuckin Paki slag" (*T* 49) and telling her to "fuck off back tae yir ain country" (*T* 50). Apparently in an effort to degrade the woman in her non-whiteness, they "made a chorus of ape noises" (*T* 50). In an attempt to form solidarity with the "Asian woman", Stevie lightheartedly and ironically comments on the incident ("What charming, sensitive young men") but rather scares the woman (she "looked at him like a rabbit looks at a weasel"):

> She saw another white youth with slurred speech, bleeding and smelling of alcohol. Above all, she saw another football scarf, like the one worn by the youths who abused her. There was no colour difference as far as she was concerned, and she was right, Stevie realised with a grim sadness. It was probably just as likely to be guys in green who hassled her. Every support had its arseholes. (*T* 50)

What Stevie experiences in this chapter is a challenge to his white subjectivity, enabled by his empathy towards the "Asian woman", that lets him switch perspectives and reconsider his outward appearance from her non-white position as the victim of racist abuse. This form of auto-perception is analogous to white people's hetero-perception of non-whites who, just like the unspecified "Asian woman", are commonly perceived in broad and vague categories depending on their physiognomic features. In the situation described here, however, Stevie not only sees his white self challenged but is also confronted with the fragility of identity positions as a whole. The football scarves that are supposed to signify belonging[8] are put into question as Stevie fails in his attempt at "passing" as a fan of a German club in order to avoid violent confrontation. The arbitrariness of the football scarves as identity signifiers mirrors the equal arbitrariness of physiognomic features or other assumed indicators of ethnicity – the woman may or may not be from Pakistan despite her Asian looks, just as Stevie may or may not be a Hibby or a supporter of a German club.

Thus, Stevie experiences the arbitrariness of ethnic markers in general, and the paradoxical invisibility of whiteness in particular – what Richard Dyer calls white people's "absence of colour" (1997: 207), which is here made visible when he reflects on himself through what he imagines as the woman's gaze on him.[9] Within the novel's cultural context of 1980s and 1990s Britain – the Britain of Thatcher, the race riots, revived imperialism and the Falklands War – this experience of the fragility of white British identity's "transhistorical power" anticipates the challenges of multiculturalism and at the same time questions the supposedly monolithic nature of whiteness. This whiteness is, after all, shot through with the intranational differences of class, gender, age, or (sub)cultures, to name but a few. Stevie's "grim sadness" can ultimately be read ambivalently in that respect: it might be the empathetic sadness of him realising that there is a long way to go until there will be a common basis for people of all colours in Britain and an end to racial discrimination and abuse, and that he, as a white boy, is enjoying white privilege even if he is not necessarily guilty of actively maintaining the racist status quo. But it might as well be the melancholy sadness of the white subject "left to wonder if it is a subject at all" after realising that its identity is no longer stable and fixed, and that it is a "subject without properties" (Dyer 1997: 207).

8 | For a closer look at the semantics of football fandom within the context of British class-relations, see my analysis of King's *The Football Factory* in chapter IV.

9 | Of course, what is ironically implied in this passage is that the football scarves are a means to distinguish different groups of white people who otherwise would be ethnically indistinguishable (invisible) and hence need other forms – that is: other colours – of individuation.

Uncanny Thatcherism: The Past in the Present

The ambivalence between the white person's recognition of his or her potential lack of a distinguishable subject position and the awareness of whiteness as a dominant position which oppresses other racial groups can also be connected to Richard Dyer's discussion of whiteness and its symbolic relation to death. Richard Dyer argues that "the idea of whites as both dead and as bringers of death" (1997: 210) lies at the heart of horror fiction, particularly in the vampire myth and in the zombie films of George A. Romero, which he reads as a critique of American hegemonic whiteness and capitalism (1997: 210–211). It is this connection of whiteness and the undead of horror fiction that I want to use here to approach Irvine Welsh's interrogations of fragile British whiteness in Thatcherite Britain. Dyer expresses his initial hesitancy to write about the connection of whiteness and death because it could lead to another "me-too" by making whites look "tragic and sad" (1997: 208) and ultimately resorts to the construction of whites as both dead in terms of their absence of colour and as enforcing their superiority as bringers of death for non-whites as epitomised in the Ku-Klux Klan and the Nazis (1997: 208–209).

However, I rather want to suggest considering this oscillation between whiteness as deathlike absence and whiteness as bringer of death for non-whites as an ambivalent status that can be combined with Michael Gardiner's concept of the Thatcherite "neo-gothic" (2012: 110–137). More explicitly, I want to take up the notion of the undecided, aporetic "un" in order to grasp the notion of British white trash. After all, the whiteness or non-whiteness of the white trash subject is by definition unstable, meaning that the subject, marked by a "trashed" or tainted form of whiteness, may either enjoy privilege or experience marginalisation depending on the given context. The white trash subject can thus be conceived of as unwhite – a subject position that is caught in between states of being either properly white or properly non-white. Just like the undead (vampires, zombies, etc.), the white trash subject oscillates between two states of being – and, like the Irish in Noel Ignatiev's account *How the Irish Became White*, they are caught in a process of becoming.

This notion is encapsulated in *Trainspotting* – a text that can be described as a novel of inversion in which "positive is negative (as in HIV-positive); so is sharing (as in sharing needles)" (Morace 2007: 45). The patterns of inversion do not stop there, however, nor can they be reduced to clear dichotomies. Rather, they must be conceived in terms of the aporetic "un". This can best be seen in the chapter "Growing Up in Public" (*T* 32–40), a chapter that is easily overlooked within the heteroglot and diverse context of the novel since its focal character, Mark Renton's teenage cousin Nina, is only a marginal one that never reappears throughout the rest of the novel. Nevertheless, it can be interpreted as the culmination of the novel's guiding poetics of aporia precisely due to its oddity. Like several chapters,[10] it describes a funeral, yet, significantly, it is set in the more middle-class suburbs of Bonnyrigg rather than in working-class Leith. Mainly conveyed through indirect thought representations by a heterodiegetic narrator, Nina is characterised as a girl at the apex of puberty who has lost her childlike connection to the grown-ups around her, yet still struggles to get connected to another age-appropriate peer group.

The sense of alienation, which is also reflected in her uncontrolled body (she is not yet used to her period, *T* 35), is mirrored by most of her adult relatives who bemusedly notice her gothic style: "That lassie never wears anything but black. In ma day, lassies wore nice bright colours, instead ay tryin tae look like vampires" (*T* 33). Nina's endorsement of 1980s gothic subculture is thus rendered as the expression of generational conflict, and it simultaneously represents the motif of death that looms large in many facets of the novel. Nina is "dressed for grief", as the adults mockingly remark (*T* 33), although she is supposed to embody the youthful future of the nation. Such ideas of progress are constantly questioned in the chapter (and in the novel), with the adults laughing like "frightened children trying to keep on the right side of the school hardcase" (*T* 33) and thus being a further instance of inversion (old – young, mature – childish), and with future prospects being rather bleak, as becomes evident in a conversation that Nina has with her older cousin Geoff who has just finished his university degree: "You could go tae University. — Whit fir? Geoff had to think for a while. He had recently graduated with a degree in English Literature and was on the dole. So were most of his fellow graduates. — It's a good social life, he said" (*T* 38).

---

10 | Apart from this chapter, "Bang to Rites" (*T* 209–222) and "Memories of Matty" (*T* 290–299) centre around funerals, while one of the main characters in "Bad Blood" (*T* 239–262) is lying on his deathbed. Throughout the novel, the passing of characters is frequently mentioned, making death an omnipresent topic for the characters of *Trainspotting*.

The teenage goth Nina here functions as a focaliser for the "truths" hidden underneath the surface of 1980s British society. Her aporetic in-between position as neither adult nor child allows her to perceive the faults hidden by pretentious cultural rituals and empty phrases like the one about the "good social life" of higher education that is supposed to hide the devastating situation of the job market by referring to the significance of symbolic cultural capital. This capital, however, is not worth anything in the world depicted in *Trainspotting* – after all, the novel undermines the concept of a functioning and caring society ("Nae friends in this game. Jist associates", as Mark's dealer Johnny Swan states, *T* 6). In this respect, Nina's endorsement of gothic culture as a symbolic reversal of life and death can be interpreted with Michael Gardiner, who argues that while "the 1790s Gothic, or 'terror writing', made thinkable that which had been rendered unthinkable by the still relatively new and defensive state" (2012: 110) and can hence be regarded as "the underside of English Literature's British-imperial story" (2012: 111), the emerging interest in the genre that can be found in 1970s and 1980s literary criticism as well as in the emerging neo-gothic literature and gothic/Industrial youth subcultures and musical genres must be interpreted as a reaction to the emergence of "the liberal-conservative Toryism of Margaret Thatcher" (2012: 116). This period, as Gardiner argues, was complexly marked by a new form of "Burkean Europhobia" that "saw the European Economic Community as a threat to evolved, instinctive heredity" (2012: 116) and resulted in a form of neo-imperialism visible in the Falklands War as well as in the increasing fear of Soviet activities, and further saw an unprecedented form of violent measures against one's own people as the reaction towards the Miners' Strike showed (2012: 117). However, it was precisely the Miners' Strike that at the same time endangered this new "strengthening of the state" since it "caused a counter-British reaction" because the measures "alienated even natural conservatives among the strikers" (2012: 117).

Thus, the new gothic literature of writers like J.G. Ballard, Angela Carter and Alasdair Gray had their backdrop in "an economy turned deathly, cannibalistic and sterile, with empty factories and housing estates left to crumble like ancient ancestral piles" as well as in "the combination of strong state and zombified neo-imperial 'free markets'" (2012: 117). Thus, according to Gardiner, the neo-gothic culture is part of "a political contest against the 'democratic deficit', which revealed a nation getting the opposite of its voting intentions" (2012: 117). For Gardiner, the characteristics of this political neo-gothic are, among others, the evocation of the past in the present and an emphasis on double consciousness – "a clash of incommensurate personalities and different registers within the same person" – that Gardiner especially detects in the Scottish branch of neo-gothic that takes up new realist modes of dialect writing. Such instances of incommensurate personalities and split linguistic registers can also be found throughout Welsh's work and form something which I would call a Thatcherite socio-political uncanny, and they can also be retraced within the context of Welsh's renegotiations of (un)whiteness.

The gothic, which "lets the dead walk the earth" (Gardiner 2012: 115) literally and figuratively, can be found in the chapter "Growing Up in Public" when Nina mistakenly believes her uncle Andy to still be alive due to a heating blanket accidentally left switched on underneath the dead body: "There was something different about him. He was sweating. She saw him twitch. God, she was sure she saw him twitch. She touched his hand. It was warm" (*T* 39). Uncle Andy for a few moments appears to be alive, or rather: undead, and thus embodies the past-in-the-present that symbolically haunts the characters in *Trainspotting* and turns seemingly natural orders upside down – just like Nina, who reacts to the shock with hysterical laughter that then turns out to be crying and who briefly returns her to the childlike stage that she as a pubescent teenager had abandoned: "Sweet childhood memories [...] flooded her consciousness. [...] Memories of [...] the happiness and love that once lived here, in the home of her auntie and uncle" (*T* 40). On the one hand, Nina's painful realisation that there is no return from death and that "happiness and love" as well as her childhood have died with her uncle is an individual coming-of-age-story. But on the other hand – given the novel's wider political context and especially considering that Nina does not seem to have another central function for the several plots and does not appear again in the novel – it can be read as an allegory of the bleak prospects and realisations of post-Falklands and post-Miners' Strike Britain that saw the re-emergence and simultaneous failure of an imperial (white) nationalism as well as the decline of a once distinguishable, now scattered working-class identity and the crumbling of a once prosperous national industry.

Trainspotting envisions the casualties of this decline as the living dead roaming the "empty factories and housing estates left to crumble" (Gardiner 2012: 117). After all, the novel's HIV-infected unemployed heroin addicts, years away from proper medical treatment of the disease, can be seen as dead in life, hence "undead". Similarly, Mark's detoxification-induced hallucination of his friend's recently deceased baby, tellingly named Dawn, coming back to life to mock and terrorise him ("The bairn has sharp, vampire teeth wi blood drippin fae them", *T* 196), symbolises the notion of a country whose young generations will not promise a "new dawn" or any future progress whatsoever for the nation in crisis. This sense of disintegration is all-encompassing and affects all forms of cultural identity and political action. It is therefore close at hand to interpret Welsh's deconstructions of white British identity within the context of the leitmotifs of death and decay.

Despite Richard Dyer's misgivings that a conception of whiteness as death might provide for a melancholy "me-too", no such options are offered in *Trainspotting* because there is no indication that race and genealogy were ever proper sources of identity in the first place. On the contrary, the prevailing scepticism towards any form of state-sanctioned ideology does not offer any sentimental mourning over nostalgic ideas of an untainted whiteness, as Mark Renton's rants about Scottish white trash and English colonisers indicate.[11] What further becomes evident in the given examples is that images of grotesque and uncontrollable bodies dominate *Trainspotting*, undermining any trust in the clean surface of the human body as a signifier of racial belonging. After all, a body that cannot contain its fluids is permanently at risk of excessively and uncontrollably oozing, defecating and ejaculating; it will always be "trashed" and tainted. That this holds true not only for whiteness or race as identity categories but affects human identity across intersections is for instance epitomised by the transsexual character Chrissie and her scarred and useless genitals in Welsh's short story "Eurotrash" – another in-between character who tellingly hails from one of the Channel Islands, Jersey, a place that is neither properly British nor properly French in terms of national belonging (*AC* 10–30).

11 | What is more, the novel highlights the constructed and fragile character of any form of identity in many facets; one notable instance is the construction of the sociopath Frank Begbie as a Scottish hardman: Frank's power over his "friends" results in them dutifully retelling glorious and impressive stories about him in company. As Mark observes, this alterocharacterisation has the advantage of seeming "more authentic comin fae somebody else" (*T* 308).

II.2 *Marabou Stork Nightmares*

Intersectional issues of race and class are even more pronounced in Welsh's second major novel. With Roy Strang as the sole first-person narrator, the narrative is more focused than in *Trainspotting*. As is the case with Mark Renton in *Trainspotting*, Roy Strang eloquently relates his own life to broader social issues and thus situates his position as representative of more general conditions. The decisive difference between Roy and Mark, however, is that the former is a highly unreliable narrator both factually and morally.[12] Roy has unsuccessfully attempted suicide over the guilt induced by his participation in the gang rape of a young woman in Edinburgh. When the novel begins, he is a coma patient being nursed in hospital. The novel's narrative takes place on three interrelating levels. On the first level, Roy gives an account of the things going on around him on the coma ward. He is still capable of recognising aural sensations, and he comments on the several visitors and hospital staff that he recognises in his state.

On the second level, which is closely linked to his semi-conscious state, he also gives a detailed autobiographical account of his upbringing in the housing schemes of Edinburgh's Muirhouse, his family's emigration to apartheid South Africa in the 1980s, and the events that led to his crime. Later it becomes clear that several bits of his narrative are factually inaccurate (e.g., his role in the gang rape), which consequently might compromise the moral reliability of his account. It is important in that respect that this level of narration also includes most of Roy's socio-political musings. Hence, these must be considered to be affected by Roy's complex unreliability as a narrator and should not be mistaken as the actual socio-political "message" of the book as a whole. On a third level, Roy finds himself in a deepened comatose state, which, in its dreamlike quality, is closely connected to what might be called his subconscious. On this level, Roy embarks on a quest in an imagined South Africa to hunt the vile Marabou

12 | Of course it might be argued that Mark Renton can to some degree be considered as an unreliable narrator at least for most parts of the readership since his outlook on life is drastically influenced by his consumption of drugs, which might distort his capability of proper judgment. However, this is entirely dependent on the individual moral standards of each reader. For a problematisation of unreliable narration and its relation to cultural discourses, see Zerweck 2001.

Stork, an animal that he constantly had nightmares about ever since his childhood experiences in South Africa.

The division of the narrative structure into three parts that are representative of different stages of consciousness is also linked to different semanticisations of race and class. While on the second level, the memories of growing up in deprived circumstances in Edinburgh revolve around the economic and psychosocial situation of the narrator's family, the third level marks an idealised revision of the relations of class and race that inform the second level. The two levels thus reflect each other and can, as I will show in the following analysis, be interpreted as a critical comment on the way intersectional identities are constructed and normalised by means of boundary work (Wray 2006; see chapter I).

A "Genetic Disaster": The Strang Family

Early in the accounts dominating the second narrative level, Roy gives a detailed description of his family and the troubled circumstances which resulted in the marriage of his parents and his birth. His judgment of his upbringing is rather unforgiving and extreme: "I grew up in what was not so much a family as a genetic disaster" (*MSN* 19). The parameters by which Roy defines the "genetic disaster" that is his family are the normative standards set by his environment – i. e., the other people surrounding him in the neighbourhood of the housing schemes that he grows up in. Even at an early age, he realises that his family must deviate from the norm that others seem to embody: "I sensed that there was a general, shared quality kicking around which we seemed to lack. I suppose it was what people would call normality" (*MSN* 19). The realisation that his family is not the embodiment of normality already signals Roy's immature level of reflection – or so he wants to suggest retrospectively – and it also signals his strong desire to distinguish himself from his family and what they represent.

That this is primarily a desire to leave behind the deprived working-class environment of his childhood becomes stylistically evident in the use of Standard English rather than Scottish English in his narrative accounts. Scots is usually featured in direct speech and in those moments in which he loses control over his reconstruction of memory or the forging of his dreamt South Africa on the third level (see *MSN* 5). Here, Welsh once more employs dialect and sociolect as a marker of class, albeit in a reversing manner: Just as Mark Renton employs a mockery of Standard English as a strategy of passing in different social situations like in the chapter "Courting Disaster" in *Trainspotting*, Roy opts for the standardised "official" variety of English to assume a privileged position in terms of class and "to assimilate himself into this language of power" (Kelly 2005: 109).[13]

The description of his family as a "genetic disaster" in connection with their situation within the lower classes of Edinburgh is reminiscent of biologist conceptions that consider members of the lower classes genetically and racially inferior. In the vein of conceptions of white trash as the embodiment of both excess and lack, a liminal figure that signifies moral and genetic anomaly, the Strangs embody a state of exception and denormalisation – Roy's diagnosis of his family's "lack" of "normality" can in this context be directly connected to their abject lower-class whiteness. This also becomes clear in the family's desire to be assimilated by the racist apartheid system in South Africa in order to gain back their white privilege, as I will point out later. With regard to his mother's emotional instability, Roy remarks that before his parents' marriage, his mother "had a sort of mental breakdown, or rather, had her first mental breakdown. She would have these breakdowns intermittently until it got to the stage it's at now, where it's hard to tell when she's *not* having one" (*MSN* 19). Like his father, who is prone to violence and choleric outbursts as well as paranoia, his mother represents a reversal of normality that is typical of conceptions of white trash as deviant and excessive. This behavioural and emotional deviance corresponds to the family's physiognomy, which, according to Roy's account, the neighbours refer to as "'the Strang look'" (*MSN* 20).

This particular look consists of "a concave face starting at a prominent, pointed forehead, swinging in at a sharp angle towards large, dulled eyes and a small, squashed nose, down into thin, twisted lips and springing

13 | Kelly also notes that Roy's efforts towards assimilation are disrupted by the persons gathering around him in hospital, keeping him from further descending into his escapist dream world and also disrupting his attempts at immersing himself in the standardised language of power by speaking Scottish dialect around him. Thus, when the novel starts with Roy's complaint that "they were trying to disturb me" (*MSN* 3), this not only refers to the disruptions of his African fantasy recounted on the novel's third level but also to efforts of passing from one social sphere to another via language and register.

outwards to the tip of a large, jutting chin. A sort of retarded man-in-the-moon face" (*MSN* 20). Roy further has "additional crosses to bear": "two large protruding ears which came from my otherwise normal-looking mother" (*MSN* 20). The implications of such detailed physiognomic descriptions regarding class and race are close at hand if one recalls the biologist discourses at the end of the nineteenth and the beginning of the twentieth century,[14] and they become even more clear in the patronising descriptions of the Africans that Roy and his imaginary friend Sandy Jamieson encounter on their quest in the dreamed-up version of South Africa on the novel's third narrative level.

The natives that Roy and Sandy, in a colonialist fashion, want to hire on their quest appear to Roy as "morally deficient" (*MSN* 4) and "manifestly unfit for the physical demands" (*MSN* 4–5) of their journey. Further, he detects an "attitude of 'something for nothing'" in what he calls the "non-white races" (*MSN* 5). Although he blames the "white colonialists" for this attitude (*MSN* 5), the logic behind his argument can all the more be interpreted as a satirically exaggerated and distorted racism that lies at the heart of this patronising, supposedly 'non-racist' and understanding attitude towards the Africans. This image of native Africans as childlike and in need for the help of "the white man" conveyed by Roy's dream-ego might be read as a fantasised compensation for the discrimination and marginalisation experienced by Roy in his youth in the Muirhouse housing schemes. Roy's dream persona as well as his imaginary friend can be interpreted as satiric embodiments of white colonists who have returned to an older, pre-Mandela version of South Africa. This spatial fantasy is nourished by different sources of Roy's (and possibly a generalised white Briton's) racist imagination and can thus be interpreted as a conglomerate of a white supremacist notion of South Africa.[15] On this

14 | For a historical overview and a critical reading of cultural products with regard to the British endeavours at phrenology and the classification of the race types on the British isles, see Brannigan 2009, esp. 78–143.

15 | The telling names employed in the novel are also notable in that respect. As Aaron Kelly has pointed out, the name of Roy's sister, Kim, echoes Rudyard Kipling's 1901 novel of the same name. According to Kelly, Kipling's protagonist "is the site wherein incommensurate narratives of coloniality collide and this charged liminality informs the unraveling imperial fabric woven by Roy's visions in *Marabou Stork Nightmares*" (2005: 115).

third narrative level, Roy displays the same tendency towards racial type-casting that informs the detailed descriptions of his family and himself. His preoccupation with linking physique to race and even class stands in the tradition of racist discourses in which the body becomes what John Brannigan describes as the "site of racial figurations" (Brannigan 2009: 7). "Epidermal and corporeal figurations" (Brannigan 2009: 7) thus become the bearer of racial and class identity. Roy's character is designed as a figure that has internalised discourses around race and class in British society during the Thatcher and Major years. What is crucial in the design of his character is that his perception links the attitude towards class and race in the 1980s and early 1990s to the more explicitly classist and racist attitudes common in late nineteenth and early twentieth century Britain. Roy's account actually implies that such attitudes have not yet vanished from British culture and that they have rather become less overt over the post-war decades. Welsh's novel thus suggests a historical continuum in the racialisation of class in British culture that is most prominently represented by Roy's father, John Strang.

Spectres of Thatcher

John Strang's frequent references to the British politics of the times of World War II and his simultaneous endorsements and mythifications of figures like Winston Churchill as well as Margaret Thatcher – he regularly listens to the recorded war speeches of the former (*MSN* 29) and even names his dogs after him, and glorifies the latter's treatment of the unions ("She pit the fuckin unions in their place right enough", *MSN* 83) – indicate a process of disintegration in the self-conception of the British working class in the post-Thatcherite period that is of fundamental importance for the complex intersectional processes of subject formation that Welsh's characters undergo.[16] In that respect, it is rather telling when

16 | The loss of a shared identity and a sense of belonging and purpose within the disintegrating working class is a motif frequently examined by Welsh. While *Trainspotting* and *Marabou Stork Nightmares* focus on the aftermath of the Thatcher era, *Glue* (2001) attempts to sketch a complex portrait of working-class characters spanning several generations, and his recent *Skagboys* (2012) returns to the point of origin of this disintegration as reflected by the character of David Renton Sr. (Mark's father) who experiences the riots of Orgreave and laments the decline

Roy's impaired leg and resulting limp are attributed to an attack by the family's second dog, called Winston Two (*MSN* 21), suggesting the irony behind a working-class father who, in his aspiration towards upward mobility, detests anything that is related to a more liberating politics that would empower the working class and therefore endorses an ideology that has frequently been blamed for severely affecting working-class culture in Britain. That such an attitude is a form of classist self-loathing and, to use a more literal expression in the vein of Welsh's employment of symbolism, ultimately self-devouring, is thus symbolically represented in the beloved family dog biting the father's male offspring – the only child in the family that is, according to John, deserving of the name Strang: Before he sets up fights between Roy and his step-son Bernard, he repeatedly tells him: "You're a Strang son, mind that. He's no. Mind that. Right? Mind, yir fightin fir the Strang name. He [Bernard] might git called a Strang, but eh's no. Eh's a crappin eyetie bastard son" (*MSN* 29).

The remaining chronic pain and disfigurement are the corporeal manifestations of the classed paradoxes and tensions inscribed in Roy's body – another significant instance in which the body is rendered as a bearer of symbolic and intersecting markers of social belonging in the novel. While I emphasise the symbolic significance of Roy suffering from the mutilations by the family dog in terms of his paradoxical classed subject status, Aaron Kelly, among others, has interpreted this aspect with regard to Roy's problematic masculinity: "John decides further that Roy, due to his limp, and his brother Bernard, who is viewed as effeminate by the rest of the family and later turns out to be gay, should prove their questionable masculinity by boxing each other in the living room. Masculinity in this environment is regulated through an economy of pain" (2005: 107). That aspects like these can lend themselves to such varied readings is further proof of the huge significance of intersectional relations in the (un)making of identity positions and processes of subjectification in the novel. Ultimately, it is almost impossible to divorce one identity category (race, class or gender) from the others in the case of Roy Strang and his family.

---

of industry and resulting fragmentation and demise of a traditional working class (see *Sk* 285-292). For a reading of Skagboys as a reflection of the erosion of the working class, civil society and the changing nature of labour in the 1980s, see del Valle Alcalá 2016: 110-132.

John Strang's endorsement of Thatcherism and his admiration for Winston Churchill signal the wish for traditional forms of leadership as well as the sentimental longing for a Britain that was seemingly united in the fight against German fascism during World War II.[17] The narrator's rendering of his father's obsession with politics, British history and class, however, indicates that John Strang's aspirations are not only delusional but border on a form of mental instability: "The only things which seemed to give Dad enjoyment were drinking and listening to records of Winston Churchill's wartime speeches. Pools of tears would well up behind his thick lenses as he was moved by his idol's stirring rhetoric" (*MSN* 29). John's attempt at appropriating an idealised British history (Churchill) and an anticipated new dawn of British economy and society (Thatcher) also finds its expression in his desire to distinguish himself and his family from the rest of the working-class neighbours in Muirhouse by indulging in a consumerism that he fathoms to be middle class:[18]

> We were the first family in the district to have all the key consumer goods as they came onto the market: colour television, video recorder and eventually satellite dish. Dad thought that they made us different from the rest of the families in the scheme, a cut above the others. Middle-class, he often said. All they did was define us as prototype schemies. (*MSN* 27)

Roy's comments on his father's delusional class aspirations reveal John Strang to be a parodic figure representing the paradoxes that a Thatcherite and post-Thatcherite notion of a classless society must inevitably produce if it is contrasted with the actual cultural and material realities of a classed society. As Anna Biressi and Heather Nunn observe with regard to the Thatcherite notion of classlessness,

---

17 | As I will show in my subsequent analysis of John King's *The Football Factory*, working-class disillusionment with the notion of a united Britain after the war is a central component of British post-war working-class culture.

18 | This habit seems like an illustration of Stuart Hall's analysis of a "sense of classlessness" during the post-war period of the 1950s when "the worker" was conditioned "to the new possibilities for consumption" (2017: 36). In the post-war years, the working class had "been built into the market itself" – i. e., they are now not only the producers, but also the consumers of the products of their work – commodities which now "have accumulated a social value as well" (Hall 2017: 37).

> The Conservative imperative to be dependent on no-one but one's self and one's family served as an outright rejection of the earlier failed 'social contract' model of 1970s Labour administrations which had tried to negotiate a 'social wage' with workers in return for universal benefits. [...]. [...] the *promise* of Thatcherism, its rhetoric and presentation of the *possibilities* of social change, was as important as its actual policies. (2013: 8)

John Strang can thus be said to embrace the self-improvement, entrepreneurialism and individualism that Thatcherite rhetoric wanted to convey, while at the same time unconsciously embodying the actual "rising inequalities of income and status" that Biressi and Nunn observe in the 1980s, "cross-hatched by a political rhetoric of choice, entrepreneurialism and individual aspiration towards social mobility which seemed to make sense for many people" (2013: 7). In that respect, John Strang is reminiscent of several stereotypes that were popular with audiences during the 1980s and 1990s – Essex Man and Essex Girl – as well as comedian Harry Enfield's routine Loadsamoney. Those are described by Biressi and Nunn as "emblematic figures" in the "classed landscape" of 1980s Britain, who

> bear the traces of the originating moment when consumerism, entrepreneurialism and aspiration were fuelled by and woven into the political discourses and fantasies of Thatcherism and its aftermath. [...]. They represented an ostentatious desire for the good life and for personal respect, together with a refusal to quietly and carefully brand themselves with markers of mannered, discreet good taste and decorum. They are emblematic figures who also expressed, for those who understood them more empathetically, a classed longing and a defiant belief in their own self-worth. (2013: 42)

Strikingly, Roy Strang's description of his family as a "genetic disaster" implies the same kind of behavioural and bodily inadequacies and excesses that were attributed to the aspiring working-class figures of the Essex Man and Girl. Of the latter, Biressi and Nunn say that this stereotype "is burdened with multiple labels rooted in British social difference, including that she is working class, that she is class-less (i.e., post-working class) and that she has no class (i.e., she lacks good taste)" (2013: 38). The representations of the former likewise connect "working-class male identity with the body and with bodily fluids" in a move that is, according to Biressi and Nunn, typical of "class-based snobbery" (2013: 30). In that, figures like Essex Man, Essex Girl and Loadsamoney can be described as boundary figures (Wray 2006) that help to establish and maintain symbolic and, consequently, material boundaries which are, in these cases, primarily class-based. Similarly, John Strang is in the eyes of his son a classed boundary figure that despite his efforts in terms of consumption never can and never will overcome the complex obstacles of class difference that are inscribed in the cultural landscape of late 1980s and early 1990s Britain as it is depicted in the novel.

With that in mind, the complex narrative situation of *Marabou Stork Nightmares* must once again be emphasised: after all, it must be noted that the characterisation of John Strang as this classed boundary figure is established by his narrator son. Roy's view of his father and his particular outlook on British and Scottish society more broadly are informed by his own self-loathing and insecurity, which, however, might be an internalisation of British society's "classedness". Thus, the construction of the novel produces a complex portrait of a person ridden with culturally induced scorn and guilt so that all the central events and turning points of the novel can in some way or another be traced back to the psychosocial injury of living in a classed society. That former analyses have not only highlighted the questions of class raised by the novel but have predominantly focused on the aspects of Scottish identity politics as well as masculinity and sexual violence is further proof of the complex intersectional dimensions that the novel dissects with respect to class.[19]

The sense of injury and internalised guilt associated with being a member of the working class or the lower classes in a society that denies the existence of class-based difference and emphasises individual responsibility is a leitmotif in much of Welsh's early fiction. His novels examine the emergence of boundary figures in their intersectional and psychological complexity and their inherent contradictions, as will also be seen later in the analysis of his third full-length novel *Filth*. In *Marabou Stork Nightmares*, the complex intersections of race, class and gender and the ways they mutually reinforce themselves in different contexts is shown to culminate in the paradoxical continuum of whiteness. This primarily becomes evident in two aspects that I will regard in the following sections in order to conclude my reading of *Marabou Stork Nightmares*: the first is the Strang family's emigration to South Africa and their subsequent

19 | See Whyte 1998, Herbrechter 2000, Schoene-Harwood 2000 and Jones 2006.

return, which demonstrates the shifting continuum of working-class whiteness, and the second is Roy's involvement in the gang rape of a young woman and the subsequent treatment by the legal authorities of the white male perpetrators, which is represented by Welsh as the intersection of white male privilege and rape culture.

The Continuum of White Privilege

As I have outlined above, John Strang puts considerable effort into a performance of middle-class respectability which, in its emphasis on consumerism, becomes a distorted parody that in fact has the unintended reverse effect of making him and his family appear to be more working class in the very attempt to efface class-specific attributes. In another attempt to gain a more privileged class status, John decides to move his family to South Africa, which in the 1980s was still in the grip of white supremacist apartheid. Displaying an awareness for the intersections of class and whiteness, John assumes that in South Africa his family will enjoy the privileges that they are being denied in Edinburgh: "Sooth Efrikay, that's the place. [...]. That's cause it's a white man's country, like ah sais, a white man's country. White is right oot thair, ah kid ye not" (*MSN* 24).

John Strang's assessment at first glance seems to be in line with Alasdair Bonnett's argument that the whiteness of the British working class is not a self-evident trait but a time-specific construction and attribution which depends on different historical and cultural factors such as the imperial project (see chapter I). However, a decisive difference is that John Strang does not seem to have a sense for the intricate complexities at work in his and his family's perceived marginalisation. Since he denies his own working-class identity, he ignores the class factor in his disadvantaged social position and assumes that he lives in a society which does not value whiteness as much as it should. His insistence that South Africa is "a white man's country" where "white is right" implies that Scotland and the United Kingdom are a place where white is *not* right, and where whiteness is not a property which induces a sense of supremacy and pride.

In fact, his views imply a xenophobic sense of foreign infiltration which nourishes a fight over entitlement to resources and privileges. Such a sense of competition with non-white residents is, as Steve Garner (2012) has shown in a study of qualitative interviews, at the heart of a specific set of working-class notions of national, racial and class identity. Garner argues that "where there is so little *obvious* benefit in whiteness, it is sometimes easy to lose sight of the complexity of [...] power relationships" (2012: 460, emphasis in orig.), and this is why, in a desire to reduce complexity, "despite claims that we are living in times of 'cultural racism', 'new racism', 'colour-blind racism', etc., in which culture is the key theme of discourse, people still simultaneously make sense of difference through the old-school visual distinction of skin tone, hair type, facial features, etc." (Garner 2012: 459). Thus, when 'white culture' is perceived to be at a perceived disadvantage and threatened with marginalisation, those who believe their culture to be in this position will still think along the lines of phenotypical markers of racial difference. This is why to these people, 'white' appears to be in "a position of injury and beleaguredness" (Garner 2012: 460). In other words, whiteness as an identity position is constructed as inherently meaningful, precious, and therefore in need of preservation from non-white influences. This obfuscates the actual roots and causes for the disadvantages of the working class. In fact, as Garner argues, "the national evidence that does exist quite strongly underscores class, 'race' and gender as compounding sources of impact on life chances, with class appearing as slightly more decisive" (2012: 460, referencing Rhodes 2011). John Strang's obsession with finding a place where he will benefit from his whiteness can in this context be considered as a repression and displacement of the more complex causes for his and his family's social situation in Scotland.

At first, it even seems as if John Strang's dreams of living in a country as a privileged white will come true, and his son recalls that "everyone seemed lighter, happier" during their time in Johannesburg (*MSN* 62). Roy's father not only hopes to profit from the apartheid system but also from his brother Gordon's business in Johannesburg. In retrospect, Roy describes his uncle as "what I suppose I'd now call an unreconstructed pro-apartheid white supremacist" (*MSN* 62). Gordon had the career that John hopes for in South Africa:

> There was no doubt Gordon had done well, at least materially, from the system. After taking a few menial but well-paid-compared-to-the-blacks-doing-the-same-thing sort of job, he set up a property management agency in Johannesburg. It took off, and he diversified into property development. [...]. I think the old man thought that he was just going to walk into a top job in Gordon's business. (*MSN* 62–63)

John's hope turns out to be a misconception, and when Gordon sets him straight, a family row ensues and spoils the happiness the Strang family (and especially young Roy and his siblings) had felt in Johannesburg: "This was the end of my father's South African dream" (*MSN* 63).

Welsh's novel renders some profound points about the British white working class, and specifically its Scottish members, by letting John Strang hope for a better life in apartheid South Africa and having his hopes crashed. The logic behind John's plan is informed by what Alasdair Bonnett has identified as the paradigm shift in the perception of the British working class as white – namely, the imperial project. As I have outlined in the previous chapter, Bonnett identifies the non-white colonies of the British Empire as the Other against which the racial position of the working class was newly measured, and it was only after encounters with colonised black subjects that the working class was perceived as embodying British whiteness (see chapter I and Bonnett 2000). In *Marabou Stork Nightmares*, the context of colonisation and imperialism is hyperbolically present in Roy's comatose dream world. In its narrative peculiarities, which parody children's adventure novels (see Kelly 2005: 108–112; Morace 2007: 105–107), Roy's dream narrative is his realisation of the fantasies that he indulged in in order to escape the boredom of his housing-scheme childhood. In both cases, adventure fiction offers the blueprint for his fantasies, as becomes clear when he reminisces about the games he played as a child in Edinburgh: "Sometimes me and my pals used to go out of the scheme, but it was usually just doon the beach. [...] we would think aboot running away and going camping, like in the Enid Blyton books" (*MSN* 26).

In both his childhood and his later dream world, the narrative and thematic framework of adventure stories helps Roy to maintain a coherent and stable worldview in order to escape the identity struggles he has to face in reality. Thus, as Aaron Kelly observes, *Marabou Stork Nightmares* plays with "the discourse of adventure [and] the social conflicts of class, gender and race that it traditionally seeks simultaneously to both order and repress" (2005: 110). Through the novel's threefold narrative structure, Roy's fantasy of colonial empowerment via the "discourse of adventure" is, however, continuously disrupted, and the novel thus "significantly destabilises the escapist teleology of some readings of adventure fiction" (Kelly 2005: 109). In that respect, then, the idea of empire assumes a double meaning within the ideological frameworks Welsh's novel deals with. On the one hand, empire, with its clear-cut boundaries between powerful British whiteness and dominated black Africa is present in Roy's dream world as a stabilising framework to assert his superior and stable identity as white, male and Anglo-Saxon – and it is worth noting here that the passages at level three of the novel's narrative (Roy's coma fantasy) have Roy speaking in a peculiar version of Standard English, a parodied version of the English likely to be found in adventure fiction, rather than in his Scottish dialect, with the occasional mild exclamation like "holy cow!" (*MSN* 7), "gosh" and "golly" (*MSN* 13) being used as well. With the use of a stylised literary Standard English and such "Enid Blyton-esque exclamations" (Kelly 2005: 108), Roy tries to efface his Scottishness as well as his working-class background. As Robert Morace remarks, "Enid Blyton's children's fiction plays an especially important role in Welsh's novel and in the formation of a distinctly British character based on the English model. In reading and attempting to emulate Blyton's children, Roy [...] was learning to become British and more especially English, not Scottish" (2007: 105). Similarly, if one follows Alasdair Bonnett, colonialism and imperialism ensure Roy's (and, during their stint in South Africa, his family's) whiteness.

Roy's attempt at "passing" as English rather than Scottish functions in analogy to his father's quite similar attempts which manifest themselves in a consumer behaviour and the support of ideologies that he perceives as middle class, and in both cases, whiteness plays a central role to achieve this passing. While John Strang perceives South Africa as a place where his whiteness will be acknowledged, Roy enjoys a privileged position as a white explorer in his fantasy world. On both levels, whiteness as a privileged subject position is produced and maintained by the exploitative model of power imbalance that is central to the colonial project as well as to South Africa's apartheid society. However, the novel subverts any sense of stability of the hegemonic position of whiteness by disrupting Roy's fantasy with the other narrative levels. This is made clear from the outset when Roy's fantasy persona makes his way through the African jungle in a jeep and struggles to "regain some sense of control over the vehicle" (*MSN* 6). The steering of the vehicle mirrors his struggle to maintain narrative control over his fantasy world in order to avoid undesired memories seeping in:

> The deeper I get, the further from *them* I get, the happier I feel. [...]. But they keep trying; even from here I can feel them. Trying to stick another tube up my arse or

something similar, something which constitutes a breach of my personal no no can't have this... change the subject, keep control. (*MSN* 7)

While in Roy's case the desire to escape his history is also linked to his despicable actions in the past, that is, the gang rape of the young woman who will eventually take revenge by castrating him and letting him choke on his own testicles in the coma ward, it is also representative of his lack of agency as a Scottish working-class subject with no control over his own biography or over the proper representation of his own identity within cultural narratives. Thus, when Roy at the beginning of the novel "defeatedly observed" with regard to his vehicle that "I've absolutely no control here", this symbolically prefigures and summarises the novel's project of demonstrating its narrator's and its characters' inability to properly shape their own lives and identities to a satisfying degree (*MSN* 7).

Thus, neither Roy nor his father have control over their identities. John's "South African dream" (*MSN* 63), which is ultimately a fantasy of class and racial superiority, is as much an illusion as Roy's comatose attempt to escape his past into a dream world. Both fantasies are dependent on the notion of empire and the racist dichotomy of black and white, and they fall apart in the very moment these respective systems collapse: Roy's fantasised quasi-colonialist enterprise must fall apart because it is an imagined construction that relies on an image of the British Empire which at the time of his dreaming has, despite being kept alive in literary narratives (particularly the naively jingoist adventure intertexts),[20] already been lost. Hence, the novel's first part is titled "Lost Empires", and the first chapter is "Another Lost Empire". In a similar way, John's aspirations in South Africa, based on the idea of apartheid, are nourished by a simplified genealogy of the "white man's" position in the country, which Roy's uncle Gordon explains to the young Roy in the following way: "As a race, they [black Africans] are murderers and thieves. It's in their blood. [...]. They

20 | Apart from adventure novels, there are a number of other complex intertextual references which highlight the colonial context of *Marabou Stork Nightmares*; these can particularly found in the names of Roy's siblings (his sister's name, Kim, as mentioned before, alludes to Kipling's novel). While it would exceed the scope of this thesis to discuss them at length here, Schoene-Harwood (2000: 152-153), Kelly (2005: 115) and Morace (2007: 105-107) provide detailed analyses of the novel's intertexts.

are one stage up from the baboons you'll see out in the veld. We had to take this land and show them how to develop it. We made this beautiful country, now they say they want it back" (*MSN* 64). This explanation of racial hierarchies as well as Gordon's treatment of black servants in his house shapes Roy's thinking as a child and informs his later observations on social injustice both in South Africa and Scotland. He compares the housing schemes of Edinburgh to South African townships:

> I realised that it was exactly the same situation as Johannesburg; the only difference was that the Kaffirs were white and called schemies or draftpaks. Back in Edinburgh, we would be Kaffirs; condemned to live out our lives in townships like Muirhouse or So-Wester-Hailes-To or Niddrie, self-contained camps with fuck all in them. [...]. [...]. Edinburgh had the same politics as Johannesburg: it had the same politics as any city. Only we were on the other side (*MSN* 80).

This assessment, somewhat problematically, implies that systems of sub- and superordination, be they based on race or on class, can always be mapped onto each other.[21]

This simplified conflation has provoked some objection from critics and literary scholars, which are most poignantly summarised and rebutted

21 | Considering the South African context, Roy's problematic equation is also reminscent of the attitudes of white South Africans after the election of Nelson Mandela and the end of apartheid. As Melissa Steyn has pointed out in her analysis of qualitative interviews with white people in post-apartheid South Africa, there was a common sense of being subjected to a "reversed apartheid" and a dramatic change in the status of one's whiteness and racial privilege among Afrikaans communities. One statement by a person interviewed by Steyn is particularly telling within the context of tainted whiteness and racial abjection: "Nowadays you are dirt itself. Nowadays it is said, try something white and you are dead. Yes, now we are dirt itself, and we have no say in the economy" (2001: 70–71). Thus, as Steyn points out, many white South Africans remained unaware of the actual system of racial discrimination and white privilege from which they benefited during apartheid and continue to think and feel along the lines of their racist indoctrination. *Marabou Stork Nightmares*, having been published only in the year after the election of Mandela, to some extent seems to foreshadow this sense that South African "whiteness just isn't what it used to be" (Steyn 2001).

by Carole Jones in a comparative analysis of masculinity and whiteness in contemporary Scottish novels (2006):

> The 1980s and 1990s setting of *Marabou Stork Nightmares* is a postcolonial era when national liberation for ex-colonies and civil rights for the marginalised have been won, apartheid has been defeated and racism fought on all fronts. The pathologies of domination indulged by the colonialists in the construction of their own identities have been recognised for the injustices that they propagated and the victims they produced. In some controversial ways, Irvine Welsh aligns his central character, the working-class 'schemie' Roy Strang, with such victimhood; part of the shock value of *Marabou Stork Nightmares* lies in Welsh's engagement with these narratives of oppression. [...]. The outrage here is caused by a white appropriation of black suffering. But [...] this move does connect, albeit in an oblique way, with a history of the policing of the working class through the discourses of race; in the post-liberationist era, however, the moral authority is reversed, making the association with blackness a positive aspiration. (n. pag.)

However, it must be clarified here that it is not Irvine Welsh the author who, as Jones describes it (thereby somehow unintentionally repeating the very mistake she sets out to rebut in this passage), "aligns his central character" with black victimhood, but the character Roy Strang himself – and Roy is, as I have emphasised above, a profoundly unreliable and morally dubious narrator whose political views must also be considered in this light. In that respect, blaming Irvine Welsh for his character's polarising political views on race and class would be as unjustifiable and misguided as blaming him for Roy and his mates' downplaying of their gang rape[22] – a point I will return to in the next section.

In addition, it must be noted that Jones is not entirely accurate in describing the world depicted in Welsh's novel as a post-apartheid one. In fact, it is precisely the still ongoing violent fight against apartheid that forms

22 | On the subject of rape, the novel (and, as could in this case be justifiably argued, Irvine Welsh the author) provides a clear and unmistakable moral stance by using material of and aligning itself with the Zero Tolerance campaign. This campaign is in the acknowledgements described as "the first campaign [in Edinburgh] to use the mass media to challenge male violence against women and children. The campaign believes that there is no acceptable level of violence against women and children" (*MSN* n. pag.).

the backdrop for those passages taking place during Roy's childhood in Johannesburg, and the Strang family's time in South Africa significantly ends with a bombing attack allegedly committed by guerrilla sections of the ANC: After the family is forced to move back to Scotland because John cannot manage to get a profitable job as he hoped and is sentenced to prison for six months for beating up a taxi driver, Uncle Gordon dies in a car bombing while he is on an excursion with Roy. Within the novel's logic, Gordon's death plays out as the outcome of poetic justice. In Roy's account, he is a child molester who frequently abused Roy during their trips and threatened him to turn his parents against him if he thought about telling on him. In addition to that, he is characterised as a vicious and committed racist who, only moments before his death, "seemed seriously disturbed" by the state of affairs in current South African politics (*MSN* 84). Scared by the political changes in what was then called Rhodesia, prefiguring the changes in South Africa, Gordon looks at his land and explains to Roy: "This is mine. My farm. I'm a Jubilee boy Roy, a penniless Scotsman from Granton. There I was nothing, another skinny teddy boy. Here, I count. No fucking Kaffir is going to take this away from me!" (*MSN* 84). Gordon's story is another inflection of the belief in white supremacy, or rather, white entitlement, which is equally shared by Roy's father.

However, Roy's retrospective description of his uncle reveals Gordon to be a morally corrupt racist, which causes young Roy to rethink his uncle's racist indoctrination: "Gordon's death [...] left me unmoved. As far as I was concerned Gordon was a sneaky, bigheided poofy auld cunt and it was good riddance. The only person really hurt was John, when we went to visit him in the prison, and his sadness seemed to be based on the loss of Gordon as he was fifteen years back, a 'skinny fucking teddy boy', rather than a crusty old Boer" (*MSN* 86). This image of the "crusty old Boer" becomes emblematic for the continuum of whiteness that Welsh's novel intends to illustrate: while Gordon considers himself to be socially upwardly mobile because his racial status is of different value within the apartheid system, he simultaneously appears (at least in Roy's retrospective account) as a figuration of white trash – in this case, a form of abject hyperwhiteness. Gordon is indicative of whiteness as a "position of relative privilege" which is "highly uneven, contingent and relational" (Garner 2012: 446): as political and racial relations gradually shift in South Africa, Gordon, who enjoyed white privilege during apartheid, is in post-apartheid times degraded as a figure of shameful whiteness. In Roy's descriptions,

Gordon (and with him the white racist Boer population which benefited from and maintained an oppressive racist system) now becomes a sexually deviant, excessive, degenerate and dirty ("crusty") figure of white trash.

This shift on the continuum of whiteness is not confined to Gordon but affects the entire Strang family. This is most poignantly expressed by Roy's controversial observation of his family being "on the other side" of oppression, but it is also represented in smaller details such as his observation that his "accent mattered less to the teachers in South Africa than it had done to those in my native city", and he is even "less embarrassed by Mum and Dad" because "they seemed lighter and happier out here, and strangely, their eccentricities were more tolerated as there was quite a mix of different white kids in our neighbourhood, likesay Greek and that" (*MSN* 77).

Eventually, Roy gains "a perverse sense of empowerment; an ego even" (*MSN* 88). Roy grows increasingly confident that he will be different from the rest of his despised family. In this metamorphosis, his peculiar family name becomes representative of Roy's morphing whiteness. While at home, the name Strang is often misread as "strange" by other people (*MSN* 28) – indicating the "strangeness" of a Scottish working-class family within a cultural environment which strives for the ideals of Anglo-Britishness and the middle class – Roy, in his newly gained self-consciousness, reinterprets his name as "strong": "Ah wis going to be strong. Strong Strang. Ah wis gaunny make sure every cunt kent ma fuckin name" (*MSN* 89). Berthold Schoene-Harwood interprets the semantic ambivalence of the family name within the context of Scottishness, British Empire and notions of masculinity:

> Serving and no doubt benefiting as indispensable helpmates in the construction and maintenance of the British Empire, Scottish men – and those of a lower social rank especially – have never won perfect equality with their allegedly superior English counterparts. Quasi-English colonisers abroad, their acculturation at home has remained spurious and incomplete, a circumstance perhaps most poignantly illustrated in Welsh's novel by the mistranslation of the Strang's family name into 'strange' rather than 'strong'. While living under the South African apartheid regime Scottish 'schemies' may pass for legitimate members of the master race. In Britain, however, they represent a severely disadvantaged underclass, of which the men especially find themselves at risk of 'losing their marbles' to the constant taunts and provocations of systemic emasculation. (2000: 152)

Roy Strang's status as a Scottish white working-class male is thus a very peculiar one, which demonstrates the ambivalence and context dependence of intersectional identity positions. Following Schoene-Harwood, Roy's working-class whiteness is an in-between identity which assumes different significance in each cultural context and can thus range from normative invisibility to abject hypervisibility.

Thus, especially in the contexts of Roy's mapping of class-based oppression onto racial oppression, which equates the marginalisation of the Scottish white working class with that of black Africans, Roy "exists somewhere in-between these two social poles, between oppressor and oppressed, a situation that can be said to reflect the complexity of Scottish-British identity" (Jones 2006: n. pag.). However, it has of course to be noted that in most cultural contexts where black and white subjects and populations are interacting, the racialised position of blackness would not enjoy whiteness's flexibility to shift from abject to normative. Thus, even if (white) working-class identity might be subjected to oppression, it would still have more potential than a black subject position and thus still enjoys the privileges of whiteness.

Scottishness is thus rendered as a contested cultural and national identity, which is here mapped onto whiteness as a semiotic carrier of this national identity. In the process, both whiteness and Scottishness are proven to be profoundly ambivalent and shifting categories. Consequently, Aaron Kelly concludes that *Marabou Stork Nightmares* suggests that

> Scotland is itself not a homogeneous entity that can be positioned as either coloniser or colonised. Rather, it is a collision of both that benefited large sections of Scotland's upper and middle classes in addition to aspirant working-class imperialists who gain provisional access to its benefits. Yet simultaneously, it further oppressed the rest of its own working and subaltern classes. So colonialism does not merely seek to dominate and control overseas, it also strives to maintain specific sets of unequal social relations relating to class, gender, sexuality and place at home. (2005: 118)

These complex and at times ambiguous intersectional relations are also at work in *Marabou Stork Nightmare*'s key event, the gang rape of Kirsty. As I will show in the concluding section of my analysis, this event further complicates Roy's (and, by extension, his family's) whiteness and his class status by focusing on the intersections with gender and sexuality.

Masculinity, Abject Sexuality and Whiteness

Roy's sexual and gender development complexly interlink with the development of his class consciousness and his awareness for the sociopolitical contexts he was raised in. In his retrospective account, he repeatedly emphasises the effect of his low self-confidence regarding his outward appearance – that is, what he previously referred to as the "Strang look" – on his male identity. This becomes evident in a passage quoted above where John forces Roy and his half-brother Bernard (who later turns out to be gay) to fight each other, calling for Roy to fight for his family name and hence prove his masculinity. After his time in South Africa, where Roy rebuilt his self-confidence, he returns to school in Edinburgh in his early teenage years and takes revenge on those who he feels pick on him. When one of his classmates, Caroline, flicks "the back of ma fuckin ear", he considers this as "humiliation", recalling the many times he had been called "Dumbo Strang" before: "I was always sensitive about my ears" (*MSN* 106). His revenge plays out in a violent first sexual experience when he stalks Caroline, threatens her at knifepoint, forces her to pull up her skirt to expose herself and starts to masturbate. What he refers to as his "first ride" whets his appetite for male power and violent domination of women:

> I enjoyed the look in her eyes. Enjoyed having the knife at her throat. Enjoyed the power, I remembered thinking, you just had to take it. When you took it, you had to hold on to it. That was all there was to it. My cock was stiffening in my pants. Everything seemed to be so bright. [...]. Roy Strang is ma fucking name. Nae cunt fucks aboot wi me. (*MSN* 106)

What is important in this passage is the emphasis on appellation and the reassurance Roy gets from hearing his name said out loud. When he threatens Caroline with his knife and she asks "what ur ye daein, Roy", this is also, as he realises, "the first time she'd spoke tae ays: the first time the cunt hud said ma name" (*MSN* 106). Roy's compulsive desire to hear his name spoken out loud is ultimately indicative of his lack of control over his own identity and his narrative – an aspect which is a central leitmotif throughout the novel and culminates in the revelation that his self-description as a rather unattractive young man is not reliable. When his rape victim, Kirsty, takes revenge on him and suffocates him with his own genitals in the coma ward, she first tells him that the funny thing is, Roy, Roy Strang, that I actually fancied you. Honest. Crazy eh? I genuinely thought that you were a bit different. Thought that you were a nice-looking felly. I know that you were shy aboot your ears, anybody could see that, but I liked them. [...]. The only reason I hung around with these morons was to get closer to you. (*MSN* 228)

Subsequently, while he is choking on his genitals, Roy finally concludes his distorted narrative with the following revelation:

I have no visible ears, I never really had much in the way of ears, it was always my nose, Captain Beaky, they used to call me at the school ... it wasn't the ears, my memory hasn't been so good [...] I have the gait of a comic scarecrow, I shuffle like an old man who has shat his pants. I'm so tired ... I spread my large, black wings ... (*MSN* 264)

His sudden revelation and modified self-description as having a large, apparently beak-like nose as well as his "black wings" not only indicate the novel's final and ultimate drift into the realm of the surreal and dreamlike, with Roy himself now resembling the dreaded Marabou Stork, previously alluded to as a demonic dream incarnation of various people from Roy's past such as his paedophile uncle Gordon or his hooligan friend Lexo whom he (falsely) accused of forcing him to take part in Kirsty's rape, but also of Roy's fundamental unreliability as a narrator. Thus, at the end of the novel, the reader is left with a profound sense of uncertainty regarding the descriptions of Roy himself, but also of the other characters, especially his victim Kirsty. This, in turn has repercussions for the novel's final plot turn – Kirsty's metamorphosis from a passive victim of rape and abuse of justice into a mass-murdering avenger. As Robert Morace explains in relation to the "surprising [...] willingness of some critics to read Kirsty's transformation at the novel's ending so literally":

The novel never makes clear, and never can make clear, whether Kirsty is physically present in the hospital room or not and whether what Roy hears is what she says and how much overlap there may be between the real Kirsty and an imagined one. Kirsty is a real person who is nonetheless also, like Roy's African fantasy, an imagined construct, one that produces the final image of Roy in Roy's hallucinating mind. (2007: 114–115)

This is of enormous importance for judging the construction of Roy's character and identity throughout the entire novel, and especially his self-victimisation in relation to the issues of race/whiteness and class. What the novel in this final turn of events reveals is the ultimate distortion and incompleteness of Roy as a person, but also as a raced and classed subject. This ending conveys a profound sense of uncertainty, which also performatively probes and deconstructs the capacities of literature to account for raced and classed subject positions and identity models. In that respect, *Marabou Stork Nightmares*'s play with the reliability of signifiers in the construction of identities is no self-indulgent end in itself, and by no means denies or downplays the interplay of symbolic and material boundaries erected through the interplay of intersectional identity factors. Rather, the novel serves as a representation of the paradoxical continuum of whiteness and its intersections and the way whiteness is always bound to an interplay of personal-individual factors and collective cultural histories, both of which are more often than not conflicted and inconclusive.

For the case of tainted whiteness, this is further complicated through the abjectifying mechanisms at work in constructing this particular subject position. It is here that what Sara Ahmed calls "sticky signs" comes into play again as it is precisely the "sticky" and therefore stigmatising effect of signifiers of disgust that creates the tainted whiteness and white trash identity positions that deprive those subjects who inhabit them the ability to signify their identities themselves. The subject attempting to signify his or her own subject position has always already been labelled disgusting. One of the most poignant examples of this can be found in John Strang's attempts to label himself and his family as "middle class" by purchasing certain consumer goods when, in fact, the excessive consumerism solidifies their status as "prototype schemies". Consequently, Kirsty (no matter whether it is the 'real' Kirsty or one of Roy's projections) finally comes to a conclusion about Roy's own desperate attempts at reversing the effects of boundary work by listing his racist, classist, misogynist and homophobic obsessions: "who do you fuckin hate Roy Strang you hate schemies Kaffirs poofs Weedgies Japs snobby cunts jambos scarfers English cunts women only you don't do you Roy Strang the only cunt you really hate is // Roy Strang" (*MSN* 262).

After the rape, Roy's struggles with the "sticky signs" labelling him as disgusting gains more complexity when he (successfully) struggles to convince his parents that he is not guilty. While the case is still pending, he cannot muster to leave the house as he "felt that everyone was looking at me and I knew what they'd be saying under their breath: Dumbo Strang interbred mutant fuckup sick psychopathic rapist vermin" (*MSN* 195). Here, he fears that the stigma of being a rapist will add to the white trash stereotypes of deviant sexuality associated with the Strang family. For his father, the case is another test case for his attempts at creating an air of middle-class respectability around himself and his family in order to escape the stigmatising signs of "schemie" life. When he interrogates his son to find out whether Roy has actually raped Kirsty, he convinces them that "it was her but, Dad [...] she wanted it" (*MSN* 192). His mother, all too ready to be convinced of his innocence, as he is, after all, an upwardly mobile young man who holds a "job in computers" eagerly projects the stigmatyping images of white trash schemies associated with her family onto Roy's hooligan friends whom, apart from the rape victim, she believes to be the root of the problem:

> That's wit it wis! [...] A slag! A fuckin slag's gaunny ruin ma laddie's life! N you're gaunny jist stand thair n take that slag's word against yir ain flesh n blood! [...]. Eh's a good laddie, John! Eh's goat a job in computers ... thing ay the future. Wi eywis brought um up right! It's jist that rubbish eh's been hingin aroond wi, they idiots fi the fitba... (*MSN* 192)

Roy's "job in computers" in fact becomes the sign for his respectability that distinguishes him (and, by extension, his family) from the rest of the scheme. Thus, John and his wife, Vet, repeat his job description to comic effect as John utilises the rape case to support his bizarre worldviews:

> We've goat ma laddie thair whae's workin in computers n he's treated like a leper in his fuckin scheme because ay some slut. [...]. The shotgun solution's the only one, like ah sais, the shotgun solution. [...] eftir ah'd wasted aw that junky trash, ah'd be right up the council n ah'd blaw they cunts away n aw! [...]. Cause the junkies n the single parents n that, they're just the symptom ay the disease. (*MSN* 197-198)

Ironically, the abjectifying rhetoric of disease John employs here is, as I have shown earlier, an important part in the repertoire of middle-class boundary maintenance. John's use of it thus is another instance of his attempts to pass as middle class when it is in fact people like him – perceived as uncontrolled, misbehaved, excessive "schemies" who are prone to violent outbursts (as is evidenced in the incident he was sentenced to prison for in South Africa) – at whom stigmatyping labels such as "junky trash" are usually directed in classist discourse. In John's view, the "fuckin stupid communist cunts on the council" (*MSN* 197) are guilty of supporting "that junky trash", when, ironically, it is people like himself and his family who benefit from the council by being granted affordable housing on the scheme. The entire rape case thus threatens John's attempts to pass as middle class. It further demonstrates the paradoxical continuum of whiteness as it is (white) male solidarity which here temporarily overcomes and evades class boundaries.

This becomes evident in the defence strategy developed by Roy and his mates' lawyer, Conrad Donaldson, who, as is obvious to Roy, "didn't believe a word we were saying" (*MSN* 206). While Donaldson, in Roy's perception, can barely hide his "distaste" for the bunch of hooligan racists (*MSN* 207), he constructs the mates as a group of respectable young men which plays out as a transforming episode of class passing:

> For the trial we had to move out of being Lexo, Stangy, Ozzy and Demps, top boys. We were now Alex Setterington, businessman (Lexo had his second-hand furniture shop in Leith), Roy Strang, Analyst with a reputable Edinburgh insurance company, Ian Osmotherly, Sales Manager with a busy nationwide retailer, and Allan Dempsey, who was a student. Dempsey had enrolled to do a Social Care course at Stevenson College before the court case. It gave a better impression than dole-mole. [...]. We were described by Donaldson as 'a far cry from the picture of rampaging soccer yobbos [...]; in fact decent, articulate, upstanding professional young men with excellent prospects, from good families.' (*MSN* 207-208)

Two thing become evident from this transformation: First, it suggests that all forms of social identity are the result of performance – neither the men's "official" civil identities nor the identities they assume amongst one another, as part of their homosocial, subcultural male bond, are in any way "natural" identities. Rather, they are all forms of masquerade which, to come back to Deleuze and Guattari's notion of "faciality", draw on certain sets of predetermined semiotic inscription.

This, however, does not mean that these performances and inscriptions can be put on arbitrarily and at will; they are strongly dependent on given cultural contexts and preconditions. Here, it is through the appellation of the lawyer as a social and legal authority that Roy and his friends can assume an identity which leans more towards the bourgeois notion of "normality" than their subcultural and deviant identities. This, as the satiric presentation of the court trial suggests, is exclusively possible for them because of their male privilege, which in this situation even transcends the class boundaries between the friends and the lawyer. For while Roy and his mates can convincingly accomplish their performance of middle-class respectability, their victim, Kirsty, has no such privileges. On the contrary, she is transfixed in her position as female victim and, even worse, responsibility for the crime she suffered is shifted towards herself when, as Roy observes,

> it became like she was on trial; her past; her sexuality, her behaviour. She looked really strange in the court. It was the wey she moved. She walked like the centre ay balance in her body had irreversably shifted. It wis like the movement ay some cunt that had come oot fae under the surgeon's knife and who was recuperating from a chronic and ultimately terminal illness. (*MSN* 208)

Within the male-dominated context of the courtroom, her identity is rendered irrelevant by male law, and consequently, during Roy's account of the trial, she is only being referred to as "Miss X" (*MSN* 210) after she had previously already been reduced to a "fuckin lovely piece ay meat" by Roy and his mates (*MSN* 182). Her female sexuality is abjectified through the (male-dominated) discourses of law, sexual medicine and psychology – a process of abjectification which temporarily nullifies Roy and his friends' abjection as white trash schemies: "Donaldson then presented an 'expert' who claimed that gang-rape fantasy was a common female sexual fantasy" (*MSN* 210). In addition, the judge's attitudes, as Donaldson assures his clients,

> are very much influenced by his practicing of criminal law in the fifties where the dominant school of criminology was the Freudian model. This essentially does away with the concept of the crime of rape by proving that there are no victims. Female sexuality is deemed by nature to be masochistic, hence rape cannot logistically take place since it directly encounters the argument that all women want it anyway. (*MSN* 207)

Within the broader context of the novel, Kirsty's rape and subsequent humiliation and stigmatisation as a demonstration of male dominance play out as an analogy to the colonial project, and the novel, as Aaron Kelly argues, "seeks to place [violence] in a social context of power relations" (2005: 119). Violence against women, in the way it is supported (by, among others, the legal authorities, psychiatry and medicine) and condoned systemically by a predominantly male-led society, is exposed as a system of oppression equalling those of classism and racism. This oppression as well as the supportive system of male solidarity – "an aggressively patriarchal society where power is gendered in oppressively male terms" (Kelly 2005: 119) – which in this case transgresses all other social boundaries is then again linked back to Britishness and whiteness through the comic figure of John Strang who celebrates his son's acquittal by cheering about the British justice system as a noble achievement of the white race: "Ye kin fuckin well say what ye like aboot British justice bit it's still the best in the world! Thir's some countries whair innocent laddies wid be rottin away behind bars! [...] in a wog country or that" (*MSN* 212–213).

John Strang's crude conception of the British justice system does not only imply that non-white cultures ("wog countries") are incapable of proper legal work, but that they would also be likely to be fooled by corrupting women and, as lawyer Conrad Donaldson expresses it, by "some dykey feminist group" (*MSN* 207) agitating against "innocent laddies". Following this logic, such a "corrupt" system which does not maintain the privileged status of men would be inherently effeminate – and as John Strang's attitude towards Roy's half-brother Bernard shows, (British) whiteness is for him intricately linked to an ideal of heteronormative masculinity, best exemplified by the Scottish hard man. In the previously quoted passage in which John lets Roy fight against Bernard for the "Strang name", he refers to the homosexual Bernard as a "crappin eyetie bastard son" who is not fit to bear the "Strang name". Using the derogatory slur "eyetie" for Italian (because his wife, Vet, had her son with an Italian man), John renders Bernard as 'not quite white', much less British, and, in a common racist association with Italian masculinity, as unmanly. In his desperate and at times delusional attempt to be respectably middle class, John thus endorses hyperbolic images of whiteness and masculinity that mutually reinforce each other.

In the context of the court case, John and his son's performance of middle-class respectability ends immediately with the victorious acquittal: Having successfully done his job, lawyer Donaldson withdraws his male solidarity when John, in Roy's eyes, makes "a tit of himself, a tit of me" by inviting Donaldson to celebrate the triumph at their home "doon the scheme, ken? Muirhoose likes [...]. Nowt fancy, like ah sais, jist a wee drink" (*MSN* 213). His Scottish dialect is in stark contrast to Donaldson's uninflected speech, and from the lawyer's reaction it is evident that he does not wish to be associated with the milieu of Muirhouse, which, as a council estate, is subject to "territorial stigmatization", which in the words of Imogen Tyler is "inscribed upon the bodies of those who [live] in these abjectified zones" (2013: 162).[23] The novel continues: "Muirhouse... Donaldson repeated slowly, — ... sorry, I don't think so. I'm pretty busy at the moment" (*MSN* 213). In contrast, John's behaviour and speech appear as embarrassingly lower class and inappropriate considering the context, revealing him to be a grotesque caricature of the very "trash" that he wants to distinguish himself from when he congratulates Donaldson on his "fuckin magic, if yll pardon ma French like" (*MSN* 213). The boundaries of class are once again in full effect.

In continuation of the court case narrative's satiric tone, the chapter concludes with John Strang celebrating his son's acquittal and "British justice" by taking "quite a bit of blow" (i.e., cocaine) and "[putting] on Churchill's victory speeches full blast": "Shaking with emotion, he shouted, raising his glass, — THIS IS STILL THE GREATEST FUCKIN

23 | Tyler identifies the beginning of the "pathologization of the council estate" in the "public imaginary" during the Thatcher years (2013: 160), peaking during the years of the New Labour government with the introduction of Anti-Social Behaviour Orders (2013: 161). In fact, as Tyler argues, Britain's housing estates as the home for what Tony Blair has called "a new class: a workless class" became emblematic for a specific kind of Blairite neoliberal class consciousness when Blair, "hours after winning the 1997 election" delivered "his first address as prime minister" on the Aylesbury council estate in Southwark (2013: 159). Thus, during the Blair years, the "council estate became metonymic shorthand for this 'new class of problem people', and the poverty associated with these places was imagined as a self-induced pathological condition. Blair's speech in 1997 signalled how, by drawing on neoconservative theories of welfare dependency and the conceptual categories of underclass, poverty would come to be unshackled symbolically from economic inequalities and reframed as a psycho-cultural problem" (Tyler 2013: 162). Published two years before Blair's speech and set in the 1980s and early 1990s, *Marabou Stork Nightmares* can thus be regarded as a representation of the social precondition for the "territorial stigmatization" of the council estate.

COUNTRY IN THE WORLD!" (*MSN* 214). The chapter's final sentences – "Most people nodded approvingly, thinking he meant Scotland. I was one of the few present who knew he meant Britain" – once more illustrate John Strang's delusional aspirations towards hegemonic, middle-classed Britishness, which, for him, is still associated with the values of the Empire. These aspirations are rendered particularly comic since John is throughout the novel incapable of even switching linguistic registers and is one of the characters in the novel with the thickest Scottish dialect and "schemie" speech register. Unlike his son, who ultimately even fools the reader into going along with his deceptions at least temporarily, John is unable to successfully and convincingly pass as middle-class white. Within the context of what my analysis of *Trainspotting* has established as one of the underlying ideas of Welsh's early novels, the uncanny past in the present, John Strang's desperate yearning for Britain's glorious time of empire where white was "right" (which he can neither reach in his home country nor in South Africa) appears as a similarly uncanny desire for clinging onto a national and racial past which is no longer available in the present and, as is suggested by the novel's troubled narrative, probably never was available to people of the lower classes like John Strang. John's longing for the past is mirrored in Roy's desire to come to terms with his own past as is evidenced by the fantasy narratives he spins during his comatose state and by the increasingly unreliable forgings of his memories which neglect his full responsibility for a crime.

In that respect, when he tries to start a new life in the Manchester rave scene after the acquittal and starts to take ecstasy in order to make peace with himself and the world around him, thereby further repressing his guilt, his attempts at dealing with the past become representative of a naive national wish for reconciliation and returning to a perceived pristine primal state – a state which Roy believes he could find in an idealised version of South Africa: "I wanted to go back, no as it is now but as I imagined it was or as it could be. Once those fuckin white cunts had been kicked out" (*MSN* 234). Here, his individual guilt and responsibility for violating a woman and getting away with it are mapped onto the collective historical guilt of the "white cunts" (i.e., British imperialists and their descendants). This sudden streak of white guilt and self-loathing (culminating in his suicide attempt), however, must be questioned in their sincerity when considering how Roy acts them out in his coma fantasy where he becomes a colonial explorer who treats black natives in the most patronising manner. Ultimately, when he is being confronted by Kirsty (or an imagined version of her), it becomes clear that he will not get away with such attempts at personal or (to take up Gavin Miller's criticism of certain strands of Scottish literary criticism) collective, transhistorical reconciliation. The white trash "schemie" Roy Strang, despite becoming an aspiring upwardly mobile yuppie who has a "job in computers" ("a thing ay the future", as his parents do not tire of repeating),[24] a rapist and the caricature of an adventure novel explorer, is not able to escape the past, be it his personal or familial one, or a collective-historical past of white Britain. These complexities haunting the Scottish-British white (male) subject are further explored by Welsh in his third novel *Filth*.

24 | It could be argued that his parents' comic and pathetic repetition of this phrase demonstrates the very impossibility of fully progressing into the future. Instead, there is only the promise of progression and future being repeated in a circular rather than a progressive structure.

II.3 *Filth*

If *Trainspotting* can be regarded as a novel of inversion, and *Marabou Stork Nightmares* makes explicit the torn and conflicted consciousness of the white male working-class subject, then *Filth* can be considered to elaborate on the issues of the first two novels by adding to the perspective from the bottom of society that dominates *Trainspotting* and *Marabou Stork Nightmares* the point of view from the institutional top of society in the form of a corrupt policeman. For Aaron Kelly, who examines the novel's take on racism and racist violence within the context of 1990s scepticism towards the systemic preconditions of racism as well as towards the police force in the aftermath of the Stephen Lawrence murder (see 2005: 156–157), this shift of perspective is not a move towards mainstream forms of presentation as they can be found in popular genres like the detective novel[25] but another example of Welsh's subversive literary project:

> A large part of the dissident political force of *Filth* resides in its refusal to dismiss racism as either a problem of rogue individuals in an otherwise equitable system or as an abstract and impersonal structural fault to which individual officers are helplessly bound despite their better intentions. Instead the novel excoriates both the institution and those who maintain its oppressive culture. (2005: 157)

It is precisely the novel's focus on the depth and complexity of raciology that allows it to be read in reference to boundary work and the construction and maintenance of symbolic/material racial boundaries. *Filth* functions as a companion piece to *Marabou Stork Nightmares* not only in the construction of its unreliable narrator but also in the way it presents the human body as the site of racial configurations, and it further explores the way institutions inscribe themselves in the body and consciousness. In the continuation of a neo-gothic exploration of the post-Thatcherite socio-political uncanny, *Filth* also continues Welsh's occupation with the inversion of bodily and psychic orders to lay bare the aporetic character of intersectional forms of identity, and also adds emphasis on the inversion of spatial orders related to these identities. Once more, the (this time monstrous) body emerges as the major signifier and semantic battleground

25 | Robert A. Morace (2007) shows that the protagonist of *Filth* is designed as a parody of Ian Rankin's detective hero John Rebus, see 87–88, 90.

on which these tensions and conflicts are carried out. As the novel's title already suggests, it also adds further layers to the semantics of trash and dirt in the context of whiteness.

From the Pits to the Top

Politically and psychologically, the narrator of *Filth*, Detective Sergeant Bruce Robertson, is in many ways a refined continuation of *Marabou Stork Nightmare*'s John Strang. Like Strang, he is an admirer of Margaret Thatcher who bemoans the end of Thatcherism and the subsequent shifts towards a multicultural and politically correct Britain. Several time markers indicate that the novel's plot takes place in the winter of 1997/98, that is, shortly after New Labour's and Tony Blair's victory in the elections, the death of Lady Diana, and the Scottish devolution referendum. Within the context of the emerging politics of New Labour, Bruce Robertson appears as a conservative chauvinist relic from the 1980s, with his name evoking an even broader historical context stretching back to the fight for Scottish independence led by Robert the Bruce, the King of Scots. Like Roy Strang in *Marabou Stork Nightmares*, his name also recalls Rob Roy, another Scottish national hero. Thus, Robertson also embodies the past in the present, and, if perceived as a type rather than an "authentic" character, lets medieval history and national myths converge with the cultural and political developments of 1980s and 1990s Scotland. Moreover, Robertson is far from representing an authentic and original Scottishness. Rather, he is comprised of several mythic components and is yet another instance of inherent identity deconstruction in the work of Irvine Welsh.

One of the novel's central episodes in which this deconstruction of identity culminates in relation to questions of whiteness is the chapter "Equal Opportunities". Having dedicated several days to solving the murder of the African Efan Wurie (which, as it turns out, Bruce committed himself) in Edinburgh, the leader of the investigation, Amanda Drummond, has decided to launch a racial awareness workshop for the officers involved. Several issues of intersectionality and boundary work become evident in this episode. First, it becomes increasingly clear that Bruce is not the only white male officer harbouring right-wing and chauvinist attitudes. In the workshop, which is facilitated by Drummond and an Asian-British female, the confrontation between the female instructors and the male officers is staged as the eruption of more complex ideological conflicts that betray the connection of abstract systemic racism and the individuals who represent and actively enforce (to stick to the terminology of police work) these attitudes, as Aaron Kelly has indicated in the passage quoted above. Before the workshop, in an instance of male bonding that is performed throughout the seminar, Bruce and his colleagues complain about the politically correct formalities of contemporary law enforcement under Blair:

> – Aye, says Gus Bain, – Scotland's a white man's country. Always has been, always will be. That's the way ah see it at any rate, and ah'm too long in tooth tae change now, he chuckles cheerfully. A good auld boy Gus. – Precisely Gus. Ah mind when I took Carole and wee Stacey tae see that *Braveheart*. How many pakis or spades did ye see in the colours fightin for Scotland? Same wi *Rob Roy*, same wi *The Bruce*. [...]. We built this fuckin country. Thir wis nane ay them at Bannockburn or Culloden when the going was tough. It's our blood, our soil, our history. Then they want tae waltz in here and reap all the benefits and tell us that we should be ashamed ay that! We were fuckin slaves before these cunts were ever rounded up and shipped tae America! (*Fi* 46-47)

This passage illustrates the involuntary self-deconstruction of the speaking male white subject. After all, Bruce is not talking about the actual historical events that are part of the construction of white Scottish national identity, but rather contemporary filmic representations of these events, all produced throughout the mid-1990s – and it should be kept in mind that, ironically, *The Bruce* is the only film that is actually a UK- and Scotland-based adaptation, whereas the other films mentioned by Bruce are American productions or international co-productions.[26] Thus, the national consciousness of the white Scottish male is shown to be the product of, among other factors, fictional representations produced for an international market. Lacking any actual basis for its claims, the conflation of national and ethnic identity is revealed to be a forgery and a form of pastiche – and Bruce Robertson, as his name's alteration of the names of Scottish heroes already indicates, can likewise be considered to be a forged identity that lacks any stable basis just like any supposedly essential form

26 | Morace appropriately describes Gibson's *Braveheart* as a film in which "outlandish caricatures and historical inaccuracies are rendered as if real by means of cinematic verisimilitude coupled with postmodernism's attenuated historical sensibility" (2007: 91).

of identity in Welsh's work, as Gavin Miller has argued (see my introduction to this chapter).

A similar inconsistency can be detected in the repeated shift between the poles of racialised active perpetrator and passive victim: Bruce moves from painting a picture of the white Scots as prevailing fighters who by virtue of soil and blood have inherited the right to inhabit the country, to the white Scots as victims being sponged by non-white immigrants who simultaneously weaken the Scottish nation by invoking a discourse of white shame and guilt (notably, both these aspects have been recurrent motifs in the rhetoric of far-right parties like the BNP and the NF ever since Enoch Powell's "Rivers of Blood" speech). Similarly, the rendering of the Scots as "original" slaves who allegedly experienced victimhood and exploitation before the African slaves evokes a paradoxical "me-tooism" and a quest for the 'authentic victim' that undermines the image of the white Scot who is superior by heritage. Going back to the two previous novels, Bruce's argument can be compared to Roy Strang's observation that "Back in Edinburgh, we would be Kaffirs; condemned to live out our lives in townships like Muirhouse or So-Wester-Hailes-To[27] or Niddrie, self-contained camps with fuck all in them [...]" (*MSN* 80) – however, this statement comes from one of the "schemies" that Bruce Robertson so utterly despises for their inferiority in terms of class (*Fi* 273, 327).[28] And as Biressi/Nunn and Collins have argued, the discourse of white victimhood is part of the stereotyping of the contemporary white working class. This leaves the question why a character like Bruce would reference this discourse. Aaron Kelly has shown convincingly how Bruce is rendered as a paradoxically classed subject that constantly shifts between different performances of class identity. Kelly particularly argues that this paradoxical tension is most evident in Bruce's avid consumption of the tabloid press: while he distances himself from the "pleb" readers of the *Sun*, not a day goes by that he does not study the paper. However, he does not want to be associated with its regular readers, as becomes clear fairly early in the novel:

> I'm upset at the cheerfulness of the shopkeeper. – The *Sun*, he shouts loudly, – very good, thirty pence. This disgusts me as I'm not like the rest of the festering

27 | A play on the names of Wester Hailes and the South-African slum Soweto.

28 | Strikingly, Roy's gang of hooligans and rapists return for some guest appearances throughout *Filth*.

plebs who read the *Sun*. I'm more like somebody who writes the thing, edits it even. Know the difference, you pleb, always know the fuckin difference. (*Fi* 25)

Kelly interprets passages like these within the context of what Stuart Hall calls Thatcherite "authoritarian populism" that takes up "popular discontents" to "cut across and between different divisions in society" (Hall 1988, qtd. in Kelly 2005: 161).[29] Kelly's interpretation of Bruce's attitude and his identity as an embodiment of "Thatcherism's irreconcilable contradictions" (2005: 163) in that context can be linked back to John Strang's attempt at passing as middle class through certain forms of behaviour and adjustment of habitus.[30] Just like John wants to overcome the assumed stigmatisation of his working-class origins, Bruce is eager to conceal his upbringing in a miner family – a fact that is systematically hinted at throughout the novel in allusions that only in the final concluding chapters is fully revealed by Bruce's unconscious in the form of his speaking and extremely perceptive tapeworm – an aspect of the novel that will be looked at more closely in the following section. In many ways, Bruce is the kind of person that John Strang could have been if he had been completely suc-

29 | Richard Hoggart's analysis of the "Them" and "Us" worldview of the British working class fits in with Bruce's characterisation as a former working-class child who aspires to be middle class and to police and humiliate the working class in his professional capacity. In describing "minor officials" who have been recruited from the working classes and thus become superior to their peers, Hoggart notices that these minor officials "will now be regarded as on the side of 'Them'. Some minor officials have a doubleness in their attitudes. They tend to be sharp towards the working-classes because they would like to feel more securely separate from them; they know in their hearts by just how little they are separated and do not like to think of dropping back. Their deference towards the middle-classes can conceal an animosity; they would like to be one of them but realize they are not" (1968: 74). In *Filth*, Bruce can be interpreted as an embodiment of this "doubleness" taken to the satiric extreme.

30 | I here follow Daniel Bernardi who sees "whiteness, and thus race, as a performance: a performance about passing. As I have suggested, there are no white people per se, only those who pass as white. And passing as white, at least in the United States, has almost always had something to do with 'acting' and 'looking' - making - white. [...] Whiteness, clinging as it does to common sense notions of genetic or divine difference, is the perfect performance: the actors' method is accepted as natural" (2001: xxi).

cessful in his passing.[31] Bruce decided to join the police force in order to be part of the police brutality against the striking miners in 1984/85 (see *Fi* 385), and, as his tapeworm lets the reader know, admires Thatcher not only for her harsh treatment of the strikers but also for her ruthlessness in the Falklands crisis:

> You idolise Thatcher over the Falklands. You try to imagine the buzz she must have felt when the word 'rejoice' came from her lips. It makes you feel like you did when you were a child. While other children fantasised about killing in wars, you wanted to be in the position to send others to their deaths from the safety of an oak-panelled office. In your head you practise speeches condemning the enemy. (*Fi* 389)

Thus, while John Strang sentimentally listens to Churchill's wartime speeches and establishes his own system of surveillance within the realm of the housing scheme to monitor his potentially deviant neighbours from the point-of-view of the omniscient authoritative state but never actually manages to overcome the boundaries of class even in apartheid South Africa, perceived by him as a utopian haven for the white man, Bruce has successfully managed to pass beyond his family background into the realm of state power, the middle class, and – ultimately – proper Scottish-British whiteness. He is therefore the complete embodiment of the Thatcherite uncanny within the new "Cool Britannia" of New Labour, a gothic haunting from the past that nevertheless is not unique in its political backwardness but rather, as Welsh's novel clearly suggests, hints at more complex, subtle and perfidious structures of racism and classism in contemporary Britain. The notion of passing is of central importance in that respect and for the figurations of whiteness in Welsh's novels.

The Uncanny Politics of Passing

For the purpose of analysing Welsh's fiction with regard to the notion of passing, I would like to draw on a working definition provided by Sinéad Moynihan in her recent publication on the subject, *Passing into the Present* (2010):

31 | "Robertson is a variation on the type represented earlier by Roy Strang's father, another reactionary, racist, Anglophile Scot" (Morace 2007: 88).

> Broadly defined, to 'pass' is to appear to belong to one or more social subgroups other than the one(s) to which one is normally assigned by prevailing legal, medical and/or socio-cultural discourses. To pass as white, if one is 'black', or male, if one is 'female', is to challenge assumptions that the evidence of one's race and/or gender is always visually available by recourse to a set of characteristics considered immutable - skin colour, hair texture, fingernails, genitalia and so on. By contrast, to pass into a different class is more likely to be an invisible form of passing. (8)

However, while Moynihan (and others) have put race and gender to the fore as crucial identity categories of passing, I would only partly agree that "class is more likely to be an invisible form of passing". Rather, as Welsh's work frequently shows, class might usually not be considered to be linked to specific physiognomic attributes like skin colour and genitalia, but nevertheless is in the public imagination and in the symbolic construction of boundaries that manifest in visible (and, in the case of the sociolects which are so carefully represented in Welsh's novels, audible) signs. In Welsh's fiction, passing takes place in varying intersectional contexts – among the many examples are Mark Renton, who switches sociolects to avoid a prison sentence by convincingly passing as an educated ex-student interested in Kierkegaard,[32] or John Strang, who believes that a certain set of material possessions would be likely to suggest his aspired middle-class status. The most important aspect, however, is the racialisation of class.

---

32 | In his study of the "dialect and dialectics" of the modern Scottish novel, Cairns Craig reads Renton's courtroom speech as the unfolding of a social dialectic that could also be described in terms of an uncanny passing: "The novel of dialect becomes, almost inevitably, the novel of dialectics. *Trainspotting* acknowledges this when Renton, in court for stealing a book, outlines the philosophical basis of his opposition [...]. Renton's philosophical exposition is 'talk' which can get him a 'higher sentence' - both the higher rhetoric in which he is engaged and the sentence he might get in jail. The 'higher sentence' belongs to a culture which he is now stealing as effectively as he stole the book. He is engaging in precisely the kind of dialectics which the society of which he is a part must suppress in order to maintain its own control, because what he is expressing is the philosophy of individual isolationism which appears to challenge society but is actually a justification of society's economic individualism, its negation of the heterocentricity of which his dialect speech is but the ghost" (1999: 99).

As Alasdair Bonnett shows in his chapter on "How the British Working Class Became White" (2000: 28), class status has been closely linked to visible physical markers of class, at least in the nineteenth century. To give another example from *Filth*, one of the most obvious means to express classedness and hence to visibly pass as member of a certain class, is clothing: Bruce is intent on wearing nothing but flannel pants in an attempt to distinguish himself from the common people, and he scoffs at the sight of "a student with that nigger hair and rags these rich white kids like tae wear" (*Fi* 37). The last instance is particularly relevant since it suggests another, possibly inverted, form of the visible racialisation of class, with markers of "blackness" being ambivalently interpreted.[33] The inherently contradictory arbitrariness of racial attributes as markers of class and racist-classist assumptions is further parodied in the novel in an alcohol-fuelled dialogue between Bruce, who is an avid music fan but has destroyed all his Motown records because he considers it a "weakness to have coon music in the hoose" (*Fi* 172), and his mate Clifford Blades:

> – How can you be a racist and like Motown? He's whining, – I mean, how can you be a racist and like Marvin Gaye? – Marvin Gaye was not a black man. – How can you say that? – He wasn't a black man to me. The cunt that shot him, that was a black man. That was a fuckin nigger. – But that was his father! – Yes. A black man. (*Fi* 172)

Apparently, Bruce feels caught out by Blades in this absurd conversation, as he involuntarily gets up and has "some sense of grabbing Bladesey round the neck and him shouting: — What are you doing Bruce? It's me! It's me! But I know it's him and I want to choke the living shite out of the cunt [...] cause he's just one of the cunts who's got it in for me" (*Fi* 172–173). Within the context of "passing", Blades could thus be interpreted as what Amy Robinson calls a *clairvoyant,* that is, the person who can actually see the passing person for what he/she is (1994: 715).[34] In this instance, Bruce's turning against his drinking mate (the demise of whom Bruce is constantly plotting throughout one of the novel's subplots) is the reaction of the passing subject being caught for what he is.

33 | "Black" attributes can be connected to both the "rich" and educated classes as well as to the community of "schemies" in Bruce's racist-classist worldview.

34 | See also Moynihan 2010: 3.

Yet the forms of passing are rather complex in Bruce's case and run across several intersectional axes. As is revealed towards the end of the novel, Bruce is not only the descendant of a mining family, a member of the very class of people he desired to oppress and oppose by joining the police under Thatcher, but he is also a bastard child fathered by a rapist who throughout the novel is known as "The Beast" (see *Fi* 381–386). This fact is revealed by the tapeworm long after Bruce and his comrade Ray Lennox have played "the Beast routine", a method to "spook" criminals in interrogation (*Fi* 85). In such instances, the interrogated person is intimidated by the officers' extensive accounts of convicted criminals who allegedly have been incarcerated on the same ward as The Beast, leaving them in "The Beast's vile clutches" (*Fi* 92), subjected to the danger of being raped repeatedly and being infected with HIV. The depersonalisation of the rapist called The Beast, his stylisation as a nonhuman bogeyman and the revelation that Bruce is actually The Beast's offspring eventually suggest that Bruce himself is a form of bogeyman, the uncanny personification of society's evils. Thus, he can be interpreted as the embodiment of the ultimate stigmatype – a figure that demarcates the boundaries of race, class, gender, and, by extension, moral and immoral, cleanliness and dirt, but simultaneously incorporates the very contradictions and aporias of these boundaries.

As will be shown in the following section, this is particularly significant in connection with the novel's main motif of filth, dirt and uncleanliness. In fact, Bruce's origin as the unwanted outcome of a horrible crime not only explains his own disposition towards mental illness (The Beast is said to suffer from "acute schizophrenia, depression, anxiety attacks", *Fi* 381), but also his classism that is directed against his family. As the tapeworm – the central clairvoyant in the novel – explains, Bruce's stepfather, Ian Robertson "stood by his wife, but every time he looked at the baby he saw the face of the man from the front page of the *Daily Record* and the caption: THE FACE OF A BEAST burned in his skull" (*Fi* 381–382). Ian Robertson's disgust subsequently results in him scorning and taunting the young Bruce by forcing him to eat the coal he had gathered throughout the day as a miner (see *Fi* 291–292, 295, 315). Bruce struggles to escape the stigma of The Beast and manages to overcome the prejudices his roots engendered in the mining community he grew up in. As the tapeworm states: "You were different to that monster. They wanted you to be the same, right from the start, you were the one thing an isolated, terrorised people could kick out at. That was the role you took on. But you're different Bruce, you're different from him" (*Fi* 388). Although he is innocent, he is secretly held responsible by the community for the unfortunate accidents that caused the deaths of his half-brother and his first girlfriend due to his heritage and has thus become something like a gothic villain, the stigmatype-bogeyman of the village: "The people in the village seemed to glance at you as if you were a freak" (*Fi* 355). Hence, Bruce's basic motivation is to pass as "normal" by leaving his village and his family for London, becoming a policeman, and starting a family – that is, overcoming his stigmatised working-class identity and fulfilling the standards of heteronormativity, which then again, with Judith Butler, can be interpreted within the broader context of the "production of bodily contours" (2011: xxv). The move from Scotland to London and back is also conspicuous in Bruce's construction of "normality", especially when considering the cultural geography and the dichotomy of England/Scotland evoked in all of Welsh's novels. One might say that Bruce wants to become normal by becoming more English, and by getting closer to the centre of Thatcherite power in the 1980s.

Here, in line with Butler's ascertainment that normative heterosexuality is by no means the "only regulatory regime" in that respect and that the "social regulation of race" is clearly as important and is working in conjunction with heteronormativity in "contour[ing] the materiality of bodies" and in "setting the limits of bodily intelligibility" towards what she calls a "racial industry" (2011: xxv), one can identify the intersectional effects of producing a normative existence. By fulfilling the standards of white heteronormative identity, Bruce's existence becomes "symbolic" and therefore functions within the "register of regulatory ideality" (Butler 2011: xxv). However, Butler argues that "the social regulation of race emerges not simply as another, fully separable, domain of power from sexual difference or sexuality, but that its 'addition' subverts the monolithic workings of the heterosexual imperative" (2011: xxv). Butler examines this subversion within the context of passing in one of the best-known passing novels, Nella Larsen's *Passing* (see 2011: 122–138). In the following, I propose that this process also functions in the other direction (i. e., the monolithic workings of race/whiteness can be subverted by adding the component of sexuality) in order to adapt Butler's concept of the subversion of demarcated bodies to an examination of Bruce's passing as a British white male in the context of his marriage.

The ostensible main plot of *Filth*, i.e., the detective story around the Efan Wurie murder case, is turned around in Christie-like fashion[35] when Bruce himself is revealed to be the killer. The random murder is motivated by Bruce's anger about his wife, Carole, who cheated on him by sleeping with a black man. Here, a first instance of passing is remarkable: while Bruce assumes to be safe from being suspected, his boss Toal finally reveals to him that his colleagues not only knew about the adultery but also covered up the murder:[36]

> We're no as daft as you think. Your wife. We know she was having an affair with a black guy. It's no a big city Bruce, and it's a very white one. Things like that get noticed, no matter how discreet the parties are. But, as I said, you've got friends. We look after our own. (*Fi* 364)

This revelation is not only surprising within the overall structural makeup of the novel and for the increasingly delusional Bruce himself: considering the social and political mechanisms depicted in the novel, it devastatingly suggests that the entire justice system of Edinburgh, and quite likely of the United Kingdom as a whole, is a racist apparatus that uses overt assertions of political correctness and equity in the form of the aforementioned racial awareness workshops and the policies attached as part of a scheme to "pass" as racially aware and to cover up its actual actions that testify to the contrary.[37] While a form of white solidarity is put forward here, Toal also implies the importance of male bonding. While

35 | As Aaron Kelly points out, *Filth*'s narrative structure bears strong resemblance to Agatha Christie's *The Murder of Roger Ackroyd*, another detective story whose investigating narrator turns out to be the murderer (2005: 154).

36 | With regard to the novel's logic of (textual) doubling, it is also notable that Toal secretly aspires to become a screenwriter, and works the case into one of his scripts. Bruce realizes that his boss must have known about his crime when he reads the script that he has ripped from Toal's hard drive in order to thwart him in his aspiration.

37 | *Marabou Stork Nightmares* similarly presents a satirically exaggerated version of the British justice system when Roy's rape victim is eventually accused of provoking the rape with her sexual attitude, and Roy and his gang are being celebrated as the redeemed actual "victims". Thus, the trial turns out to be a bizarre affirmation of systematic misogyny.

Butler states with regard to Bellew, the white male protagonist in Larsen's novel who discovers the passing of his mixed-race wife Clare, that "his masculinity cannot be secured except through a consecration of his whiteness" (2011: 137), Bruce is characterised in a similar way. His superior British whiteness must be secured and protected from tainting through a consecration of his heteronormativity and his masculine strength, which is weakened and called into question by his wife's adultery. This is particularly important regarding the male bonding of *Filth*'s police officers and their Masonic activities.

The interrelation of heteronormativity and whiteness is also tackled in another central instance of passing in the novel: among the many plot twists and revelations culminating towards the finale, it is also revealed that Bruce occasionally dresses up as his wife, Carole, and that the chapters allegedly providing her perspective, distinguished from Bruce's (and the tapeworm's) monologues by a different typography, are actually Bruce voicing the imagined thoughts of his wife while he is playing her. It is implied that he has also slain Efan Wurie in that mode.[38] During the peak of Bruce's mental breakdown, he is attacked by a group of thugs, and his identity is revealed after one of them, who Bruce interrogated using The Beast routine earlier, recognises him. Here, Bruce's attempt at passing as a woman fails, and the text, which had previously subsumed his identity under Carole's, performs this failure by collapsing into fragmented sentences, a mingling of pronouns and typographies, shifting from Bruce to a multiplicity of voices consisting of Bruce, his wife and his daughter Stacey and back again:

> They laugh. They just laugh at me. We pull off the wig we have been wearing. We still hold on to our handbag. Carole's handbag. My present. Last Christmas I gave you my heart. The car seems to be moving so slowly, and there is a sickness in my stomach, a sickness which makes us feel as if we have eaten too much candyfloss at the fairground and gone on the waltzers. Stacey liked the waltzers. Us and her, her tucked in the middle. The nuclear family, spinning, twisting, disorientated, but still huddled together. (*Fi* 342)

Simultaneously experiencing the unity as well as the disintegration of his family – the fact of which should have consecrated his integrity as a white

38 | The novel's prologue, which presents an account of the murder from the point-of-view of the yet undisclosed killer, is written in the same type as the Carole chapters.

British male – Bruce experiences what Michael Gardiner has labelled the "Gothic doubling" that can also be found in Stevenson's *The Strange Case of Dr. Jekyll and Mr. Hyde* and many other Scottish novels (2012: 120). Here the doubling undermines notions of monolithic identity through the presence of a continuously disintegrating subject. Once more, the strong connection between race, class and gender/sexuality becomes evident when Bruce is mocked by the thugs – "the scum they put in the prisons" (*Fi* 343) – as a "queer", "twat" and "buftie" (*Fi* 344) and is thus ridiculed as unmanly (and in that, Bruce resembles Roy Strang in his hospitalised state and after his castration),[39] to which Bruce remarkably reacts not only by biting off the tongue of one of the thugs in a fight, but also by using the language of racism and classism: "Who's fuckin next spastics! We are the Edinburgh polis! We kill spastics! WE HATE NIGGERS! ESPECIALLY THE WHITE ONES THEY CALL SCHEMIES!" (*Fi* 350). While the use of the plural pronoun "we" for the first person is not uncommon in Scottish dialects, this feature assumes a different quality in this context. In the case of Bruce, the pronoun "we" now potentially connotes a double consciousness, and it is now undecidable whether the "we" still signifies the unity of Bruce/Carole/Stacey or the institutional collective of the Edinburgh police. If the latter is the case, Bruce here becomes the pars pro toto of a racist-classist apparatus, and by conjuring its collective power, he attempts to reinforce his individual identity. With his "bellowing", to take up Butler's interpretation of the white male racist's telling name in Larsen's *Passing*, Bruce thus tries to prevent the "shattering" of his "veneer of whiteness" (Butler 2011: 127) that is threatened by the discovery of his "queerness" by his white trash enemies. Thus, while Butler reads *Passing* as the articulation of race as one of the "convergent modalities of power by which sexual difference is articulated and assumed" (2011: 123), Bruce Robertson's doubled passings can be read as a figuration of racial and class difference that, among others, is convergent with and upheld by conflicted and doubled forms of sexuality and gender.

39 | It could be argued that these homophobic interpellations work in the same way as the racial interpellations of Bellew in Larsen's *Passing* when he discovers his wife's "blackness" – the "symbolic bellowing 'Nig! My God! Nig!'" (Butler 2011: 137). According to Butler, "Bellew's bellowing can be read as a symbolic racialization" to sustain his masculine dominance on the "social map of power" in the face of his unconscious miscegenation with a mixed-race woman (2011: 137).

This passing is simultaneously performed and undermined by the novel's text itself, proving Sinéad Moynihan's observation that passing is a "useful meta-critical and meta-fictional tool" particularly in postmodern fiction that highlights a notion of textuality, with passing being mapped onto the text itself (2010: 5). Thus, when the revealing tapeworm monologues are mapped onto the text of *Filth*, literally overlapping with Bruce's account, the text itself assumes a bodily materiality: the tapeworm text infiltrates Bruce's text like the tapeworm itself infiltrates Bruce's body and mind. The ensuing disintegration reflects the disintegration of the white male subject and its attempt at upholding a monolithic white identity against the threat of tainting.

Bruce's varied forms of passing across the intersections of race, class and gender reveal him to be the embodiment of the aporetic "un" that dominates Welsh's literary interrogations of the failure to achieve a stable form of cultural identity. Bruce is an aporia in practically all aspects of his personality. In hindsight, this already becomes clear in the first sentences of his interior monologue in the first chapter, titled "The Games". Here, Bruce is conceiving of the structural makeup of organisations and institutions as the conglomerate of games played by and against every member of any organisation. In this case, the games are intricately linked to his coping strategies concerning his job as a police officer:

> All that's left behind is the residue. That's the games. The games are the only way you can survive the job. Everybody has their wee vanities, their own little conceits. My one is that nobody plays the games like me, Bruce Robertson. [...]. The games are always, repeat, always, being played. Most times, in any organisation, it's expedient not to acknowledge their existence. But they're always there. (*Fi* 3)

While "the games" mainly consist of schemes directed at mates and colleagues, the demise of whom Bruce plots to benefit his own career or simply for his own sadistic amusement, his continuous activities of deception and passing likewise are part of these games. This leaves the reader to wonder whether Bruce actually exists beyond his games and deceptions – and this question leads to the way intersectional identities are conveyed and physically inscribed.

Apart from the many examples given in this chapter, two particularly illustrative instances shall be examined in order to prepare for the analysis of conceptions of the (white) body and its tainting in *Filth*. The first instance is a surprise Christmas party at the office where Bruce instigates another game to seduce the "Size Queen", one of the precinct's secretaries. Bruce has made a bet with his colleague Ray "on who'd be the first yin to get into the Size Queen's knickers" (*Fi* 202). In order to attract her attention, Bruce instigates a competition, allegedly a party game he learned from his Australian colleagues during his time at the New South Wales Police Department: "The guys would take it in turns tae go into the photocopier room and photocopy their wedding tackle on to a sheet of paper. Then they'd write their names on the back, and put them into an envelope. [...]. The lassies would then try to match the cock to the guy" (*Fi* 203). After the suggestion has been appreciated by his colleagues, Bruce secretly turns up the copy machine's enlarger switch when it is his turn to photocopy his penis, and when the images are turned over to reveal the names, they are "put in descending order", representing a phallic male hierarchy with Bruce, as expected, on the top (*Fi* 204). His plan turns out to be successful when the Size Queen "vampishly announces, — The winner deserves a prize" (*Fi* 205). The ensuing sex scene is of importance for Welsh's rendering of Bruce's activities of passing: "I push in and watch the Size Queen thrust and buck with an increasingly puzzled look on her face. [...]. After a while I shoot my load and leave her wondering what's been happening" (*Fi* 205).

The Size Queen's puzzlement in this situation, mentioned by Bruce almost en passant during the account of his triumph, can of course foremost be understood as her personal and individual disappointment given the discrepancy between what the enlarged image of Bruce's penis promised and the actual size of his genitals,[40] but in the light of the novel as a whole it is generally representative of the fragility of Bruce's games of passing and deception: despite his self-assured bearing, he never quite is what he attempts to make others believe. The comic incongruence between the literally enlarged image of his masculinity and his actual physical appearance thus metonymically stands for Bruce's incongruent subjectification on all axes of intersectional identities. In fact, this incongruence takes monstrous forms when considered within the context of his excessive body and his infamous parentage.

40 | In the recent screen adaptation (2013) of the novel by director and writer Jon S. Baird, this interpretation of the scene is pronounced by having the "Size Queen" (played by Pollyanna McIntosh) exclaim an irritated "What?!" during intercourse, which is also a clearer indication of Bruce's "passing" being exposed.

While the Size Queen here assumes the status of the clairvoyant because, as her derogatory nickname indicates, she measures his (actual and alleged) size, it is in another central instance involving clairvoyants that his parentage becomes particularly evident as a monstrous fracture within his struggle for subjectification by passing. Its centrality only becomes clear when interpreted with respect to the aforementioned disclosures at the end of the novel. While Bruce is eating his bacon rolls in the canteen, one of his opponents, "that lippy fucker Conrad Donaldson Q. C. who spends his time coining it in from the tax-payer by defending the kind of fucking scum that we risk our lives to try and put away: rapists, murderers, child molesters and what have you" (*Fi* 62), approaches him with the sarcastic comment "Practising cannibalism Bruce?" (*Fi* 62), and Bruce counters, "Remember what I told you that PIG stood for? Pride, Integrity and Guts". While the multilayered plays on the word *pig* emerging in this dialogue already hint at the centrality of the aspects of dirt and uncleanliness that will be discussed in the next chapter, Donaldson's subsequent reply, directed at his pals, is indicative of his status as a clairvoyant who is aware of Bruce's hidden social background as well as of Bruce's uncanny denial of these facts: "Detective Sergeant Bruce Robertson. One of the force's leading reactionaries. Comes from a mining family as well, I hear". At this stage, the reader is yet unaware of Bruce's conflicted class background, and so Donaldson's awareness does not yet seem significant. Likewise, Bruce's reply – "— You hear wrong, I say softly, looking him hard in the eye. — You must be getting me mixed up with someone else. [...] I feel sick and dizzy" (*Fi* 62) – is only revealed to be meaningful by the final revelations, and already hints at the conflicted double consciousness with regard to the identity embodied by Bruce.

It is in this instance that Bruce's passing is also rendered not only within the context of class, but also with regard to his body and his status as a policeman: the word *pig*, in Donaldson's initial pun, is meant as an insult degrading Bruce not only as a person of lower status but also in his professional function as a policeman, with "pig" being a derogatory term for officers especially in anti-establishment discourses. Here, the use of the term also brings full circle the semantics of the novel's title, with "filth" similarly denoting not only dirt and uncleanliness, but also being a derogatory term for the police. Accordingly, Robert A. Morace connects the frequent plays on words in the novel to Sigmund Freud's *The Joke and Its Relation to the Unconscious*, arguing that in *Filth*, puns and double entendres are instances of subversion and parody of authoritative structures (2007: 92). However, as the confrontation with Conrad Donaldson shows, Bruce is not a sovereign agent when it comes to jokes. Although he himself frequently and ironically plays on words throughout the novel, this instance reveals him to be a victim of the pitfalls of language, and his attempt to regain the upper hand with his reinterpretation of the anagram "PIG" must be considered as a defeat in the face of the knowing and thus more sovereign "New Labour rising star Conrad Donaldson" (*Fi* 63).

Here, it becomes clear that *Filth* can be regarded in terms of the gothic uncanny, since, as Morace argues, one can find "in the vulgarity of language and situation, an example of unbridled *id* and a study in repression, guilt and shame" (2007: 92). The novel enacts the undermining of Bruce's language and the language of the British authorities by undercutting it with double meanings and double discourses that literally interrupt the text in the form of the tapeworm's interior monologues,[41] and thus performs the surfacing of repressed and shameful issues of class and race in contemporary Britain. To put it more concretely in terms of tainted whiteness, Bruce thus becomes a figuration of the aporias pervading Welsh's early texts. While his attempts at passing cannot contain these aporias, it is particularly through his grotesque and uncontrolled body that they become manifest.

"Chasing Dirt": The Unruly Body

Both Aaron Kelly and Robert A. Morace have elaborated on the semantics of pigs and filth in their interpretations of the novel. Kelly particularly connects these aspects to his general analysis of Welsh's treatment of post-Thatcherism and the "antinomies" of Bruce's "class-identities" (2005: 166). He considers the restructuring of the working class in the face of "Thatcherite and Blairite Britain and the solidification of the monetarist state" in which "some workers became consumers, some citizens became shareholders and then stakeholders, whilst others became a seditious enemy or disenfranchised underclass" (Kelly 2005: 166) as the background for Welsh's descrip-

41 | To think the novel's logic of puns and double meanings even further, one could argue that the tapeworm's speech is not only an interior monologue according to the terms and definitions of literary analysis, but simultaneously and literally a monologue taking place *within the interior* of Bruce's body.

tion of the police as filth and pigs, and draws on Peter Stallybrass and Allon White's Bakhtinian analysis of the pig as a "deeply ambivalent and ambiguous creature which diffuses and confuses social boundaries and categorisations" that "troubled the demarcation between human and animal" (ibid.). Stallybrass and White trace the etymological development of the word *pig* from the Greek and Latin slang (porcus/pocelus) in which it denoted the female genitalia through to the modern use of the term to derogatorily refer to the "police, the fascist and the male chauvinist" as well as the cultural relevance of the pig as an animal that was at the same time kept close to the human household but was not quite like other productive livestock due to its rather "human" dietary habits and its skin colour (Stallybrass/White 44–45, qtd. in Kelly 2005: 166). The pig thus became an ambivalent animal "at the intersection of a number of important cultural and symbolic thresholds" (Stallybrass and White 1986: 45, qtd. in Kelly 2005: 167).

Kelly, in line with Stallybrass and White, argues that the use of the term *pig* to name the police "developed out of the response of the urban working class to resist their own status as despised slum dwellers in urban 'filth' and squalor" (2005: 167). This makes the words *pig* and *filth* instances of resignification of hate speech[42] and boundary terms that can be connected to the phrase *white trash* and its semantic layers. Considered within the context of *Filth* this means that the novel's "metaphor of pigs and filth subtly elucidates contemporary Britain's convulsive disruption of social identities as impacted in Robertson's own character" (Kelly 2005: 167) – and consequently, the attempts at passing that I analysed above are bound to fail as becomes evident in Bruce's attempt to resignify the derogatory term *PIG* in the confrontation with Donaldson. The clear boundaries that Bruce wants to establish between himself and the social "filth", the "supposed criminal working-class filth that he so demonises" (Kelly 2005: 167), must break down in these moments of passing. In analogy to this erosion of clearly separated class identities, Bruce's body likewise literally disintegrates (see Morace 2007: 93).

Robert Morace considers the semantics of the word *filth* within his interpretation of the novel's puns, of which filth is "the most punningly playful and powerfully, as well as ambivalently, deployed" (2007: 93). Like Kelly, Morace remarks on the power tensions expressed in the term since it is both used by the state authorities to denote social outcasts and criminal

42 | On hate speech and resignification, see Butler 1997.

elements as well as by the groups opposed to these authorities in order to denounce the police. Regarding the latter's reversal of the use of *filth*, Morace argues that it implies "filth as the synecdochic representation of modern society's obsessive desire to rid itself of, or at least manage, filth, which is to say its own waste products" (2007: 93). In addition, Morace briefly suggests understanding *pig* in connection with "prohibitions against unclean food" (2007: 94) – a reading that can be supported with reference to the aforementioned canteen confrontation between Conrad Donaldson and Bruce in which the pun revolves around the latter's eating habits. In support of Morace's argument, a point can be made about the novel's overall emphasis on Bruce's bad diet, which consists mainly of fast food, the description of which is central to Bruce's narrative discourse.

Food is a particularly dominant topic in relation to the tapeworm who starts to talk whenever Bruce is eating, urging its host to eat more (see *Fi* 69, 119–120, 140, 219). His eating habits are also of concern during his frequent visits to his general practitioner Dr. Rossi who suggests a more balanced, fat-free diet in order to get rid of the rash on his buttocks, another frequent motif in the novel that is also connected to the issue of filth and insanitariness: "— It's some aggravated skin disorder, probably a form of eczema. I can't emphasise strongly enough that you should keep that area clean [...]. [...] you may be allergic to a certain foodstuff" (*Fi* 54). Here, it is not only important that Bruce is reluctant to practise personal hygiene (he also frequently complains about the absence of his wife, whose job it would be to take care of the laundry), but that he also might be polluted from the inside through a bad eating habit – an aspect that is confirmed by the tapeworm diagnosis, since, after all, the tapeworm has very likely entered his body through improperly prepared, "unclean" food. Thus, the tapeworm signifies the permeability and resulting uncontrollability of Bruce's body that corresponds to the uncontrollability of his identity: Bruce can never quite have a proper identity just as he can never quite control the confines of his body. This has significant repercussions for concepts of the body as the signifier of raced and classed identities.

Welsh's bodies represent the failure of the idea that a body can properly signify a coherent and fixed identity in any way since, after all, they cannot even contain their own interior. Like Bakhtin's grotesque body (a concept frequently mentioned in relation to Welsh's corporeal aesthetics), the bodies in Welsh's texts are open to the world surrounding them rather than closed entities. This can be seen in the bodies of the heroin addicts in *Trainspotting* and *Skagboys*, connecting with one another through shared needles and HIV infection – and as the addicts and HIV victims are polluted by intravenous drug use and viral infection, Bruce's body is polluted from the inside by the tapeworm.[43]

The notion of bodily pollution can be directly linked to white trash discourse, especially when considering the hookworm-infested "dirt-eaters" of the nineteenth-century South that Matt Wray has examined in his analysis of the concept of *white trash* and which, as I have shown in this chapter, bears analogies to the resignifications of the British working class as white at the turn of the nineteenth and twentieth centuries along the lines of the semantics of dirt and blackness. It is within this transformation of the British white working class, in analogy to American poor whites, that *Filth*'s figuration and deconstruction of British whiteness must be considered. Taking into account the historical and discursive background of the tension between whiteness and non-whiteness, cleanness and dirt, national inside and non-national outside, Bruce Robertson can be comprehended as an aporetic figuration in which the desire to represent an elitist British-Scottish whiteness (best expressed in Bruce's historical revision of white Scottish victimhood and empowerment) that takes care of enforcing the moral and sanitary virtues of a white master race (expressed in the notion of the police as the cleansing force of society) paradoxically conflates with his appropriation of whiteness as the property of an ordinary working class (expressed in Bruce's disdain for the Asian workshop facilitator whom he suspects of coming from a posh school and suppressing decent ordinary men like him). This aporetic figuration shows whiteness itself to be a nexus of aporias in which historical and discursive coordinates simultaneously meet and level one another out. Given Bruce's family and class background, he is additionally constantly haunted by the spectre of lower-class tainted whiteness that continually threatens to undermine his self-constructions as properly white.

In this, Bruce Robertson is by far the most concentrated, complex and difficult figuration of whiteness in Welsh's fiction, and thus functions as

43 | Morace also remarks that the tapeworm is a recurring trope signifying heroin addiction in another Scottish writer's texts, Alexander Trocchi's short piece "Tapeworm" and his novel *Cain's Book*: "Trochhi's tapeworm is the need for heroin which compels him to write to earn the money to support his habit; as long as Trocchi writes, the worm sleeps" (2007: 94).

a monstrous signifier. If a monster is, in a Foucauldian sense, to be comprehended as "the major model of every little deviation" (Foucault 2003: 56), then Bruce can be interpreted as a monster since he is the conglomerate of all the fault lines inherent to constructions of whiteness exhibited in Welsh's previous texts. And within the novel's text, he is a monster in many aspects. To stick to Foucault's definitions, he is a moral monster (and to some degree certainly a sexual monster) and simultaneously shows signs of a monstrous body in all its excess, while the symbiosis with the tapeworm as well as his dubious origin as the child of a rapist to some degree make him a biological monster (see Foucault 2003: 55). What makes Bruce an even more aporetic figure, however, is that he not only embodies the monstrous object as it is defined in juridico-biological discourses of power (Foucault 2003: 55) but that he can also be considered the subject of power. As a corrupt policeman with a longing for Thatcherist power, he also represents what Foucault calls the "maximization of effects of power" – that is, "grotesque sovereignty" (Foucault 2003: 12). Foucault

> call[s] 'grotesque' the fact that, by virtue of their status, a discourse or an individual can have effects of power that their intrinsic qualities should disqualify them for having. [...]. Political power, at least in some societies, and anyway in our society, can give itself, and has actually given itself, the possibility of conveying its effects and, even more, of finding their source, in a place that is manifestly, explicitly, and readily discredited as odious, despicable, or ridiculous. This grotesque mechanism of power, or this grotesque cog in the mechanism of power, has a long history in the structures and political functioning of our societies. (2003: 12–13)

Bruce – like most of his colleagues who are just as bigoted, racist and misogynist as him – represents this "grotesque cog in the mechanism of power" in all its despicability and ridiculousness. Whether Bruce uses his authority to force minors into fellatio, manipulates colleagues, covers up his murder of an immigrant, supports the production of animal porn and prostitution or indulges in excessive drug use while on duty: he is the morally corrupt and grotesque element within the mechanisms of power – and he can have his way precisely because he partakes in this power. One of the many politically incorrect conversations among Bruce and his colleagues sums up the political workings of power in *Filth*: Bruce and his male colleagues are arguing with Amanda Drummond about the new ministers of the Blair government and how the police is supposed to represent the political shifts. While Drummond "squeaks, in polis rhetoric" that the police is supposed to enforce the law made by the "democratically elected government of the day" (*Fi* 244), Bruce and his mates imagine their own cynical version of the situation:

> – Hmm, I say teasingly [...]. This new Drugs Führer wants to attack demand rather than supply. This means sending more kids to jail. If that works and kids are scared to take illegal drugs, then they'll turn on to legal ones like alcohol as a substitute. – Which means more violence! Ray gives us the thumbs up. – Tougher sentences! I say. – Mair polis! Ray laughs. – And, mair promoted posts, I rub my hands. – It also means mair prisoners, mair prisons, mair wardens, mair security guards. Pump-priming, basic Keynesian economics! Then we'll get Maggie back in ten years' time telling us we've been spending too much! – But we can cut back on education, social work and health and aw that shit, Lennox nods. Drummond's looking horrified. (*Fi* 244-245)

Strikingly, it is during this wilful endorsement of potential despotism that Bruce's uncanny double consciousness emerges. When the conversation shifts to the miners' strike as an example of the police force upholding the law of the respective government ("we upheld the law, Drummond's screeching"), Bruce unexpectedly bursts out: "If unions had never broken the laws, we wouldnae have any democracy... in the first place, I say, wondering why the fuck I'm coming out with all this wank" (*Fi* 245). This seemingly involuntary incongruence in his political attitude, marked by the hesitation mid-sentence, is accompanied by a textual interruption by the tapeworm who, provoked by the mention of the miners' strike, recalls Bruce's stepfather force-feeding his son with coal: "Ian Robertson. He made you eat, Bruce. His methods were his methods. Did you learn those methods from him? He made you eat coal. Black, shiny, filthy coal" (*Fi* 245). Thus, what emerges in this conversation, prompted by the turn towards the miners' strike – Bruce's moment of awakening that made him pursue a position in the grotesque mechanism of Thatcherite power by joining the police force – is Bruce's double consciousness in the form of his repressed past, re-emerging in the present like the Thatcherite spectres in Welsh's previous novels. Bruce's past is – literally – a dark secret, directly linked to filthiness and blackness. Here, as in the entire novel, blackness is semantically multifaceted. Literally, it connotes the filth of the coal pits as well as a dark skin tone, and in the case of young, humiliated Bruce, both conflate when his white skin is painted black by the filthy coal. Figuratively, blackness evokes Bruce's unconscious and his repressed past as well as the opposite of Bruce's desire to enjoy the supremacist power that is connoted with the privileges of whiteness as a social formation. In other words, to take up Toal's statement (*Fi* 364), Bruce wants to be in charge in the "very white" city of Edinburgh, but he cannot shake off the heritage of the remote mining village he comes from, and he is still "the Other Laddie" (*Fi* 353), the bastard son of a rapist. As Aaron Kelly notes,

> the *leitmotifs* of blackness and filth become recodified by the reader's awareness of Robertson's need to denigrate all the threats to his self as a homogeneous, hostile otherness, whether it is the 'black, shiny, filthy coal' [...] that Ian Robertson made him eat, the blackened flesh of his brother Stevie as he lies buried under the coal, or the skin of his wife's new partner and of his victim Efan Wurie. [...]. Yet [...], Robertson's own sense of himself as a 'pig', and as 'filth', his own pinioning at the collision of conflicting social identities, perpetually frustrates his effort to construct a superior and sequestered subjectivity [...]. (2005: 169–170)

In turn, the semantic variability of blackness and filth has repercussions for the status of whiteness, which is shown to be just as semantically varied. What the character of Bruce Robertson ultimately shows in its aporetic make-up and in the failure to achieve a superior and uniform identity is that whiteness constantly betrays its own antithesis and facilitates its own deconstruction once it is evoked or made manifest as a coherent and homogeneous form of individual and collective identity.

Consequently, the notion of tainted whiteness that becomes evident throughout *Filth* implies that whiteness as an actual identity-related property more often than not oscillates within a continuum rather than becoming a fixable identity position. This does not mean, however, that the notion of whiteness does not have structural effects in society, and Welsh's text by no means cosily anticipates a future that sees the futility and eventual disappearance – or "unthinking" – of whiteness as a model of superior identity.[44] Rather, whiteness is shown to be an often fatal prin-

44 | In fact, an episode in *Trainspotting* sums up the bleak outlook that Welsh's texts provide in that respect. In "Na Na and other Nazis", Spud recalls a pub fight with a group of Nazi skinheads that he and his black mixed-race uncle Dode got involved in. When the white Spud comforts his injured uncle in hospital, Dode tells

ciple that does yield significant material effects, particularly for those individuals who are not regarded as white due to either their non-white ethnic origin or their lower-class status precisely because whiteness still holds symbolic power – and is thus part of the grotesque mechanics of power. This surfaces in the bigoted management of the Efan Wurie investigations, and it becomes similarly evident in the recurrence of boundary figures, the "white niggers" or "schemies", in Bruce's framework, who emerge at the intersection of race and class. Only at first glance do these white trash figures merely function as Bruce's other.

Considered in the context of Bruce's aporetic double consciousness, they also function as a revealing mirror for this aporetic non-identity since, after all, Bruce must himself be considered white trash, at least if one follows his belief in what Gavin Miller calls "quasi-racial mythology" (2010: 98). Bruce thus represents a paradigmatic character for Welsh's project of exposing the aporetic intersection of Scottish white male working-class identity. Desperately struggling with his own belief in the hereditary 'nature' and the "curious transformation of economic class into cultural identity" (Miller 2010: 99), Bruce's attempts to abjectify the tainted white trash working class lead to his mental breakdown and personality disorder since, ultimately, this abjectification must affect Bruce himself. Struggling with his own abject status as well as with both his cultural heritage and his past guilt, Bruce thus becomes the concluding point of Welsh's treatment of tainted whiteness: a self-devouring white trash subject who denies his own abject status and whose striving for a coherent self-narrative must finally implode.

---

him "– S awright Danny. Ah've hud a loat worse n the past, and ah'll huv a hellay a loat worse in the future." Spud, who is rendered as the most uncynical and innocent member of the group of friends portrayed in the novel and could be interpreted as a representation of an implied naive reader who hopes for such an anticipation of a post-racist society, reacts with denial: "Dinnae say that man. Dinnae say that, ken?" However, even Spud must finally realise his naiveté: "He looks at us like ah'll never really understand, n ah ken that he's probably right" (*T* 129). Just like Stevie in the chapter analysed above, Spud represents the incapability of the white subject to appropriate a black perspective. Welsh's literary strategy could here be described as a reversal of what Toni Morrison observes in her analysis of the narrative absence of whiteness (1992: 72): whiteness, and particularly the discrepancy between a white experience of life and a black experience of life, is made critically visible in the blank spot that the black experience poses to the white experience.

III How Southern Gothic Came to Wales

Race, Class and Post-Britishness in the Novels of Niall Griffiths

Even in the as of yet manageable amount of research on Niall Griffiths's work, it has become a cliché to reference the numerous press reviews of Griffiths's earlier work comparing him to Irvine Welsh. To quote just one example, from a review in the *Daily Express* on the back cover of *Grits*: "If you liked Irvine Welsh's *Trainspotting* you'll love *Grits*". Of course, this comparison is part of the marketing strategies and a somewhat understandable move on part of the publishing house Jonathan Cape, which, as it happens, is also Welsh's publisher. However, recent scholarly work dealing with Griffiths's texts have attempted to move beyond superficial comparisons to identify more complex stylistic and thematic similarities between the two authors' texts while at the same time decidedly moving beyond rather one-sided comparisons to study Griffiths's work in its own right. As Jarrad Keyes states,

> Stylistically, each probes the shifting relationships between dialect and grammatical form, whilst thematically both are concerned with discourses of addiction, gender, and nationalist politics, aspects which compliment their mutual interest in the construction and enunciation of identity. Depicting a nation politically deracinated by Thatcherism, its legacy of social atomism [...], Griffiths' works [...] together resemble the political topography of *Trainspotting*. (Keyes 2009: 134)

Likewise, Aleksander Bednarski sees similarities in style ("vernacular setting, demotic transcription") and even more so in subject matter in that

> Griffiths's work is commonly associated with the off-centre tendency in the contemporary British novel, epitomised by the fiction of Irvine Welsh as well as other Scottish writers associated with the publishing company Rebel Inc. What characterises the trend is, generally, a vernacular setting, demotic transcription, and a tendency to focus on the lower classes and controversial topics such as drugs, sex or crime. (Bednarski 2012b: 9)

While these stylistic and thematic similarities are certainly central aspects (which Griffiths and Welsh, of course, also share to some part with John King), I propose a comparison that goes into more detail concerning the aspects of class and race. At first sight, Griffiths's texts, while clearly dealing with the aforementioned issues of lower-class life, disenfranchisement and the social aftermath of the Thatcher years for a considerable segment of the British population, do not seem to share Welsh's explicit focus on issues of race and whiteness, meaning that readers will hardly come across such explicit mentions of whiteness or white trash as can be found in the three novels by Welsh analysed in the previous chapters. Yet, a reading of Griffiths's work that likewise focuses on figurations of race and their intersections with class and national belonging, can find similarities with Welsh's engagement with tainted whiteness.

In the following, I will examine selected novels by Griffiths under the aspect of bodily inscriptions of national and cultural belonging and the interrelation of these bodies with their similarly inscribed surroundings in the form of social collectives as well as landscapes. While, as the aforementioned interpretations by Bednarski and Keyes indicate, Griffiths's engagement with the lower classes is self-evident in his texts, it requires much more in-depth examination to register a similar (and yet at times much more subtle) engagement with race as in Welsh's work. Therefore, it is necessary to consider Griffiths's work firstly within a context which forms yet another often-perceived similarity with Welsh's work, i.e., the devolutionary process in Wales and Scotland,[1] and secondly with regard to its intertextual and intercultural engagement with the American South, most notably the fiction of Cormac McCarthy, which is, as I will show, a major point of reference for Griffiths and thus informs the characterisations of landscape as well as of his protagonists.

1 | See my analysis of Griffiths's *Sheepshagger* in the context of Welsh devolution and post-British communities (Schmitt 2015).

With regard to the former aspect, it is important to consider Griffiths's novels as part of the devolution of British literature described by Robert Crawford and Michael Gardiner (see chapter I). Hywel Dix (2008) has proposed to consider several protagonists of the contemporary Welsh and Scottish literary scene as actors in a literary project of devolution that he explains, in Raymond Williams's terms, as cultural materialist:

> Since 1997, English literature has been devolved just as much as political power and representation has been devolved from Westminster to Edinburgh and Cardiff. What many recent writers in Scotland and Wales have in common is that their historic imagination is able to subvert the imagined harmony of an earlier period. This in turn can be read in tandem with the process of undoing to which the United Kingdom has more recently become subject. Since devolution has to be understood as an ongoing process rather than an accomplished fact, it can be said that the writing plays a part in the continuing process. (Dix 2008: 128)

Although not going into analytical detail with respect to the two authors, Dix explicitly mentions Irvine Welsh and Niall Griffiths, among others, as major examples of this process (see 2008: 133).

Building on Dix's suggestion to consider a contemporary trend towards literary devolution with the conceptual tools of Raymond Williams, I contend that Williams's writings on Welsh cultural identity within a British context can also serve as a starting point for considering questions of race and ethnicity in relation to the context of devolution, since it is precisely the myth of distinct British races that Williams frequently criticises: "Where there are real gaps there is not only inquiry; there is also the making of myths. Trying, under pressure, to define our identity, we have invented and tolerated many illusions. That we are physically distinct, for example: a specific race; the last of the old Britons, hanging on in the west" (2003: 8). It is noteworthy here that Williams alludes to a mutual construction ("invented and tolerated") of the myth of a Welsh race in that it is used by both oppressed and oppressor to either enhance or degrade the status of the Welsh people. However, he goes on to point out that the "physical mix of the people of Wales is essentially that of the whole island, though in different areas, including the different regions of Wales, the proportions in the mix vary" and that "it was not the race that changed; it was the history" (Williams 2003: 8).

As I will demonstrate in the following analysis of Griffiths's *Grits* and *Sheepshagger*, it is precisely this idea of a distinct Welsh race (and other British races) that is interrogated in the novels and shown as intersecting with (lower) class status. The two texts thereby allude to another problem discussed by Williams, namely that of the inherent differences not only between the different nations of Britain but also intranationally within these single nations, including England. Recounting a conversation with a friend from the north of England who expressed his envy regarding the Welsh and Scottish peoples' "available national self-definitions, to help them find their way out of the dominance of the English ruling-class minority culture" since "what the world knows as English" was not the northern way of life (2003: 10), Williams proposes this predicament as an actual opportunity to "get through, quicker, to the real differences, the real conflicts", meaning the actual social and political zones of conflict easily overseen in the construction of monolithic national identities (2003: 10). This observation corresponds to a suggestion made by Charlotte Williams, who states that "we need to point to conflicts *within* nation states and not simply to lines of conflict between them. Renationalisation [...] remains inadequate in the face of contemporary realities" (2009: 73).

As will become clear throughout my analysis, these zones of conflict, with the problematic intersections of race and class, are highlighted by Griffiths as actually underlying the devolutionary tensions in the British nations. Thus, while Raymond Williams's emphasis is predominantly on class as the major issue of inequality, Griffiths's novels point towards the fact that class cannot be viewed as an isolated factor outside of broader intersectional relations. Although supposedly hidden by the trajectories of devolutionary national conflicts, these trajectories are in fact one of the zones in which these conflicts are played out.

These aspects are examined by Kirsti Bohata in her study *Postcolonialism Revisited* (2004) in relation to Welsh writing in English. Bohata proposes holding Welsh culture as postcolonial, despite several pitfalls that might be posed by certain definitions of the term.[2]

2 | Bohata refers to Anne McClintock to defend her choice to employ the theoretical framework of postcolonialism to the Welsh context: "Anne McClintock has famously attacked the tendency of the term to universalize a single colonial/postcolonial condition, thereby replicating the binary between colonizer and colonial other, she thus draws attention to the prefix 'post', which suggests an adherence

The wide appeal of postcolonialism is surely due in no small part to this concern with shifting identity, with 're-membering' the self, and is of immediate relevance to and for a nation such as Wales, which has relied in recent centuries on a fairly self-conscious imagining of nation. It is therefore not surprising that the concerns of postcolonial writers and theorists from elsewhere chime so resonantly with the concerns of a significant number of writers from Wales. (2004: 2)

Bohata puts forward the thesis that while Wales might not be postcolonial in the same way that countries such as India or Zimbabwe are, the Welsh people have in similar ways been subjected to the enforcement of notions of racial hegemony imposed by the English during the period of the Anglo-Norman conquests and the political assimilation of Wales[3] – and "this colonization included violent displacement of peoples from fertile land, the planting of foreign peasantry as well as alien overlords, and attempts to wipe out difference even while maintaining racial hierarchies and racially differentiated laws" (2004: 8). This entailed the notion that the Welsh were culturally and racially inferior to other Anglo-Saxon peoples, a "backward people in need of the enlightening influence of the

to the very idea of progressive linearity that postcolonial theory has tried to undermine. The problems of any such postcolonial model are evident in the case of Wales, whose history and literature in no way conform to the progressive-linear model of moving from colonization (and colonial literature) to decolonization (and postcolonial literature)" (2004: 2–3). In addition to that, Bohata acknowledges critics who object to referring to Welsh culture in the terms of postcolonialism, stressing the complicity of the Welsh and Scottish nations in the British imperialist project (2004: 4–6). Yet, she remarks that "the fact remains that the position of Wales within the British Empire and the United Kingdom was not, and is not, coterminous with that of England. In Wales we may find the proportions in which we have been and are colonial, imperialist and post-colonial [...] are subtly and sometimes significantly different from those of other countries of the UK and the rest of the Empire" (2004: 5).

3 | It must be noted, however, that such far-reaching historical approaches are in danger of nourishing mythically constructed notions of monolithic national cultures. Interestingly, such problematic notions are critically anticipated in Niall Griffiths's fiction, most notably through the subtly ironic presentation of those characters who are representing Welshness like Sioned in *Grits* (see my corresponding observations in this chapter) or the critical assessment of the discourse on devolution in *Sheepshagger* (see my analysis in Schmitt 2015).

English language" and "an unruly bunch who needed to be brought under control" (Bohata 2004: 9). The overall construction of Welsh culture as "degenerate" thus "worked to interpellate the Welsh in a discourse which constructed them in binary opposition to Englishness – as other" (Bohata 2004: 10). A postcolonial reading of Welsh culture and in particular of Welsh literature in English therefore works towards offering a "structure within which the past can be interrogated with the aim of (re)constructing the present" (Bohata 2004: 15) and, more specifically, supports the aim of "extricating Britain from hegemonic Anglocentricity" as part of a "dehomogenization of whiteness" (Bohata 2004: 6–7). Bohata analyses several authors' texts with respect to, among others, their use of Welsh racial, gender and sexual stereotypes of alterity and their (politicised) construction of the Welsh landscape – central aspects of Welsh literature in English that are taken up in Griffiths's novels and that I will return to during my analysis of his work.

Within the context sketched in Bohata's study, it is close at hand, then, that Aleksander Bednarski suggests to read Niall Griffiths's fiction as embedded in an Anglo-Welsh literary tradition that is "not free from the (post)colonial predicament" (2012b: 7).[4] Like much of Welsh writing in English, Bednarski argues, Griffiths's work displays "language strategies characteristic of postcolonial literatures, hybridity, dramatisation of borders, sense of loss and exile and constructing of fictional home space" (2012b: 27). Quite similar to Dix, Bednarski, in an analysis of *Sheepshagger*, argues that the novel is an example of a literature that constitutes "the domain that is particularly responsive to any significant processes of social change", and, more concretely, reflective of a post-1998 Wales that is still "deeply divided on the grounds of language issues, culture and national identity" (2012a: 111).

In my analyses of *Grits* and *Sheepshagger*, I will build on this assumption while at the same time extending it with a more detailed examination of racial issues and how notions of British whiteness are scrutinised in Griffiths's treatment of the conflict between Welsh culture and British hegemony within the larger context of what Michael Gardiner calls 'post-Britishness' – the devolutionary move towards a "democratic restructuring of each nation within union *and* each nation still affected by Anglophone

4 | Bednarski also makes this point more clearly in connection with Griffiths's *Sheepshagger* in Bednarski 2012a: 115.

imperialism" (Gardiner 2004: x). In that respect, I will follow Chris Haylett's observation that:

> The process of political devolution for Scotland, Northern Ireland, and Wales has instigated questions about the shape of English representative democracy and of English identity per se, with 'Englishness' standing for white British identities. The idea of an English identity 'in crisis' has promoted discussion of Englishness as a culturally and historically distinct ethnicity like any other. (2001: 356)

Following Haylett, whose argument ties in with Bohata's thesis about the dehomogenisation of British whiteness, I contend that the cultural phenomena that can be subsumed under the term 'post-British' are linked to an increasingly problematic notion of British whiteness, or, to be more precise, *whitenesses*. While the monologues of Irvine Welsh's narrator Mark Renton about Scotland's white trash are symptomatic and prototypical for this increasing instability of whiteness in the face of the British break-up and similarly instable class positions, Griffiths's first two novels offer a similar literary take on issues of post-British whiteness from the Welsh perspective. I will read *Grits* and *Sheepshagger* as texts that interrogate questions of British whiteness within the context of post-Britishness and a postcolonial Wales – a context that Griffiths simultaneously intersects with questions of social class and the human body.

III.1 *Grits*

Post-British Plurality of Voices

Grits is told from the interchanging perspectives of eleven narrator-characters,[5] all of them disillusioned young people who originate from different corners of the British islands, including Ireland. Their paths cross at the Welsh coast in Aberystwyth while each of them is searching for something in their lives to give them purpose and stability. Some of them have left their home countries due to political tensions, like Liam who has come from Northern Ireland, or poverty or both. All of the characters struggle with the fact that they no longer know where they belong. At some point, some of them even become literally homeless when trying to escape their predicaments. Like many of the protagonists in Griffiths's later novels, the characters in *Grits* are characterised by a sense of spiritual and cultural 'homelessness'. The tension between a superior Anglo-British culture and its sub-British counterparts is one of the many facets tackled by Griffiths. The prototypical protagonist in a Griffiths novel is of mixed cultural origin or does not quite feel at home in his or her place of birth, is constantly in search of personal fulfilment in some way or another, be it due to social or political circumstances, physical or emotional lack or a mixture of all of these. While some struggle to escape their social predicaments, others try to deal with their lack by turning to drugs or excessive sex.[6]

In *Grits*, the coastal town Aberystwyth assumes the role of a symbolic place for the novel's characters. To them, it is a place of hope for new beginnings and thus becomes fraught with symbolic meaning within a post-British context since it attracts people from all over the archipelago, which is also reflected by the group of befriended narrator-characters.[7] Early on

5 | I adapt this term from Aleksander Bednarski's narratological analysis of *Grits* (2012b: 31).

6 | The idea of actual homelessness and its symbolic meaning within a post-British context is most pronounced in Griffiths's second novel *Sheepshagger*, as I will point out in the next chapter. Further forms of cultural and "emotional" homelessness are explored in *Kelly + Victor* (2002).

7 | Jon Anderson identifies Griffiths's portrayal of Aberystwyth's community of drifters as "a subculture within society that identifies no roots in the traditional

in the novel, its first narrator, Paul, reminisces about his friends and how they came to meet each other in Aberystwyth despite their diverse origins:

> Intrestin, tho, how wir all from diffrunt parts uv the country, apart from Sioned, oo was born ere; Roger's from South Wales somewhir, Merthyr a think, Colm's a Scouser, Malcolm's an Essex lad, Mairead's from somewhir in Yorkshire... tuh ask why wir all here, in this town like, is like askin why wir here on this planet. A doan av a fuckin clue about either. (G 31)

Aberystwyth thus appears as a trans-British melting pot that reflects the entire spectrum of cultural difference to be found on the British islands. The town is a condensation of these differences and offers a counterimage to hegemonic concepts of a culturally homogenous Britain and Anglocentrism. Situating his friends' situation within a larger British cultural context, Paul goes on to reflect how the friends' personal backgrounds reflect the cultural tensions of the British islands:

> People offun say that yuh can choose yuh friends but am not entirely sure about that; sometimes it's like yuh just find yuhselves next tuh each other, like stuff washed up on thuh beach. What is it that binds yuh together? Thuh local Nationalists like ul talk about nationhood, cultural unity, stuff like that; a doan rirly know what ther talkin about [...]. But a think that the stuff that binds yuh together as probly got more tuh do with, erm, a dunno, recognising somethin in others that either yuh want tuh see in yuhself or are too scared tuh see in yuhself. (G 31)

Aberystwyth thus becomes a microcosm in which British national conflicts manifest themselves, but in which at the same time the potential of overcoming these conflicts becomes visible. These differences and conflicts are also enacted on the novel's stylistic level, with each narrator-character having his or her own distinct voice and dialect, performed by a demotic writing style that represents a "manifestation of the society's hybrid character" (Bednarski 2012b: 32; see also Roberts 2002: 107). As Bednarski argues, the characters' different dialects form a literary language that is "far from forming a common, universal and comprehensible language" (Bednarski 2012b: 32).

---

sense, he identifies a drifting class who are disconnected and dissociated from their social and geographical communities" (2014: 159).

However, it is not only the mix of cultures to be found among the characters gathering in Aberystwyth itself that makes for a hybrid environment. The individual characters themselves are already hybrid personalities who experience themselves not as homogenous individuals that can be seen as representatives of a single culture. Colm, who identifies himself as a Romany Irish Traveller, for instance, reflects upon his culturally mixed upbringing in Liverpool, a city which he describes as "some fuckin babel", an "Anglo-Celtic city" whose "version uv English ardly sounds fuckin English" and should have "its own government" (*G* 318). Like many of his friends, he scrutinises the notion of cultural and racial unity in his monologues ("It annoys me tho, the wey people alweys need ter categorise" [*G* 318]), and describes the process of unlearning one's cultural and linguistic heritage in order to adapt to new cultural contexts. He recalls his parents and grandparents, who, after having to leave Ireland for England, were forced to give up their first languages Gaelic and the "Bog Latin", i.e., the Travellers' language (*G* 318). Colm's and the other characters' reflections on their own cultural hybridity and their positions as speaking subjects within a plural cultural context show that in *Grits*, post-Britishness is the underlying theme that dictates the novel's specific structural-formal approach, which makes it a radically plural text.

Despite his anger about the normative and oppressive influence of cultural hegemony which oppresses minor cultures and their languages, Colm likewise expresses his disgust for those people whose "desire fer martyrdom, righteous indignation, an the display uv false suffering as a badge uv belonging" (*G* 318–319) leads them to assume a minor cultural identity, as can be seen in the militant Welsh nationalism expressed by other characters throughout the novel. Colm's awareness of cultural oppression and simultaneous scepticism regarding exaggerated victimhood can be interpreted as an overall rejection of any construction of cultural unity as forced and potentially dangerous. From this tension, however, a certain restlessness arises which is closely linked to the theme of homelessness. Colm is characterised as a permanently moving person who regularly adapts to new environments and is uncertain as to whether he will stay in Aberystwyth for much longer: "This driftin round this fuckin island. Wher will a go after Aberystwyth, wher will a end up? Out ther into the darkness, behind glass: England, Scotland, Isler Man, other partser Wales…" (*G* 308). In a dramatic turn, Colm ultimately succumbs to his drug habit and ends up homeless and deranged on the streets of

Aberystwyth, having been kicked out by his equally unstable and addicted girlfriend Mairead. Still, while his restlessnessness (and that of other characters) is also clearly connected to his drug habit, the novel never insinuates in a one-directional construction of causality that this is the sole root of his unsteady life. Rather, it is implied that the origins or explanations for his addiction and unstable, promiscuous and self-destructive personality cannot be easily pathologised, and although it might go hand in hand with his problematic cultural and social background, it cannot be decided which came first. Rather, the cultural tensions seem to be inscribed in the bodies and psyches of the protagonists, while a clear monocausal explanation is denied – the novel thus plays with common explanatory patterns and abandons the idea of cause and effect in the context of personal and collective pathologies, a tendency that is mirrored by the novel's narrative style, which privileges no one speaker over the other.

In a similar way, Liam is described as a restless fugitive from Northern Ireland. Having temporarily been homeless, he has now made a living on the Welsh coast:

> Uf anny fucker deserves a fuckin rest, ut's me. Diddun ah long ago get off me fuckin ahrse an do summun fuckin positive wuth me life? Too fuckin right ah did. Left the place which was bad fe me (both Donegal *and* uni), wurked on a site, found a flat, a good wommun... When ah furst came hur ah had thurty fuckin quid in me pockut. Ah slept on flurs, in the fuckin public sheltur with the winos, ah ate fuckin dulse an crabs off the beach... (G 118)

Colm and Liam are thus the clearest examples of what I call cultural precarity, a condition which is directly reflected in their equally precarious living conditions. For both, this condition of precarity is not only evident in their material and social living conditions, but is also associated with the issue of ethnicity. Colm repeatedly refers to his Romany Traveller origins when he contemplates leaving Aberystwyth ("Gypsy blood. Itchy feet" [*G* 339]) and especially the racism he was confronted with during his childhood in England: "am offen gerrin accused uv things tharrah haven't done. Like when a was a kid, all the fuckin other kids ud be like: Gyppo, gyppo, derty fuckin gyppo, pooh gerrah bath yer smelly tinker bastard. All tha shit" (*G* 326). Thus, Colm, as part of an ethnic minority, is the victim of hate speech and a racialising discourse that marks him (and his body) as the dirty Other. This, as I will show later, can be linked to the particular representation of his body in the novel as well as his own relationship with his own body and the human body in general.

While Liam is not immediately and explicitly marked as racially other, he nonetheless experiences comparable forms of exclusion as a Catholic in Northern Ireland. In a remarkable scene in the chapter narrated by Sioned, she observes him while he drunkenly tries to associate with a Protestant from Northern Ireland, saying "A doan fuckin curr if ye are a fuckin Proddy. Suren wurr ahl fuckin brothers now eh? Ceasefire, mahn, the fuckin war's ovurr so ut is, the fuckin warr's ovurr" (*G* 406). When Liam defines the Protestant as a fellow Irishman despite the latter's insistence on his self-definition as British, the situation escalates, as observed and commented upon by Sioned:

– No yurr fuckin not, mahn, yer a fuckin Irishman. Will yis lissen te wha ahm sayin? British in me fuckin hole, yeer –
– See if ah fuckin wanter call meself British en ahl fuckin call meself British! Ooer fucker *you* ter tell me wha fucken nationality ah am?
– I'm a fuckin Irishmahn, is what! An am fuckin tellin yis that yurr wahn too!
Oh God. Not for the first time I find myself thinking of Liam's sister - how well he copes with her disability like - the bomb and all that - but I also realise now that - whatever capacity for forgiveness we - all of us - have - it's not enough. There is hatred - real, true hatred - everywhere.
The Proddy's mates are pointing at Liam and singing:
Ee aye ee aye ee aye oh! [...]
Paddy was a bastard - ee aye oh! (*G* 407)

This scene shows how the national conflicts that have shaped contemporary British culture are still prevalent and continue to define encounters between the different peoples of the archipelago – and what is more, Griffiths's novel demonstrates that these conflicts can take shape within a number of overlapping discourses.

Yet, while all views expressed by the leading characters are basically rooted within a left-wing, alternative and/or subcultural worldview, they are still distinguishable in a lot of aspects, with no single perspective explicitly privileged over the others. Thus, while the narrative strategies of *Grits* to some degree resemble those of Welsh's *Trainspotting* in its episodic, nonlinear structure and multiperspectivity, Griffiths's novel manages to provide different, sometimes conflicting views on issues of post-Britishness by letting the different narrator-characters contribute to the overall narrative in equal parts with their own distinct voices and views. This reflects the same conflicts and aporias that surface in the drunken dispute between Liam and the Protestants which is representative of a sense of unsolvable cultural conflict that is in significant part due to people's need to define themselves in national, cultural or, as I will demonstrate in the following with regard to the Welsh character Sioned, racial terms. The argument between Liam and the Protestants escalates not necessarily because of the latter's hostility towards Irish Catholics based on a hegemonic pro-British position but, rather, because of Liam's overbearing sense of entitlement when it comes to defining somebody else's national belonging. With this situation, the novel demonstrates one of its main themes, the fragility or impossibility of community, especially when it is based on cultural constructions such as nationality. Ultimately, this problem affects the entire group of friends at the heart of *Grit*'s narrative. While Paul's aforementioned monologue about their friendship can already be read as sceptical regarding any form of human community or sociality, epitomised in his baffled (and ultimately unanswered) question "What is it that binds yuh together?" (*G* 31), the final chapters describe the rapid disintegration of the group due to relationships breaking apart (or being held up despite the partners' inherently destructive behaviour) and the drastic physical and mental decline provoked by substance abuse.

Race in the Devolutionary Discourse

In the representation of the only major Aberystwyth-born narrator-character, Sioned, the impossibility of human community based on cultural identity constructions is directly linked to Wales as a minor nation and culture. Upon seeing a graffito by the Welsh separatist organisation Meibion Glyndŵr, Sioned links her theories about Welsh political independence to the status of Aberystwyth as a place that attracts social outcasts:

> It's this fucking simple, right – if Wales ruled itself, the Welsh people would be different – more confident – more laid back – less disposed to self-destruction and infighting – it's as simple – and as complex – as that. [...]. That's why this place – Aberystwyth like, this west Wales area – attracts all the fuck-ups – on the surface, like, people come here to escape – or that's what they say – but underneath it all like what they're really doing is answering the call – the external realisation of their

inner chaos – it calls to them across the countries – this little place on the western windy rim of Europe – this place between mountain and sea – this small colony of sadness and insanity. (*G* 415)

Strikingly, Sioned here evokes the notion of Wales as a (post)colonial minor nation that is still affected by a lack of proper political representation within the United Kingdom. This sense of remaining cultural and political oppression is also alluded to in the repeated mention of RAF airplanes roaring above the coastline and thus creating a sense of intimidation. After once more being scared "shitless" by one of the jets, Sioned interprets this as a "a show of strength – a threat – like, see what we've got to destroy you with – we can blow you to fuckin bits if we want" (*G* 396). The RAF planes are symbolically perceived as a representation of Anglo-British oppression of minor nations like Wales, as if the RAF was not in fact sustained by the United Kingdom as a whole. Thus, Wales appears as something entirely outside of the British nation state, all the while being affected by its politics and cultural hegemony. Apparatuses like the military are thus conceived as not belonging to Wales, as not being part of the people.

This sub-British sense of detachment and separation also informs Sioned's perception of the Welsh and English peoples as culturally and even racially distinct. In her rhetoric, she frequently alludes to the vocabulary of race in order to make her points about the cultural and political tensions – "I mean, I'm not overly keen on the English myself, like, in general – you know – as a race – but some individuals are perfectly alright" (*G* 404). While her comment about the English as a race is subsequently relativised by herself and put into perspective by some of her friends, it nonetheless is remarkable in the way the rhetoric of race is turned upside down. If one follows Chris Haylett's assumption that Englishness as a cultural identity implies a normative form of (British) whiteness, then Sioned's "racing" of the English as a culturally hegemonic group (which is therefore racially invisible, or, to reference Richard Dyer once more, "just people") can be interpreted as an act of making this whiteness visible. To put it differently, and to slightly rephrase Sara Ahmed, Sioned makes visible the "unmarked mark" of (Anglo-)Britishness (Ahmed 2004b, par. 13). Her insistence that she distinguishes between a generalised English 'race' and some "perfectly alright" individuals who are an exception to the rule mimics and inverts a common anti-black racist rhetoric that, to quote the main character of

John King's *The Football Factory*, is epitomised by the line "People say they hate niggers but if they know one then he's okay" (*FF* 5) – and consequently directs it back at the supposed hegemonic oppressor.

However, Sioned is still intent on maintaining a balanced view on these issues by objecting to radical anti-English sentiments held by many fellow Welsh people whom she accuses of using the Welsh concept of *hiraeth* as a justification for racism: "It's not only the English who are racist – oh no – that's a fucking myth, boy, that racism's an English thing like – sometimes what starts off as anti-racism can become mutated into racism itself – and something as precious as hiraeth becomes like Aryanism was to the Nazis" (*G* 404). *Hiraeth*, a word that means "'longing', 'homesickness' or 'nostalgia' but escapes precise definitions" (Bednarski 2012b: 51) becomes a leitmotif throughout the novel,[8] especially in the context of the protagonists' post-British cultural homelessness. In that respect, it is striking that race is a ubiquitous, if not necessarily always explicitly pronounced, issue in the narrative accounts and interior monologues of almost all characters. It is especially striking since most of the central characters handle the issue with a certain degree of ambivalence, most of them being well aware that race is the least suitable option for maintaining a sense of individual or collective identity.

While Sioned is eager to stress that she is pro-Welsh, yet anti-racist, and that she even despises anti-English racism in other pro-Welsh friends, her actions reveal that her attitudes in this regard are more complicated (and problematic) than she would likely admit. This becomes evident when her chapter closes with the lines "Nos da'r, spwriel Saeson. Nos da'r, twpsyn" (*G* 425) – meaning "Good night, English rubbish. Good night, nitwits" (transl. in Bednarski 2012b: 49) – after she has put on a tape with exclusively Welsh bands for the night's collective drinking excesses. While the reduction of the English 'race' to "rubbish" can be seen as a (problematic) counterstrategy by a postcolonial subject (after all, Sioned is described as a native Welsh who was forced into learning and using English as a second language), some of her friends reflect her political and cultural views as particularly extreme ones.

Probably not by coincidence, it is during the final chapter (narrated by Malcolm, an Englishman), describing the demise and disintegration of

8 | See Bednarski 2012b: 51 for a detailed look at *hiraeth* and its relevance for the novel.

the group, that Sioned's position is explicitly scrutinised. Malcolm, who is increasingly alienated by the self-destructive group dynamic among his friends and who finally decides to leave Aberystwyth to return to his Essex home, recollects a dispute between Colm, at this point already on the verge of complete physical and mental collapse, and Sioned about racism in Britain:

> ee sent Sioned off in a huff befaw by callin er a racist cow (prompted by a stawry Sioned towld abaht er sista playin a joke on er by arskin er tha Welsh word fa 'dog' – which is 'cŵn' – as they were wawkin parst a black fella.)[9] Eee went on abaht ow racism ain't purely an English disease, it's endemic throughaht tha British Isles, which Sioned, in er dangerous idealisation of awl things [sic] Welsh an blinkered demonisation of awl fings English, disagreed with, which was tha trigga Colm needed ta gow on tha offensive. Personally, I agreed wiv Colm, but ... best just ta keep ya gob shut. (G 451)

In introducing Malcolm's level-headed view towards the end of the novel,[10] the radical views expressed by some of the characters – labelled "dangerous" by Malcolm – the novel proves to be an agglomeration of views and standpoints about race, culture and national belonging in a post-British context that defies one-directional approaches and ultimately proves to be ideologically aporetic.

In addition to the problematisation of Sioned's radical positions through altero-characterisations, her position is also on an ironic meta-level conspicuously presented in formal terms, for, as Bednarski remarks,

> what is striking about Sioned's narrative is that her speech, in contrast with the other monologues, reflects hardly any dialectal features and is closest to literary, standard English. In other words, her language, contrary to the other narrators', is literarily modelled and processed. Interestingly, Sioned's speech, when quoted in

9 | The pun being that *cŵn* is pronounced like the racial slur *coon*.

10 | Despite this "level-headedness", the readers' potential initial impression that Malcolm might therefore be a more dominant voice or morally more reliable figure than the others is put into perspective by the fact that even though he eventually decides to leave Aberystwyth and his friends behind, he still uses drugs and considers them to be a substantial component of his excessive lifestyle. His "escape" in the end is therefore framed as potential self-delusion despite his final impression that "there's happiness ahead" (*G* 482).

the monologues of other characters, manifests dialectal pronunciation in a more noticeable way than in her own narrative. [...]. Therefore, the element undergoing stronger fictionalisation (Sioned) is at the same time unquestionably associated with Wales. (2012b: 48)

This contrast between the formal and linguistic representation of Sioned's narrative voice and the rendering of her speech by other characters introduces an alienating element of narratorial and compositional interference which stresses the novel's deconstructive and critical interrogation of notions of monolithic national cultures both from a hegemonic, Anglocentric as well as from a sub-British minority standpoint. Thus, it is not only Sioned as an individual character who is put into perspective by this alienating interference – it is the entire notion of a monolithic and essentialist notion of Welsh national culture as well as the novel's own engagement with it which are highlighted in their (literary) constructedness and thus denaturalised, especially when considering that Sioned "is the only character whose first and most natural language is Welsh and she is the only character-narrator with access to both linguistic universes" (Bednarski 2012b: 48). The underlying theme of post-Britishness and the plurality of voices are thus also scrutinised in the formal representation of the novel as neither the victimising postcolonial discourse about Wales nor radical nationalism offer the characters any solace in their search for a fixed cultural identity – and those who subscribe to such radical ideologies without questioning themselves mostly appear as marginal caricatured characters – and it is through such a character that the term *white trash* is introduced in the novel.

White Trash and the Trans-British Community

An episode in Colm's account focuses on Oxford John, called a "Nazi cunt" by Colm due to his obsession with the history of World War II and his endorsement of Hitler (*G* 333). Commenting on a monologue by John about the moral relativity of war crimes and his attempt to convince his listeners to read *Mein Kampf*, Colm comments:

A doan wanner listen ter some Nazi prick blather on about inferior races and life unwerthy uv life, as if some ugly white trash from some scummy council estate in the heart uv some sinking, stinking island is some'ow superior. Ther's alweys some cunt like John around ter spoil things, ter taint things with is diseased ideas. As if things arn bad enough. As if the werld needs another gobshite like im. (*G* 334)

Despite the thematic similarities between Irvine Welsh's *Trainspotting* and Griffiths's novel – particularly in their post-British sensibility and focus on socially marginalised characters with a penchant for iconoclastic, dissident thinking (Colm's musings resemble those of Mark Renton in Welsh's novel), Colm's use of the term *white trash* significantly differs from that of Mark Renton. While Mark uses the term to refer to his Scottish home country and its people as the sub-British victims of colonisation within the context of the United Kingdom, the term, while at the same time referring to socioeconomic marginalisation and deprivation (in the reference to the council estate), is in this case clearly used to reference John's racism. Thus, Colm's use of the term assumes a similar semantic dimension as in the Stephen Lawrence murder case where *white trash* was used to denounce and demonise the perpetrators of a racist crime that was condemned by liberal middle-class whites as the deed of people whose whiteness was viewed as the monstrously visible marker of their moral inferiority. In other words, Mark's use of the term stresses victimisation (despite his explicit contempt for the Scots and their passive behaviour as victims), while Colm uses the term to describe a (potential) perpetrator. This is all the more important since Colm, who is of Irish-Romany descent, describes himself as the victim of racism and could, from a racist perspective, in the words of Matt Wray be described as "not quite white".[11] In conclusion, Welsh and Griffiths's uses of the term, despite their similar contexts, demonstrate the ambivalent semantics of *white trash* and other stigmatypes from the American South.

---

11 | In fact, a recent novel by Simon Thirsk, *Not Quite White* (2010), which offers a satirical account of a Welsh-speaking small-town community coming to terms with the history of English colonialism, is based on the presumption that the Welsh, in the eyes of the colonisers, were not considered white. The novel's title is based on a quote by Welsh artist Osi Rhys Osmond: "The Welsh are blessed in the smallest of ways – by being not quite white" (*NQW*: n. pag.). Since the novel cannot be linked directly to the corpus of texts under consideration in my thesis in that it does not explicitly draw on images of white trash or related stigmatypes, I will not analyse it in depth. However, its sentiments and approach strongly resonate with the issues of trans-Britishness and race that can be found at the heart of Niall Griffiths's novels.

The semantics of dirt and pollution are also emphasised by Colm when he refers to the "scummy" estate and the "tainting" with "diseased" ideas. In this case, however, the fear of pollution does not necessarily derive from a notion of 'pure' whiteness which is in danger of being tainted through lower-class status – a notion which still would hold whiteness up as an invisible norm and parameter. Rather, Colm's choice of words implies that whiteness as a vessel for racist ideologies is a form of contagious pollution. In this notion, whiteness is no longer assumed to be an invisible ideal but is seen as the product of racist discourses which form cultural hegemonies through ethnicity. For Colm, then, it is the multicultural, trans-British community to be found in Aberystwyth that is in danger of being polluted.

The semantics of dirt and pollution in relation to Britishness, race and class are also central in the monologues of Roger, a veteran who fought in Ireland during the Troubles and who is described by his friends as a sociopath because of his regular violent outbursts. He grew up on the New Gurnos estate in Merthyr Tydfil in South Wales – a place which he describes as the

> biggest fuckin estate in-a ole uv Ewrop, fucked fuckin place like am fuckin tellin yew, Merthyr fuckin Titfeel, a fuckin *real* Wales fyer boy, none uv-a fuckin mountains or lakes yer jes fuckin sewage an dumps n boxes t'fuckin live in like, a *real* Wales, a place whir am fuckin *from*, Indyin fuckin reservation in-a middle-a Great fuckin Britain like [...] a pleyce-a gwehilion[12] o boblach boy, too fuckin right, ewman fuckin weyst like, waste-a ewmans, gahbidge like, rubbish, shite. (*G* 57)

In fact, the Gurnos is to this day infamous for being one of the most deprived areas in Great Britain, with one of the highest unemployment rates, one of the highest suicide rates and an overall low healthy life expectancy.[13] In Roger's rants, the Gurnos becomes the epitome of the "real"

12 | The Welsh term *gwehilion* translates as *trash* or *dregs* (my translation).

13 | The estate came to infamous attention in 2011 when the *Daily Mail* reported about the allegedly "low life expectancy" of 58.8 years among male residents, and originally stated that life expectancy was lower than in Iraq or Haiti. It was later revised and specified to a "low 'healthy' life expectancy" rather than an overall low life expectancy, also relativising the comparison with Iraq and Haiti. However, the initial comparison still shows the conspicuous way in which places like the Gurnos

Wales that contrasts the country's bucolic construction in the collective imagination. This also implies that the Gurnos is in fact the place where 'real' oppression is being felt, as opposed to the stylised sense of oppression that Roger accuses the proponents of Welsh devolution of:

> A tell yer, ey think eyv ad it bard like, with-a pressure from-a English, but ey wooden larst two fuckin minutes on-a Gurnos like. No fuckin wey. Now *yer's* fuckin pressure for yer, livin on-a Gurnos; yer wunner see oppression? In action, like? Look-a a New fuckin Gurnos, boy, down in Merthyr Tydfil. At's-a real fuckin Wales fer yer, yer twat. (*G* 83–84)

According to Roger's logic, 'real' oppression is predominantly class-based oppression, resulting from economic inequality and material circumstances, whereas the cultural oppression by the English appears mainly as a construction that people who are otherwise far from being underprivileged indulge in. His rhetoric combines the semantics of dirt ("human waste" and "wasted humans") with racial imagery when he describes the Gurnos as an "Indian reservation" (a comparison that is repeated by his friend Gerraint, see *G* 369), likening the lower-class inhabitants of the estate with disenfranchised and displaced natives in colonised America. Thus, race, or more precisely, racial imagery, is used by Roger to say something about class-based oppression. This rhetoric underlines the particular intersection of race and class in the form of speech and rhetorical figures, and is underlined by Gerraint, another narrator, who describes the Gurnos as "a fuckin piece-a the Third World in the middle of wha is supposed t'be the First" (*G* 369).

Strikingly, the comparison of a deprived estate with an Indian reservation resembles the comparison of Edinburgh's Muirhouse estates with South African townships by Roy Strang in Irvine Welsh's *Marabou Stork Nightmares*. Within the context of sub-British nations like Wales and Scotland, such racial analogies for class relations have a twofold effect at least: firstly, they seem to prove what Raymond Williams has said about the need to get through to the real conflicts of class and economic inequality

---

are constructed and othered within the national imagination, as well as the way in which poverty is compulsively approached via racialising frames of reference and comparisons with 'foreign' cultures associated with "non-whiteness" (see "Future?" 2011: n. pag.).

that underlie the imagination of racial differences between the different British nations. However, in a second step, such analogies prove to be a de facto repetition of these racial stereotypes. That is, they cannot seem to break out of the matrix of racial imagery and rhetoric, reproducing the same racial hierarchies while attempting to define class as the actual and primary problem underlying issues of inequality in Britain.

In a further step, Roger ties the two trajectories of race and class together with the rhetoric of trash and waste when he speaks of the Gurnos being full of "human waste", and, stretching the image with a play on words, a "waste of humans". Roger's take on "human waste" resembles Zygmunt Bauman's idea of "human waste" as the by-product of the design of "human togetherness": "Where there is design, there is waste. [...]. When it comes to designing the forms of human togetherness, the waste is human beings. Some human beings who do not fit into the designed form nor can be fitted into it" (2004: 30). According to Bauman, this order building is the preoccupation of the modern nation state which "has claimed the right to preside over the distinction between order and chaos, law and lawlessness, citizen and *homo sacer*, belonging and exclusion, useful (= legitimate) product and waste" (2004: 33).[14] In Roger's view of social relations in Wales, class is the main category according to which people are designated as useful or waste, and places like the Gurnos (and Muirhouse respectively) are the designated area to dispose of this social waste. His use of racial imagery indicates that race is a factor by which people are additionally qualified as waste or non-waste. Appropriately, then, "yer's fuckin graffiti on-a wall in-a New Gurnos: [...] Croeso i uffern"[15] (*G* 57). The estate thus almost seems like a heterotopic space, a "hell" for those individuals who do not fit the dominant social and racial design.

However, Roger's monologues reveal even more complexity in Griffiths's treatment of the intersections of race and class in a trans-British context. It is the use of stereotypes from the American South that is employed here to illustrate this complexity. When Roger observes a group of English hikers, he deliberately acts in a threatening manner only to imagine the foreign tourists – pictured as "posh" middle-class English hikers – retrospectively talking about their "experience" with a local Welshman. In

14 | I will use Bauman's concept of human waste more extensively in my analysis of John King's novels *The Football Factory* and *White Trash* in the next chapter.

15 | "Welcome to hell" (my translation).

this imagined dialogue, Roger mockingly adapts the novel's strategy of rendering demotic speech to caricaturing effect and plays with different auto- and hetero-stereotypes:

> Some fuckin hikers pass by, rambler tossers like with eyr fuckin rucksacks an stewpid fuckin boots on, an a look on eyr fuckin feyces when ey fuckin clock me like, me with the muscles all warped like an a fuckin ead uv a lion on me fuckin shoulders, ewge fuckin gun in me ands which now look like bunches-a fuckin bananas... A stick me tongue out at em an meyk a growly noise as ey pass by an ey nir fuckin shit emselves like, ey fuckin leg it over-a hill an a piss me kex larfin at eyr fuckin feyces, Christ, yew should-a fuckin seen em, mun... Ey probelly fuckin loved it. Madgin-a fuckers back ome over-a fuckin border, tellin eyr poncey meyts over-a fuckin cheese an wine about eyr fuckin hikin olidey in Wales:
> 'Oh yarse, rilly rahther hex-hiting. Hauthentic Welsh hill-billeh, ite hanting his suppah... Rilly rahther quaint. Toby was all fawer hinviting him back to thar hotel, bat Hi poo-poohed thet hi-dear: hay mean, cen you imargine what he wad hev dan with the san-dried toe-mahtoes?' (*G* 70)

Roger's attitude towards the English tourists displays his awareness for the possible stereotypes he is subjected to in their eyes, particularly including colonial imagery of the same kind that Kirsti Bohata draws attention to in her studies on (post)colonial Wales and its racialised representations in Anglo-British literature. Although it must be emphasised that none of the English explicitly express such stereotypes themselves, the images Roger anticipates convey the same racist sense of "authenticity" and atavism that is associated with the rural Welsh population. In one of his later novels, *Stump* (2005), Niall Griffiths further explores this mindset through one of the main characters: a gangster from Liverpool expresses his fear of the Welsh countryside in a way that is exemplary of the racist and colonial imagery of the backwards Welsh population:

> Don't like this fuckin place, lar. This fuckin country. Never fuckin av. Fuller fuckin wollybacks, sheepshaggers. They're fuckin, thee've been fuckin left behind. Still fuckin sacrificing their kids to the fuckin sun-god n stuff, I shit you not. [...]. I mean, a place with this many mountains an lakes an woods, it's just not fuckin right. Fuckin witches n all sorts out here. Creepiest fuckin place. [...]. Just don't fuckin like it, lar. Don't fuckin like it. Wanner be back in town. (*St* 56)

The associations with the atavistic and supernatural, although coming from a rather simple mind, are nonetheless indicative of the status of Wales in the racial (and, in its imagined opposition to [English] cities, spatial) national imagination of an Anglocentric Britain.

With his behaviour and his performance as an "authentic Welsh hillbilly", Roger appears as a sub-British subject empowering himself by appropriating and parodying Anglo-British constructions of a Welsh 'race'. What is more, he appropriates colonial language strategies by caricaturing a class-conscious linguistic hypercorrection (such as the "h"-insertion in "rahther hex-hiting"). With his exaggerated imitation, Roger plays with culturally dominant versions of British English and marks them as yet another dialect among many on the British islands. Thus, far from being the privileged mode of speech of a culturally dominant group, the English hikers become just another voice in the trans-British plurality of voices that the novel presents. Consequently, for Griffiths and his characters, there is no "pure" form of speech as much as there is a "pure" British race. Rather, speech as well as the concept of race (and here, it must be recognised that dominant as well as less dominant, "impure" forms of speech are markers of race and [sub-]Britishness).

By using the "hillbilly" stereotype, a slur directed against the rural population of the American South, Roger (and, accordingly, Griffiths's novel) evokes once again the specific dynamics of race and class. But unlike Colm's use of "white trash" for the Nazi Oxford John, Roger appropriates the phrase in his performance and his imagination of the English tourists' prejudices against him and the Welsh, and uses it in a form of postcolonial mimicry of stereotypes that parodies and de-essentialises positions of subordination and power.[16] Thus, by adapting American stereotypes in order to illustrate similarities in the racial and social dynamics in both the United States and the United Kingdom and by consciously playing with their ambivalent semantics and showing how race "changes shape, size, and color as the need arises" (Niro 2003: 1), Griffiths presents the reader with an interrogation of race and its intersections that demonstrates race to be a category that, at best, is constantly in flux and made up of similarly

16 | Harri Garrod Roberts discusses Homi K. Bhabha's concepts of hybridity and mimicry in the context of abjection, claiming that Bakhtin's grotesque implies similar strategies of resistance to postcolonial power structures and processes of social and cultural abjection (2009: 17-19).

fleeting and unstable, if not entirely arbitrary signifiers. This awareness of the semantic instability of race and the tensions in British culture reflected in the recourse to race is also reflected in Roger's relativising attitude when it comes to easy solutions on part of the supposedly oppressed Welsh:

> a mean, ferget-a fuckin English, like, eyr not wirth fuckin worryin about mun. Ther jes pricks, fergettable fuckin pricks; yer ar wirse fuckin... oh yeh, a mean, al sey a hate-a fuckin English so's ter wind-a cunts up like, but it's sometimes-a fuckin Welsh emselves, a fuckin Wales v. Wales fixtures, a small fuckin neytion-a fuckin fuck-ups... Carn even pley fuckin rugby enny more. (*G* 86)

Echoing Mark Renton's contempt for the Scots and what he considers their incapacity to properly deal with the oppression of their culture in *Trainspotting*, Roger similarly deconstructs the notion of a victimised Welsh people that blames any shortcomings on Anglo-British cultural oppression. If compared with Irvine Welsh's protagonist and his use of the white trash stereotype for a similar context, Roger's blunt yet subtle and consciously chosen hillbilly performance shows the same awareness for the construction of racial intersectional stereotypes in a trans-British context. In both cases, cultural and economic disenfranchisement are intercut with racial components.

Although in both cases, the judgments expressed are those of two rather unstable individuals and therefore should not be taken at face value, their emotional outbursts nonetheless reveal a degree of intuitive insight into the matters of race and how it is employed as a signifier in contemporary Britain. Roger even goes beyond the level of criticism expressed by Mark Renton in *Trainspotting* when he performatively presents both sides of the spectrum. On the one hand, he reflects the view of the oppressed (or, respectively, the critique of those who feel oppressed abuse a sense of oppression for other means) – including a distinction between perceived and actual oppression, with the deprived urban estates marking the "real" Wales as opposed to the countryside that the English imagine as "authentic" in Roger's imagination. On the other hand, he incorporates the imagined view of the oppressors represented by the tourists, who perceive the Welsh as raced and therefore as presumably more "authentic", i.e. more rooted in place than those Britons who are racially unmarked in their view. This view works according to the logic that Richard Dyer has summarised in the oft-quoted phrase "[other] people are raced, we are just people" (Dyer 1997: 1).

The question of racial authenticity, which could be translated as the desire to define something like a cultural "essence", is thus dependent on certain signifiers which hide the fact that there is no such thing as cultural "essence", and hence no racial authenticity. If one were to define the novel's political poetics, it could be defined as the radical representation of cultural plurality, reflected in its unsettled language and plurality of voices, its Bakhtinian dialogism, which ultimately demonstrates the impossibility of fathoming cultural essence. Consequently, the novel seems to anticipate its implied readers' struggle with intelligibility, which proves this impossibility. However, the novel's de(con)structive form is also accompanied by its recurring themes of bodily decay and death which similarly serve to undermine a sense of cultural essence and stability. This also implies the stability of the symbolic regime of race and class which are signified by the human body. The human body as a cultural marker is denaturalised and undermined in its discourse on the mortal body.

The Body, Decay and Grotesque Poetics

While the entire novel can be interpreted as a grotesque text designed to illustrate a morbid teleology in order to finally make the plain point that everything has to die and, until that end, is to some extent already involved in the process of decay, Colm and Malcolm – perhaps not coincidentally bearing similar names – can be identified as the two narrators who dwell the most on this aspect. Quite fittingly, they are reflected by Liam – perhaps the most optimistic, yet at the same time no less complicated and hypocritical character: "Fuckin Colm and Malcolm an thur endtime nonsense. The wurld ul go ohn, like ut ulweys fuckin has; if they havunt lurnt tha yet then they nevurr fuckin will" (*G* 139). However, the novel implies that Liam is wrong as it denies its characters (and its readers) a sense of closure or purpose underneath its imagery of decay. At the end of the novel, many of the characters, most significantly Colm himself as well as his girlfriend Mairead are shown to be disintegrating mentally and physically due to their substance abuse and life in poverty, while some of their friends attempt to keep up the facade of a liberal, alternative and fulfilling lifestyle on the fringes of the establishment.

One of the most significant observations regarding the role of death in the novel comes from Sioned during the funeral of one of the friends' remote acquaintances, Fat Charlie. Remarkably, death even seems to undermine language and literature as sense-making mechanisms when she describes the circumstances of the funeral and is failed by her rhetoric devices while attempting to make a comparison:

> The sky was blue and huge and hung over the valley like a – like a – oh I don't fucking know – it just hung there. And that was Fat Charlie's funeral – he choked on his own sick and was laid to rest – no, was burned – was cremated – was scorched into ash – among groups of fucked-up, grumbling, useless and rejected people who all seemed to be trying their best to follow him into the flames. The whole thing baffled me – bewildered like – none of it made the slightest bit of sense. (G 417)

The way literary language and its conventions are denaturalised by the rupture "oh I don't fucking know – it just hung there" denies and ridicules aesthetic elevation that would attribute greater meaning to what is accounted in this passage.

Signification and symbolisation, and even the process of mourning itself, seem to have lost the power to contextualise death. At the same time, the graveyard becomes the locus at which the trans-Britishness scrutinised in the novel seems to converge when Sioned observes: "I'd never heard such a variety of accents in such a small place before – it was like the whole of the British Isles compressed into one graveyard" (*G* 416). But instead of attributing any sense of reconciliation or symbolising the possibility of a future of British cultural unity, the funeral is just that: the plain farewell to a dead body devoid of any sense of new beginning. In fact, Sioned immediately adds an observation regarding the mourning community: "And funny how people form cliques even at funerals like – death the great leveller – my arse" (*G* 416). While death is presented as a "great leveller" when it comes to the meaning attributed to bodies as culturally marked, death does indeed not affect the way people perceive each other in terms of these cultural markings. Even the reflection on death and decay as such does not seem to add up to anything in the novel: although the different narrators devote themselves to morbid chapter-long philosophical musings, no deeper insight is gained. On a performative level, the novel illustrates this nihilistic tendency in several instances like the ironic rupture in Sioned's narrative account or when the verbose and self-educated Colm, watching a woman's body floating in a canal, acknowledges his language's incapacity in the face of death:

My use of language merely masks the fact tharrah doan have a fuckin clue, no fuckin idea uv wha any uv this is about. Am completely fuckin baffled. [...]. ... is this it, then, is this all ther is? (*G* 320)

As Harri Garrod Roberts makes clear in his interpretation of *Grits*, scatology and the grotesque body are of central importance for Griffiths's poetics. In regard to a passage in which Colm is asked by Sioned why he is "so obsessed with arses an shit an stuff?" and replies: "I feel the need to mask my divine essence in scatological camouflage. In order to protect it like" (*G* 398), Roberts writes that "Colm's 'scatological camouflage' hides nothing; it *is* his 'essence'" (2009: 157) – that is, human beings are nothing but assemblages of bodily fluids held together by cell tissues: "That's all wer made up of" (*G* 277).

That the human body can be seen as a mere vessel of biomass has ideological repercussions if this fact is considered in the context of race and class. Like the novels of Irvine Welsh, Griffiths's *Grits* employs the grotesque as a political mode that radically denaturalises body-centred ideologies that attribute meaning to human bodies that would go beyond their mere biological functions. The grotesque thus denaturalises ideological concepts of cultural belonging. Following Harri Garrod Roberts, who argues for considering the poetological similarities between Bakhtin's two concepts of heteroglossia and the grotesque because "each is described as disrupting the state of unified stasis characteristic of official linguistic/bodily normality" (2009: 143), I contend that Griffiths's novel, with its radical emphasis on the plurality of trans-British voices as well as with his equally radical dissection of the human body, can be read as a literary project of social transformation – a reading that is supported by Aleksander Bednarski, who similarly situates the novel within a tradition of the Bakhtinian grotesque that aims at "inverting and transgressing boundaries between different categories, mainly between the high and the low, the official and unofficial, the inner body and the outer world" (2012b: 35).

Like in Irvine Welsh's novels, the grotesque is not only a literary aesthetics but a political mode with which the literary text works through the human body in order to dissect and undo the ideological inscriptions of race, class and gender it bears. Thus, the literary text simultaneously undoes the cultural separations that distinguish between precarious and less precarious subjects. Along the lines of Judith Butler's arguments, *Grits* can be interpreted as a text that demonstrates its characters' precarity, which might be intensified by their individual living conditions, but which affects individuals and populations irrespective of their race or class. Colm's description of and reflection on a woman's body floating in the canal is representative of this all-encompassing precarity:

> White n bloated, floppin about in the waves? Bein eaten by fish an crabs, floppin uselessly about, naked, rotting, bloated ... aw fuck. She's as white as, wha, a dunno, boiled fish flesh, white an purulent an pasty an yer imagine tha if yer touched er a piece uv flesh ud just, like, squelch off in yer hand ... yud be able ter break er inter little bits with yer ber ands [...]. (G 320)

This meditation on mortality suggests a disintegration of the body that lets its inscribed values die with it, and the fact that every body will eventually meet the same fate implies that such inscriptions – as well as the notion that some bodies might be less precarious or more safe than others – are futile in the first place.[17]

The disintegration of the woman's body is particularly remarkable since Colm repeatedly refers to her white skin, which in this case is completely devoid of whiteness as an ideological construction. The body is reduced to its mere corporeal fabric, and the colour of her skin is far from being a cultural marker. In fact, reduced to a biological fact, the white skin appears as something abject, reminding of Julia Kristeva's statement that the corpse is the "most horrifying of all bodily wastes" (Roberts 2009: 7), the "utmost of all abjection" (Kristeva 1982: 4). However, Griffiths's grotesque poetics do not imply the "normalising compulsions" (Roberts 2009: 17) that Kristeva's conception of the abject has often been criticised for. I would argue that Griffiths's grotesque similarly resists normalising forms of abjection in that abjection is not merely challenged as a hegemonic mode of normalisation, but rather in that virtually every living matter is rendered abject in his novel. This is in line with Imogen Tyler's critique of Kristeva's ultimately conservative and dangerously Eurocentric conception of abjection (2013: 27–38) and her call for a Butlerian alternative practice of citation that lets abjection give "rise to resistance" (2013: 38). The abject – in the form of an all-encompassing fate of decay – is elevated to such a degree that any inscription onto the human body must

17 | That Fat Charlie's corpse is being cremated and thus is immediately erased with all its possible inscriptions makes this episode even more dramatic.

be rendered futile and meaningless. In that regard, Griffiths's novel to a certain degree accomplishes the subversive effect of the Bakhtinian carnival, turning social and corporeal orders upside down. With Aleksander Bednarksi, who identifies the literary grotesque in *Grits* as a means to "[undermine] the rules of realistic representation" (2012b: 37), I read the novel's strategies of fragmentation and the effacement of boundaries between individuals and their surroundings as a critique of literary signification in the sense of naturalising realist representation – a literary endeavour which ultimately reaches beyond the confines of the literary and challenges broader ideas of the human body as culturally inscribed.

Thus, when following Chris Haylett's assertion that "black" and white "degenerate working-class others" are figured within the "same symbolic register" as signifiers of the "abject, as residual matter, defilement, and disorder" (2001: 361),[18] Griffiths overthrows this symbolic order of racialised British nationality, grounded on a naturalisation of the biological fact of skin colour as a political inscription, by subjecting this symbolic order to a hyperbole of decaying matter. One might even say that Griffiths's novel discards the politically symbolic altogether – something which it accomplishes not only through a grotesque aesthetics on the level of representation, but also on the semiotic and formal level: at almost five hundred pages, *Grits* leaves nothing unsaid, unexplored or unsignified. The cacophony of thoughts, political views, introspections and social observations, rendered in a radically demotic, abominable language – a language that likewise might be defined as an abjection of 'proper' English – spells everything out and reveals the narrators' semiotic struggle with the literary. This struggle is epitomised in passages such as Sioned's description of the funeral and her failure to grasp the situation in literary comparisons, and highlights the characters' difficulties with coming to terms with a symbolic order that is not of their making and yet to some degree defines their cultural and political identities. When the novel's final narrator, Malcolm, evaluates the demise of his friends and asks "what's appenin ta awl of us? Where did tha fuckin rottennes begin,

18 | "Where 'black' is the originary signifier of the abject, as residual matter, defilement, and disorder, 'white' embodied in degenerate working-class 'others' come to share the same symbolic register [...]. In this way, poor whites can be seen as dangerous to the symbolic order of British nationhood where hierarchies of national belonging and privilege are still naturalised by skin colour" (Haylett 2001: 361).

where are its roots?" (*G* 453), this marks his realisation that the decay is all-encompassing and cannot be put into perspective or incorporated into a symbolic order no matter how eager he and some of his friends are to read the decay around them as symbolic, as becomes evident in Malcolm's and Colm's thoughts on the sheep suffering from the footrot epidemic in Wales (see *G* 138–140).

However, the novel's characters still cannot operate outside the literary. In fact, their frames of reference (and Niall Griffiths's) are most prominently defined by, among others,[19] Cormac McCarthy's Southern Gothic novels, once again reaffirming the intercultural links that have already been established with the references to white trash and the racial dynamics in the American South. Colm at one point explicitly mentions McCarthy's novel *Suttree* (1979),[20] and Malcolm's disillusionment and decision to leave Aberystwyth's subculture towards the end of the novel mirror *Suttree*'s titular character who, after attempting to live an outsider life in the slums at the shores of the Tennessee River – *"a world within the world"* inhabited by the *"illshapen or black or deranged, fugitive of all order, strangers in everyland"* (*Su* 4; italics in original), abandons his alternative lifestyle among the outcast African Americans, the hillbillies and white "crackers".[21] Even his remark on his friends' fate – "but it neva ends, tho, does it? It just gows on, extremity on extremity on extremity. Human misery knows no absolutes" (*G* 479) – is a reference to Suttree's similar-sounding realisation "but there are no absolutes in human misery and things can always get worse" (*Su* 372). Similarly, the fact that the narrative of *Grits* denies its protagonists the conclusive character of symbolism and other processes of signification as a sense-making mechanism on the diegetic level, does not mean that the novel itself operates outside the symbolic. The radical

19 | In his monograph on Griffiths, Aleksander Bednarski has analysed the intricate references to Welsh mythology and literature in his novels, and he has referred to the meta-reflexive construction of *Grits*'s cast of characters as well as to the rendering of Wales as a "theatrical stage" (2012b: 39–45).

20 | "Amazin fuckin werds, in Cormac McCarthy. [...]. So ther a was, readin *Suttree*, all warm an sheltered from the rain. Oner the best nights av ad in fuckin ages" (*G* 282).

21 | A point could also be made that *Grits*'s conclusion resembles that of Irvine Welsh's *Trainspotting*, whose main character Mark Renton escapes the destructive environment of his Leith home.

materialism that its characters and their cultural belief systems are subjected to seems likewise to be informed by Cormac McCarthy's radical sense of materialism, which shines through in *Suttree*'s meditations on sewage and processes of decay.[22] Thus, while Griffiths's characters are left in a world devoid of meaningful symbols, the novel itself still employs its grotesque imagery symbolically.

Griffiths's transatlantic engagement with McCarthy's texts is crucial in several ways: First of all, in directly drawing on the Southern literary tradition of the grotesque, Griffiths not only stresses the analogies in relation to intersectional aspects of race and class that come to the fore in Griffiths's repeated allusions to forms of tainted whiteness like white trash and hillbillies, but he also stresses the constructed and fictional character of his representation of Wales. Thus, while Griffiths might not necessarily display his own text's constructedness using ostentatious postmodernist gestures, he still crafts his text in a way that performs its own de-naturalisation. Wales as an "authentic" national culture and its issues of race and class, so it seems, can only be rendered through recourse to either ancient Welsh mythology or to imagery from another culture, in this case the Southern Gothic – and in doing so, Griffiths's text subtly demonstrates the actual unrepresentability of cultural essence. To put it differently: Wales must be represented by reference to other cultures and their literary representation because there is no actual essential Welshness to be represented. This, among other passages, is most poignantly illustrated by Roger's play with Welsh stereotypes – or, rather, what he *thinks* the English perceive as a Welsh stereotype – namely, a "Welsh hillbilly" – that is, an Americanised version of the sub-British Other. In order to understand this aspect, it is useful to recall Flannery O'Connor's laconic definition of the grotesque in Southern fiction: "I have found that anything that comes out of the South is going to be called grotesque by the Northern reader, unless it is grotesque, in which case it is going to be called realistic" (1972: 40). If one substitutes the terms *Northern* and *South* with *English* and *Wales* respectively, one has a fitting description of what is demonstrated in Griffiths's novel.

The American South is therefore not only used to express the view that Wales and Britain are dealing with similar issues of race and class,

22 | This radical materialism is also central to McCarthy's earlier novel *Child of God*, which I will consider later as a pretext for Griffiths's *Sheepshagger*.

but is also employed to allude to the novel's construction of Wales as what Aleksander Bednarski has identified as a "doubly fictive space (in the mode of an image-within-an-image)" (2012b: 23). I would argue that Flannery O'Connor's ideas about the tension between the grotesque and realism are echoed in Bednarski's observation that "the important feature of the grotesque is that, underscoring the deformed, the freakish and the bizarre, it makes literature non-mimetic. The reality penetrated by the grotesque is no longer analogous to photographic representation" (2012b: 36) – an assessment that once more underlines my argument that Griffiths's grotesque poetics is a means to denaturalise cultural essentialism and identity positions at the intersection of race and class. This stance as well as the intercultural references to McCarthy's Southern Gothic are even more condensed in his second novel, *Sheepshagger.*

III.2 *Sheepshagger*

Postcolonial Monstrosity

The novel starts with what could best be described as a "dramatic script" (Scott 2009: 199) reproducing a conversation between four young men – Marc, Griff, Danny and Llŷr – recounting their experiences with their former friend Ianto. Since there is no narratorial interference, it is at times hard to identify who is speaking, and the reader only occasionally learns the identity of the speakers when they address each other directly by name. This technique is conspicuous since it is the only level in the novel that is not explicitly marked by narratorial interferences, whereas the two other levels, chronologically taking place before the friends' conversation, are clearly presented by heterodiegetic narrators. Bednarski provides a thorough and helpful examination of the novel's narrative levels and the temporal axis they run on (see 2012b: 62–67). To simplify matters, I will here take up his definitions of the three levels and narrators as level/narrator A (the conversation between the friends), level/narrator B (the passages reporting events from Ianto's adult life and his death) and level/narrator C (the passages in italics reporting Ianto's childhood memories).

The purpose of the friends' conversation, as it turns out, is to make sense of Ianto's horrible actions that are reported on level B, namely the killing of several English tourists and the abuse of their dead bodies. Throughout the dialogue, the speakers make reference to the social and political context that some of them hold responsible for Ianto's development. While some of them are convinced that Ianto resembles something of a "demon" ("Hell of a boy's right, aye. Straight from-a fuckin place he was if yew ask me, like"), others object by arguing that the circumstances of his upbringing have formed him: "He wasn't put yer on this earth fully as a murderer [...]. I reckon Ianto's childhood would've turned Mother fuckin Teresa into a murderer, mun" (*Sh* 1). However, this is countered by Griff's argument that Ianto's childhood was nothing unusual during the Thatcher years, which, however, did not result in more violence: "That's bollax. Hundreds, no, fuckin *millions*-a people have a shitey upbringing and they don't turn into killers, do they? [...]. Jesus, if that was the case yerd be murderers all-a fuckin time, mun, all over these fuckin islands. Left, right and bastard centre" (*Sh* 1). In addition, Marc argues: "Griff's right, mun. Under fuckin Thatcher? Major? The poverty, the repossessions?

All that shite? New fuckin Labour's no bastard better, either. So, fuck, by yewer reasoning, Danny, we'd all be fuckin murderers. Awful fuckin lot uv shitey upbringings in-a past couple-a decades, mun" (*Sh* 1).

Despite the disagreements between the friends, it becomes clear that Ianto and the events he set in motion can to some degree be related to the political issues affecting Welsh culture during the 1980s and 1990s, with Thatcher once again looming large as an influential figure and a haunting historical presence. As is the case with Welsh's novels, *Sheepshagger* can be read as a text dealing with the aftermath of Thatcherism, and Griffiths's characters express the same pessimism about the succeeding governments that is implied in Welsh's later novels, particularly *Filth*. At the same time, the discussion between the friends (who, as it turns out later on in the novel, are responsible for lynching Ianto after they discover his victims' bodies, which compromises their status as reliable and 'upright' moral figures) clearly leaves open the interpretation of Ianto's actions as symptomatic of a social and political climate. However, his actions are considered too extreme, too deviant, to be readable in terms of a clearly defined meaning, as I will show in the concluding part of my analysis.[23]

Thus, Ianto can be understood as a monster in the Foucauldian sense: "The monster is the limit, both the point at which law is overturned and the exception that is found only in extreme cases. The monster combines the impossible and the forbidden" (Foucault 2003: 56). As I will show in this chapter, this monstrosity can be applied to several aspects concerning Ianto's racial, social and legal status. As far as the conversation between the friends is concerned, it becomes clear on the very first pages of the novel that Ianto is to them semantically and morally a monster in that they can hardly make sense of him and his actions: he is to them a "Fuckin enigma. Mystery, like" (*Sh* 29) and a "closed book" (*Sh* 30). Within the cultural and political context evoked by them, then, Ianto must likewise be regarded as a monstrous return of the past in the present. As Jeffrey Jerome Cohen states:

> The monster is that uncertain cultural body in which is condensed an intriguing simultaneity or doubleness: like the ghost of Hamlet, it introjects the disturbing,

---

23 | The characters' search for 'meaning' and reason behind Ianto's actions and their attempt to read him as a symbol echoes the interpretive struggles of *Grits*'s narrators.

repressed, but formative traumas of 'pre-'into the sensory moment of 'post-,' binding the one irrevocably to the other. The monster commands, 'Remember me': restore my fragmented body, piece me back together, allow the past its eternal return. The monster *haunts*; it does not simply bring past and present together, but destroys that boundary that demanded their twinned foreclosure. (1996a: ix–x; emphasis in orig.)

The conversation that runs as a thread through the novel can symbolically be interpreted as a restoration of the fragmented body posed by Ianto, and in that, the friends try to come to terms not only with the challenge that is posed by Ianto's very appearance and being, but also with the social and cultural context posed by their Welsh and, by extension, British home. The "doubleness" that "pre-" and "post-" Ianto represents in *Sheepshagger* can be connected to Michael Gardiner's arguments about the Scottish literary renaissance and its relationship to the haunting aspects of Thatcherism. Ianto can thus be interpreted as a culturally specific sign, in line with Cohen's definition of the monster as the "embodiment of a certain cultural moment":

The monstrous body is pure culture. A construct and a projection, the monster exists only to be read: the *monstrum* is etymologically "that which reveals," "that which warns," a glyph that seeks a hierophant. Like a letter on the page, the monster signifies something other than itself: it is always a displacement, always inhabits the gap between the time of upheaval that created it and the moment into which it is received [...]. (1996b: 4)

While the friends try to 'read' Ianto as a monstrous sign, the reader is likewise faced with the challenge of making sense of what is conveyed about Ianto; up until the climax on narrative levels B and C, the reader can only guess what happened. However, the discourses of narrators B and C, concerned with Ianto's adolescent and adult life respectively, regularly give hints as to the nature of the climactic events as well as at the nature of his childhood traumas that may have affected his mental and behavioural development. Thus, in the first chapter devoted to level B (*Sh* 14–27), Ianto is described by the narrator with a proleptic reference to how he has been presented by the media after his crimes:

Nondescript Ianto, remarkable only in the prominence of his ears and upper front teeth; average height, underweight, nothing like the grotesque troll the newspa-

> pers will later depict him as, no similarity with the hulking hirsute beast image that the collective fears and neuroses will be fed. They will dig up an old mugshot of him taken after a pub brawl and that is how he will be apprehended in the public imagination, huge and bruised and bulging with blood. Scruffy skinny spotty Ianto, tiny in this vastness. (*Sh* 15)

This passage alludes to the dimension that Ianto's case will assume; he and his crimes will not merely be registered as regrettable, yet singular events, but apparently gain significance on a much broader scale. Ianto seems to posthumously become a public figure, an icon, and hence a monstrous sign all of its own, possibly precisely because of the singular nature of his crimes. This also means that his case is publicly open to interpretations within a broader cultural context and develops a semantic dynamics of its own in the collective cultural imagination, hence becoming an example for Cohen's thesis that the monster, as a surface for collective projections, is "pure culture". Given that Ianto's victims were English and that his appearance echoes stereotypes of rural Welshness, he can more precisely be considered as a monstrous manifestation of aspects of Welshness within the Welsh and, more so, the British and English imagination. The novel's vagueness in this regard actually contributes to the enigmatic quality that Ianto possesses for the characters and for the reader, and thus highlights his semantic monstrosity and its haunting aspects.

Although the narrator contrasts the description of Ianto's actual physical appearance with the "grotesque" image that is conveyed of him by the news media later on, Ianto nevertheless appears to be a conspicuous sight. His physique is obviously slightly out of proportion, with the "prominence of his ears and upper front teeth", and resembles a simianised figure – an impression that is supported by later descriptions of him by narrator B as resembling "a hillbilly caricature" (*Sh* 35), situating Ianto's physical appearance among common descriptions of degenerate Southern white trash. Similar descriptions evoking the context of the backward American South can be found in the scenes describing encounters with English holidaymakers.

The novel's title, *Sheepshagger*, is one of the common insults yelled at the Welsh protagonists during rows and conflicts (*Sh* 19, 232), alluding to the inhabitants' rural backwardness and their moral and sexual deviance. Given that the narrator even describes Ianto's friend Llŷr as having "full almost African lips" (*Sh* 20), the novel could be said to consciously play with the biologist stereotypes associated with the Welsh and, according to Kirsti Bohata, reproduced in a range of literary texts published at the end of the nineteenth century. Among others, she demonstrates how the notion of ancient races, alluded to as non-white and primitive, informs the gothic fiction of Arthur Machen who in his short story "The Novel of the Black Seal" (1895) depicts a Welsh hybrid child with "sallow skin" and "of another race" (qtd. in Bohata 2004: 32).[24] As Bohata points out in her examination of representations of Welsh alterity, "in Welsh writing in English the colonial status of Wales as peripheral nation within the United Kingdom is reflected in the way the Welsh are themselves often cast in the role of the racial other" (2004: 58). In that respect, the allusions to non-whiteness in Griffiths's text can be said to echo and complicate a tradition of representations in Welsh writing in English. *Sheepshagger* thus transfers a common set of literary significations of race known from texts that are at least a one hundred years old into the literary and cultural present, thereby suggesting that traces of these conceptions are still a part of the British cultural imagination. In the same manner, these allusions also hint at the common descriptions of the Irish as resembling Africans (see chapter I). Since the novel's setting, the town Aberystwyth and its surrounding rural areas, located on the west coast of Wales and bordering the Irish Sea, has historically seen an influx of Irish immigrants, it is not unlikely that this context is implied here.[25] Thus, the sphere of racist stereotypes dominant on the British and Irish archipelago can be said to inform the symbolism of Griffiths's novel.

It is also notable that these peculiar descriptions of Ianto and Llŷr's faces by the narrator occur around and during a central episode of conflict between the two Welshmen and a group of English holidaymakers. Within the context of this conflict, which assumes a political and national dimension, the emphasis on the two mens' faces becomes significant as a marker of physical deviance and even monstrosity. The episode (*Sh* 14–21) takes place on level B and describes a day in Ianto's adult life during which

24 | Bohata, like Anne McClintock (1995) for the working class and the poor during Victorianism and John Brannigan (2009) for the Irish, points out the centrality of new ideas of anthropology and phrenology for racialising constructions of the Welsh as a British Other during that time (2004: 29-30).

25 | After all, the relation between Aberystwyth and Ireland is also explored through the character Liam in *Grits*.

he and his friend climb up a hill in the countryside where Ianto grew up. As it turns out, his old homestead, a cottage, has been taken up as a weekend residence by an English family, most likely the result of the infamous repossessions that took place during the 1980s under Thatcher and that were alluded to on the novel's initial pages. The narrator situates the mens' bodies within the landscape so that the importance of the relation between man and land is indicated:

This vast land they climb, its peaks and its plains like furniture designed by and for some titanic race was wind-stripped and rain-flayed of anything soft and yielding aeons earlier under a low rising sun. There is nothing of any comfort here [...]. Ordovician country, named after the dark squat tribes it once sustained. [...]. You must dirty your knees and knuckles to let this land lift you up. (*Sh* 14-15)

The novel's extensive descriptions of the Welsh landscape characterise the country as inscribed with ancient history and shaped by inhospitable conditions, through the often almost lyrically stylised descriptions, assumes a sublime and humbling quality that seemingly contrasts with the worldly and sometimes almost banal goings-on.

Griffiths's descriptions of the Welsh landscape, much like his allusions to the discourse of race, echoes those employed in older Welsh fiction. In her analysis of "The Novel of the Black Seal", Bohata examines Machen's description of the Welsh countryside and concludes that "Machen uses the Welsh landscape [...] to evoke images of a mystical borderland between the contemporary world of Victorian rationality and scientific investigation and the dark, sinister realm of an atavistic, supernatural past. The descriptions of the surrounding countryside are central to the creation of a suitably oppressive, ominous and mysterious atmosphere, and this area of Wales is represented in terms reminiscent not just of gothic literature but of colonial texts, which produce the otherness of foreign landscapes and peoples: the hills are repeatedly referred to as 'wild' and 'savage'; rocks are of 'fantastic form'" (2004: 31).

The allusions to ancient races and "dark" tribes and the organic quality of the landscape, the soil of which is described as "like a reptile's back" (*Sh* 14), not only let the country appear as inscribed with history of which humanity is but one factor, but also implies that the human inhabitants of this country are similarly inscribed with the land and its history. This "repellent and ragged" land in which "upright motion is abhorred"

(*Sh* 14–15) is thus clearly a country which lets humans appear as humble and as surrendered to the land's power. One of the defining anatomic characteristics of humans, upright motion, is denied by the country.[26]

However, the intimidating sublime landscape does not incite humbleness in the English holidaymakers described on the subsequent pages. Blasting Phil Collins, who "sings about another day in paradise" (*Sh* 16), which mockingly contrasts with the description of the hostile land in which the cottage is situated and the living conditions of Ianto, the new inhabitants elicit a "high and happy chatter, accents traceable only to a vague South of England locale, where none seem to have been or go but from where many originate" (*Sh* 16). They own "shiny cars" and wear "expensive sunglasses", "thin bright dresses" and "untucked loud shirts" (*Sh* 16) that contrast Ianto's scruffy appearance and "dirty hair slapping the collar of his brown-checked shirt" (*Sh* 16). The new inhabitants' accents as well as their demeanour are presented as a strong and almost ironic contrast to the sublime landscape surrounding them. Accordingly, Llŷr observes that "Yew'd hardly recognise-a old place now, would yew, eh? Bloody hell. Lost all its fuckin character it has, yew ask me. Looks like a fuckin holiday chalet or something" (*Sh* 16). The house's "fuckin character" arose, as is indicated during the conversation presented on level A, from the natural cycle adhering to which the house was supposedly built: "It was built ages ago when that law was around, y'know that law which said something like if you could have four walls and a roof with a fire going in-a hearth between sunrise and sunset then yew wouldn't have to pay for the land, something like that" (*Sh* 9). Like the people inhabiting the land, Ianto's family home is intricately related to the land to the point where it seems impossible to separate the two.

While this almost essentialist idea of the natural and of ancient races might seem ideologically suspect and problematic at first glance, it quickly becomes clear that the narrator's emphasis on these aspects is part of a more complex hyperbolic poetics that consciously plays with stereotypes on both sides of the imperial conflict between Wales and England, taking

26 | In that respect, the almost atavistic features of the two men's faces might also imply their close relationship to the similarly atavistic geological structures; they are of this land in a deeper sense that is connoted with the idea of an ancient race. The mentioning of "African lips" thus becomes another indicator for the novel's postcolonial character.

up the similar tone apparent in Roger's mocking of English tourists in *Grits*. The description of the verbal quarrel between Ianto and the holidaymakers demonstrates the mutually reinforced auto- and hetero-stereotypes about the Welsh and their racial distinctness (see Williams 2003: 8 qtd. above). As Ianto yells at the English homeowners that "I just want-a stand on the fuckin soil, mun. That's all I want-a do. Fuck all wrong with that, is there, just standin on-a fuckin soil? Fuckin dug in that soil when I was a kiddie I did" (*Sh* 17) and accuses them of "trespassing" on his land (*Sh* 19), the English laugh at the "sheepshaggers": "Run back to your hovels, peasants! Bloody Welshies don't even know how to look after your own country! Should all still be living in caves!" (*Sh* 19) The English in this passage are sketched as stereotypically as the two Welsh men, as Aleksander Bednarski remarks:

> The incident and Ianto's sense of property revealed by it can be seen as a reflection of a set of issues which have been a *cause célèbre* in 20th century Welsh history. What is dramatised in the fragment is [...] the tension between England and Wales. The new inhabitants of the cottage are described as stereotypical upper class English holidaymakers with an imperial attitude to the place they are in and no real connection to it. (Bednarski 2012b: 73-74)

The use of the derogatory term *sheepshagger* and the suggestion that the Welsh should be living in caves take up the notion, implied in the narratorial descriptions preceding the conflict, of the Welsh as an ancient and distinct race living in close relation to nature. Thus, the episode illustrates the reciprocal relationship of the racial stereotypes anchored in the British cultural imagination. The image of the Welsh as peasants devoted to bestiality ("sheepshagging") is part of the stigmatyping of the Welsh within the semantics of this cultural imagination (see Bohata 2004: 52) and bears close resemblance to figurations of the sexually deviant, racially degenerate and backwards American poor white trash in the nineteenth century. This resemblance is also emphasised via the aforementioned description of Ianto as a "hillbilly caricature" by the narrator, while at the same time this notion is transferred into the context of British imperialism, connected to the idea of different and racially distinct British peoples.

British imperialism is alluded to not only through the description of the English holidaymakers as claiming a Welsh boy's ancestral land for their weekend retreat but also through the image of them as being superior in number, as is indicated by Llŷr: "What the fuck did yew go and do *that* for? Near got us both beaten bastard well up yew did, yew soft twat. What-a hell were yew fuckin playin at, mun? Only fuckin two of us, Christ... fuckin loads-a them..." (*Sh* 20). Likewise, Ianto growls at what he perceives as material excess on parts of the English: "Got nowhere to live an that's my fuckin house. Those bastards use it as a second home like for eyr holidays an I haven't even got *one*" (*Sh* 20). As I pointed out earlier, Ianto seems to have an almost symbiotic relationship with his land. Here, the English "occupation" of his home must be read as physical abuse affecting his very bodily structures. This becomes clearer when analepsis on narrative level C (*Sh* 227–237) finally reveals the childhood trauma that severely affected Ianto's mental development and left his body mutilated.

When he is ten years old, Ianto is sexually abused by an English hiker, once again presented as an embodiment of "stereotypically imperial Englishness" (Bednarski 2012b: 70) who is carrying an "Ordnance Survey map" as well as the *Pocket Guide to Celtic Britain* (*Sh* 228). As Bednarski remarks, the survey map "may be associated with the attempt of a centralised imperial power to, through mapping, control and extend its authority over subjugated territories" (2012b: 70). In the same way, the Englishman's ignorant and dismissive attitude towards young Ianto testifies to his imperial attitude when he inquires about Ianto's family in order to feel out if he is easy prey for him. When Ianto uses the Welsh word "mamcu" for grandmother, the hiker complains: *"What's a bloody 'mamky'? Can you not talk bloody English?* [...]. *Expect every visitor to your little province to know your bloody language, do you?"* (*Sh* 229; italics in orig.). The conflict between the Welsh language, which had been repressed well until the end of the mid-twentieth century and thereby turned into a minority language, and the dominant language of those responsible for this cultural repression here represents the overall cultural conflict between the Welsh and the English, and the language barrier becomes another marker for the perceived cultural and racial inferiority of the Welsh. The hiker blames sexual deviance in the form of incest, another common stereotypical trait not only of the rural Welsh populace but of American "white trash" as well, for Ianto's incapability to properly communicate with him: *"I give up. Stupid. You're all bloody stupid. All that inbreeding has rotted your brains"* (*Sh* 230; italics in orig.). Thus, the (in)ability to speak is here intricately linked to its physical and cognitive preconditions. As I will show later by referring back to the conflict between Ianto and the holidaymakers, speaking is thus linked to matters of bodily inscriptions of cultural belonging and social and racial minority status in *Sheepshagger* – an aspect that is comparable to similar issues concerning language and speaking in the work of Irvine Welsh.

During the traumatic confrontation with the hiker, Ianto's body is occupied in a very corporeal sense and in a symbolic sense. When the man starts to touch the young boy, Ianto experiences this not only as the break-down of personal bodily barriers but also as an act with implications going beyond the personal:

He doesn't want this man here. He wishes he would go away. He feels as if he has done something terribly wrong and this man has been sent to punish him, but he does not know what it is. The man's fingers on his chin feel rough and foreign and intrusive, yet intrusive with some strong rights of trespass, some ineffable legal backing. (*Sh* 229; italics in orig.)

Ianto's abuse, as suggested by the narrative voice, is a symbolic expression of broader cultural issues and is more or less consciously experienced as such by Ianto whose later actions against English tourists, as is inferred in this causal construction, are informed by this experience. This contextualisation is continued when the English paedophile forces Ianto to fellate him, calling him a *"filthy little Welsh SLUT"* (*Sh* 233; italics in orig.).[27] The ultimate physical marking is accomplished by the hiker when he in turn forcefully fellates Ianto and mutilates his penis, biting into his urethra (*Sh* 234). As a consequence, Ianto, who must have spent several months hospitalised afterwards, has suffered impairment of his ability to speak:

All he will do is lie in this hospital bed and say not one word and let them do to him what they seem to feel must be done [...]. [...], he hears others talk, of 'wounds con-

27 | Of course, the feminisation of Ianto is noteworthy here, and recalls the construction of Welsh women by the English as particular examples of the Welsh's racial degeneracy during the nineteenth century that, according to Kirsti Bohata, bears similarities with the construction of black women at the same time. In a manner similar to Anne McClintock's analyses in *Imperial Leather*, Bohata states that "the ostensibly unrelated discourses of race and sexuality inform and influence each other" and that the "recognition of the interrelation of such discourses in our re-reading of 'white' texts has been one of the most significant contributions of postcolonial studies" (2004: 37).

sistent with human dentition' and 'psychoneurotic aphemia' and 'motor aphasia' and 'possible brain damage' and 'tremendous shock-trauma'. Words from an alien dialect descriptive of him and of the fever and greed of human need and all its extended fallout. (*Sh* 237)

Ianto's body, and consequently his physical and behavioural monstrosity as perceived by others, can be read as inscribed with what Deleuze and Guattari have called the "territorial signs that plant their flags in bodies" (Deleuze and Guattari 2009: 145). Literally marked by the English tourist-trespasser, his body once again resembles the land he originates from in that he too has been inscribed with the hegemonic power and has been territorialised by it. Ianto's later violent crimes are precipitated by this territorialisation and inscription of his body. Consequently, Ianto becomes the monster that he is later perceived to be as the result of the symbolic desecration of his body and land by the English. This development also fuels his transformation into a being that the narrator as well as the friends conversing on level A refer to as something transgressing the physical bounds of the human. Watching a spider waiting for its prey at his hospital bed, the desire for revenge manifests within him:

Not once does he see it feed but his recovery is hastened by the spider itself, its patience, the annihilation imminent in its soft thorax throbbing and spread suspended legs. This insect [sic] is restorative, its hunger in his healing. And he will wait like the spider for whatever the wind will bring. For however long it takes. He will wait like the spider unaccompanied except by an urge for murder for whatever the wind will bring to him, and for however long it takes. The burning in his middle. (*Sh* 237; italics in orig.)

Ianto, as a hybrid figure that blurs the border between human and animal as well as human and natural environment, thus represents not only a monstrous and haunting return of Wales's colonial past, but also a case of a monstrous blurring of bodily boundaries that, among others, is central to many figurations of tainted whiteness. Likewise, Ianto's impaired ability to speak and properly (or, rather: conventionally) communicate is a challenge to the way interpersonal interactions bridge the liminality of the (human) body and the world. In drawing on Harri Garrod Roberts's analysis of the grotesque in Welsh fiction and in comparing Ianto to similarly blurred bodily boundaries in Irvine Welsh's fiction, I will demonstrate further aspects of the kind of postcolonial tainted whiteness presented in *Sheepshagger* before focusing on the intertextual relations to Cormac McCarthy's Southern Gothic novel *Child of God* (1973).

Hybrid Bodies

Like other figurations of tainted whiteness, Ianto is an embodiment of paradoxes. The central paradox defining him is his perceived inability to properly connect with the world and with other people around him on the one hand, and the obvious lack of boundaries between himself and the world on the other. Interestingly enough, although the novel suggests that Ianto's image as a monstrous figure is produced by the media, his status as a self-contained and autonomous, clearly defined subject is put into question by the many approaches to characterisation provided by the novel. While his former companions (and later murderers) during their conversation at times emphasise his demonic or monstrous status, they nonetheless have to come to terms with the fact that they tolerated his presence among them for a long time, with some of them even having considering him a friend. As their initial conversation shows, they are at pains to fully grasp Ianto's being. Despite their tolerance for such a wretched and outcast human being in the past, they must face the fact that they never fathomed him in the first place, concluding that he remains an "enigma" to them. In a way, it seems that Ianto only gains a status as a "full" subject in the subsequent construction of him as a monstrous symbol that semantically hints at something more profound beyond the mere fact of his socially incompatible existence. Ianto's enigmatic quality, as indicated above, can be described with Cohen's definition of the monster and its "uncertain cultural body" that presents itself as a "doubleness" (that is, a paradox). Three aspects of the novel's characterisation are central to this uncertainty and doubleness: the lack of boundaries between Ianto and the surrounding landscape and nature, which blurs his status as human; his relation to dirt; and his inability to communicate.

The first aspect is already evident in the friends' conversation when they wonder about Ianto's asocial behaviour:

out of every given month, Ianto would on average spend two weeks in-a town like, y'know in society, with people. Two weeks. That's half his whole fuckin life. Anny

> other half spent wanderin over-a mountains or doin what ee did. Fuck knows what he used to do. Should've been born a fuckin fox, ee should uv. (*Sh* 54)

Ianto's asocial behaviour is linked by his friends not only with his later crimes and his deranged character but also with his close affinity, or symbiotic relationship with, nature. It is thus implied that he is not entirely of the human world, an aspect that has repercussions for the racial construction of Ianto as a paradigmatic and symbolically overdetermined Welsh outsider figure. In addition to his friends' musings, the narrators on levels B and C stress Ianto's relation to nature and particularly the animal world. In one passage, Ianto defecates in the woods, making the act of excretion appear like an atavistic ritual: "He places the old skull and a chunk of rotten wood over his steaming dark coils, burying his spoors as an animal would, covering his tracks and individual stench as a wild animal would" (*Sh* 39). Ianto becomes one with nature through the act of defecation. As Harri Garrod Roberts makes clear in his interpretation of *Grits*, scatology and the grotesque body are of central importance for Griffiths's poetics, and *Sheepshagger* is no exception, as it extends his exploration of the conflict zone between bodily contours and the space outside them.

In another passage similar to Ianto's defecation, Ianto masturbates on a public toilet in Aberystwyth after looking at some porn magazines at a newsstand. He

> wanks into the open bowl [...] his semen plops onto the shit-smeared porcelain and into the oval of water reflecting his loosened face and he imagines his sperm balled in tresses of auburn hair quivering and blue-tinged like the clutch of some mythical bird. [...] the droplets of sperm on his fingers stick to his skin like scum [...]. (*Sh* 43–44)

The mingling of faeces and sperm represents the convergence of decay and renewal, and, like the distorting reflection of his loosened face, becomes a further instance of bodily disintegration. Furthermore, not only are semen and faeces mixed in the act of ejaculation; semen itself assumes the quality of dirty excretion when it is likened to "scum".

This realisation of a Bakhtinian poetics, turning corporeal orders inside out and thereby challenging cultural orders that demand a closed bodily surface, resembles similar strategies in the novels of Irvine Welsh, most notably Mark Renton's lustful engagement with bodily fluids and excrements in *Trainspotting*, most poignantly realised in his rebellious and almost ritualistic attempt at anal sex during his brother's funeral with his brother's pregnant widow. Here, the sexual act, with the narrator's foregrounding of the stench of male and female smegma and his assumption that it must have to do with his family's ancestral Glaswegian background (the "soapdodging white trash"), becomes a Bakhtinian ritual of revolt which also plays with the racialisation of the Scottish population. In a comparable way, the body of DS Bruce Robertson in *Filth* turns inside out in many ways, making it impossible to define his identity through the markers of his skin: the novel strategically undermines the cultural codedness of the human skin as an identity marker by literally letting Robertson's skin disintegrate in the form of eczema and letting him assume different identities by symbolically slipping into someone else's skin during his cross-dressing phases. And ultimately, his tapeworm can be said to wear his body as a skin, making it hard to identify Robertson as a corporeally embodied and confined subject.[28]

The same kind of disintegration of bodily surfaces is evident in Ianto, who at some point is described as "a bedraggled mountain man dragging himself up towards the heavens on fingers ripped and bleeding soaked to the cold bone and caked from the knees down in mud like some peculiar centaur, some horrid hybrid of flesh and filth" (*Sh* 196). The "hybridisation" of flesh and filth makes the one indistinguishable from the other and thus, like the comparable disintegrations in Welsh's texts, reflects not only a tainting of the character's racial identity but similarly precipitates what Judith Butler calls the "production of bodily contours" (2011: xxv; see chapter II.3). To take the Butlerian reading of Ianto further, one could say that the ultimate task of his literary construction is to challenge the very idea of a confined corporeal materiality of the human subject. After all, Ianto seems to be less of a human subject and more like a conglomeration of filthy matter. As is the case with Bruce Robertson in *Filth*, it is suggested that Ianto is not only symbolically representing filth, but rather has literally become filth.

The narrator's language on levels B and C, evoking this transgressive and at times contourless monstrous body, is complicit with this mon-

28 | In addition, the tapeworm, inhabiting Bruce's intestines, draws attention to what is supposed to be concealed by the human body's smooth surface – i.e., processes of digestion, defecation, etc.

strosity in that it refuses to provide the reader with concrete information that would illuminate the enigmatic entity Ianto becomes in the friends' conversation at level A. Thus, although political context in the form of the Welsh move towards increased governmental independence and the evocation of Wales's colonial past is clearly a backdrop for what is going on in the narrative, and although Ianto is affected by these political processes in a very personal way, he still remains highly enigmatic until the end due to his corporeally unconfined, hybrid quality. This hybridity is also evident in the constant flow that Ianto's body seems to be in. His body merges with the landscape surrounding him, or with animals when he becomes the "Iantolamb" (*Sh* 5), while as a child he tries to help a lamb whose eyes have been hacked out by crows by putting stones into its gory eye sockets – "The lamb cries and cries again, the dark and bubbling holes in its face expanding into howling voids which begin to draw little Ianto in" (*Sh* 5). With this hybridity, the figure of Ianto corresponds to Bakhtin's description of the grotesque body as a being that blurs the boundaries between "plant, animal and human forms" (1968: 32) and challenges the dichotomy between wildnerness and the city as well as between the primitive and civilisation.[29]

This is suggested when Ianto, after having returned from the wilderness to claim benefits at the Job Centre in Aberystwyth and being confronted with the disgusted reactions at the centre, goes to the beach to wash after days without a bath. The episode is constructed as Ianto's passage from the wilderness with which he seems to exist in a kind of symbiosis into the estranging experience of town life, representing what the narrator calls "officialdom": "how it unsettles him; the irrefragable opprobrium, the irrepressible disapproval" (*Sh* 46). The representatives of this "officialdom", for the homeless Ianto a necessity to be dealt with, meet his grimy appearance with disgust: "The person directly in front of Ianto turns nose-wrinkled to scowl his way, probably at the smell of him, and Ianto just returns his stare and the man turns away again" (*Sh* 45). Similar reactions coded by the structures of social abjection are visible in the clerk handling his matters at the centre: "He can see the bridge of her nose crinkle as his stink reaches her and can almost hear her thinking:

29 | Jon Anderson offers a reading of Griffiths's fiction as "non-anthropocentric, or ecocentric" (2014: 165); see also Anderson 2014: 168–176 for a reading of the hinterland and the wilderness in Griffiths's *Grits* and *Sheepshagger*.

Good Christ, he reeks. He does" (*Sh* 46). After having accomplished his encounter with "officialdom" successfully and having been treated by the clerk in a condescending manner, Ianto goes to the beach to wait for his benefit cheque, and he becomes aware of his own uncleanliness: "his own smell rises to his nostrils" (*Sh* 48). Thus, "he strips to his scrawny white nakedness, a greasy black band belting his waist", (*Sh* 48) and takes a bath in the sea, emerging with "a new-feeling-body to live in and that will surely do" (*Sh* 49).

Taking place after the degrading experience at the Job Centre, the bathing scene gives the impression of a cleansing ritual that regenerates Ianto's body after several pages of what can be described as a literary celebration of his grotesque and unclean body (with particular emphasis on the semantics and symbolism of "black" and "white" when his "white" skin is described as being encrusted with dirt which is so thick and persistent that it forms a "greasy black band"), marauding from the Welsh wilderness (Ianto's sphere and place of origin) into the town centre (the sphere of social sanctioning and his 'domestication'), spilling and mixing body fluids (the masturbation scene takes place immediately before Ianto enters the centre) and offending the townspeople with his stench. While in the wilderness, his uncleanliness makes him become one with his surroundings, turning him into more of an animal, the filth covering his body takes on a different meaning as soon as he enters town. Here, he is immediately perceived as an outsider who does not fit society's sanitary norms – a digression that becomes all the more significant due to his status as a member of the lower classes, dispossessed, homeless (or of "no fixed abode", as he is registered at the Job Centre [*Sh* 46]) and unemployed. In addition, his mental impairment, or, rather, his impaired ability to "conventionally" communicate particularly within official contexts, single him out as other. This becomes apparent in the dialogue between him and the Job Centre clerk who is described as "the black-bobbed battleaxe" (*Sh* 46). Having told her he is of no fixed abode but is staying at a friend's where he has left a form required for claiming benefits, he is condescendingly reprimanded by the clerk who tells him it "might be a good idea" to tell his friend to give him a set of keys to the shared flat (*Sh* 46).

Ianto is dealt with as one would with an unruly child, and although he gets what he needs, i.e., a benefit cheque, the humiliating treatment at the centre reasserts his status as a borderline figure in several ways. Thus, getting rid of the dirt encrusted on his body as a kind of tainting second skin, Ianto temporarily ensures, at least to some degree, that he can for a short time pass in civilised society with his "new-feeling body to live in" (*Sh* 49). In line with Deleuze and Guattari's idea of faciality that assumes faces not to be an individual physiological property marking off an individual per se but rather something that one slides into, Ianto's body is described as something that allows or hinders passing as "normal" in certain socially determined situations. In suggesting that Ianto's (or anybody else's for that matter) body is not strictly confined to itself, but is open to the world rather than closed, in a manner best described with the openness of the Bakhtinian body, the stable workings of the system of faciality that designates racial and class statuses is unhinged, and the confines of the body are exploded.

The aforementioned masturbation scene where Ianto sees the blurred reflection of his face in a mixture of watered excrements is symptomatic of this unhinging. Here, the signifier (the reflected image on the water's surface) for his face becomes unstable, representing the actual instability of his body and showing the "horror story", as Deleuze and Guattari call it (see chapter I), of the human face. To Ianto, the body ultimately represents as much of an enigma as he himself is to other people in the novel. When he tries to give eyes to the eye sockets of the attacked lamb, he significantly does so because, as we are told, he wants "to put something where there is nothing, to bring substance upon emptiness" (*Sh* 5).[30] In a certain way, albeit to different ends, his killing sprees serve the same purpose. Murdering someone is in this case not only a random act of revenge against the English that caused him harm. When Ianto kills the English hiking couple, who function as caricatures of pretentious bourgeois post-hippies eager to "feel" the "ancient power" of the site of the massacring of English troops by Owain Glyndŵr (*Sh* 202), he

> is shocked at the facility with which the man's physiognomy disintegrates, the eyes leaving their orbits in twin geysers of ichor and plopping into the mud to squint cross-eye upwards and the whole cranium shifting the rippling movement beneath

30 | Bednarski also describes the hybrid "Iantolamb" and the blurred borders between the two as a Bakhtinian feature (2012b: 80–81). In the same vein, Martyn Colebrook (2016) interprets Ianto as a "chimera" (34) that exists in the "grey area between human and animal" (35) and represents "a skeletal form wearing the history of a nation" (38).

> the clotted hair and beard and the skull abruptly collapsing flat on one side and that ear bubbling pink porridge and the lower jaw sliding prognathously out and up and over the nose, which itself sinks or is sucked back into the imploding face, all this in a small red maelstrom. (*Sh* 206)

The description of these acts of violence, which Aleksander Bednarski describes as a "grotesquely exaggerated and theatricalised" (2012b: 89) restaging of history where the killing of the English hikers mirrors the massacring of the English by Owain Glyndŵr in the year 1401 at the same place (*Sh* 89), stylistically resembles the descriptions of the Welsh landscape that can be found throughout the novel in their almost lyrical manner that blends the depiction of the dramatic act and the undoing of the human body with vocabulary that evokes both descriptions of natural phenomena ("maelstrom", "geyser") and medical and scientific language ("prognathiously", "ichor"). However, the choice of words and the "hyperbolic character" achieved through the description's "hyperrealism" (Bednarski 2012b: 89) also serve a comic effect. Once again, it is the human face that is at the centre of this spectacle of bodily disintegration. Within the context of an interpretation focusing on the aspects of postcolonialism and race, this disintegration of the English hiker's face can be read as the unmaking of the normative English face as a site of racial and social inscription. Of course, the very act of violence itself is a drastic and all too literal form of inscription through the colonised subject as well. Viewed in this light, one of the novel's primary poetic devices to realise its postcolonial project is the systematic literary examination of the human body as a site of inscription for such traits as race, social position and national identity (including all its connotations like "blood", "origin", "home[land]" or "soil") and its simultaneous disintegration or explosion by means of the literary grotesque. Thus, with Bednarski I contend that Ianto can be read in "allegorical terms as an emanation of Wales" that, through the animalistic features emphasised in the narrative, simultaneously recalls and subverts racial stereotypes:

> Associating Ianto with a predatory animal inescapably brings about the modes of representing the colonial other, frequently imbued with atavistic, hybrid or animalistic features. Instead of a stereotypical, imperial projection, however, the portrayal of Ianto seems to suggest a rather *post*-colonial strategy where the stereotypical image is internalised and used *against* the oppressor. (2012b: 79)

In that regard, it is important to bear in mind that not only Ianto is described as a "hillbilly caricature" but that likewise most of the representatives of the 'colonising' power of England are ostentatiously designed as caricatures throughout the novel, be it as nasty rapists who feminise and victimise the Welsh, as yuppie-like and snobbish holidaymakers or as ridiculous esoteric weekend hippies who indulge in the perceived exoticism of Welsh myth and history.

To fully grasp how Ianto works as a "hillbilly caricature" (*Sh* 35) and consequently not only as an emanation of a colonial Wales but also as a representation of white trash, it is necessary to regard its American intertext, McCarthy's *Child of God*, as a blueprint for the use of racial boundary figures and stigmatypes in the tradition of the Southern Gothic. Taking up the notion of "hyperrealism" proposed by Bednarski's interpretation of the grotesque violence in *Sheepshagger*, I will conclude the analysis of Griffiths's novel by focusing on similar poetic strategies in McCarthy's novel and how they in turn inform Griffiths's Anglo-Welsh text by drawing on Kenneth Lincoln's suggestion to read McCarthy's fiction as "hyperreal" "gothic distortion" (*Sh* 21).

Transatlantic Southern Gothic: Niall Griffiths and Cormac McCarthy

For readers who happen to be familiar with McCarthy's *Child of God*, it is hard to ignore the many nods towards McCarthy's early novel ranging from motifs and structural elements to whole passages apparently designed as homage to the older text. For a reading of *Sheepshagger* as a novel that not only treats a postcolonial conception of Wales in the wake of its political devolution at the end of the twentieth century but also negotiates corresponding notions of race and class, it is important to look at *Child of God* as a central intertext. As I have shown throughout this chapter, *Sheepshagger* draws on several Welsh and Anglo-Welsh intertexts and can be regarded as a contemporary take on a particularly late-nineteenth-century gothic concept of Wales and the Welsh as a distinct race. Similarly, *Sheepshagger* can be read, as Aleksander Bednarski has done (2012b), as a "theatricalisation" of Welsh culture by drawing on Welsh and Celtic mythology as important intertexts. All these intertexts serve to construct the main protagonist as an "emanation of Wales".

Sticking to the terminology used in this study, one might substitute the term *emanation* with *figuration*: to recall Imogen Tyler's definition of figuration, Ianto can be described as a distorted and caricatured condensation of aspects of Welshness, and ultimately represents a paradox. While, for example, heritage, ancestry, soil and landownership represent a "natural" given, these aspects assume an altogether different quality when viewed by the English holidaymakers or even by his friends and later murderers. Here, the version of Welsh identity embodied by Ianto becomes an image of backwardness and primitivity that is expressed in stigmatypes like the incestuous "bloody Welshies" or the bestial "sheepshaggers". In that respect, Ianto is a prime example of the way processes of figuration produce ultimately ambivalent meanings in which certain traits intersectionally define each other. And while, as I have argued above, the aspect of whiteness is not as pronounced in *Sheepshagger* as it may be in other texts, the aspect of race nevertheless looms large as a central and defining characteristic implicated in the issues of Welshness depicted in the novel. Aspects of race are evoked in the frequent and exaggerated, distorted descriptions of Ianto's (and some of his Welsh lower class friends') physique in the tradition of the grotesque and gothic.

The two latter aspects are also the stylistic and poetic element that connects Griffiths's novel not only with the British and Welsh tradition of (among others) Arthur Machen's gothic, but also transnationally with the American tradition of the Southern Gothic. While descriptions of Ianto as a "woodland imp" or "hobgoblin" situate him within the imagery of Welsh folklore, descriptions like "hillbilly caricature" explicitly connect Ianto to well-known figurations of the backward American South. Once again, it is particularly in the appellations through obnoxious English tourists that these American stereotypes come into play. One of Ianto's murder victims, a teenage hiker, provokes the attack by saying about Ianto: "You're a local. [...]. Something weird about you sheepshaggers. I'm tellin yer. Fuckin banjo-players round here" (*Sh* 87). As noted above, the ascription of being "local" assumes negative qualities in this appellation that, in the insult "sheepshagger" once more becomes an instance of anti-Welsh (and anti-rural) hate speech, while for Ianto, to be of this place and of this land is part and parcel of his identity construction and self-perception. Apart from that, however, the term *banjo-player* alludes to one of the best-known figurations of white trash degeneracy in contemporary popular culture: the iconic "banjo duel" scene in John Boorman's film adaptation of James

Dickey's 1970 novel *Deliverance* (1972).[31] In this scene, one of the main protagonists, a middle-class family man going on a river rafting tour in rural Georgia, "duels" a local mentally challenged (and, as is suggested, inbred) boy in a spontaneous jam session. It turns out that the "inbred" boy is an outstanding banjo playing talent, and the two seem to have a moment of mutual understanding through their music just before the middle-class men fall prey to the local gang of rapist hillbillies. Evidently, Ianto's teenage victim is drawing from a cultural imagery of racial stigmatypes available transnationally through the film (and novel) *Deliverance.* A similar strategy is employed in the use of *Sheepshagger*'s most important intertext, *Child of God.*

By comparing the two novels, I will show how Griffiths's use of McCarthy's Southern Gothic serves two central tasks. First, the cultural, social and political situation of contemporary Wales is mirrored in the context of McCarthy's novel, the American South during a stage of transformation from the pastoral, premodern republic into a class-based capitalist society of progress, as I will demonstrate by close-reading two corresponding scenes in the two novels with reference to Deleuze and Guattari's analysis of capitalist inscriptions in *Anti-Oedipus.* Secondly, the subtext of race and the mapping of class identity through race in *Sheepshagger* is pronounced by constructing Ianto as a mirror image of the hillbilly Lester Ballard in *Child of God,* who himself is seen in the novel through the distorting and exaggerating lens of Southern Gothic's grotesque imagery that plays out

31 | The boy's observation of local people's "weirdness" also resembles a similar observation by the narrator in James Dickey's *Deliverance*: "There is always something wrong with people in the country, I thought. In the comparatively few times I had ever been in the rural South I had been struck by the number of missing fingers. [...]. There had also been several people with some form of crippling or twisting illness, and some blind or one-eyed. [...] You'd think that farming was a healthy life, with fresh air and fresh food and plenty of exercise, but I never saw a farmer who didn't have something wrong with him [...]" (*D* 48). Yet, even the narrator of this 1970 novel is aware of the pre-existing stigmatypes attached to images of Southern folks and their transmedia circulation, as is evident in this description: "He looked like a hillbilly in some badly cast movie, a character actor too much in character to be believed. [...]; everything in Oree was sleepy and hookwormy and ugly, and most of all, inconsequential. Nobody worth a damn could ever come from such a place" (*D* 47).

as a hyperbole of racial features. In the following, I contend with Lydia R. Cooper, who argues that in McCarthy's early Appalachian novels,

> like other fiction in the American southern gothic genre, these novels combine a horror-drenched and heavily allegorical aesthetic style with historically rooted commentary on social ills, such as issues of race, class, urbanization, and industrialization, to bring into focus repressed social anxieties. [...]. The grotesque, often used to illuminate notions of evil and the abject, transforms ordinary objects into something bizarre – otherworldly, transcendent, demoniac – to reveal the sublimated and the mysterious. [...]. The Appalachian novels employ prominent figurative patterns of the "southern grotesque" in the form of obscene and sometimes comic exaggeration, often of physical deformity or sexual deviance. In these novels, an image is made grotesque to function as a visual catalyst for the apprehension of uncomfortable, perhaps even terrifying, realities. (2013: 41–42)

Kenneth Lincoln argues in the same way in writing that McCarthy achieves a form of "hyperrealism" in his "Gothic distortion" that shows a "reality unnaturally exaggerated" (2009: 21) to the effect that it demonstrates notions of normalcy to be futile: "From the sublime to the grim, deviations from the norm are the norm in human history because there is no controlling norm, only assumptions about middles based on denials of extremes all around us" (2009: 23). This similarly holds true for the depiction of white trash as a monstrously exaggerated, excessive stigmatype – an abnormal form of racial and class identity that produces norms of race and class through difference.

From Pastoral to Capitalism

Griffiths's engagement with McCarthy's *Child of God*, apart from paying homage to another individual literary work and taking up its motifs and modes of representation, can be considered within a broader context of Welsh-Appalachian cultural and literary relations. As Sarah Roberston (2007) has argued in a comparative study of Welsh and Appalachian coal mining and industrial novels, both regions share distinct characteristics:

> both places are othered within wider national discourses, with Appalachia bearing the weight of hillbilly stereotypes and Wales regarded, particularly during the nineteenth and early twentieth centuries, as backward by its English neighbours.

> [...]. The two regions, then, share not only similar industrial heritages but are also perceived as othered spaces within their larger national cultures. (504)

While both are much younger texts than those examined by Robertson, and while neither deals explicitly with the tradition of the mining novels in question, both *Sheepshagger* and *Child of God* can still be considered as texts which take up similar issues and which build on the same awareness for the respective regions' place in the British and American national imaginary, not least in the way the texts reject the idea of the pastoral vision which is commonly associated with the Welsh or Appalachian setting. Thus, while both Griffiths and McCarthy play with the notion of the pastoral, they bring to the fore that which lies underneath the pastoral setting as much as the texts analysed by Sarah Robertson do: "the characters in these novels can never retreat into a completely pastoral setting since the mining industry leaves its mark not only underground but also on the surface. That which the characters seek to escape inevitably returns to haunt them" (2007: 509). The deconstruction of the pastoral in Welsh and Appalachian industrial fictions can, in addition to Griffiths's clear intertextual references to McCarthy, be considered as a further *tertium comparationis* for *Sheepshagger* and *Child of God*. Both novels, while not explicitly dealing with the mining industry, nonetheless deal with the effects of capitalism on rural cultures, which, ultimately, can be linked to issues of race and class.

Like *Sheepshagger, Child of God* takes place in a rural setting, more specifically in Sevier County and the forests and mountains of East Tennessee, and features a deranged and somewhat backward central character who has been dispossessed and expelled from his family home (after his father committed suicide by shooting himself, just like Ianto's grandfather) and subsequently roams the country's woods, "preying on the population with his strange lusts", as the blurb of the Picador edition (1989) fittingly has it. Living isolated in the woods and incapable of communicating and bonding with people, as proven by a few pathetic and comic attempts to the contrary, he succumbs to his necrophilia when he stumbles across a dead couple apparently asphyxiated in their car during intercourse. Having acquired a taste for dead girls' bodies, he, very much like Ianto, turns to killing people in order to not run out of supply. While his literary Welsh successor hides his murder victims in "the disused silver mine where, as a child, he knew a dragon slept" (*Sh* 40), Lester stores his victims in the caves riddling the Appalachian underground (that also serve him as an occasional hideout from the law and a lynch mob), and they are found by accident long after Lester has died from pneumonia in a mental institution. On the structural and narratorial level, *Child of God* seems to be a blueprint for Griffiths in its threefold structure. However, *Sheepshagger* adds more narrative layers to this basic structure. While *Child of God* is divided into three parts that are clearly distinguishable in terms of narrated time and time of narration, *Sheepshagger* is more playful when it comes to interweaving the different time levels of its narration. What *Sheepshagger* also takes from *Child of God* is the element of oral narration, which in McCarthy's novel can be found in the beginning where the narrator addresses the reader as if he/she was partaking in a conversation that details Lester's life in retrospect – an element which in Griffiths's *Sheepshagger* can be found on narrative level A. As in Griffiths's novel, this supports the impression of a kind of folklore that is devoted to the figuration of an outcast.

Apart from these general similarities, explicit homage is paid by Griffiths in a passage where Ianto, shortly before going to the Job Centre in Aberystwyth, is trying to make some purchases at a grocery store (*Sh* 40–43). For readers who are familiar with *Child of God*, the scene is easily recognisable as an overt mirror image of a similar scene in which Lester Ballard is buying food at a store in the local village (*CG* 124–126). The mirroring of this particular scene proves to be more significant upon closer examination. In McCarthy's novel, Lester tries to go about the everyday business of buying groceries as naturally as possible, assembling several goods. When the storekeeper tells him the price ("Five dollars and ten cents"), Lester, making no attempt to pay, asks him to "put it on the stob for me" (*CG* 125). The storekeeper, apparently used to this procedure, tells him that he owes him "thirty-four dollars and nineteen cents" from previous purchases. Lester proposes to pay him four dollars and nineteen cents on the spot, leaving it "thirty even" (*CG* 125). In one of the novel's few comic moments, the storekeeper tries to figure out when Lester will be able to pay him:

> The storekeeper looked at Ballard. Ballard, he said, how old are you?
> Twenty-seven if it's any of your business.
> Twenty-seven. And in twenty-seven years you've managed to accumulate four dollars and nineteen cents?

> The storekeeper was figuring on his pad.
> Ballard waited. What are you figurin? He asked suspiciously.
> Just a minute, said the storekeeper. After a while he raised the pad up and squinted at it. Well, he said. Accordin to my figures, at this rate it's goin to take a hundred and ninety-four years to pay out the thirty dollars. Ballard, I'm sixty-seven now.
> Why that's crazy.
> Of course this is figured if you don't buy nothin else.
> Why that's crazier'n hell.
> Well, I could of made a mistake in the figures. Did you want to check em?
> Ballard pushed at the scratchpad the storekeeper was offering him. I don't want to see that, he said. (*CG* 126)

The dialogue and the storekeeper's humorous handling of the situation shows the extent to which Lester is out of touch with everyday human interactions and his attempts to "pass" as normal by trying to imitate other people's behaviour like purchasing food. The scene's punchline – Lester is actually able to pay the price for his current purchases, "laying out the five dollars and slapping down the dime" (*CG* 126) – emphasises his absurd behaviour even more.

The counterpart to this scene in *Sheepshagger* is characterised by more interference in form of free indirect speech and narratorial interference that explicates the scene's intended effect and therefore also functions as an interpretive comment on the scene's underlying meaning in *Child of God*:

> Ianto busily scours the single aisle, doing his daily shopping, that's all he's doing for his necessary purchases. That's all he is about, he's just shopping. Everybody does this: they need certain items to see them comfortably through their days so they go to the shop and they buy those things. The simple rhythms of normality. [...]. He is smiling, Ianto is, but still emanating this air of efficiency, of diurnal chores being carried out with aplomb.
> – Will that be all?
> Ianto misses the sarcasm in the merchant's voice. –That's it, yeh. (*Sh* 40-41)

In both novels, the transactional aspect of the shopping scenes serves to illustrate the conflict between the childlike protagonists who seem to have no concept of value exchange, let alone the basic principles of finances and mathematics. The episodes mark the endpoints of the protagonists' estrangement from society: although in both cases the storekeepers are shown as persons who have to some extent tolerated the outcasts' behaviour, this tolerance is shown as coming to an end in both passages. In *Child of God*, the storekeeper is trying to "minimize my losses" (*CG* 126), and in *Sheepshagger* the Welsh storekeeper clearly demands his money back but also shows pity for Ianto when he separates his desired groceries into necessary and less necessary goods:

> To the left he places cigarettes and whisky and chocolate and crisps and cheese and crackers, leaving on the right the loaf of sliced white and the Curried Chicken Slice. [...]. – You can take them. That's today's dinner. Give you the fuel to get into town so you can pick up your money and come back out here to pay me your bill. (*Sh* 42)

For Ianto and Lester, the times during which they could live off the goodwill of others seem to come to an end in these passages. Despite Ianto's self-assertion that he is acting like normal people do on a day-to-day basis, he is no longer able to maintain this form of passing in a society based on monetary values and transactions. Like Lester, he represents a relic from premodern times and tragicomically clashes with the contemporary.[32] For both of them, the shopping scenes and their failure to successfully pass in these situations marks the point of escalation from which their descent into madness and violence seems to be inevitable.

Lester and Ianto can be interpreted as the savages that according to Deleuze and Guattari's analysis of capitalism in *Anti-Oedipus* have a direct relation to the earth rather than to the socius that will later form the "Urstaat" and civilised capitalist society.[33] For Deleuze and Guattari, it is precisely the notion of debt and credit that forms one of the modern effects of social inscription; it is "important to see debt as a direct consequence of the primitive inscription process, instead of making it – and the inscriptions themselves – into an indirect means of universal exchange" (2009:

32 | Which is also visible in the goods that Ianto perceives as necessary equipment.

33 | For a detailed interpretation of Lester Ballard as a "virtual savage" whose "largely unreflected, primitive, if faintly articulate" point of view is supposed to communicate an "authentic representation of wilderness" that echoes "antecedent figures of American pastoralism, such as Natty Bumppo, Daniel Boone, Kit Carson, Melville's Ishmael, or even Thoreau", see Guillemin 2004: 39.

185). Building on the work of Claude Lévi-Strauss, Deleuze and Guattari perceive debt systems as a superstructure, "a conscious form whereby the unconscious social reality of exchange is converted into cash" (2009: 185).

Within this logic, Lester and Ianto can be seen as pure precivilisatory desire: "Desire knows nothing of exchange, *it knows only theft and gift*" (2009: 186; italics in orig.). Hence, the two outcasts act only according to their desires, believing that they are entitled to get what they want because they cannot see the grocery stores for what they are apart from their perception of them as sources for satisfying their desires. What they essentially ignore, then, is the logics of debt and credit that mark them as inferior in terms of class: the moment that they are denied the products in the stores is the very moment that the inscriptions, gaps and boundaries of class become visible for them. In addition, it is precisely the intersection of class and their racial status that likewise becomes visible in these moments – apparent in the backwardness and the patronising attitude of the storekeepers towards them, a behaviour reserved for children and savages. It is certainly no coincidence, then, that Griffiths's narrator once more emphasises Ianto's peculiar physique in this passage: "Ianto gives the man [the storekeeper] his profile. Shows his sharp nose and low brow and prominent epiglottis" (*Sh* 42).

The same logic of class, inscription and exchangist processes is apparent in the triggering events of eviction from ancestral land that both Ianto and Lester fall victim to, and in that respect, the shopping scenes can be read as a continuation of the processes that led to the evictions. According to Deleuze and Guattari, developing notions of private property and commodity production, the bases for the development of capitalism, mark the end of the classless "Urstaat" ("the eternal model of everything the State wants to be and desires") that was defined by communal possession (2009: 217):

> It is beneath the blows of private property, then of commodity production, that the State witnesses its decline. Land enters into the sphere of private property and into that of commodities. *Classes* appear, inasmuch as the dominant classes are no longer merged with the State apparatus, but are distinct determinations that make use of this transformed apparatus. At first situated adjacent to communal property, then entering into the latter's composition or conditioning it, then becoming more and more a determining force, private property brings about an internalization of the creditor-debtor relation in the relations of opposed classes. (2009: 218)

Deleuze and Guattari's account of capitalism as the result of shifting notions of property can help to interpret Lester Ballard's eviction from his ancestral land. On a "pastoral morning" (*CG* 4), Lester interrupts the auctioneer who, commissioned by the county to sell the property, praises the benefits of investing in property:

> They is real future in this property. As much future as you'll find anywheres in this valley. Maybe more. Friends, they is no limit to the possibilities on a piece of property like this. […]. If I had a million dollars I would have it ever [sic] cent invested in real estate within ninety days. And you all know that. They ain't no way for it to go but up. A piece of land like this here I sincere [sic] believe will give ye ten percent on your investment. […]. Your money down here in this bank won't do that for ye and you all know that. There is no sounder investment than property. Land. You all know that a dollar won't buy what it used to buy. […]. But real estate is goin up, up, up. (*CG* 5-6)

The auctioneer's cheerful monologue transports the ideology of progress that is connected to property ownership and what Deleuze and Guattari call the "internalisation of creditor-debtor relation". One can no longer claim one's land as long as it is not yet inscribed with and integrated into the new system of commodity and property. This makes Lester a premodern figure, which is also signified by the rifle that he constantly carries with him. As John M. Grammer explains, the rifle

> identifies him as an anachronism, left behind by history […]. [In] the mythology of the pastoral republic, with which *Child of God* is suffused, weapons like Lester's rifle carry enormous symbolic value. An armed man, prepared to defend the country and his own liberty and property, was for our ancestors the ideal republican citizen, the foundation of stable order. (1999: 39)

So, Lester, confronting the auctioneer rifle in hand, "is claiming a role for himself in one of the central dramas in the pastoral republican mythology" (Grammer 1999: 39). The "pastoral morning" mentioned by the narrator must then be interpreted as a sarcastic paradox since the morning is actually the end of Lester's pastoral existence and the beginning of a new ideal of market and property relations based on privatised property. The end of the pastoral republic can be seen as the end of the Deleuze-Guattarian "Urstaat" that then triggers the appearance of capitalist class systems.

With his land, Lester will inevitably lose the basis for his day-to-day existence, making him the dispossessed member of a new form of lower class. His "Saxon and Celtic bloods", mentioned by the narrator fairly early in the account of this morning (*CG* 4), will no longer grant him a privileged position in the shifting social relations of the American South. No longer the master of his own land, he has neither soil nor noble blood to claim for himself since these have lost their value in the newly emerged exchangist society he resists becoming a member of. In other words, he is becoming white trash, and so, as a figuration that defies the ideology of progress that gets a hold of the "backward" and "lazy" South (see Wray 2006), comes to symbolise anti-modern sentiments. In contrast to Lester, the auctioneer and the sheriff are "figures of modernity" (Grammer 1999: 39) who cannot share Lester's premodern understanding of landownership, which is based on a personal relationship of man and soil.

This premodern idea of property is also shared by Ianto in *Sheepshagger* who likewise is degraded from the status of a person outside of a modern capitalist class system into a member of the lower classes, dispossessed and homeless, relying on benefit payments and well-meaning friends who let him squat in abandoned houses. This social degradation, of being forced into a new kind of class system through dispossession of something that has by both characters been taken for granted based on notions of "natural" heritage, is a major component in the processes of figuration that Ianto and Lester are examples of. Their premodern qualities and beliefs are subject to forms of auto- and hetero-stereotypes that make them into figures in which conflicting notions of race and class converge, for it is precisely their premodern character that is perceived by them as "traditional" and "natural" (with positive notions of soil, blood and heritage attached to it) and as "backward" and "anti-modern" by others.

These figures' socially symbolic qualities are reflected in their environment's reaction to their behaviour. For both Ianto and Lester, it is not just their refusal to obey the existing laws robbing them of their land, but also their social habitus that is questionable. While Ianto's yelling insults at the English yuppies and accusing them of trespassing is viewed as inadequate and excessive behaviour that elicits mocking laughter, Lester breaches the boundaries of good behaviour when he tells the auctioneer and the potential buyers to "get your goddamn ass off my property. And take these fools with ye" (*CG* 7). The auctioneer apparently not only considers himself entitled to enforce the existing property laws of the county but also feels the need to teach Lester proper behaviour. His first reaction merely consists of reprimanding Lester: "Watch your mouth, Lester. They's ladies present" (*CG* 7). However, Lester's indecent tone continues: "I don't give a fuck who's present. [...]. I want you sons of bitches off of my goddamned property" (*CG* 7). Ianto's yelling at the English on his property, enunciated in a "voice rusty with disuse" and in the "longest speech" he has ever made (*Sh* 17), is, like Lester's obscenity-laden language, an 'improper' mode of speaking that represents an ultimately futile attempt to mark their territory and to restore ancient order that prefigures the later acts of violence. In Lester, the urge to impose his order on things in a changing world articulates itself in observations on the natural landscape; and his relation to it is reminiscent of descriptions in *Sheepshagger* illustrated above:

> A winter dreadful cold it was. He thought before it was over that he would look like one of the bitter spruces that grew slant downwind out of the shale and lichens on the hogback. Coming up the mountain through the blue winter twilight among great boulders and the ruins of giant trees prone in the forest he wondered at such upheaval. Disorder in the woods, trees down, new paths needed. Given charge Ballard would have made things more orderly in the woods and in men's souls. (*CG* 136)

The wish to make things "orderly" is then in a macabre way expressed in Ballard's growing necrophiliac and homicidal drives. John M. Grammer interprets his necrophilia as his "mad protest against history itself, against the passing of time. Among his corpses, there is a timeless order, immunity to change" (1999: 40). It is in the last half of the novel when Lester descends deeper into his madness that the text increasingly assumes the quality of a Southern Gothic tale. In the following concluding examination, I will show how race and particularly the white trash stigmatype are expressed through the gothic grotesque and put into a broader cultural context in both novels.

Race, Gothic, Politics

Fairly early in *Child of God*, Lester, who has not yet fully succumbed to his urges, watches a couple have sex in a car near the forest – a scene that is of central importance for an interpretation of Lester in terms of race:

> He raised himself up and had one eye to the windowcorner. A pair of white legs sprawled embracing a shade, a dark incubus that humped in a dream of slaverous lust.
> It's a nigger, whispered Ballard.
> O Bobby, O god, said the girl.
> Ballard, unbuttomed [sic], spent himself on the fender.
> O shit, said the girl.
> On buckling knees the watcher watched. The mockingbird began.
> A nigger, said Ballard.
> But it was not a black face that loomed in the window, that looked so enormous there behind the glass. For a moment they were face to face and then Ballard dropped to the ground, his heart pounding. [...]. The door opened on the far side of the car.
> Ballard, a misplaced and loveless simian shape scuttling across the turnaround as he had come, over the clay and thin gravel and the flattened beercans and papers and rotting condoms. (*CG* 20)

The scene starts out with Ballard's perception of the sexual act, a glimpse of white legs in contrast to a dark figure that the narrator immediately transposes into the realm of the gothic with the choice of the words "incubus" and a "dream of slaverous lust". Considering Ballard's interpretation that this "incubus" must be a black man recalls common stereotypes and accusations of black men in the South sexually preying on the white female population – a common reason given for lynchings. There is also, however, a hint of incredulity in Ballard's repeated identification and appellation of the man as a "nigger". This may be interpreted as astonishment in the face of an act that Ballard, as a backwoodsman in the American rural South of the 1950s, might certainly find egregious.

First of all, considering the fact that he is portrayed as a young man who is not the most successful when it comes to courting (living) women, as several clumsy attempts show, the mere fact of watching a couple having sex only emphasises a feeling of lack on his part. Secondly, seeing a black man having sex with a white woman, that is, doing what he desires to do, may unhinge notions of racial hierarchy that, given the narrative's time and place, might still be shared by Ballard (and many others). In the next turn, the narration suggests that Ballard's assessment of the situation was wrong ("But it was not a black face") and that he realises that he is dealing with someone else. What is more, the reader cannot be sure if he actually sees the man or merely a reflection of himself in the glass, as the narrator immediately proceeds to describe Ballard's own "simian" shape, thereby once more calling up racialised forms of physiognomic descriptions.

In a sense, then, this scene constitutes a moment of distorted recognition of Ballard's racial self in which physiological traits signifying "blackness" in racist discourse are mapped onto him, the white outcast. This is precipitated by Ballard's experience of sexuality, and particularly of unheard-of and scandalous interracial sexuality, as something abject – in this case, it is something which he cannot experience for himself (he is merely capable of being the "watcher") but which nonetheless arouses him (he "spent himself on the fender").[34] Ballard's moment of recognition appears as a form of uncanny doubling in which he seems to see himself reflected in the (imagined) face of a black man; his attempt to dominate the situation linguistically by naming and banishing the racial other fails.[35]

It is here that racial abjection exposes a peculiar double bind. Since it is suggested that Ballard considers the idea of a black man and a white woman having sex as abject, this form of abjection is projected onto himself. In this scene, then, Ballard – possibly more clearly than ever – can experience and "live" (Tyler 2013: 26) the abjection that he presents to the people of Sevier County. The final sentence of this paragraph likewise implies his recognition of himself as abject when he runs back to where he has come from, that is, back into the dirt – "over the clay and thin gravel and the flattened beercans and papers and rotting condoms" (*CG* 20).

In this key moment, the novel suggests a form of racialised abjection – a threat that is running through the rest of the novel, often in conjunction with gothic motifs and modes of depiction, and is taken up by Griffiths in *Sheepshagger.* What is more, the racialised abjection and the sexual and

34 | Of course, this scene also invites interpretations with regard to object fetishism, especially so in regard to the fetishisation of the automobile and of technology.

35 | To some extent, the uncanny identification of the delusional racist Bruce Robertson with his adulterous wife in *Filth* resembles the situation of Lester in *Child of God*. In both cases, it is interracial sex, considered 'unacceptable', even 'unspeakable' and shameful (Bruce tries to hide the fact from his equally racist and misogynist colleagues who, however, already know about the fact), that triggers forms of disassociation in the white male subject.

behavioural deviance represented by Ballard becomes, in its condensation, a figuration that connects the racial and gothic imagery from different historical contexts. Looking at the literary influences of *Sheepshagger* – nineteenth-century gothic descriptions of landscape and the Welsh indigenous people to be found in the likes of Arthur Machen as well as McCarthy's brand of the Southern Gothic – one can detect a common denominator in the way modes of gothicisation are employed and reflected as a means of figuring social deviance as racialised. In his study of gothic images of race in nineteenth-century British culture, H. L. Malchow draws attention to the way travel accounts of Europeans visiting the islands of the South Pacific focused on descriptions of the strange landscapes all the while fixating on the taboos of anthropophagia and necrophilia, ascribing these to the non-white Other encountered in these foreign countries:

> An important example of the gothicizing of geographical and anthropological discovery in the nineteenth century is the juxtaposition of scenic and floral beauty with the most disquieting form of the cannibal taboo – the eating of the dead and buried. "Mortuary cannibalism" served as nothing else to sensationalize and dehumanize the non-European, violating as it did taboos against both necrophilia and cannibalism. It also, at the very least, violated the principles of sanitary health, an area of domestic discourse already resonating with gothic fears of the contagion of decomposition. This provided an ideal field for the gothicization of racial difference. (Malchow 1996: 52)

These forms of gothicisation via the attribution of cannibalism or necrophilia were also relevant for the projection of the racial Other onto parts of the population at home considered to be deviant and dangerous – that is, the unruly poor as well as any group deemed to deviate from the racial and physiological norm of the white Anglo-Saxon such as the Irish (and the Welsh) in the "poetics of degeneration" (see McClintock and chapter I). Malchow considers the legend of Sweeney Todd as well as Bram Stoker's Dracula as embodiments of the cannibal Other (1996: 45–48), and particularly demonstrates how several adaptations of Sweeney Todd employ racialised stereotypes of Irishness in the depiction of the cannibal barber (see reprinted figures of drawings in Malchow 1996: 46–47). Cannibalism was a decisive indicator of delineation between whiteness and blackness, European and non-European:

> To a very large degree, the nineteenth-century middle-class Englishman imagined the cannibal realm of the black by projecting upon it the gothic images he found most disturbing in his own world. This served him well in the era of imperial expansion in shifting responsibility for the ugliness of white brutality. (Malchow 1996: 122)

What is crucial about cannibalism as a "black" paradigm in its nineteenth-century constructions, however, is its shifting semiotics from something that is entirely situated in the realm of the Other to something universal:

> By the end of the century, Joseph Conrad, James Frazer, and Sigmund Freud each turned to the cannibal tradition as sensational means of exploring the private, hidden nature of the European [...]. These theories demote the cannibal abroad by making him no longer a uniquely demonic force but merely an atavistic signifier of a buried universal. That is, they shift the cannibal out of his own realm and into that of the European. (Malchow 1996: 122)

This means that the cannibalism as well as its "inherent aggression and sexuality" (Malchow 1996: 122) was no longer exclusively attributed to non-white populations in remote countries but was seen as part of humanity's evolution, and therefore as inherent even in white European populations. It was feared, then, that the perceived degeneration of large parts of the British population would succumb to such atavistic drives. Notions of the wild, animalistic and atavistic within the bourgeois individual consequently informs nineteenth-century gothic narratives such as *Dracula* and Stevenson's *The Strange Case of Dr. Jekyll and Mr. Hyde* (see Malchow 1996: 126–127).[36]

Coming back to *Child of God* and *Sheepshagger*, then, the two novels and their focus on gothic imagery and acts of necrophilia can be interpreted as an echo of these nineteenth-century narratives and the fears of degeneration and the "non-white within" conveyed by them. When Lester Ballard, escaping from a mob into the cave system underneath the Appalachians, uttering "a sound not quite crying that echoed from the walls of the grotto like the mutterings of a band of sympathetic apes" (*CG* 159), the semantic realms of the gothic grotesque (note the use of the word *grotto*, the etymological origin of the word *grotesque*) and of racial degeneration are made

36 | For an interpretation of Stevenson's novel in relation to race, class and whiteness, see Hartigan Jr. 2005: 43–48.

to converge in one literary image. Similarly, the descriptions of Ballard as a "gothic doll in illfit clothes, its carmine mouth floating detached and bright in the white landscape" (*CG* 140) who is "wearing the underclothes of his female victims" and who by now has also taken to "appearing in their underwear as well" (*CG* 140), create notions of hybridity that let Ballard not only oscillate between man and animal but also between male and female, and, in his appetite for dead bodies and use of his victims' clothes, life and death. During the escalation of the novel's events, Ballard is also described as wearing "a wig [...] fashioned whole from a dried human scalp" (*CG* 173). He thereby becomes a figuration that not only encompasses older notions of racial degeneration, but also connects these to images and fears that were of more imminent actuality during the time of the novel's publication.[37]

Similarly, Ianto's crimes are linked to a political context that suggests that he is mediatised as a bogeyman for these issues. After Ianto has murdered the hiking couple, and the local police search the hills and find the bodies of his victims, the narrator accumulates the voices of the populace, the politicians and the media reacting to the incidents. Ianto hears

> their low talk of missing persons [...]. Of a young couple gone missing, disappeared into the mountain fastness, two flames of life snuffed in the colossal rises and sky-puncturing crags and perpetual downpour as if simply swallowed by that terrain and not as yet spat or shat out again. He hears their whispered surmises of lunatics escaped, of nationalist outrages unprecedentedly extreme, of a hill half-wit gone feral and psychotic [...]. On the local news he sees facial images, one a scowling mugshot and the other two tanned smilers on a sweaty sunburned holiday and he recalls those features swelling, spurting, breaking apart, bursting and collapsing and pleading through blood. He hears talk in a chip shop of devolution fever, of millennial psychosis. Of drug-crazed teenagers, of community care. [...]. Outside early-morning chapels he hears the bellowing about Lucifer returned, about punishment and apocalypse [...]. (*Sh* 226)

The apocalyptic panorama evoked in these lines suggests that Ianto's actions have triggered the collective imagination and fears which range from religious and eschatological positions to political interpretations

37 | "The novel is rife with case-specific details that suggest Ballard is perhaps based to some extent on James Blevins, the 'Lookout Mountain Voyeur,' and Ed Gein, the Wisconsin necrophile" (Cooper 2013: 48).

fuelled by the national tensions between the Welsh nation and the constitutional unity of Britain. The perpetrator of these crimes, yet unknown to the media and the citizens expressing the aforementioned accusations and fears, is constructed as a monster, a sign that may stand for multiple unresolved cultural issues. When Ianto is later revealed to be the murderer, these fears are projected onto his body. Ianto's friends, by killing him, physically attempt to ban this monstrous body and the dangerously multifaceted and potentially endless semantics of cultural decline implied in it. That Ianto's grotesque body immediately becomes the target of his shocked friends after they learn about his crimes not only implies that this violent outburst is the release of an anger that probably had been implicitly directed against him and his conspicuous otherness within the group, but also fits the hyperbolic character of the collective fears expressed in the media.

Within the context of the grotesque, the monstrous and the Southern Gothic, Ianto and Lester Ballard are examples of how white trash can be figured as an incommensurable sign that must be interpreted within specific cultural contexts. The white trash protagonists can thus become scapegoats that must be erased in order to purge the collective. In both novels, however, the semantic riddle posed by the respective white trash monsters, is not solved with their deaths – and this aspect can be connected to McCarthy's sense of materialism that is likewise adapted by Griffiths in his radical denaturalisation of cultural essence and ideologies inscribed in human bodies. In *Sheepshagger*, this becomes evident in its narrative construction, with the friends' retrospective account of the events as a sense-making process that attempts to figure Ianto as a readable and commensurable sign. This retrospective struggle with the incommensurable monstrous sign is adapted from *Child of God*, which in a similar way does not simply conclude with its protagonist's death. Rather, the novel goes on to describe in detail how, after Lester has died in a mental hospital, he is dissected by scientists who, as Steven Frye states, see his body "as a mass of material parts, seemingly absent of spirit, implying a rigid philosophical materialism" (2009: 49): "His entrails were hauled forth and delineated and the four young students who bent over him like those haruspices of old perhaps saw monsters worse to come in their configurations" (*CG* 194). The contrast between the medical students' strictly material interest in the functioning of the body and the comparison with haruspices – ancient soothsayers attempting to predict the future – is conspicuous, as Frye notes: "In the end, he is a configuration of flesh, flayed and systematized, and at the same time he is a sacred text" (2009: 49). The same could be said about Ianto, who becomes a "sacred text" for his murderers to be interpreted.

In conclusion, Griffiths's intense engagement with McCarthy's Southern Gothic pretext shows how raced bodies, especially in their monstrous figurations, serve political functions in their construction as scapegoats who, with their grotesque bodies, become culturally overdetermined signs. In engaging with the poetics of (Southern) Gothic and grotesque literature, Griffiths uses their aesthetics to interrogate and denaturalise the production of such images. While in *Grits*, the emphasis was primarily on a radical materialism that denaturalised the human body's cultural significance by reducing it to mortal and decaying matter while simultaneously reflecting on the literary mechanisms of representation, *Sheepshagger* goes a step further in demonstrating the subsequent symbolic elevation of a deviant individual's body in a hyperbolic fashion. In that way, the novel offers something that could be described as a double caricature: since white trash, as a semantically condensed figure, is often already a caricature, as I have shown in reference to Imogen Tyler's analysis of the chav (see chapter I), Griffiths's hyperbolic description of his characters' struggle with interpreting the exaggeratedly grotesque figure of Ianto, as the amalgamation of transatlantic and historical figurations preceding him, can be read as a caricature of the figuring processes that produce such figures. In short, Griffiths demonstrates how literary texts, by employing grotesque aesthetics, can turn the means that produce racist and classist stigmatypes against themselves.

IV Trashing the National Centre

England's Human Waste in the Novels of John King

While the novels by Irvine Welsh and Niall Griffiths can be situated within the context of questions regarding the status of individual national cultures within Britain, with an emphasis on the interrogation of Scottish and Welsh marginality, John King's work, focusing on England and often specifically on London, the supposed centre of English cultural and political hegemony, does not seem to fit into this context at first sight.[1] However, King's texts share the same preoccupation with the intersection of race and class, and, as I will argue throughout my analysis, white trash is here similarly used as a figuration of notions of post-Britishness. As Miguel Mota proposes, King, rather than being marginalised as a mere writer of popular hooligan novels, "may be more fruitfully placed in a tradition of twentieth-century writers, ranging from T. S. Eliot to George Orwell to Hanif Kureishi, who have attempted to define what it means to be 'English' in a postcolonial age" (2009: 262). Referring back to Raymond Williams's suggestion that within England, without a supposedly marginalised national identity to claim as one's own, one might "get through, quicker, to the real differences, the real conflicts" (2003: 10; see my discussion in chapter III), meaning the ones concerning social (and, by extension, racial) inequalities, King's engagement with social and racial marginalisation could be regarded as a literary means to complicate notions of Englishness – and Britishness – from within, rather than from the Scottish or Welsh perspective of the margins. With regard to

1 | King's novels have so far been predominantly analysed with regard to their representations of hooliganism. For a comprehensive examination of King's trilogy of football novels, *The Football Factory* (1996), *Headhunters* (1998) and *England Away* (1999), see Piskurek 2015: 202–241.

King's third novel *England Away* (1999), for instance, Mota argues that it "provides insight into how the white hooligan culture that has surrounded English football is compellingly implicated in the articulation of specific nationalist discursive practices" (2009: 262).

As I will argue throughout the following analyses of *The Football Factory* (1996) and *White Trash* (2001), these novels can in a similar way be read as reflections of post-Thatcherite issues of whiteness, class and masculinity that view the hooligan and other white trash protagonists as figures of tainted whiteness, constituted through discursive and performative practices as a monstrous internal threat to English and, by extension, British society and the national body.

I will further argue that the sentiments expressed by the characters in the novels concerning their class and racial status within British society can be productively read in analogy to Zygmunt Bauman's theories about the "wasted lives" of capitalist modernity (2004). The concept of wasted lives also offers a broader framework that allows for comparing King's hooligan novel *The Football Factory* with his later novel *White Trash*, which, as is apparent in the title, takes up similar ideas about race and class but moves beyond the exclusive realm of male hooligan culture and envisages a broader socio-cultural scope. Since King's novels, even more so than those by Griffiths and Welsh, focus on changed concepts of labour and the market as well as the values they represent in contemporary British society, Bauman's examinations of modernity's "wasted lives", expelled from a quickly changing global market, is an apt model for explaining how people become "disposable" and how their resulting redundancy is then reflected in the alignment of race, class and trash.

For Bauman, the process of designing "human togetherness" results in the production of human waste (2004: 30), which in turn is defined by the rules of the nation state and the economic market. During modernity's gradual shift from a "society of producers" to a "society of consumers", those people who do not seem to be employable or who are being made redundant become "flawed consumers" – "people lacking the money that would allow them to stretch the capacity of the consumer market, while they [the poor] create another kind of demand to which the profit-oriented consumer industry cannot respond and which it cannot profitably 'colonize'" (Bauman 2004: 39). The semantics of waste also imply the potential threat of contamination: "All waste is potentially poisonous – or at least, being defined as waste, it is deemed to be contaminating and disturbing to the proper order of things" (Bauman 2004: 86). Consequently, as Bauman argues, 'human waste' has to be regarded within the management of (social) hygiene, necessitating the compartmentalisation of the social fabric for waste to be assigned to its proper "dumping site" (2004: 63) because contemporary social structures do not allow for removing "human waste" to "distant waste disposal sites" (2004: 85). It therefore needs to be "sealed off in tightly closed containers" (2004: 85), provided for by the penal system and other institutions. Looking at the previously discussed primary texts, the social housing estates of *Marabou Stork Nightmares*'s Muirhouse, *Trainspotting*'s Leith or *Grits*'s New Gurnos could be regarded as examples for such metaphorical dumping sites – and in fact, as I have shown in the previous chapter, Griffiths's narrator Roger actually calls the New Gurnos a "dumping site" for "human waste". As I will show in my following analyses of *The Football Factory* and *White Trash*, King's novels are concerned with depicting these "dumping sites" in England's urban areas, and they show these areas to be highly conflicted spaces where social order and matters of belonging are being fought over. It is especially in the forms of state surveillance and maintenance of public order depicted in King's novels that the segregation of the public sphere into areas for proper consumers and "flawed consumers" becomes visible. And as I will argue in my interpretation of *White Trash*, King's texts appropriate a particular mode of expression in the form of what Gael Sweeney (1997) has called the "White Trash Aesthetic", which brings the notion of "human waste" full circle by appropriating a 'trashy' aesthetics.

King's novels (and, to some degree, Griffiths's and Welsh's novels) seem to illustrate the obstacles of the Generation X that Zygmunt Bauman considers to be most severely affected by what he calls the "liquidisation" of modernity and the subsequent changes in the understanding of work and productivity:

> The so-called 'Generation X' of young men and women born in the 1970s, in Britain or other 'developed' countries, knows ailments of which older generations were unaware; not necessarily more ailments, or ailments that are more acute, distressing and mortifying, but ones that are distinctly different, novel – one could say 'specifically liquid modern' maladies and afflictions. (2004: 10)

What distinguishes the "ailments" of the Generation X from previous ones in terms of economic security is the concept of "redundancy". Bauman argues that whereas the term *unemployment* signifies a temporary condition which is not the norm, the term *redundancy* signals a permanency, a condition of disposability which cannot be altered because it is a quality supposedly inherent in the redundant person as such – redundancy is therefore a form of "social homelessness":

> Unwelcome, tolerated at best, cast firmly on the receiving side of socially recommended or tolerated action, treated in the best of cases as an object of benevolence, charity and pity [...] but not of brotherly help, charged with indolence and suspected of iniquitous intentions and criminal inclinations, [Generation X] has few reasons to treat 'society' as a home to which one owes loyalty and concern. [...]. So why should the suddenly disqualified employees respect the rules of the political-democratic game if those of the world of labour are blatantly ignored? (2004: 13)

Bauman's observations on the paradigm of redundancy and the resulting alienation from one's work (or from the product of it) and society at large corresponds with Imogen Tyler's analysis of the racialising discursive strategies surrounding the "underclass" that culminated with the English riots in 2011 when public discourse was buzzing with terms like *scum, vermin* and *waste* (2013: 181). These discourses are fraught with a strong eugenic paradigm that distinguishes between "deserving" and "undeserving" poor (Tyler 2013: 190–191), the former of which would consequently correspond to Bauman's redundant members of the Generation X, who, in Tyler's terms, are cast out as "moral abjects" and "unemployable 'human vermin'" confined to the "periphery of the body politic" (2013: 191). With respect to the English riots and the looting of shops by this so-called scum, Bauman's prediction that "[flawed] consumers would not know when they might be declared criminals" (2004: 14) seems in hindsight a very accurate assumption about the development in Britain from the declaration of a "classless society" and the drastic re-emergence of the socio-economic conflict zones (and not least its dangerous biopolitical rhetoric) during the last couple of years. With that in mind, King's novels prove to be fictional examinations of a gradually evolving sense of alienation from society by the people who would even in Tony Blair and John Major's classless Britain be cast onto the fringes of these new concepts of British society, thus betraying such rhetoric's inherent illusions.

King's figurations of white trash are also remarkable with respect to another aspect brought up by Bauman. Bauman sees 'human waste' as the by-product of social order building, yet, with Mary Douglas, he argues that "no objects are 'waste' by their intrinsic qualities, and no objects can become waste through their inner logic. It is by being assigned to waste by human design that material objects, whether human or inhuman, acquire all the mysterious, awe-inspiring, fearsome and repulsive qualities" (2004: 22). King's novels attempt to dissect the way certain groups of the population are being treated and constructed as waste, yet the question remains as to what exactly makes them waste in the first place. In my analysis, I will focus on this issue, and specifically on how King's novels reflect the role of racialised figurations for the construction of human waste and of what one might call a British Generation X class system. I will also show how King reflects on a society of control that polices (and produces) such figurations, and how a particular aesthetics of white trash reacts to such policing. Throughout my analysis I will show that it is not only the configuration of race and class that determines one's positions within that system, but also (especially in the hooligan novel *The Football Factory*) a post-imperial sense of national and cultural history that assigns to the British (and, in this case more precisely, the English) working class the role of 'waste' as, in Bauman's terms, the "dark, shameful secret of all production" (2004: 27).

IV.1 *The Football Factory*

Ways of Looking at Trash

With his novel *The Football Factory*, John King provides a text whose narrative and structural composition is intended to give a comprehensive and multifaceted impression of the state of the British working class during the turning point between the John Major and Tony Blair years. Like the novels by Welsh and Griffiths, *The Football Factory*'s awareness of class and its intersections with race and gender is thus strongly interlocked with the novel's formal approach. With its multiple focalising characters and a range of narrators, King's debut shares similarities with the debuts by both Welsh and Griffiths. What distinguishes it from the two other authors is King's emphasis on a sense of historicity of the British, or, to be more precise, the English working class. While a sense of decline of working-class communities is also hinted at in Welsh's novels, with an indication that it is particularly a post-war development in British politics that led to this decline, King stresses this point especially by introducing the perspective of elderly people, thereby expanding the historical scope and adding a sense of post-imperial melancholia, to use Paul Gilroy's concept (2006). The attempt to shed a broader light on Anglo-British class relations is also visible in the range of political views the different characters express. *The Football Factory* can therefore be considered as a novel of ideas, echoing books like Aldous Huxley's *Point Counter Point* (1928), with each focaliser representing a unique political viewpoint related to the issues of race and class.[2] Quite obviously, King's novel, with its focus on football fan culture, is in that respect interested in intersections with gender (and with masculinity in particular), and in that regard could be compared with Welsh's *Marabou Stork Nightmares*.

Considering the political scope of King's novel, which also makes sure to juxtapose views and opinions from the cultural margins with perspectives from the centre, one could make a case for it being the most balanced text examined in this thesis. While I called *Grits* the most plural text when it comes to rendering the different British cultures in a trans- or post-British sense, *The Football Factory* attempts to depict a broader ideolog-

2 | Huxley's influence on King's poetics is also apparent in an epigraph from *Brave New World* (1932) in *White Trash* (*WT* n. pag.).

ical and political spectrum not evinced by Griffiths. As I will show in my subsequent analysis, *The Football Factory* juxtaposes its primal focaliser's working-class hooligan perspective with the views of middle-class social workers and students of journalism as well as the elderly and radical neo-Nazis. The inclusion of more established views serves as a mockery of these very perspectives because it primarily establishes the white male hooligan as the ideological centre of its narrative, thus challenging and intervening in dominant figurations of the hooligan as a stigmatype of tainted British whiteness. One of the few non-hooligan perspectives in the novel that is not designed as a parody of established or hegemonic positions but that claims a seriousness and psychological depth in its own right is that of pensioner and World War II veteran Mr Farrell, who, as I will argue in my analysis, provides a broader historical scope through which the hooligan is socio-historically situated and rendered as a post-war working-class phenomenon.

The centrality of different narrative focalisations and the political and ideological implications of structures of seeing as a major motif are highlighted early on in the novel during one of several accounts of hooligan actions when Tommy talks about CCTV surveillance:

> We wait for the next train a couple of minutes later, watched by London Underground lenses. Video cameras see everything. You have to be sharp to achieve your ends because there's a market for Peeping Toms. Like this crime programme on the box hunting a serial killer wiping out sado-masochist queers. [...]. Cameras have a lot of power, but they won't stop anything. If you've got the urge to do something then it takes a special kind of strength to resist the desire. You don't have to get caught just because London's turning into a surveillance arcade. Not if you're clever. (*FF* 25)

Here, Tommy identifies the ways of looking at hooliganism as a public disturbance as something that is firstly utilised to observe and control certain segments of the population deemed unruly and secondly that satisfies a scopophilic desire conceived by the social mainstream. In other words, Tommy here identifies the ambivalent ways in which the monitoring of populations constructed as dangerous is intricately linked with a desire to exploit these populations as a sensationalised social other. He links this to true crime programmes on TV, but within the context of representations of white trash, this observation might as well be extended to today's so-called "poverty-porn" programmes which in recent years have taken a hold on British TV (see Hester 2014).[3] In that respect, it is also noteworthy that it is primarily areas with wealthy residents or areas of consumption that are being monitored: "the old bill don't put cameras down poor people's streets. They're only interested in protecting City wealth and the rich cunts in Hampstead and Kensington" (*FF* 30). This not only implies a persistent class inequality and attempts in political discourse to evade these differences, but also hints towards a stigmatisation of segments of the lower classes.

The figure of the hooligan finds itself at the centre of attention when it comes to ways of looking at marginalised and scandalous segments of the population, as is evident from a broad array of media representations ranging from fictional representations in films and novels to accounts of "real life" hooligans in numerous documentaries and hooligan memoirs.[4] Often, these accounts partake in what Uwe Mayer in an overview of recent hooligan films has called a "quest for authenticity" (2009: 185–200).[5] The tendency to view the hooligan as an "authentic" figure not only has implications for the target audience's voyeuristic needs, but also, as King's *The Football Factory* suggests, for the figuration of the English working class within the parameters of the authentic. What King demonstrates through the figure of the football hooligan is the way different figurations of the British working class have taken place throughout the post-war decades, peaking in a renewed form of stigmatisation of segments of the working class as excessive while idealising other segments as traditional, honourable and therefore 'authentic'. The hooligan becomes an ambivalent figure

3 | Helen Hester especially focuses on manifestations of poverty porn in British shows such as *The Scheme* (BBC Scotland 2010–2011), *The Estate* (BBC Northern Ireland 2012) and *Skint* (Channel 4 2013).

4 | Accounts of hooliganism have for several years been a considerable part of the British book market. See Redhead 2004 for a collective review of a number of hooligan memoirs.

5 | For a (brief) history of the hooligan, see Mota 2009: 264–265; for an early account of the heday of hooliganism, see Ingham et al. 1978; for an analysis of representations of hooliganism as an aspect of football fan culture, see Piskurek 2015. Like Mayer, Steve Redhead is interested in questions of authenticity and "realism" in his article on Nick Love's film adaptation of *The Football Factory* (2007).

in that regard since he can be used for figuring the working class as both authentic and excessive. Once again, the intersection with race and nationality plays a fundamental part in these figurations, as do the different ways of looking at the hooligan and the working class. By displaying the different structures of looking at the figure of the hooligan, *The Football Factory* can be regarded as a critical intervention in the figuring processes examined by Imogen Tyler.

This is most poignantly reflected in the chapter "Hooligans", one of those chapters that goes beyond the perspective of the novel's main character and narrator Tommy. It is a heterodiegetic narrative following Jennifer, a young aspiring journalist, who meets with two old football journalists during her research on hooliganism. Eager to witness some proper hooligan actions during a football game, she is disappointed to learn from Will Dobson, one of the veterans, that the hooligan is a "figment of the imagination", an "editor's wet dream" and "a thing of the past" (*FF* 52). This chapter, whose characters do not appear again throughout the rest of the novel, is set relatively early in the novel after the reader has already been confronted with several detailed scenes of hooligan violence narrated by the novel's primary narrator, Tommy. It thus belies the actual facts of hooliganism otherwise presented in the novel. Dobson's accounts suggest that the hooligan has become a figure similar to those from urban legends, something to project collective fears onto and which is to some degree elusive, as is indicated by Dobson's paradoxical attitude towards the figure of the hooligan as something which is at the same time present and absent. In that respect, the hooligan as urban legend can be compared to other figurations of tainted and abject (and often "un-British") whiteness, like, to draw on an example analysed by Anoop Nayak, the "Rat Boy" (2009: 32).[6]

This point is underlined by another journalist appearing in the chapter. David Morgan, a colleague from a rival newspaper, joins the

6 | "Rat Boy" was the nickname given to Anthony Kennedy, a teenage criminal known in the 1990s for "his elusive ability to escape the police and hide in the maze of tunnels and passageways that make up the Byker Wall estate" who consequently "constituted an anti-hero, a super-villain whose comic-book pseudonym suggested his unredeemable evil" (2009: 32). Much like "Rat Boy", the hooligans are "typical targets of social outrage" (Nayak 2009: 32).

conversation and offers Jennifer the essentials of a proper, if speculative hooligan article. He lists

> buzz-words and phrases which made for a good hooligan article – 'scum', 'mindless yobs', 'thugs', 'ashamed to be English', 'not true fans', 'bring back the birch', 'give them a good thrashing' and 'now is the time for the courts to hand down custodial sentences'. [...]. First comes the titillation and gory details, then the condemnation which masks the pleasure the reader's had from the story. Call for the return of the cat o'nine tails and demand some good old fashioned square-bashing and everyone's happy. (*FF* 58)

Morgan's list of "buzzwords" implies that the hooligan is a scapegoat figure whose figuration as a threat to society prevails despite its supposed "extinction", as Dobson calls it (*FF* 53). In that respect, the hooligan can be considered a prime example of a stigmatype, and, as the novel's main focaliser Tommy continuously suggests, the hooligan is a specifically classed and raced figure, making it a figuration of tainted whiteness.[7]

This aspect of class is also highlighted in the journalist chapter. The three characters, whose thoughts and attitudes are expressed and juxtaposed in elaborate bits of direct speech and interior monologues by an omniscient narrator, are representative of different classes. Jennifer is portrayed as an eagerly aspiring journalist, having enjoyed a good upper-middle-class education, while Will Dobson is representative of an earlier working-class generation who despises Jennifer precisely for the classist

7 | However, hooligan communities are not necessarily exclusively white. In fact, one of the most notorious British (former) hooligans, Cass Pennant, who was a member and later leader of the InterCity Firm in the 1970s and 1980s, is black. Pennant's autobiography *Cass* (2002), which can be said to have paved the way for the increasing popularity of the hooligan memoir in the early 2000s (see Piskurek 2015: 202–205) and which was made into a film by director Jon S. Baird in 2008, explicitly deals with the marginalised status of black men in the football fan culture at that time. In King's *The Football Factory*, firms also have the occasional black member, but their exceptional racial status is always signified by the nicknames given to them, usually in the form of the prefix "Black" as in the character Black Paul whom I will refer to later on in my analysis. This racialising form of address highlights the unusual status of black firm members and maintains the construction of the hooligan subculture as a predominantly white one.

attitude she has in his eyes. While he politely shares his views and information on matters of journalism and football violence, he masks his actual attitude towards her: "They thought they knew everything, these further-education people, and he wasn't conned by her mild manner. She was an arrogant bitch if ever he'd seen one" (*FF* 54). Although the insight provided into his thoughts reveals him to be aware of class and educational differences still prevalent in British society, his statements regarding the decline of hooligan culture exhibit a different stance when he argues that "society is much better balanced these days. The Tories have eradicated the class system. The angry young men of yesteryear are either sitting in bed smoking cannabis or wandering around their local homestore trying to decide what shade of paint to buy for the baby's room" (*FF* 53).

His favourable view of the Tories and his belief in their rhetoric of classlessness must be interpreted as deliberate irony intended to fool the "arrogant" young journalist in front of him, who, as her interior monologues show, is similarly aware of the social and ideological difference between herself and Dobson. Disapproving of his sexual reference in the mention of the "editor's wet dream", she thinks that "Will didn't seem bothered about such niceties though. He probably thought a new man[8] was a type of service robot, and in a way he would have been right" (*FF* 52–53). Jennifer considers Dobson a relic of past times, oblivious to shifts in social and gender relations. In similar fashion, her concluding thoughts on class provide for the chapter's final lines when she dropped off by the two men in front of her favourite restaurant where she is supposed to meet her "part-time boyfriend" (*FF* 56):

> She immediately felt at home, the clientele class-conscious and suitably confident. Looking around for Anthony, she flushed when she thought of those toads [Dobson and Morgan] sneaking glances at her legs. Then she was angry at the

8 | Jennifer's ambivalent attitude towards the 1980s and 1990s emergence of pro-feminist "new men" is indicative of one of the novel's overall themes, the crumbling hierarchy of traditional male roles which coincide with the erosion of the old working class as well as with the general shift in the perception of class and gender. I will refer to the importance of traditional male positions, which find themselves threatened by the emergence of empowered women and new forms of male gender (including non-white and non-working-class males) later in my analysis.

> boring game she had witnessed, the loss of a good evening, and not a thug inside. At least she was on familiar ground in Bo-Bo's and could act normally again. The common people really were common as muck. You could give them money, but you couldn't fake breeding. (*FF* 59)

The insight provided into Jennifer's thoughts and attitudes prove the persistence of class markers – she still "minds the gap", as Ferdinand Mount describes it in his essay on "the new class divide in Britain" (2004). Her perspective on the working class in general and the hooligans in particular is thus representative of the voyeuristic sensationalism through which the hooligan has been figured as an embarrassing relic of what certain sections of the media want to construct as the working-class youth – an attitude that can also be found in accounts that explain the phenomenon of hooliganism as a typical outcome of English working-class culture like Bill Buford's *Among the Thugs* (1991/2001).

David Morgan functions as an in-between character in that respect: he works for the tabloid press and, unlike Will Dobson, is not interested in proper journalism but in exploitative sensationalism. His reckless focus on his career is of interest for Jennifer, who immediately senses that he might be useful for her own success. It is here that it becomes apparent to the reader that Jennifer functions as a clichéd caricature of a reckless and opportunist posh student when she teases David Morgan: "she [...] adjusted her legs so David had a better view of her upper thighs, filing the old lech's face in her memory and his card in her purse. He would certainly be more useful than Dobson who was an old duffer in comparison" (*FF* 58). In the construction of the chapter and within its character constellation, Morgan is the missing link between Dobson, who claims that society is well-balanced in terms of class, but is himself a relic of an old working class, and Jennifer, who is a representative of a new generation of privileged British classism who, as her interior monologue implies, even believes in the hereditary nature of class as something that is inscribed in people's bodies. Between these two extremes, Morgan is a cynic who maintains a sense of class-based hierarchism through his journalistic representations. He "had been widely accepted as having his finger firmly on the pulse of the mid-Eighties", as Will Dobson thinks: "While he'd never pushed himself more than his contemporaries, he always seemed to be in the know. Will suspected that this was because he was a little bit more liberal with the truth than the others, which in turn reflected the attitude of the title paying his wages" (*FF* 55). Thus, Morgan supposedly was responsible for the media construction of the hooligan during the peak of hooliganism, which, as Dobson tells Jennifer, "faded away after Heysel" (*FF* 53), referring to the Heysel Stadium disaster in 1985 when the deaths of thirty-nine football fans was primarily blamed on Liverpool fans and resulted in stricter controls of fan behaviour during games and a ban of English clubs from European competition.

In his own words, Morgan similarly presents himself as someone who takes advantage of the public need for class-based stigmatyped figurations when he tells Will and Jennifer about his recent football report and complains about the "havenots" who allegedly took out their "petty frustration" on him by scratching the side of his Volvo: "the politics of envy I'm afraid to say are alive and fermenting. It might not have been football fans of course, just the local population moaning about its lot" (*FF* 57). The same sense of classism that is expressed in his suspicion about the motives behind his scratched car can be identified in his

> story of a politician who had been discovered in Brompton cemetery with a thirteen-year-old rent boy, a young lad from Burnley whose homelessness was a direct consequence of Government cutbacks. [...]. It was an excellent story, and Morgan had toyed with the idea of somehow introducing vampirism and Aids. (*FF* 57)

The way Morgan renders this story, however, reveals his class bias to be more complex. It is not merely the "envious" lower classes and havenots he targets, but it is similarly the upper class and Conservative politicians who are figured by him as excessively extreme and monstrous, knowing full well that he can attract a broad readership with images of a degenerate upper class that mingles with deviant lower-class subjects such as, in this case, a homeless and underage male prostitute.

Morgan's idea to combine the story with added speculation about "vampirism and Aids" echoes the figuration of the tyrannous monarch as a "political monster" in late-eigtheenth-century France during the Revolution that Foucault outlines in his lectures about the "Abnormal". In the revolutionary pamphlets he examines, the monarchs are imagined with the "cannibalistic, anthropophagic side of the sovereign, greedy for the blood of the people" (Foucault 2003: 97). "Sexual debauchery" and cannibalism are, according to Foucault, the two major characteristics in the imagination of the political monster that preys on the population (2003:

98). It seems as if in the tabloid press represented by King's characters, the figuration of the political monster can also be applied to the construction of the Tories. Morgan's horror stories about vampiric and sexually excessive capitalists fittingly illustrate King's attempts to demonstrate the two extremes of monstrous figurations of class on both sides of the spectrum: the lower classes are rendered as a danger to public safety, and the 'ruling classes' are demonised as excessive and debauching.[9] In both cases, the origin of the demonisation and stigmatypisation lies in a normalisation of the middle class. This approach to rendering different extremes of depicting class is a central part of *The Football Factory*'s narratorial strategy of multi-perspectivity, and it shows the different ideological positions and purposes for which figuring practices can be put to use.

In his interpretation of John King's *England Away* (1998), the final instalment of his hooligan trilogy, John Brannigan juxtaposes King's strategy of conveying his subject matter through different focalisers and the dominance of interior monologues with the "tourist's gaze" of texts like Buford's that ultimately construct the hooligans as "alienated and eccentric objects" (2003: 80). A similar observation can be made about the narrative strategies in *The Football Factory*, which uses chapters like "Hooligans" in order to provide the reader with "moral and political contexts other than [the hooligans] offer themselves" (Brannigan 2003: 80). King's narratorial construction, however, points towards a significant incongruity in the perception and reality of class in Britain. While the novel is clearly situated in the "classless" Britain of the 1990s, it consciously plays with the actual discrepancies between such political rhetoric and the lived reality of the British working class. These discrepancies are made apparent through the narrative juxtaposition of perspectives like Jennifer's with those narrated by hooligans like the novel's main character Tommy. Thus, the proclaimed "death of the hooligan" (*FF* 58), which is proven to be illusory by the narrative accounts comprised in the rest of the novel, becomes an analogy for the similarly illusory end of the British class system. Interestingly, though, the awareness of class, its markers and its liveability is perpetuated not only on the part of snobbish yuppies like Jennifer and cynical journalists like Morgan, who employs class-

9 | However, King's own construction of different classes is at times no less problematic in that it is complicit in such polarising constructions, as I will demonstrate in my analysis of his novel *White Trash*.

based stereotypes and uses them to grotesque effect, but simultaneously by hooligans like Tommy and his mates. In the case of the hooligan characters, however, a significant degree of self-awareness comes into play, as they often demonstrate what John Hartigan Jr. calls "the active way people subjected to certain debasing images are able to inhabit them in complex ways that involve critique and elaboration" (2005: 16; see chapter I), evident in many figurations and inscriptions of race and class. Thus, the hooligans in King's novel sometimes knowingly play with the performances expected from them on account of what they embody.

The chapter "Worker's Dream", again one of the few ones narrated from an extradiegetic position, follows Sid, a storage room worker, and is a case in point for this stereotyped construction of the working class. Bored by his working day routine, Sid "daydreamed the morning away, imagining he was playing centre-forward for QPR in one of the finest football teams the world had ever seen" (*FF* 33). In this rendering of 'the' male working-class mind, Sid not only imagines himself as a proficient football player, but also as the object of desire of Princess Diana who follows the dream match from the "royal box" and "cheered her favourite player with a look on her face which meant one thing and one thing only. Romance" (*FF* 33–34). In one scene from his dream, designed as the imagining of the 'worker's mind' and its social dichotomies already implied by the title of the chapter, Sid imagines himself in a bedroom, post-game, with "the expectant royal awaiting his plebeian touch" (*FF* 34).

Sid's fantasy articulates a sexual fetishisation of the physical abjection of the working class, but, conspicuously, this fantasy of the "plebeian touch" is here appropriated and internalised not by a subject of the middle or upper class but by the worker himself, and, paradoxically, for his own pleasure.[10] This image of the worker's body as something which is incom-

10 | In addition, this dream could also be read as a comment on the economic changes in British football in the 1990s: in order to prevent undesirable segments of fan culture, i. e., the working-class hooligans, changes in entrance structure, especially through raising ticket prizes, had been implemented throughout the 1980s and 1990s. This "exclusion of some fans and forms of behaviour" (Crabbe and Brown 2004: 32; for an extensive analysis of the situation, see also Piskurek 2015) was primarily targeted at the hooligans as they are portrayed in King's novel. Here, by imagining himself as a superstar player (somewhat prefiguring the media hype concerning stars like David Beckham starting later in the 1990s), Sid

patible with an upper-class body, yet paradoxically desirable in the form of sexual fetishisation *precisely because* of this incompatibility can be read as a hyperbolic play on the imagination of the working-class body as tainted. Here, the white working-class subject derives enjoyment (and even sexual pleasure) from imagining himself through the gaze of the royal class, and thereby consciously plays with the ideological inscriptions on his body.

While the novels by Irvine Welsh and Niall Griffiths feature images of such tainted bodies in grotesque detail, the degree of fetishisation that King implies in these descriptions is on a different plane in that it incorporates a version of the upper- and middle-class gaze on the working class that is largely absent from Welsh and Griffiths's texts. This internalisation of the abjectifying gaze by working-class subjects recurs throughout the novel – for example, when Tommy remembers chatting up a girl at a bar who turned out to be a police officer: "I was gutted. She was filth and I was lining up a good bit of sex and I find she's got the plague. But I got myself back in the swing and started thinking what a laugh it would be shagging a copper. It would be a crack telling the lads I'd knobbed a WPC" (*FF* 240). Tommy defines his own working-class identity, and specifically his identity as a hooligan who is permanently at war with the police, through distinguishing himself from the flirting WPC who in his eyes represents a class enemy: "That's all you need, socialising with the old bill on a Saturday night. I'll have a drink with almost anyone, but there's a limit. You have to have standards" (*FF* 241). These "standards" allude to an idea of working-class solidarity and community, epitomised by the institution of the pub as a space for enacting this sense of community and getting in touch with people. In addition, the reversed strategies of figuring the police as abject, revolting subjects by analogising them with filth and disease is noteworthy here.[11] The abject figure of white trash that Tommy perceives himself as throughout the novel (i.e., his appropriation of the hegemonic gaze onto himself) here consciously plays with the strategies of figuration and inscription that he himself is usually subjected to, and maps their semantics of abjection onto the WPC.

---

dreams himself into a situation, i.e., the actual game in the stadium, from which he will most likely be excluded.

11 | In this, *The Football Factory* could be regarded in comparison to Welsh's *Filth*, which, as I have shown in chapter II.3, also plays with the ambivalent semantics of "filth" as a derogatory term for the police in the context of tainted whiteness.

Ironically, Tommy's assertion that he would have a drink with "almost anyone" stands in contrast to the internal fragmentation of the British working class into different subcultures, part of which is the hooligan culture that he himself is a member of. As Gary Day observes in his account of British class and its representations, "it is an interesting reversal that in the nineteenth century the working class were regarded as a threat to society but in the mid-twentieth century were seen as its cohesive force" (2001: 181). The sentiment that members of the working class could share a drink with anybody and thus be on equal terms with them irrespective of social standing, thereby becoming something like the integral force holding society as such together, however, must be regarded as an anachronism during the historical moment the novel looks at: "Ironically, the very moment when the working class were perceived in this manner was the very moment when their communities were being destroyed by redevelopment" (Day 2001: 181). Gary Day identifies this destruction of working-class community as one of the central motivations behind the characters depicted in *The Football Factory*, especially the main narrator Tommy (2001: 201). Yet, Tommy and most of the other characters representative of his generation have "no sense of the working-class traditions of self-improvement or social transformation", and thus their frustration "is diverted into violence against opposing football fans" (Day 2001: 201). Therefore, Tommy's generation is characterised by their awareness of their working-class identity as well as of the market forces threatening their communities. This awareness, however, is coupled with an inability to properly deal with the predicament arising from this situation.

Despite the focus on football hooliganism, the novel also highlights other extreme forms of diverting working-class frustration as well as the perspective of other classes on the situation of the working class. The chapter "Happy Ever After" approaches the issue of a crumbling working-class community through a heterodiegetic narrative switching between four focal characters – the two pensioners Mr Moss and Mr Farrell, the social worker Michelle Watson and Billy Bright, an unemployed, "deformed neo-Nazi" (*FF* 114).[12] The two pensioners, Albert Moss in particular, serve as representatives of a past working class. They are the

12 | Bright's "deformity" seems to be related to a crippled hand, as the description "he responded to the raffle ticket he was holding in his one good hand" indicates (*FF* 114).

elderly relics of this class and struggle with their pensions and impending old-age poverty. Albert Moss, who has an appointment "at the social" (*FF* 111), is described as an old man with a strong sense of dignity: "Albert Moss was no sponger and he didn't expect charity" (*FF* 112). This attitude is mirrored in the passage focusing on Michelle Watson, the interviewer with whom he had an appointment concerning his pension. Described as "keen and sincere and working for the state" and a "dedicated socialist", she considers herself to be deeply understanding of the precarious situation old people such as Albert find themselves in: "Michelle was appalled at the way working-class pensioners had been conditioned to regard their financial entitlements as charity" (*FF* 113). Michelle, however, seems to be similarly "appalled" by the demeanour of some of her other working-class clients of younger generations:

> At times Michelle despaired of the working-class people with whom she dealt each day, especially the younger elements of the community. They had no idea of directing their anger and aggression in the cause of class solidarity, preferring to drink themselves near to a state of coma and then fight each other over trivialities. There was no logic to this self-destructiveness when the people who crippled their lives with unjust laws and oppressive propaganda were so near in the House of Parliament. (*FF* 113)

These sentiments, distinguishing a "good" and a "bad" working class, are reminiscent of what Imogen Tyler in her critique of Owen Jones's *Chavs: The Demonisation of the Working Class* (2011) describes as a typical strategy of the left to essentialise the working class – a strategy that

> revolve[s] around the axis of deserving/undeserving poor and, as such, they reproduce the same problematic opposition that Marx conjured up in the figure of the revolting feminized lumpen against which he crafted the gallant muscularity of the proletariat. It is this same myth of worthiness which New Labour appeals to in its pitting of 'honest hard-working families' against the parasitical, pathological underclass. Indeed, the use of this strategy by the left often works to the advantage of the right, which [...] also appeals to a mythical 'real working class' in order to legitimize its mockery of the poor. (2013: 170)

Michelle Watson appears as a representative of similar kinds of political hypocritical double standard, and as the narration makes clear, she is supposed to be read as a caricature, devoid of characterisation. Rather, she appears as a vessel for accumulated ideas, like many other characters in the novel. Her condescending attitude towards and demonisation of young working-class males as potential "right-wing thugs" (*FF* 114) stands in contrast to her compassion for people like Mr Moss. Further evidence for her qualities as a caricature is her view on the "black population":

> Downtrodden through the centuries they were the ultimate in crushed humanity. With the help of left-wing, educated whites such as herself the blacks would gradually fight their way up the scale, and in the black youth out on the streets there was a potential for a political cadre of fit young men ready to overthrow the barriers of white capitalist racist oppression. (*FF* 114)

This attitude, exaggeratedly outlined by the narrator, is the peak of her hypocritical attitude. It reveals that she thinks of herself as well meaning towards the so-called black population while she is in fact condescendingly paternalist and ultimately racist, a position and self-image that is a consequence of her unexamined white privilege. In line with the book's multiperspectivity, this caricature of white liberalism is immediately contrasted with another extreme, the viewpoint of Michelle's next appointment, Billy Bright, a "deformed neo-Nazi" who "had the short hair and black combat jacket she had seen on TV reports covering fascist activity in Brick Lane, and appearances while generally deceiving could easily be assumed correct in such right-wing instances" (*FF* 114).

The narrator's angle here implies that Michelle, while claiming to speak for the political needs of "the black population", in fact essentialises this ethnic group. For Michelle, black culture seems to be inherently authentic, as is evident from her interpretation of NWA and Public Enemy's "gangster rap" as the alleged medium of political expression: she listens to the music despite their occasionally "violent and sexist lyrics" not being "exactly conducive to informed political struggle" because, after all, the rappers "were talking about life on the streets of Los Angeles and New York as it appeared in the flesh" (*FF* 114). Michelle not only seems to believe that rap is the political mode of expression for *all* people of colour but also identifies "the black population" as the epitome of authentic class struggle. However, she denies this "authenticity" to contemporary white working-class culture. King's construction of Michelle's character and her political position is representative of the paradoxical tension between a contemporary working class perceived as excessively white by a middle class which in turn does not perceive itself as ethnically or culturally positioned (see Garner 2012 and chapter I). She seems to apply the same mechanisms of essentialisation in a reversed way.

While "the black population" is essentialised as a political tool for her symbolic system, the young white working-class males who attend her office hours are deemed to be racists and fascists per se based on their looks alone. In a seemingly paradoxical turn, Michelle, despite her (patronising) endorsement of black culture and her disdain for racist white working-class thugs, makes herself white by these very attitudes. This can be explained with Steve Garner's argument that the "white middle classes often whiten themselves by reference to a less sophisticated and *excessively* white working class. Indeed, a proportion of the public service middle classes actively seek multicultural capital through education, while devaluing white working-classness" (2012: 453).

The chapter construction does little to actually subvert Michelle's point of view when the passage focalising on Billy actually reveals him to be the Nazi she suspected him to be. In the passage, the narrator just refers to him as "number 46", apparently the waiting number at Michelle's office hour, which also implies his status as a victim of capitalism: "Made redundant by the captains of industry who spent their time bleating on about national identity and then invested British resources overseas" (*FF* 115–116). As an employee being made redundant, Billy fits the description Zygmunt Bauman gives of the "human waste" of redundant employees in "liquid modernity". The depersonalisation and disposability conveyed in his description as "number 46" is thus reflective of his "social homelessness" (Bauman 2004: 13), as are his political attitudes born from frustration that is bluntly expressed in his reported thoughts: "Fascism was an attractive proposition. [...]. He was white, Anglo-Saxon, heterosexual and fed up of being told he was shit" (*FF* 116). Billy Bright thus subscribes to a sense of nationhood that is closely linked to a white working-class sense of entitlement that Steve Garner in his research on white working-class attitudes to English and British national identity describes as a "set of layered belongings [...] defined by a combination of bloodlines and contributions granting entitlement to resources" (2012: 455). This "set of layered belongings" is something that is being competed over among "those of similar economic levels" – that is, many white working-class Britons consider themselves in competition with non-white members of the same class over said "set of layered belongings" which comprises, among others, "neighbourhood, estate, town, nation" (Garner 2012: 455). Billy Bright thus invests "ideological labour" in what Garner calls the "moral economy of whiteness" which "[produces] one's character as ethically valid and competent" (2012: 455).

Just as the "suddenly disqualified employees" do not "respect the rules of the political-democratic game" because "those of the world of labour are blatantly ignored" (Bauman 2004: 13), Billy turns away from democratic parties and fears the "queers and Jews in the Tory party" (*FF* 116): "Billy Bright hated the Tories even more than the scum on the Left. The Tories had taken charge of the patriotic stance, waving the Union Jack around while milking the common man as though he was a factory farm animal" (*FF* 117).

As he sits in front of Michelle Watson, he directs his hatred towards her and thereby becomes a mirror image of her own assumptions about his person based on his looks:

> The woman looked like a right Trotskyist with her specs and clear skin, scruffy long hair and roll-up stained fingers; the kind of know-nothing outsider who came onto his manor and practised so-called positive discrimination for every minority that could ever possibly exist. These people talked about the working-class but didn't have a clue what the working-class was all about. Maybe he was wrong, but he doubted it. They all looked the same. (*FF* 116)

What is crucial in this shift in perspective from Michelle Watson to Billy – and this is symptomatic for the entire novel – is that Billy's assessment of her attitude is quite precise (Michelle is indeed depicted as superficial and hypocritical) and therefore initially shifts reader sympathies towards him. However, his all-encompassing hatred for everything that deviates from the perceived norm of being white, male, Anglo-Saxon and heterosexual subsequently lets him appear as just another caricature representative of standardised ideological positions. This becomes clear towards the end of the passage when he muses about his sympathies for Hitler: "Hitler understood what was what" (*FF* 117). While Billy "didn't exactly go along with the mass extermination of a race", he still admits that "sometimes, though, he got so fucking wound up by the whole thing that he could see himself out on the streets shipping the bastards off" (*FF* 117). However, as he then comically realises, an actual reordering of society based on national-socialist principles would have drastic repercussions for himself and his lifestyle: "He would have to change a lot himself, though, if the thing became official, because there would be no more drugs, drink or random violence. He would have to become a new man and hoped his deformity wouldn't count against him when it came to the crunch" (*FF* 117).

Michelle Watson and Billy Bright thus appear as stock characters who perceive each other as stereotypes but whose interior monologues actually affirm these stereotypes. Thus, the narrative multiperspectivity does in this case not serve a subversion of respective stereotypes that can be found in novels with multiple focalisation such as those by Niall Griffiths analysed in the previous chapter. In their juxtaposition through the multi-focalised narrative, the two ideological extremes, Michelle Watson and Billy Bright, are exposed as paradoxical figures who try to get along within contemporary British culture. While the narrative stance leaves no doubt that this culture is clearly not in favour of the British working class, it is implied that people like Michelle Watson are thriving in this very culture, which is basically characterised as a society which tries to come to terms with the changing post-war class system as well as with shifting attitudes towards multiculturalism. The character of Billy implies, and this point is emphasised by other characters throughout the novel, that members of the British white working class are the most disadvantaged group in this scenario – a problematic take on the issue that echoes a similar rhetoric of victimisation which can be found in accounts of American white trash like Jim Goad's *Redneck Manifesto* (1997), in which the author laconically states: "Multiculturalism is a country club that excludes white trash" (22). However, with regard to the white British working class, it has to be questioned if it was ever part of mainstream British culture at all, and whether this exclusion really is a consequence of or even remotely connected with the idea of multiculturalism. In the next section, I will therefore analyse how *The Football Factory* pits different notions of white Anglo-Saxon identity against one another in the face of the decline of the British Empire.

The Aftermath of Empire

Regarding King's follow-up to *The Football Factory*, *England Away* (1998), John Brannigan identifies the ultimate vulnerability of his characters, which is "not their shallow addiction to the aggressive consumption of sex, alcohol and violence, but their compulsive dependence on the authority of a mythic national identity" (2003: 80). This "incessant need to relate their own individual identities to the collective, to tell their story through the group identity" (Brannigan 2003: 80) is also at the heart of the narratives in *The Football Factory*, and while it is most prominently related to the hooligan protagonists' need to reinvent their national and ethnic identity, it is not exclusively restricted to them but can also be identified as the motivation of other, non-working-class characters like the aspiring journalist Jennifer or the "keen and sincere" Michelle Watson, who similarly identify with collective superstructures such as the educated middle class or the notion of an advanced, liberal state. What can be identified as an underlying current in the novel is that almost all forms of collective identity are modelled through an intersection of race, class, gender and national identity.

In this section, I want to compare three male working-class characters and their grasp on their white Anglo-Saxon identity: the main narrator Tommy, the unemployed neo-Nazi Billy Bright and the pensioner and war veteran Mr Farrell. While the three characters accentuate different aspects of Anglo-Saxon whiteness, they all must be considered within the context of what Brannigan calls England's "post-imperial hangover" (2003: 79).[13] In the context illustrated in *The Football Factory*, this Anglo-British "post-imperial hangover" must also be seen in relation to the devastating long-term effects of Britain's participation in the Second World War on the working class, not only materially in the form of destruction of infrastructure, but also for their class and national consciousness, and through the development of "a distinctive *ideology* of welfare capitalism" (Sinfield 2004: 17) during and after the war. King's novel depicts contemporary (that is, mid-1990s) Britain as a culture which in large part still tries to keep alive the national symbols attached to the victory over Nazi

13 | Silvia Mergenthal interprets King's *England Away* along similar lines within the context of the post-war struggles with national identity among working-class men (2011).

Germany and everything that victory allegedly entailed for British society. It thereby reveals the ideological inconsistencies and frictions within this symbolic heritage.

Alan Sinfield's account of post-war Britain (1997/2004) appears as an insightful blueprint for understanding these frictions. Using characters from different generations, King sketches the same social and ideological post-war trajectories examined by Sinfield. According to Sinfield, the Second World War saw the major attempt of the twentieth-century British ruling class to mobilise the working classes for a common cause by using an ideological superstructure that was designed to evade class differences even after the war had ended. While alternative historical accounts have shown the opposite, the war was narrated and officially remembered as a catastrophe eliciting the Britons' "intrinsic virtue and their commitment to king, country, empire and freedom" (Sinfield 2004: 9). However, it was feared that the working classes, severely affected by the blitz and even before that uncertain in their commitment to the British state, would be disobedient, causing the collapse of British economy and industry. Sinfield therefore interprets Churchill's rhetoric describing the British people as "united like one great family [...] taking their share and doing their work" (qtd. in Sinfield 2004: 11) as expressive of the promise of a better and more just British society that would arise after Nazi Germany was defeated. Subsequent post-war tensions between the different strata of Britain's class-based society, Sinfield argues, are to a significant degree a result of the fact that this promise was never quite delivered upon:

> Historians dispute the idea that a historic shift towards a new kind of civilization occurred in 1945. Developments in welfare, health and education were the expected extensions of existing arrangements [...]. The reformers of the 1940s (Labour Party leaders and others) were timid, trapped in paternalistic Victorian assumptions, failed to think through what they were doing, and consequently became embroiled in disabling tactical compromises [...]. (2004: 17)

Thus, while these attempted changes were subsumed under the ideology of welfare capitalism, legitimised, as Sinfield argues, "by claiming that it is what people want" (2004: 17), the actual changes affecting class relations were more complex and were by no means erasing class inequality. As Gary Day shows, the immediate post-war period saw a drastic change in the composition of British society, with the middle class increasing in size due to a newly emerging variety in professions, while the working class decreased in proportion due to "developments in the economy whereby there was a shift from heavy industry such as coal and shipbuilding to the light industries such as automobiles and electrical goods", which in turn meant "the loss of traditional work cultures" (2001: 179). These changes were felt not only in the relation between the middle and working classes, with the middle class striving to distinguish themselves from the working class through a range of symbolic practices, but also significantly in the cultural and artistic representation of the working class. Consequently, "the language of citizenship, based on the political consensus over the mixed economy, full employment and the welfare state, seemed to leave culture as the sole marker of class difference" (Day 2001: 180).

This mode of representation shows the working class as isolated and their problems as self-contained rather than as the effects of structural inequalities (Day 2001: 180). Day identifies the subsequent idealisation of the working class as an answer to the need for alternatives in producing a collective identity after the post-war loss of imperial images of British national identity (2001: 180–181). In that respect, I would argue that the fundamental problem at the heart of John King's characters is not only, as Brannigan has argued, the need to compensate for the loss of imperial images of national identity, but also the frustration over post-war welfare capitalism's empty promises of providing alternative identificatory models for the changing working class. Seen in this light, King's redundant workers, and the football thugs in particular, appear as the "substantial underclass" which is not "consoled with the toys of affluence" and cannot be incorporated into the ethos of British capitalism, which leaves them as representatives of "the myth of savagery-that-must-be-controlled" (Sinfield 2004: 171).

These problems become evident in *The Football Factory* through the omnipresent spectre of World War II. As is already apparent in the interior monologues of the "deformed neo-Nazi" Billy Bright, the figure of Adolf Hitler is repeatedly referenced in the novel, and in fact, it is one of the very first things mentioned at its beginning, as the first sentences – part of Tommy's narrative account – demonstrate: "Coventry are fuck all. They've got a shit team and shit support. Hitler had the right idea when he flattened the place" (*FF* 1). Of course, this is a casual mention during the angry rant of a football hooligan, but nonetheless, it is conspicuous in the range of its implications for the Britain that King depicts. Tommy here evokes the horrors of the Battle of Britain and the Blitz (in this case particularly the "Coventry Blitz" of 1940), events that, as I have shown above, were used to mobilise Britain as a unity transcending a number of inherent differences within the British population, including class, gender and national differences. However, as Tommy's reference implies, it now signifies not so much a common enemy external to the British nation state (Nazi Germany) but rather refers to zones of conflict within the nation. These might consist of the banal and "playful" animosities between different football teams as they can be found in any country which counts football among its national sports, but it still implies a deconstruction of supposed national harmony if seen in the context of the novel's themes.

In fact, it could be said that while Irvine Welsh and Niall Griffiths attempt to demonstrate that Britain cannot be considered as a homogeneous national whole, but must be seen as the agglomeration of different national cultures, King demonstrates that not even the supposed hegemonic cultural centre of British culture, England, can be regarded as a homogeneous national culture. He therefore adds another microlevel to the literary project of representing trans-British cultures in their diversity and their contradictions.[14] Within hooligan subculture, these microlevel differences are even more complicated, as Tommy sums up in a crude comparison of the feuds among English teams with the inconsistent nature of anti-black racism:

> There's grudging respect for Millwall and a few names have been known to grace Chelsea in the past, but when we play them it's war. Funny how it works. It's like blacks. People say they hate niggers but if they know one then he's okay. Or if he gets stuck in then he's a Chelsea nigger. Or like when you watch England away all the English get on, although there is occasional trouble, between Chelsea and West Ham say, because some riffs run deep. Generally you're broken down into people rather than mobs so somehow the whole thing works. (*FF* 5)

This quote reveals the difficult lines of conflict dominating hooligan life, and it is also remarkable in its employment of race, and especially blackness, as a trope to explain these conflicts. This racial trope as a means to

14 | Of course, instances of this microlevel deconstruction are also apparent in Welsh's segmentation of Edinburgh and Scotland as well as in Griffiths's character Roger's rants about "authentic" Welsh culture.

intersectionally map out social and cultural differences reappears in different shapes, as I will point out later.

Later, Tommy lets the reader in on his particular construction of Englishness, which he defines against Chelsea's archenemy Tottenham:

> Tottenham away is a cracker. There's always been a healthy hatred for Spurs. They're yids and wear skullcaps. They wave the Star of David and wind us up. We're Chelsea boys from the Anglo-Saxon estates of West London. Your average Chelsea fan coming up to Tottenham from Hayes and Hounslow is used to Pakis and niggers, but go up Seven Sisters Road and it's all bagel and kebab houses. Greeks, Turks, yids, Arabs. [...]. Silver Town yids. They're the rich spivs to West Ham's poor dockers. At least that's how the story goes. You go through Stamford Hill and Tottenham and you wouldn't think you're in the same city as Hammersmith and Acton. We've got our Paddies down in West London, but none of these yids ghettoes. I'm no Christian myself, but still Church of Fucking England. (*FF* 22-23)

The deconstruction of national unity continues in this quote, but now the microlevel fragmentation is extended to the city of London. Again, race and racialisation play a central part in mapping out the differences, with anti-Semitism being employed to deny Tottenham their belonging to the "same city". Conspicuously, Tommy does not differentiate between the two clubs and the ethnicities inhabiting the different parts of London in order to relativise concepts of English national identity, but rather points towards a notion of "authentic" Englishness, or Anglo-Saxon identity, which, according to his logic, is only to be found in particular estates of London, and hence is an identity that he claims for himself.[15] Football

15 | Jarrad Keyes reads King's novels as texts dealing with the "logics of dissolution" of the urban and the "global city" in particular; London becomes a decentred capital in King's novels which highlight London's diverse character and the satellite towns surrounding it: "Far from being 'forgotten', and anything but 'nameless', these dispersed elements register a new urban paradigm, reflexively aware of its contingent and arbitrary status as 'satellite towns', since the 'centre' around which it orbits - London - is perpetually decentred. Contrary to associations with centrality and power, London becomes displaced" (2007: 115). In specifically focusing on Tommy's ideas of a "London proper", Keyes argues that "the disingenuous idea of a 'London proper' is undermined by its volatility: uncoupled from its traditional moorings of centrality, London drifts interminably. [...] the rela-

and hooliganism thus constitute the arenas in which true Englishness is fought out.

The humorous endorsement of Hitler's bombing of Coventry is striking here, as it marks a move away from remembering the blitz and World War II as an experience of English (and British) unity. A similar belittlement of the war and Nazi Germany's strikes against Britain is apparent in Billy Bright's above-quoted affirmation of Hitler's understanding of "what was what". To those generations born after the war, and especially the disaffected generation, which, with members like Tommy and Billy, can in Zygmunt Bauman's terms be described as the Generation X of "liquid modernity", the figure of Hitler seems to have lost its meaning as the paradigmatic enemy of the United Kingdom. In Billy's case, the reference to Nazi ideology even serves to support his notion of supremacist white identity, and the concept of the white Anglo-Saxon and German-fascist biologism seem to go hand in hand in his thinking.

The novel provides a third take on Anglo-Saxon identity in the form of the war veteran Mr Farrell. He takes centre stage in the heterodiegetically narrated chapter "Poppy Day", which follows him as he goes about Remembrance Day. Having fought in World War II, Mr Farrell's awareness of the effects of the war clashes with contemporary generation's ignorance of these facts as well as their ideological implications: "nobody wants to hear about the realities of mass bombing. They just want a soft memory with Churchill walking through the wreckage and the royal family taking enemy flak" (*FF* 159–160). He comes to this conclusion, which is in line

---

tions between centre and periphery, urban and suburban, city and countryside, become historically contingent, suggesting these terms to be myths that have – and continue to – perpetuate hegemonic socio-economic structures" (2007: 117). Jörg Helbig, in an article discussing what he terms the "New Angries", among them the novels by Irvine Welsh and John King, argues in a similar way that in *The Football Factory* and other novels, "there is no movement [of the protagonists] towards the centre because the centre has been lost" (2007: 230). While I agree with this reading for the most part, I would still add that King's characters display much more paradoxical attitudes in that respect, for despite their contempt for a British establishment, they still adhere to diffuse notions of a true Englishness which is expressed in certain rituals. Thus, they are far from being verbose and scathing deconstructivists of nationalism as, for instance, Mark Renton in Welsh's *Trainspotting*.

with Alan Sinfield's argument about the role of World War II for Britain's cultural consciousness, after having met Mary, an old acquaintance from his youth who used to have a "sharp brain that lost the thread during the war" and who is now publicly babbling about the murder of a "white boy" by "those Pakis again" which she identifies as the outcome of an ongoing "race war": "How much longer do us whites have to get pissed on before someone does something?" (*FF* 159–160). Like Billy and many other characters in King's novel, Mary, whom Mr Farrell encounters on his way to the newsagent, is an example of white paranoia, which consists in the fear of the black population (with the support of left-wing politicians and a liberal middle class) "[slagging] off the native way of life" (*FF* 117). With the newsagent, Mr Farrell discusses the institutional backing of such paranoia, the BNP, which "has been attracting those white working-class voters alienated by the established parties. Mr Farrell and Mr Patel agree that a right-wing local councillor would mean more racist attacks" (*FF* 159).

In other words, Remembrance Day, the day which for him means to remember his own time as a soldier fighting against the Germans, becomes for Mr Farrell a confrontation with ideological post-war shifts, with the walk to the newsagent already establishing the major zones of conflict which will then erupt towards the end of the chapter when Mr Farrell witnesses "two youths in leather jackets" who "consider themselves patriots" verbally abusing a man and his two children on the train because "they are smelly Paki bastards" (*FF* 162). Once again, it is Adolf Hitler who is evoked as a patron and who is supposed to have had "the right idea" (*FF* 162). However, it is at this point that King employs the trope of the "white Anglo-Saxon" to contrasting effect. After the youths have punched the father in the face and the assaulted family have left the train,

> Mr Farrell is alone in the carriage with the two boys. He feels no fear. He is a white Anglo-Saxon Protestant male. He served in the war. An old soldier with the mark of the bulldog on his forearms, cut into the skin and filled with blue ink. He has killed for England and the English way of life. He is proud of his identity. He wears his poppy with honour. (*FF* 163)

For Mr Farrell, the "English way of life" (*FF* 163) and the construction of white Anglo-Saxon identity seems to categorically exclude racist attitudes, and so, overpowered by his memories of his wife's suffering at the hands of the Nazis, he confronts the two racist thugs and "breaks the first one's nose with a straight punch" and sends the second one to the floor with another punch (*FF* 164).

The sequence is complexly arranged, with the diegetic action of Mr Farrell punishing the two youths interspersed with his memories of killing a young German soldier and finding his future wife during the evacuation of a concentration camp, his thoughts on the present state of English society and his place in it as an elderly person as well as his emotional struggle with his morally ambivalent status as a war veteran and the function of Remembrance Day. The entire chapter thus becomes a meditation on the novel's main themes, with the nation's past and present converging in the remembered and lived experiences of an old man. Consequently, the chapter concludes by evoking the image of Mr Farrell as a ghost who haunts contemporary England. After he has beaten up the two thugs, he

> is a dark shape walking with his head down. Nobody really notices the elderly. They are considered an outdated irrelevance. Even hospitals shun them for fear of wasting money as they strive to hit financial targets. The world has moved forward. He will leave Remembrance Day until next year. Mrs Farrell will be disappointed but the good old days can wait a while longer. (*FF* 164)

Through Mr Farrell, the novel thus reflects on the problematic relationship of the British working class, and especially those working-class men who fought overseas, to the war and its relevance for constructions of British national identity. While his wife has urged him to properly celebrate Remembrance Day because she "admires her [...] knight in shining armour", he is "embarrassed, but somehow proud at the same time" (*FF* 161). To be more precise, it is in fact Mr Farrell's *imagination* of his already deceased wife with whom he communicates. When Mr Farrell returns from the newsagent in the morning, he is seemingly greeted by his wife who says that she has "made [him] a nice cup of tea" before the narrator indicates that Mr Farrell goes into the kitchen himself to boil his tea and "looks at the old photo, a picture of his wife who has been dead for the last three years" (*FF* 160). Mrs Farrell is thus a spectral presence, a symptom of Mr Farrell's struggle with the memories of his traumatic past, and can thus be linked to my discussion of the neo-gothic and the uncanny return of the past in chapter II.1. Here, Mrs Farrell, a now deceased Jewish concentration camp survivor, is present as the haunting memory of the Nazis' white supremacist terror and its victims – an aspect that is important for Mr Farrell's overall struggle with national identity, the past and the return of the evils of the past in the post-war present.

His recollection of his mates who "sold their medals to collectors to help pay the bills, while some threw them away in disgust" hints at an alternative working-class history of the war which is not embraced by the official ritual of Remembrance Day, and which is directly linked to the problem of class relations and economic inequality, which, despite indications to the contrary in war propaganda, were not improved after the war. In line with the arguments made by Alan Sinfield and Gary Day, the war must be seen as a new rupture in class relations rather than a consolidation.

What is more, Mr Farrell's musings on the elderly as "an outdated irrelevance" and just another liability in a capitalist system recall Bauman's concepts of redundancy and human waste. If we consider his body as an inscribed body – that is, a body inscribed not only with the features of a working-class life of hard physical work, but also with the traces of the war, as the narrator repeatedly emphasises in descriptions of Mr Farrell – the concept of redundancy becomes significant on several levels. As can be learned in an earlier chapter, Mr Farrell "had become a gardener after the war"; the work "kept him healthy and now that he was retired he benefited from a life of moderately superior health". His physique is directly related to his position in society: "he walked most places to keep the flow of energy circulating through his body and also because he appreciated the ability to move freely in a democratic society" (*FF* 114). When he beats up the racist thugs, the narration emphasises that "he is a strong man who boxed in the army and worked outside till retirement" (*FF* 164) – another instance in which the novel's strategy to design Mr Farrell as a representation of a strong and healthy male working-class body becomes apparent. Due to his old age, Mr Farrell might be seen as an "outdated irrelevance", but the fact that he still manages to take a stand against a bunch of young thugs implies a superiority which is inscribed in his body as much as the army insignia in the form of bulldog tattoos – signifying his sense of English national identity – on his forearms. In addition to that, he is constructed as a character who embraces different cultures and ways of life in his own concept of Anglo-Britishness: he married a Jewish concentration camp survivor and "likes Indian food" (*FF* 160) – these attributes are being accumulated to demonstrate the idealism of a man who "tells himself that people are the same all over the world. There is good and bad everywhere. He tends to believe humans are essentially well-meaning, that evil is conditioned by fear" (*FF* 163–164).

While it could be argued that this kind of too-good-to-be-true characterisation is as blatantly obvious and one-sided[16] as the stigmatypes of white working-class identities it is designed to oppose, the novel's strategy of characterisation can still be regarded as a means of resignification which is aware of the human body as a site of inscription for abjectifying and stigmatyping figurations that produce classist and racist disgust. Instead of fully deconstructing and even annihilating whiteness, as the novels by Welsh and Griffiths do, whiteness as an identificatory model remains strangely ambivalent in King's novel, the point apparently being that, while racism and classism are acknowledged as problems, these do not seem to be rooted in the construction of whiteness per se, but rather in the construction of *bad* whitenesses.

The aforementioned Billy Bright is one of the prime examples of this 'bad' and shameful whiteness. As a stereotypical neo-Nazi, he fits the stigmatype of white, uneducated working-class men associated with the Stephen Lawrence murder case throughout the 1990s (see chapter I). Billy's assumption that he would have to be treated better as a white man in his "native" country is a fallacy insofar as there never really was a time in Britain when white members of the working class were acknowledged as a respectable, privileged part of the population. In fact, when considering Alasdair Bonnett's historical analysis of whiteness and the British

16 | That Mr Farrell mourns the fact that "[things] aren't what they used to be" and that "foreign influences have eaten away at the fabric of the society he once knew" might seem like a break in this one-sidedness, but rather than being a general expression of xenophobia, it is clearly directed against particular capitalist and neoliberal changes affecting society rather than cultural influences: "Hospitals, schools, social welfare, unions, industry, everything has been obliterated by transatlantic dogma" (*FF* 163). Mr Farrell thus laments the factors that have eroded the British working class after the war (the shift from industry to the service sector and hence from blue-collar to white-collar work) and seems to be frustrated by a US-American and British neoliberalism: the "transatlantic dogma" could be interpreted as the neoliberal alliance of Thatcherite and Reaganite politics in the 1980s, which severely affected the British economy and class life.

working classes (see chapter I), it becomes clear that someone like Billy is only able to claim whiteness as a privilege for himself because of the very element he despises and considers a threat to his white identity and way of life: the descendants of peoples colonised by the British Empire now living in the United Kingdom. As Bonnett has argued and as I have outlined in chapter I, it was only through the presence of the colonised racial Other that the British white working classes could be considered just as white as the rest of the British native population, while at home, they were not acknowledged as white at all. This attitude can also be considered in the context of a "post-imperial hangover", since through imperialism and the subsequent shift in racial relations as well as through the promise of an elevation of working-class status during World War II, the white working class can be said to have experienced a racial identity crisis, caught in a state of un-whiteness between being considered the filthy lower class of the urban slums of the nineteenth-century British metropolis and being considered part of the white Anglo-Saxon colonial power, especially, as Bonnett has observed, in the colonies overseas. King's hooligans, then, can be interpreted in this context as subcultural "warriors" for a resignification of whiteness as an identity feature of the working class.

One passage from Tommy's first interior monologue demonstrates that his urge to restore a sense of Englishness that is congruent with (white) working-class identity goes even further back in history. Reflecting on contemporary eating habits and the advantages and disadvantages of continental versus British and Indian cuisine, he muses: "What else does Europe give you apart from a few dodgy lagers? Not like the Commonwealth, shunted on the back door, you'd rather have a curry any day of the week, none of that French muck the rich bastards eat, fucking wankers, if they want to be French fuck off to France. What have the frogs ever done for the English? The cunts come over in 1066, stick an arrow in someone's head and build a load of stone churches. Then they make the rich cunts speak their language while the rest of us are told our words are filth" (*FF* 13). The use of the pronoun "us" here implies Tommy's identification with what one could call a transhistorical proto-Anglo-Saxon lower-class subject which is representative of the "true" Anglo-Saxons. For Tommy, in an appropriation of the Marxist dictum, the history of Englishness is the history of class struggle, at least ever since the Norman Conquest.

White Male Impotence

In his examination of *England Away*, Miguel Mota argues with relation to football matches of the English national team abroad that,

> as Britain declined economically, shed its empire, and was forced to confront its diminished position in a new world order, the media began to view the nation itself (and here 'Britain' and 'England' become dangerously interchangeable) as betrayed by the continued failure of the English team on the international field. (2009: 264–265)

This was intensified in the 1980s through Thatcherism's attempt "to ensure the government's political survival with revived images of empire and military victory in the Falklands", and consequently "hooligan support for England at away games became a kind of defensive patriotism in the face of a wider national decline" (Mota 2009: 265). Even while Mota's argument focuses on the status of English hooligans during away games, especially within a broader European context, it allows similar repercussions for King's concentration on hooligan rivalry within the English football league. Especially in its relation to British whiteness, which assumes different qualities if it intersects with different class and gender features, the hooligan rivalry produces distinctions which help to qualify different imaginations of working-class whiteness that maintain an inner-class hierarchy as well as distinguishing the male working-class hooligans from the rest of society. Tommy's above-quoted description of the different London football clubs and their distinction based on, among others, racial ascriptions, is a case in point.

In addition, he compares the social status of white male hooligans to that of black minorities:

> I suppose we're like niggers in a way. White niggers. White trash. White shit. We're a minority because we're tight. Small in number. [...]. We have a base in the majority which means the cunts in charge can't work us out. [...]. We're a bit of everything. There's no label. We're something the rich cunts hate and slumming socialists can't accept. (*FF* 154–155)

Tommy remarkably employs white trash as a trope to delineate a 'messy' intersectional and almost hybridised identity in which class and race identifications complicate each other. How complicated this interrelation of whiteness, working-class identity, masculinity and subcultural affiliation can be becomes apparent in another sample of Tommy's observations and musings, which is worth quoting at length due to its peculiar jumps in argumentation and topics:

> We're lower than niggers because there's no politician going to stand up for the rights of mainly white hooligans like us. And we don't want their help. We stand on our own feet. There's no easy place to hide. No Labour council protecting us because we're an ethnic minority stitched up by the system. No Tory minister to support our free market right to kill or be killed. The old bill are the scum of the earth. They're the shit of creation. Lower than niggers, Pakis, yids, whatever, because at least they don't hide behind a uniform. You may take the piss out of the bastards occasionally but you have some hidden respect somewhere. But the old bill? Leave it out. We have the cunts in our sights. We pile in and the bastards don't have a chance. The sergeant takes the worst of it because he's all stripes and mouth and we've seen him batter the kid. Somehow he's worse because he's got a uniform and authority and we've been trained to respect uniforms and believe in the idea of justice. [...]. He's getting his reward and we're so frenzied we couldn't care less if he died. [...]. We look back and they've got some kids under a bus stop, kicking them black and blue, and a black woman's screaming at them to stop, that they haven't done anything wrong. A copper turns and lays her out with a single punch. Calls her a fucking slag. (*FF* 31)

Taking place during the events narrated by Tommy in the chapter "Tottenham Away", Tommy's narrative focuses on a confrontation between Tommy's hooligan firm with the police during a game against Tottenham, interspersed with his thoughts on the event and its broader implications. For the sake of my argument, I want to highlight three steps in the argumentative line presented in the quote in order to see how Tommy's thinking on race, class and society functions. In a first step, Tommy identifies a collective "we", the mainly white hooligans, and their position in British society. His comparison of the hooligans with the status of black people implies that, in a way, white hooligans, i. e., white male working-class members of a subculture, are or have assumed the status of an ethnic minority. The use of a racial slur and boundary term for black people becomes the demarcation of what groups of the population are considered to be "low". It is assumed that people of colour occupy the lowest rung of an ethnic ladder, and the sense that white hooligans are actually, if quietly, classed even below that category leads to the conclusion that they are the most despised ethnic group of all. What Tommy describes can be subsumed under the term *white trash*, as his description of the hooligans recalls a similar sociocultural dynamics that produced this concept and demonstrates that the concept not only implies a classism against lower-class white people, but also and always a racism against black people.

In a second step, Tommy suddenly jumps from his thoughts about ethnic hierarchies in modern-day Britain to the police – "the old bill" – who, in his as well as in the other hooligans' eyes are "the scum" of the earth. He thus uses the abjectifying and dehumanising terms applied to the hooligans against the state's executive forces whose task it is to materially and symbolically enforce and maintain the social boundaries delineated by such terms. In a conspicuous twist of argument, the police, just like their "enemy", the white hooligan, are measured against the segment of the population that is allegedly of the lowest rank, i. e., the mostly non-white ethnic minorities who are consequently rehabilitated in comparison with the police. From these thoughts, Tommy proceeds to describe a sequence of immediate events taking place in front of him, the beating of a police sergeant who has "battered" a kid.

Tommy's ambivalent application of the boundary term *nigger* first singles out the white hooligans, seen from the perspective of hegemonic society and its institutions as socially (and racially) abject before switching to the perspective of the abject hooligans who perceive the state's representatives as abject and finally culminating in a third step when his narration zooms in on an innocent bystander who tries to intervene in police brutality. It is worth mentioning that Tommy notes her skin colour, implying that the policeman's lashing out at her is not only violence against some innocent woman who dared to call out against police brutality, but more precisely a racially motivated act of violence. It also implies a form of solidarity of the black woman (who, in Tommy's worldview outlined above, would have a difficult standing in his socio-cultural hierarchy) with the white thugs. It seems as if the treatment of black people marks the standard of marginalisation and abjection against which everything else must be measured, but the implications for Tommy and other hooligans is extremely ambiguous.

This is also reflected in the attitudes towards the few black hooligans in Tommy's firm, most prominently Black Paul, a "Chelsea nigger from

Battersea" who "must be six-foot four in his bare feet and his hands are full of scars. Building walls for the white man" (*FF* 23). While Paul's body is shaped and altered through his work which, as Tommy implies in his choice of words, echoes black slavery, he

> makes up for this by shagging the white man's women, winding us up something chronic with stories of the blonde birds flocking round his big black cock. It's always the same kind of birds. Blonde hair stacked up on their heads listening to digital drum beats. Your typical ecstasy girls from the inner city estates. Kids who won't touch a white bloke. They look us over like we can't compare with Black Paul and the niggers from Shepherd's Bush and Brixton. Like we're not up to scratch and it can cause bad feeling. (*FF* 23)

Through these reflections on a black fellow hooligan, it becomes clear that the crisis of the British Empire, mapped on the male white working class, is also a crisis of white male heterosexuality. By reproducing the crudest stereotypes about black virility and primitive hypersexuality (Black Paul gives the white women, in Tommy's words, "a dose of jungle spunk", *FF* 23), Tommy expresses what Richard Dyer has identified as "the extraordinary anxiety surrounding inter-racial sexuality": "Inter-racial heterosexuality threatens the power of whiteness because it breaks the legitimation of whiteness with reference to the white body. [...] if white bodies are no longer indubitably white bodies, if they can no longer guarantee their own reproduction as white, then the 'natural' basis of their dominion is no longer credible" (1997: 25).

Although Tommy does not make the matter of reproduction explicit since he rather focuses on casual sex here, the "commonly found anxiety that the white race will fade away" (Dyer 1997: 26) still seems to underlie Tommy's descriptions of his and his mates' frustration with the white women preferring someone like Black Paul – an anxiety that corresponds to the "post-imperial hangover" prevalent in the novel, for, as Dyer explains, "the theme of outnumbering has been a mainstay of white racial politics, becoming the organising principle of British post-war debate, moving from discussion of 'overcrowding' [...] to the language of 'flooding' and 'swamping' used respectively by Enoch Powell and Margaret Thatcher" (1997: 26). The (in almost Lacanian fashion) phallic anxiety surrounding Paul's "big black cock" which attracts so many white girls who, by having sex with him rather than his white mates, betray "the hopes, achievements and character of the race" (Dyer 1997: 27), is expressive of the impotence of the white male working class. This sense of impotence is omnipresent in the book and is more often than not figured in concrete sexual terms: white working-class men are either a dying "outdated irrelevance" (Mr Farrell), are being made redundant (Billy Bright), are being outdone by more potent black men (Tommy) or are being threatened by new types of (white) women who are unavailable either because they take a "break from the routine of shagging white men in London" by going abroad to have sex with "dagos or spics" (*FF* 69) or because of class boundaries, like the aspiring journalist Jennifer, the sexually aggressive WPC that Tommy fails to pull, or the social worker Michelle Watson, "a fair looker" (*FF* 115) whom Billy Bright suspects to be a "dyke" (female homosexuality here being another 'betrayal' of the white race) and "Marxist theorist" (*FF* 116).

The hooligan subculture, then, is a means to compensate for this impotence. The firms not provide only a form of male bonding, but they are also almost exclusively white, with the few exceptions immediately recognisable in their nicknames which mark them as black: Black Paul, Black John, etc. In the case of Black Paul, whose appeal to the "typical ecstasy girls from the inner city estates" is such a nuisance to his white mates, the virility of black associates is even claimed for the firm: "Paul gives them a dose of jungle spunk, but he's a Chelsea nigger first and foremost. Do the business for Chelsea and that's all that counts" (*FF* 23–24). Similarly, Big John is "worth having along because you know he's always tooled-up" (*FF* 27). By claiming these black men for the purposes of the firm (it is noteworthy that both are described as superior in physical strength), it seems as if the white hooligans attempt to channel their racist anxieties, especially those of a sexual nature, in collective and exclusively male activities which have nothing to do with sex but still assume a surrogate character in that respect. After all, as Tommy explains early on in the novel, fighting is "paradise" and a "great way to spend your Saturday afternoon. [...]. The rush is there and my body tingles. Sounds funny but it's true. It's better than shafting a bird. Better than speeding. [...]. This is what life's all about" (*FF* 32), and later, he weighs the possibility of sex against fighting an enemy firm: "a shag's a shag and no bird can compare with a trip to Newcastle" (*FF* 119).

The quasi-transcendental experience of violence is a form of expenditure which nonetheless does not have the potential to change the state of affairs, let alone a political impetus, as Tommy is clearly aware of: "It's not like the system's going to be overthrown or anything" (*FF* 170). Rather, the violent excesses are the unproductive and futile expenditure of the white male working class, the redundant Generation X. The sense of impotence or even extinction consequently corresponds to the scenes of urban decay which provide the setting for the hooligans' fights. Through Tommy's eyes, the novel conveys an image of a Britain whose material decay correlates with its, to use Paul Gilroy's phrasing, "postcolonial melancholia": the fights usually take place in "a shitty street with broken walls and small rundown gardens" and among "piles of rotting rubbish left uncollected" (*FF* 30). Tottenham in particular is framed like an interior space of the Other which resembles descriptions of nineteenth-century urban slums: it is a "broken down North London slum" (*FF* 29), and "there's holes in the pavements and more fumes than Hammersmith. Pensioners sit on benches looking into space and an old black woman pushes a supermarket trolley packed with flattened cardboards and empty cans. There's a heavy smell of kebab meat and even the niggers look different" (*FF* 27). This apocalyptic and grotesque scenery is matched by Tommy's perception of England as a whole. When his firm is on its way to Newcastle, the

> motorways are all the same by night and you don't get to see the rolling fields of England's green and pleasant land because the dark shuts out the housing estates and dead factories. Cities of the living dead; Derby and Wolverhampton and then up to Leeds and Huddersfield. England's full of shit towns. Places like Barnsley and Sheffield. They can't compare with London. We're out on our own and don't belong with the rest of England. (*FF* 123)

The imagery borrowed from post-apocalyptic scenarios and horror fictions about the undead recalls similar motifs in the novels by Irvine Welsh, and in King's debut novel, the white working class is likewise rendered as the natural inhabitant of these decaying, post-industrial landscapes. Where Welsh and Griffiths evoke such imagery in order to challenge a monolithic image of an Anglocentric concept of British whiteness, King deconstructs Anglo-Britishness from within through the eyes of the hooligan Tommy. This microlevel representation of a disintegrating sense of Britishness challenged by increasingly problematic intersections of whiteness and class is continued in his novel *White Trash* where the image of the hospital serves as a metonymic battleground for social conflicts.

IV.2 *White Trash*

Policing the Underclass

White Trash, King's fifth novel, can be seen as an elaboration on several themes and motifs of his debut, albeit in more focused form. Like *The Football Factory*, *White Trash* is composed of conflicting viewpoints, with different focal characters serving as representations of ideas about contemporary British society. Unlike the earlier novel, which featured numerous episodes ordered around loosely arranged chapters narrated by one primary focal character, *White Trash* primarily focuses on two main characters, the young idealistic nurse Ruby James and the hospital administrator Jonathan Jeffreys. Their experiences and opinions are recounted in alternating chapters, letting the two narrative strands parallel each other and ultimately converge. In addition, the chapters focusing on the two focal characters are interspersed with passages about different minor characters set apart from the two main strands through italics.

The concentration on only two main characters corresponds with the condensation of setting, with the narrative primarily taking place in the hospital Ruby and Jeffreys work at. The hospital, the novel is quick to explicitly point out in the introduction of its character Jonathan Jeffreys, is a "microcosm of the nation", and Jeffrey's role as an administrator is to "[observe] the nation's health from a higher plain than a physician" (*WT* 41). As the plot progresses, it becomes clear that Jeffreys is, fatally, far more than a mere observer, but his self-description as well as his focus on "control" as a paradigm of human civilisation already hints at another recurring theme familiar from King's first novel, which is here being treated in a more accentuated way: the concept of surveillance as a means of enacting class differences. As I want to argue throughout my analysis, *White Trash* envisages the hospital as an institution of control which can be described with the Foucauldian concept of the "heterotopia of deviation" (1986: 25). Drawing on the work of hospital ethnographers Alice Street and Simon Coleman, I understand King's literary depiction of hospitals as representing the "paradoxical capacity [...] to be simultaneously bounded and permeable, both sites of social control *and* spaces where alternative and transgressive social orders emerge and are contested" (2012: 5). As such, the hospital can be regarded as an institution of social design and order building; consequently, the hospital as heterotopia is, to come back to Zygmunt Bauman's terminology, another one of society's "dumping sites" where "human waste" is sorted and discarded (2004). In that respect, it functions according to what Gilles Deleuze has identified as the institutions through which the capitalist control society exacts its power: "the new medicine 'without doctors or patients' [...] identifies potential cases and subjects at risk and is nothing to do with any progress toward individualizing treatment, which is how it's presented, but is the substitution for individual or numbered bodies of coded 'dividual'[17] matter to be controlled" (1995: 182). Consequently, the hospital is an institution of social control and selection that also performs a crucial role in the maintenance of boundaries that separate social classes.

The motif of surveillance is introduced in the first chapter which follows Ruby, who, during a night out, accidentally finds herself in the midst of a police operation. Here, Ruby observes a group of young men being chased by the police, an event which merges with her childhood memories of her dog being euthanised by a vet:

> asylum sirens screaming drowned puppies, floppy dog corpses, giant body-armour men swinging truncheons as they run along the side of the motorway, handcuffs snapping, their fuck-fuck-fuck language mixing with the drone of engines, three boys climbing the embankment, mechanised Old Bill too heavy and slow to catch these scruffy skin-and-bone herberts. (*WT* 3)

Ruby's perception, still affected by her sad childhood memories, renders the police in a naive way as a mechanised, dehumanised force resembling "robocops" (*WT* 3). These almost futuristic associations are continued in the description of the surveillance technology employed to track down the suspects in the dark: the "chopper coppers" are "linked to millions

17 | John Marks defines the Deleuzian 'dividual' and its place in the control society as follows: "In general terms, the duality of mass and individual is being broken down. The individual is becoming a 'dividual', whilst the mass is reconfigured in terms of data, samples and markets. Whereas disciplinary individuals produced quantifiable and discrete amounts of energy, 'dividuals' are caught up in a process of constant modulation. In the case of medicine, which claims to be moving towards a system 'without doctors or patients', this means that the figure in the individual is replaced by a dividual segment of coded matter to be controlled" (2010: 55-56).

of television sets" and thus suggest a sense of permanent and ubiquitous surveillance (*WT* 3). Using "thermal technology targeting three fleeing suspects, [...] the pilot has a brilliant view of the town" (*WT* 4). As she is the "nearest shape", the "chopper coppers" are now "zeroing in on Ruby", although "she's just sitting in the background" and "doesn't have a bad bone in her body" (*WT* 6). The narrator, who throughout the novel is insistent upon repeating and emphasising Ruby's innocence and goodness using similar phrases, here contrasts the protagonist's inherently good and precious being with the de-individualising perception of the police apparatus embodied by technology: "Ruby doesn't have a face now, no name, no number, just the heat of her body, she's sexless, hardly human" (*WT* 7).

The dehumanised and dehumanising police force is analogised with the representation of American police in cinema and TV shows when "Ruby sees herself on the police monitor, she's seen these helicopters before, on the telly, the LAPD chasing gang bangers along burning freeways and into a McDonald's parking lot, the producers mixing hip-hop effects in with the voice of the controller, Los Angeles police chasing kids through the streets of England" (*WT* 8–9). This description indicates an "Americanisation" of British culture which affects numerous facets of society. In the novel's context, this can be interpreted as an allusion to the neoliberal modes of social structuring which have emerged as a result of the transnational move towards Thatcherite and Reaganite economic and social models emerging in the 1980s and which still affect British society in the late 1990s and early 2000s, the time focused on in King's novels. The technological fetish associated with the police force in the first chapter is analogous to the description of the hospital as a sphere of surveillance designed according to the parameters of economic and technological efficiency. Thus, the fact that a focus on the police force and its technologies of surveillance and control has been chosen as the opener for the novel thematically situates the novel's subject – contemporary health care and the space of the hospital – within a larger context of social control and mechanisms of selection. In other words, the police and the hospital are both institutions that are designed to work towards biopolitical citizen control.

This is apparent in Jonathan Jeffreys, the managing consultant who ultimately functions as the antagonist to the nurse Ruby James. Perceiving the hospital as a microcosm of society, he believes that "without control, human beings was [sic] no better than apes" (*WT* 47). His fear of a loss of control is repeatedly stressed throughout the novel and shapes not only his outlook on life and humanity, but also on his professional tasks and obligations. Reflecting on the different spheres of work within the hospital, he distinguishes his role from that of the nursing staff: "They had to deal with the nitty-gritty of hospital life and this was a thankless task. His role was more delicate, albeit equally thankless. Each needed the other. Without his expertise the hospital would soon be overwhelmed and sink into chaos" (*WT* 140). For Jeffreys, signs of impending chaos and anarchy are visible throughout society, most prominently embodied by the white working-class people inhabiting the unnamed new town in which the hospital is situated. The hospital's car park attendant, for instance, "was at home with anarchy, cars filled with skinheads and bleached blondes. Their children exact replicas. The attendant allowed cars to rest on yellow-lined kerbs rather than banish them on the street" (*WT* 180). Later, when his desire for control is revealed to be more than a mere compulsion, and Ruby only narrowly escapes his killing spree, her trust in humankind is shattered. She reflects on the possible grand scheme of things behind Jeffreys's heinous acts, which included the killing of several patients considered to be a burden on the health care system and society in general:

> Was Jeffreys really a social cleanser trained by the authorities? Was the government carrying out euthanasia according to the cost of treatment and a person's economic worth? [...]. She followed this line of thought swinging into a nightmare vision of the world around her, where she was being recorded and evaluated by accountants, something as pure as medicine and public health infected with a deadly strain of cynicism, and then as quickly as she went that way she was snapping back in the other direction, saw Jeffreys as nothing more than a loner, a coward whose snobbery was out of control and meant he killed anyone he didn't like, whenever he got the chance. He was a control freak, power mad, the scum of the earth. (*WT* 351)

As I will later come back to the repercussions of Ruby's reversal of the rhetoric and imagery of (human) scum in this crucial passage, I will for now focus on the notion of control conveyed by Ruby's reflections. While her concluding thoughts after almost having been murdered by Jeffreys are as naive as anything she says or thinks throughout the novel (her notion of medicine and public health as something "pure" bespeaks her outrageously naive outlook even if one does not subscribe to the harsh social Darwinism represented by Jeffreys), they nonetheless display a certain scepticism regarding the trustworthiness of governmental and state institutions, and the vague idea that one's every step might be watched by some externalised (institutional) big Other brings the novel's motif of the policing of the lower classes full circle as it directly connects with the images of surveillance and policing at the beginning. This idea is also picked up shortly before the final escalation during a decelerated moment of 'quiet before the storm' when Ruby hangs out at the airport with her new lover Charlie, one of the novel's "white trash" characters. Sitting on the roof of a car park, Charlie identifies a new sign which prohibits parking on the roof. Assuming that it must be placed there in accordance with the fight against terrorism, he more or less playfully imagines the roof being under surveillance:

> Wouldn't be surprised if there wasn't a camera on us, filming. […]. They've probably got a sniper out there looking at us through the sights of his rifle. […]. They work in the background, pick their targets out with special sights then get you when you don't expect it. As long as it's got the official stamp it's legal and they can get away with anything. […]. Some official killer sitting there weighing up the odds, wondering if he can get away with it, seeing us having a smoke and getting all righteous. Probably thinks we're scum even though he knows we're not terrorists, just looking for an excuse to tap the trigger and wipe us out. (*WT* 266-267)

The self-identification as "scum" in someone else's perception, conflating with the image of the terrorist as an enemy of the state and, in a post-9/11 context, of 'Western' culture and way of life, marks the white working-class protagonists as the Others of British society which have to be wiped out to maintain order and control. Charlie's half-joking suspicions anticipate Jonathan Jeffreys's escalating hatred for lower-class elements and his euthanasia project, which, in turn, is reminiscent of the biopolitical cornerstones of Nazism. The paranoia expressed by the protagonists, however, is not merely a reaction to contemporary forms of increased surveillance in the public sphere; it is also the expression of a fear that one has lost one's legitimate place in the order of things, which since modernity is, as Zygmunt Bauman has argued, paradigmatically embodied by the nation state: "Throughout the era of modernity, the nation-state has claimed the right to preside over the distinction between order and chaos, law and lawlessness, citizen and *homo sacer*, belonging and exclusion, useful (= legitimate) product and waste" (2004: 33). John King's novel assumes a similar state of affairs: with their legitimacy questioned, people like Ruby and Charlie are reduced to dehumanised scum.

Even more than the previous primary texts discussed so far, *White Trash* makes explicit the particular ways of looking at people classified as scum or its various synonyms. In the society of control rendered in the novel, the ways of looking at trash are not only limited to law enforcement apparatuses of surveillance and biopolitical/biomedical institutions like the hospital (which, as a selective institution, allows for the medical treatment of certain people while it excludes others), but can also be found in media representations of the lower classes. Repeatedly, the novel emphasises Jonathan Jeffreys's preferred method of gaining knowledge about the classes alien to him, which is the consumption of speculative TV documentaries and, as is revealed during the novel's climax, snuff movies. Watching the documentaries "was a vital part of his work, although sometimes rather depressing. But it was important to know his patients inside out, to be aware of changing trends" (*WT* 141). He is particularly appalled by a documentary on Ibiza, "a current favourite holiday destination for the young", and his interior monologues provide insight into the representational mechanisms of the film, shot with

> a bouncing handheld camcorder [giving] him an inside look at the behaviour of a section of today's youth. [...]. Obsessed with trivia, they screamed and giggled for the camera, one girl in particular turning his stomach. Sleeping with men she did not know and boasting about it in front of the whole nation. Had she never heard of venereal disease? Aids? (*WT* 141)

Although the term is not used in the novel, the description of the TV programme and its subjects strongly echoes common depictions of chavs. The fact that Jeffreys refers to such people as "scum, White trash. The white niggers which infested every civilised nation" (*WT* 306) once he lets his veneer of respectability and the allegedly disinterested perspective of the scientist slip, however, reflects the racialisation of the white lower classes associated with "inferior" black elements that is implied in the figure of the chav.

In addition, Jeffreys's obsession with the wellbeing of the nation which has to be protected from infection and infestation marks him as a paradigmatic figure of modernity which, following Zygmunt Bauman's theories of modernity and its construction of the nation state as well as, for instance, Ali Rattansi's explanation of nineteenth- and early twentieth-century racism as a phenomenon of modernity,[18] saw the increased racialisation of concepts of the nation state as a collective which had to be protected by racial and political hygiene. Thus, Jeffreys is depicted as an agent of control and order whose psychotic attitudes are not the symptoms of an individual but are rather presented as representative of more general attitudes prevalent in British society (or at least its middle and upper classes). This is also reflected in Jeffreys's mode of reception while watching the documentaries: the way he decodes the films as more or less authentic representations from which he can draw conclusions about British class life as a whole reflects these films' function as modes of social abjection instigated to produce and maintain symbolic boundaries between social classes. The "authoritative voice" of a voice-over suggests a superior mode of representation, while the voices of those who are depicted in the films are rendered inacceptable, with their sentences "broken by bleeps" and "hundreds of obscenities [being] painstakingly edited out" (*WT* 143). The televisual medium is pivotal here: firstly because it has been defined as one of the most important media (next to the internet) of disseminating the chav as a figure of class disgust (see Tyler 2008), and secondly because the narrative presentation of Jeffreys's trust in the power of televisual representation as an accurate image of social reality (and, consequently, in the affect it generates in him as the basis of his beliefs and actions) illustrates the power of the medium's symbolic and representative regime to create abject figures and, in terms of social boundaries, material difference.

Within the wider context of the primary texts under discussion in my thesis, Jeffreys's belief in such a mode of representation echoes the hegemonic and othering approach to representing the lower classes in the dominant canon of "English literature", which is challenged by Irvine Welsh, Niall Griffiths and John King in their privileging of non-standard,

18 | Rattansi argues that the epitome of racism in the twentieth century, the Holocaust with its particular form of racialised anti-Semitism, was made possible especially because of modernity's emerging idea of the nation state as a racial unit: "Ideas of *racial and political hygiene*, impossible in a pre-modern world view, took strong hold in early 20th-century thinking and policy making, especially in Germany" (2007: 60).

marginalised Englishes. In that way, Jeffreys is marked as a monstrously hyperbolic figuration of hegemonic British culture and can thus also be seen in the context of the monsters Foucault has identified[19] – even more so due to the fact that Jeffreys only thinly disguises his enjoyment of the sexual violence depicted in the snuff movie he later forces Ruby to watch and engages in deviant sexual acts himself. His weekly visits with Candy, a "common tart" (*WT* 185) who provides him with insight into "the nature of the women of this godforsaken town" (*WT* 182) and who gets paid by him for allowing him to urinate into her mouth can thus be interpreted as the "sexual debauchery" with which, according to Foucault's historical analyses, the political monster degrades the common people (2003: 98).

These exercises in "slumming" (*WT* 184) follow the same logic as his keen interest in poverty porn: Jeffreys denies his fascination and the sexual arousal he derives from these encounters and disguises it as necessary research for his work: "this was purely business" (*WT* 184). As with his work of monitoring the social dynamics in and around the sphere of the hospital and his allegedly scientific interest in documentaries on the lower classes, his encounters with Candy help him to establish a superior classed gaze on the common people who have created for themselves a world that "was rotten to the core" (*WT* 185). Once again, this gaze is also a controlling one. As Jeffreys urinates in Candy's mouth, "he controlled the sexual urge and he controlled the working of his bladder. She was under his spell. Bewitched. Under his control" (*WT* 183).

It is notable here that the aspect of control is emphasised not only in relation to his domination of the despised lower-class subject, but also in relation to the dominating man's own body and instinctual drives. Jeffreys thus appears as the epitome of the composed white Anglo-Saxon male whose self-control distinguishes him from uncontrolled, instinct-driven blacks and the underclass and is thus an example of "the divided nature of white masculinity" (Dyer 1997: 29) that I will return to later: "It was this desire for self-determination that separated man from the beasts, the intelligent man from the fool" (*WT* 232). In fact, it is the very sense of a loss of control which frightens Jeffreys the most. Later in the novel, he recalls an episode from his youth when he was given a visit with a prostitute in Soho for his eighteenth birthday by his friends. The confrontation with the girl who "had been low class" is remembered by him as an episode of humili-

19 | See my discussions of Foucault's analysis of the monstrous in chapter II.3.

ation, shame and disgust, leading to a loss of control: "He became angry at her for forcing him to lose control and refused to hand over the agreed fee" (*WT* 233). As he concludes, "the mind was all-powerful. [...]. Mind over matter was his motto from the earliest days" (*WT* 241). The primary means by which Jeffreys conceals the working of his mind is his face:

> The face was mere decoration and should not reflect a man's deeper thoughts. The masses did not know how to control their facial expressions. [...]. Jonathan had separated the physical from the intellectual. His mind followed one course while his expressions set the outside world at ease. (*WT* 243)

Here, Jeffreys becomes a fitting example of the "sexual drama of white men" which "have to do with not being able to resist the drives or with struggling to master them" (Dyer 1997: 27). His idea of the primacy of mind over body thus is reflective of the "greater will power" that white men are believed to have in comparison to white women (and to virtually all non-white people) in traditional conceptions of white (male) supremacy (Dyer 1997: 27). In that respect, Dyer describes white masculinity as "divided", which "is expressed in relation not only to sexuality but also to anything that can be characterised as low, dark and irremediably corporeal" – a problem that is enhanced by the notion that "*not* to be sexually driven is liable to cast a question mark over a man's masculinity – the darkness is a sign of his true masculinity, just as his ability to control it is a sign of his whiteness" (1997: 28, emphasis in orig.). Jeffreys's "self-determination", especially in the face of lower-class prostitutes, but also in his encounters with Candy, becomes an exercise of white male mastery of self. His self-control is coupled with his control of lower-class subjects, which seems an externalised projection of what Dyer calls the "darkness" within the white male subject. Jeffreys's actions prefigure his later complete loss of control when he captures Ruby and tries to kill her, and thus hints at the almost aporetic tension between the need for self-control and (regulated) excess inherent in white male heterosexuality described by Richard Dyer. Thus, race, class and gender are once more revealed to intersect, for Jeffrey's fantasies work best when he can activate all three categories simultaneously by superordinating himself in each one.

It is central to note the different levels of control that are attached to the particular ways in which King's novel presents the monitoring of – that is, ways of looking at and controlling – the underclass. King's novel conveys a sense of permanent observation of the underclass by the middle and upper classes through various institutions and designated individuals; this observation also works in and through the monitored lower-class subjects who to some degree have internalised the control mechanisms they are governed by. These mechanisms consequently work through the body of the lower class subjects who, in the case of Jonathan Jeffreys's work, become dehumanised objects of scientific study. This becomes poignantly evident in Jeffreys's bizarre relationship to Candy, whom he considers to be "rubbish" (*WT* 186) that is being dissected by his scientific mastering gaze. This gaze becomes apparent while he ritually urinates into her mouth: "He looked down at the hair. The blonde strands and white skin below. But he was not a beast. Every so often he squeezed his penis to stem the flow. This allowed her to catch up. He leant sideways to observe the swallowing motion. He continued. In control" (*WT* 183). In the descriptions of her (white) skin complexion as well as the mechanics of her swallowing, the narrator assumes Jeffreys's othering and abjecting gaze on Candy and thus recreates the structures of surveillance and control via its narrative conception.

In addition, his observation and control of the lower-class subject during his own performance of what, despite his own assertion of a lack of arousal, can be described as a (deviant) sexual act is once again a projection and sublimation of his own dark drives. As Richard Dyer argues, the ability to control this side is as much a sign of whiteness as the actual presence of these drives. However, Dyer adds that "there can be occasions when either side discredits the other, the white man's masculinity 'tainting' his whiteness or his whiteness emasculating him" (1997: 28). Jeffreys's sexual performance can be read as a balancing of these poles and significantly projects his dark side onto the lower-class woman. In this case, Candy illustrates the paradoxes of white femininity through her intersectional identity position: she is a white woman who thus carries "the hopes, achievements and character of the race" (Dyer 1997: 29). As Dyer argues, women guarantee the reproduction of the race, "even while not succeeding to its highest heights [which would be reserved for the white male]. Yet their whiteness, their refinement, makes of sexuality a disturbance of their racial purity" (1997: 29). In Candy's case, her class additionally taints her whiteness and is commingled with her sexuality – or rather, with Jeffreys's sexuality and its projection onto her class.

White Trash thus continues and elaborates the tendency of King's first novel to juxtapose the marginalised perspectives with more privileged, hegemonic perceptions of them, albeit, as becomes plainly evident in Jonathan Jeffreys, in a caricaturing manner. In *White Trash*, Jeffreys's perspective is cross-cut with that of Ruby, and the two perspectives are often designed as companion pieces, each taking place at the same day and time and thus juxtaposing their different activities at a given moment. This aspect is most prominent in the accounts of Ruby and Jeffreys's first direct encounter after Ruby has learned about the passing of a patient (who, as it turns out, has been killed by Jeffreys). Jeffreys discovers Ruby in the hospital cafeteria, devastated by the news, and comforts her. In the chapter focalising on Ruby, Jeffreys is described from her point of view as being "a gentleman. It was in his accent and the way he moved, holding back in case he offended her, picking his words very carefully" (*WT* 129), while the subsequent chapter with Jeffreys as a focaliser provides descriptions of Ruby as an "earnest young woman" who, for Jeffreys's tastes, "was obviously an emotional person. Perhaps even a bit unstable" (*WT* 135).[20] However, he continues to describe her as possessing "a modesty too often lacking these days. On the downside was her accent, which, to be blunt, he found a little common" (*WT* 136). The parallel descriptions focusing on the respective person's manner of speaking serves as a comic reflection on perception and human interaction based on class stereotypes, with a naive admiration of Mr Jeffreys's gentlemanly ways on Ruby's part, and a snobbish take on the working class on Mr Jeffreys's part. Through this narrative strategy, the novel highlights the inscriptions of classed habitus onto people's bodies, which serve as material manifestations of the unspoken, symbolic boundaries governing social activity.

Jeffreys's dissection of the lower classes relies on behavioural distinction, including conscious language use and accents. As I will argue in the following section, his professional habitat, the hospital, is in his view designed as a sphere in which such performances of distinction assume a vital function in maintaining social order and class differences, inscribed on the bodies of patients and hospital staff. This also entails his own

20 | In fact, the reader might gain a similar impression, as twelve entire pages (*WT* 122-134) are devoted to her lamentations on the patient's death, followed by a later reflection on his biography in a vignette told by Ruby in the first person (*WT* 295-302).

vision of economics and society as well as biopolitics, including scenarios of infection, illness and contamination which are manifest as concrete dangers for the human body, but which are also symbolically mapped onto his conception of society as a whole.

Social Contamination

In line with findings from the field of hospital ethnography, the hospital in King's novel can be described as "nuanced by incompatible logics, for example, political ideology, in the form of governance, and by an ethics of care, treatment, and respect for persons" (White et al. 2012: 69). These incompatible logics are primarily represented by the two main characters and later antagonists, Jonathan Jeffreys and Ruby James. The former's focus on economics and efficiency prohibits the sense of emotional engagement which is such an integral part of Ruby's character, as she is so dedicated to her nursing profession that she "wouldn't change it for anything" even if it seems as if "the more people get well and go home, the more seem to turn up needing a bed" (*WT* 23). Her sense of philanthropy is not only expressed in repeated characterisations of her as "a good girl", "kind-hearted", "doing her best to see good in bad" and similar attributions (*WT* 23), but is also implied in her interactions with and reactions to patients and their individual suffering. This is evidenced in several vignettes interspersing the heterodiegetic chapters focusing on Jeffreys and Ruby which, as turns out later, are told homodiegetically by Ruby, giving biographical accounts of those patients who are later revealed as having been victims of Jeffreys's euthanasia project. Her engagement with patients, however, would be seen by Mr Jeffreys as "inappropriate attendance" (White et al. 2012: 72) which conflicts with the "interplay between political and economic rationality and clinical rationality" (White et al. 2012: 69). Put into the context of Bauman's notion of human "order building", Ruby and Jeffreys's approaches to their work and the sphere of the hospital represent two different and conflicting concepts of design and order: the people Jeffreys considers as redundant and as human waste – "lives that cried out to be aborted" (*WT* 276) and who have to be "fed" the "cleansing fluid" (*WT* 277) of Jeffreys's lethal injection are perceived by Ruby as precious human beings, each with their own unique biographies which she listens to and preserves.

The description of the lethal injection as a "cleansing fluid" is indicative of Jeffreys's sense of hygiene, which constructs the social body as a macrocosm of the human body and its organs – and this is yet another sphere in which Ruby and Jeffreys are constructed as opposing characters. Ruby perceives sickness as something which becomes a social bond between patients in the hospital, something which causes suffering and despair to be overcome. She celebrates scientific and medical progress, with the hospital being a place of "learning and caring" where threats in the form of pandemic illnesses are overcome thanks to progress in vaccination and medication: "the point was things were always getting better, they were winning" (*WT* 133). Her optimism is contrasted with Jeffreys's vision of a health system which is temporarily working but on the brink of collapse and needs tending by people like him: "The knockers could say what they liked about the NHS, but it worked. Against the odds. It was a balancing act of course, and a rethink was long overdue, yet for the moment the state coped" (*WT* 53).

Jeffreys's view on the NHS as an economic rather than a social and philanthropic endeavour is informed by his capitalist attitude inspired by his admiration for US-American models of enterprise – an aspect which is also crucial for the novel's approach to the intersections of race and class, as I will show later: "Jonathan greatly respected American values within the workplace. Much of the culture he found shallow, based on quantity rather than quality, yet the dedication to a free-market ethos more than made up for the crassness" (*WT* 226). Later, the novel further elaborates on this transatlantic inspiration:

> Living in a civilised culture that had not yet embraced the ideal of truly free capitalism, Mr Jeffreys looked to the United States for some sort of guidance. He believed in private medicine as a matter of course, but accepted that a transfer from the old state system would take time. Misplaced idealism was a problem and tradition a heavy burden. The Americans were free from this sentimentalism and able to make brave decisions. (*WT* 275)

Such attitudes echo the alliance of Margaret Thatcher and Ronald Reagan's style of politics and economics which would come to be known as neoliberalism and would, if in altered form, be continued by Tony Blair's Third Way economics and politics. This is in line with Street et al.'s observation that the contemporary (British) hospital is a sphere where "neoliberal logics of 'efficiency' come to structure 'moments of access' alongside the welfare logic of 'care'" (Street/Coleman 2012: 13). That is, the hospital is not a space entirely permeable for anyone who considers themselves to be in need of care and treatment, but is designed to strictly control access to it. As such, the hospital reflects modes of inclusion and exclusion as well as the respective boundaries which can be found throughout society as a whole.

As Jeffreys continues his reflections on the benefits of American society, he praises the work ethic in the country and ends up contemplating the American condemnation of "laziness" and the 'benefits' of capital punishment:

> Hard work was rewarded, laziness was not. Crime, meanwhile, was severely punished. A policy of zero tolerance had been adopted for the lawless element and he fully supported humane execution for the most depraved murderers and sexual molesters, carrying as it did a guarantee of dignity in death for even the cruellest of men. [...] death by lethal injection eased the conscience of all right-thinking men and women. It offered a compromise and some sort of consensus. (*WT* 275-276)

Although he restrains himself, emphasising that he was "operating in a completely different arena", the connection between judicial killing, the control system of the prison and the hospital is clearly established here. Both the body of the criminal who cannot be corrected as well as the patient who cannot be healed are abjects who cannot be reintegrated into society, neither as productive members nor as active consumers, and must hence be disposed of according to Jeffreys's perception of social order, an exaggerated version of neoliberal logics of efficiency, or what Deleuze calls the "mutation of capitalism" that leads to the overtechnologisation of the control society (1995: 180). The narrator lets the reader further in on Jeffreys's thoughts on the matter during the novel's climax. According to him, the patients he has killed were

> pathetic cases who were a burden to their loved ones. Not to mention the state. [...] He believed in survival of the fittest. In the frugal use of resources. [...]. He was an angel of mercy who ended their misery. At the same time cleansing society of its unproductive element. Cutting costs in the best way possible. (*WT* 315)

Employing the phrase of the "survival of the fittest", coined by Social Darwinist Herbert Spencer[21] to describe the superiority of the white 'race' in the nineteenth century (Rattansi 2007: 54), Jeffreys is clearly designed as a modern-day representative of old-fashioned ideas of eugenics. His self-perception as an "angel of mercy" in this context echoes the Auschwitz doctor Josef Mengele, the "Angel of Death" who came to paradigmatically symbolise the particular atrocities of Nazi-German racism consisting of the abuse of medicine and science in the service of racial genocide. The analogy with Mengele is strengthened by his reflections on the benefits of vivisection and medical testing:

> Why waste millions treating the mentally ill and physically disabled when they could serve the greater good? Of course they would have to be willing, he was not proposing enforced vivisection, but he felt these people would be happy to assist. It was all very well pumping rabbits full of chemicals [...], but how much more efficient it would be if these tests were carried out on humans. (*WT* 232)

Furthermore, the association of Jeffreys with the context of genocide not only highlights his racist views, which become blatantly apparent towards the novel's climax, but also his endorsement of industrialised killing, be it in the form of "humane" judicial killing in contemporary America (which, in the case of lethal injection, strongly relies on the assistance and cooperation of medical staff and producers of pharmaceuticals, hence being another example of the ethically highly dubious misappropriation of medical knowledge) or in the form of his own bizarre euthanasia endeavour. Here the latter echoes both similar systematic programmes of killing the "unfit" in the hospitals and asylums of Nazi Germany and the origins of the eugenics movement in the United Kingdom and the United States in the early twentieth century. After all, the term *eugenics* was coined by the British scientist Francis Galton (Wray 2006: 70, Stubblefield 2007: 164) whose theses on the application of Darwin's ideas on the systematic breeding (and, if necessary, compulsive sterilisation) of humans informed the foundation of the British Eugenics Education Society in 1907.

In the United States, these ideas were met with acclaim and gained support, peaking in eugenic schemes which included the systematic compulsory sterilisation of "mental defectives". As Matt Wray (2006: 67–70)

21 | While often being falsely attributed to Charles Darwin.

and Anna Stubblefield (2007) have shown, this affected primarily the poor white population of the South, who were referred to by physicians and scientists of the time as "human rubbish" (Wray 2006: 67). In short, the history of the eugenics movement is also part of the history of the concept of white trash, and, as Anna Stubblefield has argued, eugenics played a significant part in constructing dichotomies of "pure" and "tainted" forms of whiteness along the lines of mental and cognitive dis/ability: "in the early twentieth century the concept of feeblemindedness came to operate as an umbrella concept that linked 'off-white' ethnicity, poverty, and gendered conceptions of a lack of moral character together, and [...] feeblemindedness thus understood functioned as the signifier of tainted whiteness" (2007: 162).

In addition, the eugenics movement reflected not only notions of racial purity, but was also "the product of a society which was still fundamentally divided along class lines, emerging against the background of heightened turn-of-the-century concerns about differential class fertility" and can thus "be seen as a direct ideological reflection of middle-class interests: it naturalized social inequality by explaining social success and failure as a direct reflection of innate inability; and it provided justification for the replacement of a social order of aristocratic privilege" (Thomson 1998: 188). In the British and American eugenics movement (and, by extension, in the German-fascist version), turn-of-the-century intersectional notions of class and race converge in a drastic way. The exchange of such ideas between the United Kingdom and the United States exposes the similarities between the two cultures when it comes to notions of race and class, and figurations of tainted whiteness (that is, racial purity compromised by a lower class status) represent the phenomenon around which the eugenicist ideas coalesced. Jeffreys's endorsement of eugenicist ideas makes him a condensed modern-day representation of these histories.

The fact that he primarily kills those patients he considers to be socially abject and deviant indicates that he is not only concerned with a dehumanising principle of efficiency in the health care system, but also with the eradication of those individuals deemed socially and politically unacceptable. Thus, his victims include an old man and former trade union activist who represented "an industrial age with petty class politics" (*WT* 150), a working-class man whom Jeffreys suspects of being a skinhead hooligan, "Nazi scum, a threat to national stability" (*WT* 318), a retired teacher who "was a typically frustrated, sadistic lesbian, twisted inside and unwilling to take her place in society, to marry and bear children" (*WT* 320), and a man suffering from HIV, infected through heroin injection, but mistaken by Jeffreys for a homosexual who had been "too stupid to practice safe sex" and "then expected the state to foot the bill" (*WT* 323) – in short, "the white scum who inhabited the terraces and flats and yet expected mollycoddling by the state" (*WT* 323).

When Jeffreys talks to Ruby about his victims and stresses their deviance, the function of the interspersed vignettes detailing the biographies and attitudes of his victims becomes apparent: they debunk Jeffreys's assumptions about their character and backgrounds, with Ruby being the one in the know of all their histories because she lent her ear while taking care of them in the hospital. When Ruby delivers the fatal stab to Mr Jeffreys's chest, another vignette in italics is dedicated to her perception of things, and she wraps up the incongruence between who his victims really were and who Jeffreys believed them to be (*WT* 341–350). She once more goes through the patients' biographies and every victim's reputation is once again restored in Ruby's musings. Ruby concludes that Jeffreys *"goes on about his superior intellect then does a parrot routine repeating everything he's been told by the media* [...] *pedalling cheap stereotypes ... and he's taken their prejudices to the obvious conclusion"* (*WT* 344; italics in orig.).

The functional problem of Ruby's honouring of the victims within the political project supposedly envisioned by the novel is that it leaves the impression that the victims' alleged deviance must be debunked by assuring the reader that Jeffreys's victims were in fact *not* the homosexuals or political deviants he believed them to be: the "skinhead" Steve was, in Ruby's words, *"a man"* while Jeffreys *"was a wimp"* (*WT* 344; italics in orig.), the retired teacher Pearl was in fact *not* a "lesbian and a twisted old maid" but, as Ruby is eager to stress, a (heterosexual) *"good woman and full of love"* (*WT* 346; italics in orig.), and with the allegedly bare-backing Danny she is equally eager to clarify that *"Jeffreys thought he was gay when it was dirty needles"* and that *"it was a shame that Jeffreys didn't know that Danny got HIV from using heroin"* (*WT* 348; italics in orig.). The problem with these rectifications is that they seem to suggest that Jeffreys's victims would have to be judged differently if they had *not* adhered to heteronormative standards (standards which are emphatically reproduced by Ruby when she compares the effeminate intellectual "wimp" Jeffreys to the real working-class "man" Steve). It is not clear, for instance, whether it would have made a (moral) difference to Ruby if Danny had actually caught HIV from homosexual encounters rather than from dirty needles. To put it bluntly: Would the killings have been less appalling (at least in Ruby's eyes) if the victims had in fact been the homosexuals, asexuals and "deviants" Jeffreys suspected them to be? This ultimately flawed debunking of "cheap stereotypes" is thus a rather one-directional affair and represents a conceptual and ideological flaw in King's novel which threatens its critical project of denaturalising dominant ideologies of class and their stereotypes of deviance.

Jeffreys's use of tropes of tainted whiteness situates his worldview in the imagining of the underclass as a race, which, to recall my discussion of Imogen Tyler and others in chapter I, serves to render poverty and disadvantage not as "economic or even properly political issues, but as a *hereditary condition*, a *disease*" (Tyler 2013: 188), which has repercussions for the hospital as the novel's symbolic setting, for it is precisely in its function as a heterotopia of social control that the hospital assumes its relevance in King's text. Thus, the patients killed by Jeffreys are not only "treated" by him because of their costly illnesses but because they themselves are a disease which threatens the body politic and, more precisely, the white British 'race'. His white anxiety about the "white niggers which infested every civilised nation" (*WT* 306), which comes to the fore towards the end of the novel when he feels caught in the act by Ruby and his composure disintegrates, is revealed to be the emotion at the core of his whole endeavour. Interestingly, he is only revealed to be a blatant racist after he has struggled to keep his composure throughout his interior monologues. Before this final caesura, his latent racism is primarily expressed through his classed attitude and his emphasis on intellectual and behavioural superiority as a decisive property of individuals and populations. Together with his endorsement of neoliberal economic and political principles as guidelines for his work, Jeffreys appears as a figure in which old-fashioned nineteenth-century ideas about class and race (including the conception of the city as a degenerate space of slums as opposed to the idealised countryside) are conflated with distorted versions of 1980s Thatcherite meritocratic ideals. This conflation then results in an exaggerated figuration of a contemporary racialised class hatred which anticipates the rhetoric and ideological developments of the twenty-first century – one could even describe King's novel, published in 2001, as a fictional anticipation of the attitudes emerging around the chav phenomenon and the rhetoric of the whites having adapted a "black gangster culture" in the wake of the 2011 English riots.[22]

An indicator that Jeffreys is specifically designed as a character representing 1980s politics and their continuation throughout the 1990s is his rhetoric of a "classless society" coupled with his condemnation of the "nanny state" and his endorsement of meritocracy: "Times had changed and the nation was now managed according to consensus. Britain had evolved into a more fair and classless society. It was true that today you truly reaped what you sowed" (*WT* 43). This sentiment echoes the ideas of American political scientist Charles Murray, who, as I outlined in chapter I, did much to popularise the concept of the "underclass" in the United States and subsequently in the United Kingdom where he was consulted to lend his expertise in coping with a growing underclass. His suggestion that intelligence (and hence genetic disposition) was the decisive factor in determining one's position in society (outlined with co-author Richard Herrnstein in the infamous *The Bell Curve* in 1994) led him to advocate the complete abolishment of welfare structures (Tyler 2013: 192–193; Jones 2011: 81–82; Welshman 2006: 167; Hartigan Jr. 2005: 178–179; 182–183). Murray not only proved crucial in the popularisation of "categories of contaminated whiteness" (Tyler 2013: 187) outside the United States, but also has, as Owen Jones argues, many common points with today's Tories: "Many of the Tories' ideas about social inequality – such as blaming people for their circumstances – have a firmly Thatcherite pedigree. But they can also be traced back to […] the American Charles Murray. […]. Like today's Tories, Murray claimed that family breakdown had triggered the rise of an 'underclass' in British society" (Jones 2011: 81). Thus, when Jeffreys claims that it "was superior intellect that led to survival" (*WT* 306), this can be read as a hyperbolic reflection of publications like *The Bell Curve* and their controversial reception – especially since it is implied that superior intellect is primarily a feature of the white middle and upper classes and not of the underclass comprised of white trash and blacks. Similarly, Jeffreys's obsession with the "white scum" or "white niggers" is symptomatic of a Murray-inspired "intraracial policing" (Hartigan Jr. 2005: 176), and his

22 | In fact, unspecified "riots" are repeatedly mentioned as having taken place prior to the beginning of the novel's events (*WT* 7, 10), suggesting an atmosphere of social unrest not unlike those having taken place throughout the last thirty years in British history.

talk of "cultureless rabble" (*WT* 151) likewise resembles Murray's coinage of a "New Rabble" (qtd. in Jones 2011: 81).

His contempt for the "nanny state" (also borrowed from Murray as well as Thatcher) is caused by the belief that welfare would sustain the weaker elements of society who are weaker due to genetic disposition. Jeffreys's satisfaction with the death of his first victim, the elderly Ron Dawes, a former trade union member, is thus due to the fact that

> in many ways Dawes had represented the past. An industrial age of petty class politics. He had lived through momentous times, but those days were gone. The West had settled down and made great strides. Britain was more streamlined and less wasteful than ever before. Organised rebellion was no longer an option. He knew that Dawes had been active in the trades union movement, and even though the unions had been broken for more than a decade he still felt that these men and women had a case to answer. Unions had forced the nation to its knees. [...]. Something of the past had died with Mr Dawes. He mourned the individual as he did all individuals, yet not the notion of the nanny state. (*WT* 150-151)

Jeffreys's critique of the nanny state and the trade unions, very much in line with Charles Murray's arguments, is based on the assumption that welfare will bring out the worst in those who depend on it. That is, recipients of government benefits are feared to remain passive, thus becoming a financial burden on the public, which will, in both Jeffreys's and Murray's predictions, sink into chaos. Jeffreys's perception of the lower class is thus in line with Murray's description of the "underclass", already referenced in chapter I, as being defined by their "deplorable behaviour" in response to long-term unemployment and their unwillingness to actively seek employment (Murray 1990: 68, qtd. in Welshman 2006: 164). In that context, it is no wonder, then, that Jeffreys, contemplating the death of union man Ron Dawes while watching a group of "thugs" in the emergency unit, conflates the two:

> If Dawes represented the past, then these thugs standing in front of Mr Jeffreys were the present. Their offspring would embody the future. A cultureless rabble who consumed with no regard for their fellow citizens. [...]. This was the direct result of years of undisciplined liberalism. [...]. In a curious way these thugs represented a natural progression from the trades union movement, even if they lived in a time of political apathy. They were rabble, yes, but highly dangerous

and organised rabble. He thought again of that documentary detailing the use of surveillance equipment in tackling street crime. These men before him no doubt gathered in football gangs and organised confrontations via mobile phones and the internet. (*WT* 151)

Notably, the political organisation and construction of class identity (unions as a means to express class interests and thus to forge a certain form of collective class consciousness) is mingled with a diffuse notion of breeding (the achievements of the trade unions will shape the way future generations will partake in society and future offspring will "inherit" certain forms of collective consciousness and individual conduct). The "thugs" thus appear as a distorted progression from the unionism that Dawes represented and which has in the decades after the Miners' Strike been subjected to political fragmentation. In that way, the literary character Jeffreys reflects the conspicuous mapping of classism onto modern-day versions of scientific racism and geneticism which have to a significant extent helped shape the figure of the chav and its multiple classist and racist implications for how British whiteness is intraracially constructed, segregated and policed. With regard to the latter, it is not surprising, then, that Jeffreys immediately jumps to the topic of surveillance and new media, which are integral parts in constructing a thuggish white underclass. And interestingly, King's protagonist almost prefigures the infamous and then much-discussed employment of social media by rioters and looters during the English riots ten years in advance (see Baker 2012).

The conviction that the "nanny state" corrupts the lower classes, which are in need of stricter policing due to their inherent incapability and lower intellect, also has repercussions for the institution of the hospital. During his final outburst, Jeffreys vents his disgust for the hospital staff and their "white trash" patients:

Every one of them acted as if it mattered whether these patients lived or died. Really, it did not. They were scum. White trash. [...]. But he had to remember his mission. He was employed to serve the interests of the state [...]. Yet he was restrained by ideology. If it was his decision, he would privatise the whole caboodle. Force those who could not pay for their health care to die where they fell. It was more honest that way and what God had intended. Why would He have invented cancer if it was not to control the population? [...] He was paying for the drug addicts and prostitutes,[23] the single parents and loafers, the criminals in their luxury prison cells, the whining pensioners and sponging asylum seekers. (*WT* 305-306)

In their ethnographic and sociological study on the mechanisms of entrance and patient control, White et al. state that hospital staff is concerned with the "labor of dividing patients" and granting or denying entrance to the hospital and its treatment facilities – a control which "reproduces moral orders of good citizenship; those who transgress the order become undeserving of care" (White et al. 2012: 72–73). Who is or is not a "good citizen" and hence deserving or undeserving of care in any given case depends on the common standards prevalent in the respective society and culture as they are reflected by the hospital. In King's novel, the hospital setting becomes a battleground for different ideologies. While the nursing staff is primarily characterised as inherently good and morally upright, if not entirely as exaggeratedly good as Ruby ("nurses are the heroes", as DJ Chromo, the leader of a pirate radio station, exclaims during a moment of pathos; *WT* 258), and altruistically fight for every patient's wellbeing, Mr Jeffreys represents the spectre of capital and dehumanising neoliberalism that haunts the hospital. Both parties and ideologies thus stand for different entrance policies in relation to the different strata of society. The egalitarian principles of Ruby and the rest of the nursing staff represent the idea of the hospital as a permeable heterotopia catering to all strata of society, while Jeffreys's vision of the hospital pictures it as a privileged sphere for a social elite able to pay for treatment. That his vision is built upon a white intraracial elitism distinguishing between categories of proper whites and white trash becomes evident throughout the book.

Within the context of scientific racism and classism, the hospital thus becomes a space where the boundary between the deserving and undeserving is drawn, and just who is deserving of maintaining good health might, according to Jeffreys, very well be defined by their genes. Here, it is worth looking at the novel's two main characters in relation to the question of genetics. The idea of genetic determination is a current running through the novel in several ways, most prominently associated with the place of the underclass in society. Jeffreys endorses the view that

23 | The irony behind this being, however, that Jeffreys actually pays for them when he goes to visit Candy.

people succeed in life according to their genetic fitness, and he himself attributes his superior intellectual abilities to genetics – the "ability was etched into his genes. Some were chosen, some were not" (*WT* 243). In addition to that, he outlines his theories about races and their genetic makeup, drawing conclusions about the proximity of lower-class whites to non-white populations. He even reproduces the old-fashioned assumption about the Irish as being less white than other populations of the British archipelago:

> Their [the "Asians"] ability to endure the behaviour of low-intelligence whites was quite amazing. West Indians fulfilled lower-caste jobs along with their English counterparts. Those people were closer to nature, more spontaneous and less hard-working than Pakistanis, Indians and Bangladeshis. Then there were the Irish of course. Many Irish girls came to England to work as nurses. They toiled next to the Asians and Caribbeans. A large number had been absorbed into the indigenous population, as indeed had Asians and West Indians. The Irish had been here longer and their DNA had filtered into the gene pool. Many were unrecognisable now. The same was beginning to happen with these brown- and black-skinned peoples. This was no doubt a good thing in terms of stability, and while he did not possess an ounce of prejudice, it nevertheless reflected the low morals of the common whites. (*WT* 188–189)

Blending scientific and cultural racism, Jeffreys argues for a correlation between behaviour, work ethos and genetic disposition. His assumption that the Irish can be genetically and phenotypically distinguished from "proper" whites and resemble non-white "races" echoes the anti-Irish racism peaking in nineteenth-century phrenological studies (see Ignatiev 1995 and Brannigan 2009). Genes, according to Jeffreys, are the basis for biologically distinguishable races, which, however, are also expressed by cultural forms and habitus. One of his greatest fears is that "the dirty little golliwogs" culturally corrupt "the [white] scum who loved their jungle music and had sex with their men", which resulted in a "whirlpool of mutant spawn, corrupted genes that moved faster and faster until they were absorbed and regurgitated as another wave of white trash" who "had no understanding of culture" and rather communicate through lesser cultural forms and a similarly corrupted language, "their ever-changing slang" (*WT* 307–308). These lines in particular are a striking example for the way King's novel diagnoses the ideological preconditions which in the present day eventually culminated in comments like David Starkey's argument that "the whites have become black" (see chapter I). As I have argued above, *White Trash* thus in hindsight becomes readable as a prefiguration that can, from a contemporary standpoint, be regarded as a text which illuminates the cultural conditions, figurations and tropes relevant for the construction of British tainted whiteness today.

However, as useful and telling as King's novel is for such cultural analyses, its flaws, calculated or accidental, prove to be equally telling when it comes to the seemingly timeless allure of "race" and scientific pseudo-explanations of cultural identities. This happens to be the case in one instance when good-natured Ruby in passing expresses her own stance on the matter of genes when, during a party, she thinks that "she was one of the little people, but it was good being ordinary, she didn't want to be famous, that was another world, she got on with what was right here, right now, it was how she was, part of her genetic make-up" (*WT* 68). Given the fact that Jeffreys is designed throughout the novel as a monstrously exaggerated figure representing class hatred and dubious, even dangerous eugenicist ideas, it seems puzzling that Ruby, the angelic antithesis to the almost satirically rendered eugenicist, would endorse similarly old-fashioned ideas about the genetic determination of characteristics which could in fact be better explained by theories of behaviourism and socialisation. I do not want to argue here that a person like Ruby should not be content with what she is and socially represents, but the fact that her own contentment rests in the belief that her position in society and of being "ordinary" is genetically predetermined seems problematic within a text which, as my analysis has shown, is clearly attempting to interrogate and challenge classist and racist ideologies, and especially those of a (pseudo) scientific persuasion.

This interrogation, however, suffers from passages like these – especially if considered in relation to *White Trash*'s designated intertext, Aldous Huxley's *Brave New World* (1932), which is presented in an epigraph, a quote from one of the sleep-learning slogans ("'Old clothes are beastly,' continued the untiring whisperer. 'We always throw away old clothes. Ending is better than mending, ending is better than mending, ending is better ...'", *WT* n. pag.). Is Ruby's belief in her "genetic make-up" to be read as a nod towards Huxley's vision of a future where, through eugenics and conditioning, humans are formed to fit into different castes in which each member is happy and content with their position in society?[24] While the quote chosen from the intertext clearly hints towards Jeffreys's conviction that the lives of people who are a burden to society should be "ended" rather than "mended", it does not become clear how Ruby has to be situated within this context. Her reliability as a focal character is compromised given the fact that she at times appears as a similarly exaggerated inversion of the cold, psychopathic and cynical Jeffreys to the point where she even gives the impression of being stuck in an infantile mental state. Her musings about her "genetic make-up", for instance, quickly blend into a possibly drug-induced stream of consciousness laying bare Ruby's childish character and her desire to live in a cartoon world – "she loved *The Flintstones*, wanted to live in Bedrock, have children like Bam Bam and Pebbles, talk to Wilma and Betty and lift rocks with dinosaurs instead of cranes, it was a dream town all right, Bedrock was where the men were manly and the women glamorous", *WT* 68–69.

One might argue that the crass and polarising construction of its main characters serves to exaggerate both positions – Jeffreys's antiquated bourgeois racism and Ruby's too-good-to-be-true and naive working-class attitude – in order to collapse the very basis of both stereotypes. However, it is much more plausible that, ultimately, the novel and its narrative make-up try to mark Jeffreys as a grotesque embodiment of racism and classism in an attempt at satire which then again is compromised by an overt romanticisation of working-class white trash culture as embodied by Ruby and her friends' simple outlook on life. This strategy, with its well-meant gestures of idealising the working and lower classes, entails the potential to reinforce rather than denaturalise stereotypes.[25] As I will

24 | In analogy to Huxley's novel, Ruby's attitude and conviction that she and her status in society are the outcome of her "genetic make-up" could be the result of a cultural conditioning – that is, the kind of conditioning which in Huxley's novel is being satirised in the concept of "sleep learning".

25 | In direct comparison, Irvine Welsh and Niall Griffiths's texts prove much more effective and subversive in that respect because, despite their own grotesque hyperboles, they emphatically resist an idealisation of any class and prove all forms of identity construction as inconsistent and inherently contradictory. King, however, might also at times attempt to illustrate the 'messiness' of cultural and personal identities, but in *White Trash*, he ultimately reproduces essentialised classed subjects.

show in the following section, this predicament can best be illuminated by dissecting King's engagement with tropes of American culture, for it is once more through employing and adapting transatlantic cultural forms that light is shed on seemingly idiosyncratic phenomena in the United Kingdom.

Adapting the American White Trash Aesthetic

References to American culture abound in John King's novel, as my previous quotes from the interior monologues of Jonathan Jeffreys indicate. To be more precise, specific ways of seeing American culture (or individual aspects thereof) from a non-American perspective are central to *White Trash* and its treatment of its eponymous subject. In line with King's attempt at dialectics, evident in its contrastive narrative construction with the two focal characters' narratives running parallel to each other, references to American themes and figurations are employed to serve the novel's particular dialectics as represented by Ruby James and Jonathan Jeffreys. While I have already focused on Jeffreys's endorsement of American economics and politics in the previous sections, I will now primarily pay attention to the direct implications of such references for the representation of British intersections of race and class. Thus, I will additionally focus on the relevance of American culture for depicting working-class culture as it is experienced by Ruby and as it is perceived from Jeffreys's bourgeois-elitist perspective.

Jeffreys's image of US culture is deeply ambivalent: while he repeatedly expresses his admiration for the country's economics and the work ethic of its citizens, certain phenomena which are specifically marked as "American" are only met with his contempt. Recalling a holiday romance with Donna, a film producer from Manhattan who "made movies for morons" (*WT* 227), he lauds the woman's "lack of tradition that freed her to make hard decisions with barely a second's thought" and her "pioneering spirit" (*WT* 227–228). Although he does not specify what those "hard decisions" might consist of, it is remarkable that he sees himself as a British citizen as "bogged down [...] by history and precedent" (*WT* 228) – an aspect which also is conflated with ideas of race and genetic heritage: "She [Donna] knew that as an American he had the one thing her own wealth could never buy. If he was to fall on hard times, gamble his fortune away or give it to charity, he would still have breeding" (*WT*

227). According to Jeffreys's logic, America is a nation without a racial or cultural history to speak of. Once more, this bespeaks his construction of race as a conglomerate of biological (or "scientific") and cultural factors. From the musings about his Anglo-European "breeding", which, in his intraracial hierarchy assumes a privileged position in comparison to American whiteness, he immediately switches his attention to the cultural-geographical makeup of his British surroundings, his home place, "the outer reaches of London" and the new town in whose hospital he works, "a monstrous carbuncle on the edge of a great capital": "This was a sordid world with no meaning or will to change on the part of dull people who walked in never-ending circles, too stupid to understand their lives were futile" (*WT* 228). Wondering whether the inhabitants of this unnamed new town – as a planned city devoid of the cultural tradition and history Jeffreys so admires about Britain's capital – are aware of cultural history, the literary "classics", "the world's finest orchestras", the "theatres of the West End and boutiques of Knightsbridge", he concludes that they are rather exclusively familiar with "low culture" and "drank Coca-Cola in McDonald's" (*WT* 228–229). Here, Jeffreys uses the clichéd accusation of a typically American shallow consumerism, epitomised by its well-known fast food chain, in order to demarcate "the difference between high and low culture, the latter term assuming a quality that did not actually exist. There was no culture there" (*WT* 229).

In associating the people he refers to as "scum" and "white trash" with American characteristics, "white trash" becomes another expression for the well-known rhetoric of anti-American cultural pessimism prevalent among many Europeans. Coming back to Bauman's definition of "human waste" as "failed consumers", "white trash" can thus be described not only as failed consumers (i.e., those too poor to spend money) but as misdirected consumers – that is, as a demographic that consumes excessively despite a lack of economic resources. Speaking from an American perspective, Gael Sweeney observes that "the construction of White Trash in popular culture is of total consumer and non-producer. White Trash is separated from the working class by their lack of connection with work or production" (1997: 250). Jeffreys's contempt for the British lower classes is similarly rooted in the value and cultural significance of consumption, which is most significantly represented in his attitude towards food. Throughout the narrative, he emphasises the importance of a healthy and exclusive diet, and when Candy, into whose mouth he urinates on a regular basis, serves him biscuits and tea made from PG Tips, he wonders how people "ate such rubbish" (*WT* 186). Hence, there is a direct connection between what people are and socially represent and what they eat – and a bad diet is in most cases directly linked to his vision of a cultureless America and its tainted whites.

This becomes especially clear in an episode he recalls from his time as a medical student when he took pity on a young woman sleeping rough – "as if London was no better than Cairo and Calcutta" (*WT* 236) – and offered to take her for a meal: "Her choice of restaurant was an American-style diner that sold hamburgers and French fries. [...]. He relived the smell of frying food and the sound of Elvis Presley's voice in the background. It was very tacky, even twenty years ago, before the globalisation of McDonald's" (*WT* 237). The visit to the diner amounts to a revolting sensual experience for Jeffreys, whose class disgust shifts from a symbolic to a very material level in the experience of eating. In addition, the aural and low-cultural experience of having to listen to Elvis adds to his disgust, which is yet another central aspect for the employment of American cultural phenomena in King's novel:

> He hated Presley as much as he hated the new punk rockers. Rock and roll was a blend of British folk music and black slave rhythms. The common people of America had accepted this abomination and danced to the tune of Satan. Naturally, this was all imagery. He did not believe it was literally the Devil's music, it was merely the language of the Southern states of the world's greatest democracy, a land of achievement with a continual war between the forces of civilisation and barbarism. Rock and roll was a cheap mixture of popular cultures and without meaning. Presley was its representative, a hillbilly with greasy black hair and a loud taste in clothes. (*WT* 237-238)

This passage is remarkable in the way Jeffreys, a privileged person of, as he would say, good British breeding, reproduces the cultural dichotomies running through the United States and its concepts of race and class. His identification of Elvis Presley as an icon of the white American South is in line with Gael Sweeney's interpretation of what she calls the "White Trash Aesthetic": "Elvis Presley is an icon of White Trash Culture: a figure of terror and the grotesque to the urban, mostly Northern, arbiters of 'good taste' and a spectacle of excess and release for his Southern white fans" (1997: 251). In line with Sweeney's reading of Elvis as a figure of the

Bakhtinian carnivalesque, I would argue that there is a direct connection between Jeffreys's disgusted perception of the "rubbish" consumed by the white trash and their musical tastes. The excessive and very corporeal aesthetics of Elvis represent the white trash body which is, "by definition, an excessive body", and therefore, "the Elvis period most beloved by the White Trash Aesthetic is the seventies: white jumpsuited, overweight, and in your face" (1997: 255). For Jeffreys, then, a taste in this excessive music coinsides with a lifestyle which is in overall bad taste and not in line with his ideals of beauty and cleanliness. The White Trash Aesthetic and its prime representative, the excessive and carnivalesque Elvis, represent the economic dialectic that is manifest in the "ideological construction of wealthy and privileged groups as simple, spare, thin, and understated" as opposed to "the fat, the undisciplined, and the unworthy" poor (Sweeney 1997: 255). In addition,

> this kind of dialectic also designates New England and the Puritan aesthetic as plain and pure, while the South is vulgar, hot, sensual, overeating, overweight, lazy, poor, backward. We can assume that the message from the dominant powers is: those who have little consume much – indeed, much more than they deserve! Hence the politics of Reaganism and trickle-down economics. Trash is always 'garbage': the excess at the margins of society. The working-class body is always read as excessive because working-class consciousness is materialized there: workers show their labor on their bodies. (Sweeney 1997: 255)

In this context, Jeffreys appears as the modern-day embodiment of Puritan morals, especially with his credos of mind over matter and the primacy of intellect. The working-class body, which eats too much and too unhealthily, is therefore the antithesis to Jeffreys's aesthetics of living. However, the novel's subtext suggests that such a worldview cannot be trusted and that a man who claims to favour intellect over the body and sustains an old-fashioned dichotomy of high and low culture must necessarily channel his drives otherwise – hence the characterisation of Jeffreys as a Foucauldian sexual monster preying on the lower classes. King's poetics aims at a simple inversion of stigmatypes: while the rude outward appearance of the "skinheads" populating the new town around the hospital are constantly revealed as goodhearted people, the distinguished "gentleman" Jeffreys, who has "very clear" skin and "neatly groomed" hair, hides his perverted and psychopathic character under a neat facade (*WT* 129).

The model for King's construction of Jeffreys is quite obviously Bret Easton Ellis's *American Psycho* (1991), whose protagonist Patrick Bateman has become symbolic of the idea of moral degeneration and perversion underneath a respectable upper class surface, satirically emphasising the shallowness and narcissism of Reaganite America. It is perhaps no wonder, then, that Jeffreys, when asking himself whether the "scum" around him had "read the classics", comes up with a curious sample canon of "classics": "Socrates, Sade, Nietzsche" (*WT* 228). While they are certainly historically significant, one would have to be at great pains to find the writings of the Marquis de Sade canonised as "classic" on any regular curriculum, and his texts might even today be perceived by many as an outrageously grotesque and deviant form, at least by the standards Jeffreys usually applies. But on a meta-level, his mention of de Sade might be interpreted as a hint towards his own sexuality, especially his urophilia, descriptions of which can be found in abundance in de Sade's work, as well as the political context within which de Sade's works have been received and adapted.[26]

Thus, King's construction of upper-class depravity connects to a tradition of depicting the well off as exploitive and monstrous. In that respect, *White Trash* reflects and employs the reciprocal strategies of constructing social abjection from both ends of the class spectrum. This is achieved through an engagement with different understandings of cultural forms as expressive of class identity – "high" and "low" forms of culture. Thus,

26 | Most notably, Pier Paolo Pasolini's film adaptation of de Sade's *Les 120 Journées de Sodome/The 120 Days of Sodom* (ca. 1785, published 1904), *Salò o le 120 giornate di Sodoma* (1975), has transposed the novel's plot from eigtheenth-century revolutionary France (the time period which served Foucault in his study of constructions of the upper-class sexual monster, taking the lead from de Sade's writings) into the final days of World War II in the Italian fascist republic Salò. One of the film's fascist libertines, the Duke, delivers one of the film's central statements, which might just as well come from John King's antagonist: "It is when I see others degraded that I rejoice knowing it is better to be me than the scum of 'the people'. Whenever men are equal, without that difference, happiness cannot exist. So you wouldn't aid the humble, the unhappy. In all the world no voluptuousness flatters the senses more than social privilege."

King connects to well-established traditions of caricaturing both the upper class and the lower classes as excessive in their respective ways. King adds another dimension of Bakhtinian carnival in that he not only constructs Jeffreys as someone who despises low cultural forms such as rock and roll and country[27] – forms which are the designated musical modes of expression for the "hillbillies"[28] and/or are "situated in what Bakhtin calls the 'lower body stratum': the center of procreation and excretion, where humans are reduced to the equality of their bodily functions" (Sweeney 1997: 256) – but also in elevating those "low" cultural forms as a proper mode of expression for his British white trash protagonists, as I will show in the following.

When Ruby falls in love with one of her patients, the pirate radio DJ Charlie, and spends time with his crew, the White Trash Aesthetic becomes apparent. Charlie lets Ruby in on his plan to buy a pink Cadillac, which he wants to rent for wedding ceremonies:

> What I reckon is you get people hiring Rolls-Royce and Daimlers, you know, for weddings and funerals [...], but when have you ever seen a bride come out of an old Norman church and jump straight into a pink Cadillac. [...]. [...] people go to a wedding and everything turns formal. They buy, borrow or rent suits that they would never think of wearing normally, then ponce around waiting for cars none of them have ever ridden in before, and the reason they've never been in a Rolls or a Daimler is they can't afford one, and that's it basically, they have to taste the

27 | In her study *Redneck, Queers, and Country Music* (2014), Nadine Hubbs shows how country music has evolved throughout the twentieth century as being connoted with the "hillbillies" of the South, thus signifying an embarrassing and tainted form of whiteness: "Long heard as an affront by those targeted with it, the word *hillbilly* marks one as being from the country, originally, from Appalachia, and it bears connotations of ignorance and lack of sophistication. Notably, 'hillbilly' was also for thirty years the standard industry label for the music now known as country. The music's name change to 'country and western' in the 1950s recognized *hillbilly*'s derogatory status, but it was not a complete image makeover. Country audiences are still associated with white working-class, provincial, and southern identities, as well as ignorance and, in recent decades, bigotry" (23-24).

28 | During a cab drive, Jeffreys asks the driver (another "skinhead") to switch the radio from the "hillbilly station" playing "country and western" to "some mellow jazz" (*WT* 99).

good life to make the day stand out, drink champagne when they'd prefer a pint. They listen to middle-of-the-road music when they'd prefer something a bit more lively. (*WT* 262)[29]

Instead of aspiring to have at least a fleeting experience of a socially privileged life, Charlie prefers "not taking yourself too seriously": "Imagine coming out in your wedding suit and wedding dress and jumping into a classic pink Yankee, big silver fins and polished chrome, playing Love Me Tender as you drive them to the reception" (*WT* 262). Charlie clearly favours a White Trash Aesthetic that highlights "the out-of-style, the tasteless, the rejects of mainstream society" and "privileges details, brightness, presentation; it fills a lack, covering every empty space with stuff and effect, powerless to do anything but collect junk and show it off" and is thus an "unwritten, folk aesthetic, the true American Primitive" (Sweeney 1997: 250).

In fact, Charlie draws his inspiration directly from American "low" culture – that is, from a trip to Las Vegas for the wedding of his friend, conducted by an Elvis impersonator. This serves as a perfect illustration of Gael Sweeney's observations on Elvis as a white trash icon: "My mate got married and he wanted Elvis to conduct the service. [...]. It worked out cheap and we loved it [...]. [...]. It was the older Elvis, he was wearing a cape and sideburns, then the bride and groom went off in a Cadillac" (*WT* 263). Conspicuously, Charlie adds that "it's not my own idea, but everything is recycled, isn't it" (*WT* 263) – and thus emphasises the quality of the White Trash Aesthetic as "an aesthetic of bricolage, of random experimentation with the bits and pieces of culture" (Sweeney 1997: 250). But Charlie's engagement with the White Trash Aesthetic does not stop here. He also explains how the trashy Las Vegas experience "got me into the rockabilly records I play with the other stuff" (*WT* 263). That is, Charlie has imported a genuinely American sense of the White Trash Aesthetic in the form of the rock music of the South (rockabilly being the hybrid of rock and hillbilly, the former term describing not only the rural population of the South, but also the music genre country and western; see Hubbs

29 | Given the context of his rockabilly fandom, Charlie's obsession with a pink Cadillac is probably a reference to Sammy Master's song "Pink Cadillac" (1955). In addition, the pink Cadillac has become emblematic of Elvis fan culture as this type of car was famously bought by the musician and given to his mother as a present in the 1950s.

2014: 23–24) into his Anglo-British home culture where it blends with the working-class culture of his home country and, it can be said, becomes a cultural-aesthetic refuge from the predicaments of this existence.

In such instances, King's novel becomes readable as a text which is quite aware of the transatlantic dimension of the concept of white trash and which is reflective of its cultural, political and semantic implications. This particular form of transatlantic white trash bricolage is appropriated as an aesthetics of (political) resistance by the subculture depicted in King's novel, which, if not necessarily informing an organised struggle, at least offers a sense of solace – even if this solace primarily consists of consumption and the aforementioned bricolage. This bricolage, in its transatlantic borrowings, presents itself as doubly escapist, for it appropriates the dreams and aesthetic frameworks of *American white trash* (who use it as an escape from their own situation) in reaction to their *British* situation, which, to once more return to Gael Sweeney's observations, highlights the White Trash Aesthetic as an ultimately "castrated aesthetic: it privileges details, brightness, presentation; it fills a lack, covering every empty space with stuff and effect, powerless to do anything but collect junk and show it off" (1997: 250). Here, King's two novels *The Football Factory* and *White Trash* come full circle, since, ultimately, the latter's white trash rockabilly pastiche characters share with the former's white hooligans a sense of political impotence and lack of political agency which leaves both to merely celebrate an aesthetics of excess.

What makes King's *White Trash*, despite or maybe because of all its conceptual and ideological flaws, the ideal text to conclude my study is the awareness of the transatlantic relations connected with the term *white trash*. Even while the novels by Welsh and Griffiths might be more complex and consciously ambivalent in their treatment of tainted whiteness in contemporary Britain, avoiding overt explanations in favour of deliberate semantic openness and contradiction which highlight the messiness of intersectional identities, King nonetheless goes a step beyond Griffiths's intertextual engagement with American representations of white trash by adding more dimensions to his texts' engagement with white trash. Apart from merely observing similarities in the intersections of race and class in American and British cultures which can be subsumed under the common denominator *white trash*, he additionally reflects a particular aesthetics of white trash, and his novel's overtly sympathetic and romanticising engagement with its white trash characters makes the text itself a white trash text, indebted to a "castrated aesthetic" which highlights "brightness and presentation". Here, it is important not to confuse this evaluation with a value statement about the literary status of the novel itself (for example, from the point of view of literary criticism). Rather, my description of King's novel is an attempt to do justice to the way it appropriates a certain form and mode.

This becomes clear towards the end when Ruby, who in her almost ridiculous goodness appears as a kitsch white trash good girl, escapes and defeats the monstrous Jonathan Jeffreys. The experience and her realisation that "she believed in evil now" (*WT* 335) does not leave her entirely traumatised, however, for the novel concludes on a happy note: her new lover Charlie, who a few days before was all too aware that he would never scrounge up the money needed to actually purchase the pink Cadillac of his dreams, had followed a tip from another patient at the hospital and backed a horse called Ruby, and "won enough to buy his Cadillac, it was his dream come true, and he'd had a bit left over, knew how much she liked the puppy in the pet shop, so he'd bought it for her as a present" (*WT* 355). Ruby calls the puppy after her dead childhood dog Ben, and thus the novel concludes: "[...] and she was happy, [...] and Ruby loved the dog and loved Charlie and was so happy it was almost like she'd died and gone to heaven" (*WT* 356). It does not take an unabashedly cynical reader to find this ending rather kitschy, but it might precisely be in this overtly happy conclusion (in terms of aesthetics, it is possibly King's version of a chav wedding) that the novel brings its White Trash Aesthetic full circle by attempting a de-stigmatisation and de-abjectification of white trash figurations by its own low-cultural means.[30] In the case of *White Trash*, the

30 | It could with some justification be argued that the novel's conclusion echoes the similarly (and consciously) kitsch ending of David Lynch's film *Wild at Heart* (1990), another example of conscious bricolage with a focus on white trash culture (including several references to Elvis Presley). Here, after a horrifying descent into human depravity, the film's couple – a romanticised and caricatured version of white trash outlaws – happily reunites under the auspices of a suddenly appearing version of Glinda the Good Witch known from *The Wizard of Oz* (1939). With this ending, contrasting the film's previous hyperbolic depcitions of violence and misery, Lynch elevates American mass-cultural forms of entertainment in the sense of a White Trash Aesthetic (see my reading of the film and its play with genre conventions in Schmitt 2012).

White Trash Aesthetic, with its fascination for junk, bricolage and shrill, 'tasteless' forms and artefacts, thus becomes the means of expression, and maybe even of revenge, of Bauman's "flawed consumer" who, as "human waste", is otherwise condemned to the periphery of the social order. If, as Gael Sweeney writes, "White Trash defines the self by display: it is not afraid to wear its philosophy on a tee-shirt or needlepoint it across a big pillow or proclaim it across the bumper of a pick-up, or tattoo it on an arm" (1997: 250), then this ending is King's version of this display.

Conclusion

During a vacation in Spain, Vince, one of the hooligans in John King's *The Football Factory*, takes the opportunity to try out a distanced perspective on his native country, England, and his everyday life as a working-class man in London, where, as he realises, "the class system was becoming so confused and distorted it took a full-time academic to break it into accurate categories" (*FF* 134). Indeed, Vince's observation offers itself as an appropriate concluding remark to this study as it can be read as a comic meta-comment on both the literary texts' complex representations of contemporary British class formations analysed here and on the theoretical and methodological framework that these analyses require. As I have shown, the intersecting vector of race is one of those factors through which class is distorted. Class runs along the lines of different gradations of whiteness, with class and race standing in – or rather, becoming modalities – for each other at different times.

Particularly by providing an off-centre "misfit" perspective from the margins of the British class system that is inhabited, among others, by today's so-called white trash, these novels testify to a critical awareness of the mechanisms of symbolic boundary work which, through processes of classed and raced abjection, creates figures of social abjection. Welsh and Griffiths in particular demonstrate a tendency towards formal literary experimentation, which serves to reflect and underline the inconsistencies and aporias of identity formations. However, all three writers' work does not merely confine itself to exposing the impossibility of coherent identities by claiming that identities are a purely semiotic affair. Rather, they clearly point towards an aspect which is central for sociological boundary theories, race and class studies – namely, that symbolic processes of boundary formation will inevitably have material effects. This becomes evident in the perfidious logic behind terms such as *white trash* and *chav*, which symbolically condemn those whom these appellations are directed at and thereby contribute to the way these identities are being lived materially. Through these processes of (symbolic) abjection, then, certain parts of the white population are perceived as less white than others.

Thus, what the critical study of abject whiteness and its figurations across discourses reveals is the way that whiteness intersects with other identity categories, the way that it plays out on and around bodies and the way that it situates them within a symbolic framework which exceeds the mere bodily markers of a particular race. In that respect, it is important to consider that whiteness must be thought "both relationally and comparatively" (Garner 2007: 1). For tainted whiteness, this means that we must take into consideration the specific social, cultural and historical contexts within which abject gradations of whiteness can become possible and how they relate to other racially marked identities. For the socio-cultural context that the novels by Welsh, Griffiths and King speak to, this concerns the particular configurations of the Britain of the 1980s to early 2000s. This is the political context of neoliberalism during and after the Thatcher years, which continued to develop throughout the years of New Labour and which has been influential in the post-New Labour era.

The current socio-political situation in the United Kingdom seems to indicate that the critical study of whiteness and class is and will remain a very crucial and timely task. The impending threat of more austerity cuts (the consequences of which are currently being studied within the field of poverty studies),[1] the political situation since the 2015 General Election and especially since the 2016 Brexit referendum as well as the 2014 Scottish independence referendum will all form the foundation upon which British national and cultural identity will be negotiated and defined in the near future. Inevitably, this will have repercussions for the status of class, race and whiteness as they intersect within the construction of British identity.

The matter of abject tainted whiteness, however, must not be viewed as a particular intersection with class that happens in isolation from other raciological factors, affecting merely segments within the white population. Rather, it must be regarded within the larger context of racism. Recently, shortly before the General Elections of 2015 and during the 2016 snap

1 | See my references to the recent work by Korte and Zipp and Korte and Regard in the introduction.

election campaign, an initiative by the non-profit organisation Operation Black Vote (OBV) proved that white cultural hegemony is still an issue in the United Kingdom. The campaign, entitled "Don't Take the Colour out of Britain", was intended to raise awareness for the relatively low election turnout among the black British population and to encourage black citizens to register to vote. Featuring campaign posters depicting black celebrities with their faces painted white, the campaign was designed to "[reverse] the deeply offensive 'Al Jolson' style Black face tradition" ("Don't Take the Colour out of Britain"). The campaign's play with racial colour symbolism in order to direct attention towards the persistent interplay of political dominance, democratic participation and the raciology of contemporary Britain gives lie to the neoliberal notion of post-raciality (see Garner 2016) as much as the figures of the chav and white trash give lie to the post-class society.

In this regard, it proves productive to return to a seminal essay from the 1970s, Ambalavaner Sivanandan's "The Liberation of the Black Intellectual" (1972/1977).[2] Dissecting the position of black British workers within the context of what he describes as the "Europocentrism" of Marxist analyses of the class system, Sivanandan criticises the notion of transracial working-class solidarity:

> In terms of analysis, what the white marxists fail to grasp is that the slave and colonial exploitation of the black peoples of the world was so total and devastating – and so systematic in its devastation – as to make mock of working-class exploitation. [...]. And it is this factor which makes black oppression qualitatively different from the oppression of the white working class. (1977: 340)

Even today, Sivanandan's assessment of the intersection of race and class in the United Kingdom proves timely and productive when considering the persistent intricacies of whiteness and class, especially as they come to the surface in the figures of tainted whiteness. Forty years after Sivanandan's critique of Marxist approaches to race-based exploitation and dominance, the debate on how to merge a Marxist approach with the study of race and ethnicity is still ongoing.[3] As Linda Martín Alcoff recently remarked,

2 | I would like to thank Clive James Nwonka for suggesting Sivanandan's text to me.

3 | See Roediger 2017 for an extensive account of the interrelation of Marxism and Critical Whiteness Studies. Roediger argues that Whiteness Studies origi-

> to have one's labor role based on one's identity was a feudal practice by Marx's definition, and to explain the fact that this practice continues today even in late capitalism requires a theoretical subterfuge if one wants to stay within Marxist terminology. It is understandable, then, that the gendered and racialized nature of labor has been consistently underplayed in the Marxist tradition. (2015: 66)

The critical study of the stigmatisation and abjectification of poor whites should by no means imply comparison of the situation of poor whites with the suffering of blacks under racism or to equate one with the other.

However, I would argue that within the logic of Sivanandan's argument, the consideration of categories like white trash (or its synonyms) and the processes of *intra*-racial white abjectification underlying these categories will ultimately serve the critical assessment and deconstruction of the symbolic mechanisms and boundary constructions of *inter*-racial oppression and abjectification. For, as Sivanandan argues, "the whole structure of white racism is built no doubt on economic exploitation, but it is cemented with white culture. In other words, the racism inherent in white society is *determined* economically, but *defined* culturally" (1977: 340). This mutual reinforcement of material-economic and symbolic factors becomes strikingly visible in the intra-racial abjection evidenced in figurations of white trash. The role of literary analysis within the project of a class-conscious Critical Whiteness Studies, then, must be to trace the processes of signification and figuration that shape these structures, and to pay close attention to the moments where class and race confuse and distort each other.

nated from an engagement with Marxist-materialist approaches to US history, including his own work in labour history, and that the relationship of Marxism and Critical Whiteness Studies needs to be evaluated in the light of recent events such as the Black Lives Matter movement.

Works Cited

Primary Sources

Literary Texts

Dickey, James. *Deliverance*. London: Bloomsbury, 2005 (1970). [=*D*]
Doyle, Roddy. *The Commitments*. London: Vintage, 1990. [=*Com*]
Griffiths, Niall. *Grits*. London: Vintage, 2001 (2000). [=*G*]
—. *Sheepshagger*. London: Vintage, 2002 (2001). [=*Sh*]
—. *Kelly+ Victor*. London: Vintage, 2003 (2002).
—. *Stump*. London: Vintage, 2004 (2003). [=*St*]
King, John. *The Football Factory*. London: Vintage, 1997 (1996). [=*FF*]
—. *White Trash*. London: Vintage, 2002 (2001). [=*WT*]
McCarthy, Cormac. *Child of God*. Basingstoke and Oxford: Picador, 1989 (1973). [=*CG*]
—. *Suttree*. New York: Vintage, 1992 (1979). [=*Su*]
McEwan, Ian. *Saturday*. London: Vintage, 2006 (2005). [=*Sat*]
Thirsk, Simon. *Not Quite White*. Llandysul: Gomer Press, 2010. [=*NQW*]
Welsh, Irvine. "Eurotrash." *The Acid House*. London, New York: W.W. Norton, 1995 (1994). 10–31. [=*AC*]
—. *Filth*. London: Vintage, 1999 (1998). [=*Fi*]
—. *Marabou Stork Nightmares*. London: Vintage, 2004 (1995). [=*MSN*]
—. *Porno*. London: Vintage, 2008 (2002). [=*P*]
—. *Skagboys*. London: Jonathan Cape, 2012. [=*Sk*]
—. *Trainspotting*. London: Vintage, 2004 (1993). [=*T*]

Films

Baird, Jon S., dir. *Filth*. Perf. James McAvoy. Lionsgate, 2013.
Boorman, John, dir. *Deliverance*. Perf. John Voight. Warner Bros., 1972.

Lynch, David, dir. *Wild at Heart*. Perf. Nicolas Cage. The Samuel Goldwyn Company, 1990.

Pasolini, Pier Paolo, dir. *Salò, or the 120 Days of Sodom*. Perf. Paolo Bonacelli. United Artists, 1975.

Secondary Sources

Aanerud, Rebecca. "Fictions of Whiteness: Speaking the Names of Whiteness in U.S. Literature." *Displacing Whiteness: Essays in Social and Cultural Criticism*. Ed. Ruth Frankenberg. Durham/London: Duke University Press, 1997, 35–59.

Ahmed, Sara. *The Cultural Politics of Emotion*. Edinburgh: Edinburgh University Press, 2004. [=2004a]

—. "Declarations of Whiteness: The Non-Performativity of Anti-Racism." *Borderlands E-Journal*, vol. 3, no. 2, 2004, www.borderlands.net.au/vol3no2_2004/ahmed_declarations.htm Accessed 29 November 2017. [=2004b]

Alcoff, Linda Martín. *The Future of Whiteness*. Cambridge, Malden: Polity, 2015.

Allen, Nicola. *Marginality in the Contemporary British Novel*. London/New York: Continuum, 2008.

Anderson, Jon. *Page and Place: Ongoing Compositions of Plot*. Amsterdam/New York: Rodopi, 2014.

Baker, Stephanie Alice. "Policing the Riots: New Social Media as Recruitment, Resistance, and Surveillance." *The English Riots of 2011: A Summer of Discontent*. Ed. Daniel Briggs. London: Waterside Press, 2012, 169–190.

Bakhtin, Mikhail. *Rabelais and His World*. Cambridge, MA: The MIT Press, 1968.

Bauman, Zygmunt. *Wasted Lives: Modernity and Its Outcasts*. Cambridge: Polity Press, 2004.

BBC Newsnight. 13 August 2011. BBC, 2011. www.bbc.com/news/av/uk-14513517/england-riots-the-whites-have-become-black-says-david-starkey. Accessed 29 Sept. 2015.

Bednarski, Aleksander. "Wales in a Mirror: Welsh Social and Cultural Issues in Niall Griffiths's *Sheepshagger*." *Literature in Society*. Ed.

Regina Rudaitytė. Newcastle upon Tyne: Cambridge Scholars, 2012, 111–124. [=2012a]

—. *Inherent Myth: Wales in Niall Griffiths's Fiction.* Lublin: Wydawnictwo KUL, 2012. [=2012b]

Bernardi, Daniel. "Race and the Hollywood Style." *Classic Hollywood, Classic Whiteness.* Ed. Daniel Bernardi. Minneapolis/London: University of Minneapolis Press, 2001, xiii–xxvi.

Biressi, Anna, and Heather Nunn. *Class and Contemporary British Culture.* Houndmills, Basingstoke/New York: Palgrave Macmillan, 2013.

Bohata, Kirsti. *Postcolonialism Revisited.* Cardiff: University of Wales Press, 2004.

Bonnett, Alastair. *White Identities: Historical and International Perspectives.* London/New York et al. Prentice Hall, 2000.

Brannigan, John. *Orwell to the Present: Literature in England 1945–2000.* London: Palgrave Macmillan, 2003.

—. *New Historicism and Cultural Materialism.* Houndmills, Basingstoke/New York: Palgrave Macmillan, 1998.

—. *Race in Modern Irish Literature and Culture.* Edinburgh: Edinburgh University Press, 2009.

Briggs, Daniel, ed. *The English Riots of 2011: A Summer of Discontent.* London: Waterside Press, 2012.

Buford, Bill. *Among the Thugs.* London: Arrow Books, 2001 (1991).

Butler, Judith. *Excitable Speech: A Politics of the Performative.* London/New York: Routledge, 1997.

—. *Bodies that Matter: On the Discursive Limits of 'Sex'.* London/New York: Routledge, 2011 (1993).

Carr, Duane R. "The Dispossessed White as Naked Ape and Stereotyped Hillbilly in the Southern Novels of Cormac McCarthy." *The Midwest Quarterly*, vol. 40, no. 1, 1998, 9–20.

Castañeda, Claudia. *Figurations: Child, Bodies, Worlds.* Durham: Duke University Press, 2002.

Center on Democracy in a Multiracial Society, ed. *Towards a Bibliography of Critical Whiteness Studies.* University of Illinois at Urbana-Champaign, 2006. thekeep.eiu.edu/eng_fac/51. Accessed 30 Sept. 2015.

Cohen, Jeffrey J. Preface. "In a Time of Monsters." *Monster Theory: Reading Culture.* Ed. Jeffrey J. Cohen. Minneapolis: University of Minnesota Press, 1996, vii–xiii. [=1996a]

—. "Monster Culture (Seven Theses)." *Monster Theory: Reading Culture.* Ed. Jeffrey J. Cohen. Minneapolis: University of Minnesota Press, 1996, 3–25. [=1996b]

Colebrook, Martyn. "Literary History of the Decade: Fictions from the Borderlands." *The 2000s: A Decade of Contemporary British Fiction.* Eds. Nick Bentley, Nick Hubble and Leigh Wilson. London: Bloomsbury, 2016, 27–51.

Collins, Michael. *The Likes of Us: A Biography of the White Working Class.* London: Granta, 2004.

Cooper, Lydia R. "McCarthy, Tennessee, and the Southern Gothic." *The Cambridge Companion to Cormac McCarthy.* Ed. Steven Frye. Cambridge: Cambridge University Press, 2013, 41–53.

Crabbe, Tim, and Adam Brown. "'You're not welcome anymore': The Football Crowd, Class and Social Exclusion." *British Football and Social Exclusion.* Ed. Stephen Wagg. London, New York: Routledge, 2004, 26–46.

Craig, Cairns. *The Modern Scottish Novel: Narrative and the National Imagination.* Edinburgh: Edinburgh University Press, 1999.

Crawford, Robert. *Devolving English Literature.* Edinburgh: Edinburgh University Press, 2000.

Davison, Sally, and George Shire. "Race, Migration and Neoliberalism." *After Neoliberalism?* London: Soundings, 2013, 1–16.

Day, Gary. *Class.* London/New York: Routledge, 2001.

Deleuze, Gilles. *Negotiations 1972–1990.* New York: Columbia University Press, 1995.

Deleuze, Gilles, and Félix Guattari. *A Thousand Plateaus: Capitalism and Schizophrenia II.* London: Continuum, 2004.

—. *Anti-Oedipus: Capitalism and Schizophrenia I.* London: Penguin, 2009.

del Valle Alcalá, Roberto. *British Working-Class Fiction: Narratives of Refusal and the Struggle Against Work.* London: Bloomsbury, 2016.

Dix, Hywel. *After Raymond Williams: Cultural Materialism and the Break-Up of Britain.* Cardiff: University of Wales Press, 2008.

Driscoll, Lawrence. *Evading Class in Contemporary British Literature.* New York: Palgrave Macmillan, 2009.

Dyer, Richard. *White.* London, New York: Routledge, 1997.

Eckstein, Lars. "Saturday on Dover Beach: Ian McEwan, Matthew Arnold, and Post-9/11 Melancholia." *Hard Times: Deutsch-englische Zeitschrift*, vol. 89, 2011, 6–10.

Emig, Rainer. "Von Neds und Chavs: Britische Jugend zwischen Ignoranz, Kreativität und Widerstand." *Ignoranz: Nichtwissen, Vergessen und Missverstehen in Prozessen kultureller Transformationen*. Ed. Achim Geisenhanslüke and Hans Rott. Bielefeld: transcript, 2008, 153–174.

Feldman, Keith P. "The Globality of Whiteness in Post-Racial Visual Culture." *Cultural Studies*, 2015, 1–23.

Foucault, Michel. "Of Other Spaces." *Diacritics*, vol. 16, 1986, 22–27.

—. *Abnormal: Lectures at the Collège de France 1974–1975*. New York: Picador, 2003.

—. *The Birth of Biopolitics: Lectures at the Collège de France, 1978–79*. Houndmills/Basingstoke, New York: Palgrave, 2008.

Frankenberg, Ruth. *White Women, Race Matters: The Social Construction of Whiteness*. Minneapolis: University of Minnesota Press, 1993.

Frye, Steven. *Understanding Cormac McCarthy*. Columbia: University of South Carolina Press, 2009.

—, ed. *The Cambridge Companion to Cormac McCarthy*. Cambridge: Cambridge University Press, 2013.

"'Future? What Fucking Future?' The British Estate Where 'Healthy' Life Expectancy Is Just 58.8 Years." *Daily Mail*, 12 February 2011. www.dailymail.co.uk/news/article-1356247/Gurnos-Merthyr-Tydfil-The-British-estate-healthy-life-expectancy-just-58-8-years.html. Accessed 29 Sept. 2015.

Gardiner, Michael. *The Cultural Roots of British Devolution*. Edinburgh: Edinburgh University Press, 2004.

—. *The Return of England in English Literature*. Houndmills, Basingstoke; New York: Palgrave Macmillan, 2012.

—. *The Constitution of English Literature: The State, the Nation, and the Canon*. London: Bloomsbury, 2013.

Garner, Steve. *Whiteness: An Introduction*. London/New York: Routledge, 2007.

—. "A Moral Economy of Whiteness: Behaviours, Belonging and Britishness." *Ethnicities*, vol. 12, no. 4, 2012, 445–464.

—. *A Moral Economy of Whiteness: Four Frames of Racialising Discourse*. London/New York: Routledge, 2016.

Gavron, Kate. Foreword. *Who Cares about the White Working Class?* Ed. Kjartan P. Sveinsson. London: The Runnymede Trust, 2009, 2.

Gilroy, Paul. *Between Camps: Nations, Cultures and the Allure of Race.* London, New York: Routledge, 2004.

—. *Postcolonial Melancholia.* New York: Columbia University Press, 2006.

Gilroy, Paul. *There Ain't No Black in the Union Jack: The Cultural Politics of 'Race' and Nation.* London, New York: Routledge, 2002 (1987/1992).

Goad, Jim. *The Redneck Manifesto: How Hillbillies, Hicks, and White Trash Became America's Scapegoats.* New York/London: Simon & Schuster, 1997.

Gramich, Katie. "Pimps, Punks and Pub Crooners: Anarchy and Anarchism in Contemporary Welsh Fiction." *To Hell with Culture: Anarchism and Twentieth-Century British Literature.* Ed. H. Gustav Klaus and Stephen Knight. Cardiff: University of Wales Press, 2005, 178–193.

Grammer, John M. "A Thing Against Which Time Will Not Prevail: Pastoral and History in Cormac McCarthy's South." *Perspectives on Cormac McCarthy.* Ed. Edwin T. Arnold and Dianne C. Luce. Jackson: University Press of Mississippi, 1999, 29–44.

Griffin, Gabriele, and Rosi Braidotti. "Whiteness and European Situatedness." *Thinking Differently: A Reader in European Women's Studies.* Ed. Gabriele Griffin and Rosi Braidotti. London/New York: Zed Books, 2002, 221–36.

Griffiths, Niall. "Paradise Is on the End of Your Nose: Voices from the Outer Dark in Contemporary British Fiction." Unpublished manuscript of inaugural lecture given at the University of Wolverhampton 8 Dec 2014. University of Wolverhampton, 2014.

Guillemin, Georg. *The Pastoral Vision of Cormac McCarthy.* College Station: Texas A&M University Press, 2004.

Hall, Stuart. "Race, Articulation and Societies Structured in Dominance." *Sociological Theories: Race and Colonialism.* Paris: UNESCO Paris, 1980, 305–345.

—. *The Hard Road to Renewal: Thatcherism and the Crisis of the Left.* London: Verso, 1988.

—. "A Sense of Classlessness." 1958. *Selected Political Writings: The Great Moving Right Show and Other Essays.* Ed. Sally Davison, David Featherstone, Michael Rustin and Bill Schwarz. Durham: Duke University Press, 2017, 28–46.

Hall, Stuart, Doreen Massey, and Michael Rustin, eds. *After Neoliberalism?: The Kilburn Manifesto.* London: Soundings, 2013. [=2013b]

—. "After Neoliberalism: Analysing the Present." *After Neoliberalism?: The Kilburn Manifesto.* Ed. Stuart Hall, Doreen Massey, and Michael Rustin. London: Soundings, 2013, 3–19. [=2013a]

Hartigan, J. *Odd Tribes: Toward a Cultural Analysis of White People.* Durham: Duke University Press, 2007.

Haylett, Chris. "Illegitimate Subjects?: Abject Whites, Neo-Liberal Modernisation and Middle-Class Multiculturalism." *Environment and Planning: Society and Space,* no. 19, 2001, 351–370.

Hayward, Keith and Majid Yar. "The 'Chav' Phenomenon: Consumption, Media and the Construction of a New Underclass." *Crime, Media, Culture,* vol. 2, no. 9, 2006, 9–28.

Heinz, Sarah. "The Relative Skin: Whiteness in Contemporary Irish Literature and Film." Unpublished habilitation thesis. University of Mannheim, 2013.

Helbig, Jörg. "Losers, Liars, Junkies and Hooligans: Irvine Welsh's *Trainspotting* and Related British Novels of the 1990s." *Towards a Dialogic Anglistics.* Ed. Werner Delanoy, Jörg Helbig, Allan James. Vienna, Berlin: Lit, 2007, 221–232.

Herbrechter, Stefan. "From *Trainspotting* to *Filth*: Masculinity and Cultural Politics in Irvine Welsh's Writings." *Subverting Masculinity: Hegemonic and Alternative Versions of Masculinity in Contemporary Culture.* Ed. Russell West and Frank Lay. Amsterdam: Rodopi, 2000, 109–127.

Hester, Helen. "Weaponizing Prurience." *Narrating Poverty and Precarity in Britain.* Ed. Barbara Korte and Frédéric Regard. Berlin, Boston: de Gruyter, 2014, 205–224.

Hoggart, Richard. *The Uses of Literacy: Aspects of Working-Class Life with Special Reference to Publications and Entertainments.* Harmondsworth: Penguin, 1968.

Hologa, Marie. *Scotland the Brave?: Deconstructing Scottish Nationalism in Contemporary Scottish Novels.* Trier: WVT, 2016.

Hubbs, Nadine. *Rednecks, Queers, and Country Music.* Berkeley: University of California Press, 2014.

Ignatiev, Noel. *How the Irish Became White.* London, New York: Routledge, 2009 (1995).

Ingham, Roger, et al. *Football Hooliganism: The Wider Context.* London: Inter-Action Imprint, 1978.

Jones, Carole. "White Men on Their Backs – From Objection to Abjection: The Representation of the White Male as Victim in William McIlvanney's *Docherty* and Irvine Welsh's *Marabou Stork Nightmares*." *International Journal of Scottish Literature*, vol. 1, 2006. www.ijsl.stir.ac.uk/issue1/jones.htm . Accessed 21 Mar. 2015.

Jones, Owen. *Chavs: The Demonization of the Working Class*. London: Verso, 2011.

Kelly, Aaron. *Irvine Welsh: Contemporary British Novelists*. Manchester: Manchester University Press, 2005.

Keyes, Jarrad. "'Archaeologies of the Future': Niall Griffiths – Pathways of the Urban." *The Idea of the City: Early-Modern, Modern and Post-Modern Locations and Communities*. Ed. Joan Fitzpatrick. Newcastle-upon-Tyne: Cambridge Scholars Publishing, 2009, 133–143.

—. "Delineating the Urban: The Global City and the Logics of Dissolution." *Transtext(e)s Transcultures: Journal of Global Cultural Studies*, vol. 3, 2007, 98–118.

Korte, Barbara, and Frédéric Regard, eds. *Narrating "Precariousness": Modes, Media, Ethics*. Heidelberg: Winter, 2014. [=2014a]

—, eds. *Narrating Poverty and Precarity in Britain*. Berlin, Boston: Walter de Gruyter, 2014. [=2014b]

Korte, Barbara, and Georg Zipp. *Poverty in Contemporary Literature: Themes and Figurations on the British Book Market*. Houndmills/Basingstoke: Palgrave, 2014.

Kristeva, Julia. *Powers of Horror: An Essay on Abjection*. New York: Columbia University Press, 1982.

Lehner, Stefanie. "'Dangerous Liaisons': Gender Politics in the Contemporary Scottish and Irish ImagiNation." *Scottish Literature and Postcolonial Literature: Comparative Texts and Critical Perspectives*. Ed. Michael Gardiner, Graeme Macdonald and Niall O'Gallagher. Edinburgh: Edinburgh University Press, 2011. 221–233.

Levine-Rasky, Cynthia. *Whiteness Fractured*. Surrey: Ashgate, 2013.

Liebig, Steffen. "Die Unruhen von 2011 im Spiegel von Politik und Medien." *Hard Times: Deutsch-englische Zeitschrift*, vol. 96, 2014, 2–7.

—. "Soziale Unruhen als nicht-normierte Konflikte: Das Beispiel der englischen Riots von 2011." *Prokla*, vol. 44, no. 2. 175, 2014, 271–287.

Lincoln, Kenneth. *Cormac McCarthy: American Canticles*. Houndmills, Basingstoke: Palgrave Macmillan, 2009.

Link, Jürgen. *Normale Krisen?: Normalismus und die Krise der Gegenwart.* Konstanz: Konstanz University Press, 2013.

Malchow, H.L. *Gothic Images of Race in Nineteenth-Century Britain.* Stanford: Stanford University Press, 1996.

March, Cristie L. *Rewriting Scotland: Welsh, McLean, Warner, Banks, Galloway, and Kennedy.* Manchester, New York: Manchester University Press, 2002.

Marks, John. "Control Society." *The Deleuze Dictionary.* Ed. Adrian Parr. Edinburgh: Edinburgh University Press, 2010, 55–57.

Marriott, John. "In Darkest England: The Poor, the Crowd, and Race in the Nineteenth-Century Metropolis." *New Ethnicities, Old Racisms?* Ed. Phil Cohen. London, New York: Zed Books, 1999, 82–100.

Mayer, Uwe. "Violent Criminals and Noble Savages: The Filmic Representation of Football Hooliganism as a Quest for Authenticity." *Paradoxes of Authenticity: Studies on a Critical Concept.* Ed. Julia Straub. Bielefeld: transcript, 2012, 185–200.

McClintock, Anne. *Imperial Leather: Race, Gender and Sexuality in the Colonial Contest.* London, New York: Routledge, 1995.

McGuire, Matt. "Welsh's Novels." *The Edinburgh Companion to Irvine Welsh.* Ed. Berthold Schoene. Edinburgh: Edinburgh University Press, 2010, 19–30.

McLaughlin, Eugene. "Recovering Blackness/Repudiating Whiteness: The *Daily Mail*'s Construction of the Five White Suspects Accused of the Racist Murder of Stephen Lawrence." *Racialization: Studies in Theory and Practice.* Ed. Karim a. J.S. Murji. Oxford: Oxford University Press, 2005, 163–183.

Mergenthal, Silvia. "England's Finest – Battle Fields and Football Grounds in John King's Football Novels." *War and the Cultural Construction of Identities in Britain.* Ed. Barbara Korte, Ralf Schneider. Amsterdam, New York: Rodopi, 2002. 262–268.

Mezey, Jason. "The Gospel of *Gandhi*: Whiteness and State Narcissism in Thatcherite England." *Thatcher & After: Margaret Thatcher and Her Afterlife in Contemporary Culture.* Ed. Louisa Hadley, Elizabeth Ho. Houndmills Basingstoke: Palgrave, 2010, 75–95.

Miller, Gavin. "Welsh and Identity Politics." *The Edinburgh Companion to Irvine Welsh.* Ed. Berthold Schoene. Edinburgh: Edinburgh University Press, 2010, 89–99.

Moore, Suzanne. "Here Come the Cuts...and the New Class War." *Daily Mail Online*, 18 Jan. 2010. www.dailymail.co.uk/debate/article-1243743/SUZANNE-MOORE-Here-come-cuts--new-class-war.html. Accessed 29 Sept. 2015.

—. "Debating the Word 'Chav' Is Irrelevant to the Working-Class Experience." *The Guardian*, 4 Jul. 2011. www.theguardian.com/commentisfree/2011/jun/04/suzanne-moore-chavs-working-class. Accessed 29 Sept. 2015.

Morace, Robert A. *Irvine Welsh*. Houndmills, Basingstoke: Palgrave Macmillan, 2007.

Morrison, Toni. *Playing in the Dark: Whiteness and the Literary Imagination*. Cambridge, MA: Harvard University Press, 1992.

Mota, Miguel. "Boys Will Be Hooligans: History and Masculine Communities in John King's *England Away*." *Critique: Studies in Contemporary Fiction*, vol. 50, no. 3, 2009, 261–273.

Moynihan, Sinéad. *Passing Into the Present: Contemporary American Fiction of Racial and Gender Passing*. Manchester/New York: Manchester University Press, 2010.

Murray, Charles. *The Emerging British Underclass*. London, 1990.

Nash, Jennifer C. "Re-Thinking Intersectionality." *Feminist Review*, vol. 89, 2008, 1–15.

Nayak, Anoop. *Race, Place and Globalization: Youth Cultures in a Changing World*. Oxford, New York: Berg, 2003.

—. "Beyond the Pale: Chavs, Youth and Social Class." *Who Cares about the White Working Class?* Ed. Kjartan P. Sveinsson. London: Runnymede Trust, 2009. 28–35.

Niro, Brian. *Race*. Houndmills, Basingstoke; New York: Palgrave Macmillan, 2003.

O'Connor, Flannery. "Some Aspects of the Grotesque in Southern Fiction." *Mystery and Manners: Occasional Prose*. Ed. Flannery O'Connor. London, Boston: Faber and Faber, 1972, 36–50.

Penley, Constance. "Crackers and Whackers: The White Trashing of Porn." *Porn Studies*. Ed. Linda Williams. Durham, London: Duke University Press, 2004, 309–331.

Piskurek, Cyprian. "Slum Sport, Slum People? Fictional Representations of Football and Its Fan Cultures after the Taylor Report." Unpublished dissertation thesis. TU Dortmund University, 2015.

Pollard, Stephen. "The Class War Is Over – Do Tell Labour." *The Telegraph*, 11 Sept. 2008. www.telegraph.co.uk/comment/personal-view/3562065/The-class-war-is-over-do-tell-Labour.html. Accessed 29 Sept. 2015.

Rattansi, Ali. *Racism: A Very Short Introduction*. Oxford: Oxford University Press, 2007.

Redhead, Steve. "Hit and Tell: A Review Essay on the Soccer Hooligan Memoir." *Soccer and Society*, vol. 5, no. 3, 2004, 392–403.

—. "This Sporting Life: The Realism of *The Football Factory*." *Soccer and Society*, vol. 8, no. 1, 2007: 90–108.

Rhodes, James. "'It's Not Just Them, It's Whites as Well': Whiteness, Class and BNP Support." *Sociology*, vol. 45, no. 1, 2011, 102–117.

Roberts, Harri G. "A Tower of Babel: Heteroglossia, the Grotesque and the (De)construction of Meaning in Glyn Jones's *The Valley, the City, the Village* and Niall Griffiths's *Grits*." *Welsh Writing in English*, vol. 7, 2002, 106–129.

—. *Embodied Identity: Representations of the Body in Welsh Literature*. Cardiff: University of Wales Press, 2009.

Robertson, Sarah. "The Green, Green Hills of Home: Mining in the Fiction of Appalachia and Wales." *Transatlantic Exchanges: The American South in Europe – Europe in the American South*. Ed. Richard Gray and Waldemar Zacharasiewicz. Vienna: ÖAW, 2007, 503–518.

Robinson, Amy. "It Takes One to Know One: Passing and Communities of Common Interest." *Critical Inquiry*, vol. 20, no. 4, 1994, 715–736.

Roediger, David R. *Race, Class, and Marxism*. London, New York: Verso, 2017.

Schmitt, Mark. "Redneck Apocalypse: Der amerikanische Süden als Raum des Anderen in Literatur und Film." *Geopolitische Fiktionen: Beobachtungen in Moderne und Gegenwart*. Ed. Linda Simonis. Essen: Ch. A. Bachmann, 2010. 55–72.

—. "Lynchian Road Movies: David Lynchs Spiel mit der Wissensordnung eines Genres am Beispiel von *Wild at Heart* and *The Straight Story*." *Kino der Blinden: Figurationen des Nichtwissens bei David Lynch*. Ed. Achim Geisenhanslüke and Rasmus Overthun. Bielefeld: transcript, 2012, 207–230.

—. "'A world separate yet within': Welsh Devolution and the Paradoxes of Post-British Community in Niall Griffiths's *Sheepshagger*." *Anglistik: International Journal of English Studies*, vol. 26, no. 1, 2015, 93–102.

Schoene, Berthold, ed. *The Edinburgh Companion to Irvine Welsh*. Edinburgh: Edinburgh University Press, 2010. [=2010a]

—. Introduction. *The Edinburgh Companion to Irvine Welsh*. Ed. Berthold Schoene. Edinburgh: Edinburgh University Press, 2010, 1–8. [=2010b]

Schoene-Harwood, Berthold. *Writing Men: Literary Masculinities from Frankenstein to the New Man*. Edinburgh: Edinburgh University Press, 2000.

Scott, Jeremy. *The Demotic Voice in Contemporary British Fiction*. London: Palgrave Macmillan, 2009.

Share, Bernard. *Slanguage: A Dictionary of Irish Slang and Colloquial English in Ireland*. Dublin: Gill & Macmillan, 2005.

Sinfield, Alan. *Literature, Politics and Culture in Postwar Britain*. London, New York: Continuum, 2004 (1997).

Sivanandan, Ambalavaner. "The Liberation of the Black Intellectual." *Race & Class*, vol. 18, no. 4, 1977, 329–343.

Skeggs, Beverley. *Formations of Class & Gender: Becoming Respectable*. London: Sage, 1997.

—. *Class, Self, Culture*. London, New York: Routledge, 2004.

Stallybrass, Peter and Allon White. *The Politics and Poetics of Transgression*. London: Methuen, 1986.

Steyn, Melissa. *'Whiteness Just Isn't What It Used to Be': White Identity in a Changing South Africa*. New York: SUNY Press, 2001.

Street, Alice, and Simon Coleman. "Introduction: Real and Imagined Spaces." *Space and Culture*, vol. 15, no. 1, 2012, 4–17.

Stubblefield, Anna. "'Beyond the Pale': Tainted Whiteness, Cognitive Disability, and Eugenic Sterilization." *Hypatia: A Journal of Feminist Philosophy*, vol. 22, no. 2, 2007, 162–181.

Stubbs, David. *1996 & The End of History*. London: Repeater Books, 2016.

Sveinsson, Kjartan P. Introduction. "The White Working Class and Multiculturalism: Is There Space for a Progressive Agenda?" *Who Cares about the White Working Class?* Ed. Kjartan P. Sveinsson. London: The Runnymede Trust, 2009, 3–6.

—, ed. *Who Cares about the White Working Class?* London: The Runnymede Trust, 2009.

Sweeney, Gael. "The King of White Trash Culture: Elvis Presley and the Aesthetics of Excess." *White Trash: Race and Class in America*. Ed. Annalee Newitz and Matt Wray. New York: Routledge, 1997, 249–266.

Taylor, Yvette. Introduction. *Classed Intersections: Spaces, Selves, Knowledges*. Ed. Yvette Taylor. Surrey/Burlington: Ashgate, 2010. 1–10.

Thomson, Mathew. *The Problem of Mental Deficiency: Eugenics, Democracy, and Social Policy in Britain c. 1870–1959*. Oxford: Clarendon Press, 1998.

Tyler, Imogen. "Chav Mum Chav Scum." *Feminist Media Studies*, vol. 8, no. 1, 2008, 17–34.

—. *Revolting Subjects: Social Abjection and Resistance in Neoliberal Britain*. London, New York: Zed Books, 2013.

Virdee, Satnam. *Race, Class and the Racialized Outsider*. Houndsmills: Palgrave, 2014.

Wacquant, Loïc. *Urban Outcasts: A Comparative Sociology of Advanced Marginality*. Cambridge: Polity, 2008.

Ware, Vron. "Perfidious Albion: Whiteness and the International Imagination." *The Making and Unmaking of Whiteness*. Ed. Birgit B. Rasmussen, et al. Durham/London: Duke University Press, 2001. 184–213.

Welshman, John. *Underclass: A History of the Excluded 1880–2000*. London: Hambledon Continuum, 2006.

Westergaard, John. *Who Gets What?: The Hardening of Class Inequality in the Late Twentieth Century*. Cambridge: Polity Press, 1995.

White, Paul, Alexandra Hillman, and Joanna Latimer. "Ordering, Enrolling, and Dismissing: Moments of Access Across Hospital Spaces." *Space and Culture*, vol. 15, no. 1, 2012, 68–87.

The White Season. BBC Two, 2007. www.bbc.co.uk/pressoffice/pressreleases/stories/2007/11_november/20/bbctwo_white.shtml. 29 Sept. 2015.

Whyte, Christopher. "Masculinities in Contemporary Scottish Fiction." *Forum of Modern Language Studies*, vol. 34, no. 3, 1998, 274–285.

Williams, Charlotte. "The Melting Pot and the British Meltdown." *Breaking up Britain: Four Nations after a Union*. Ed. Mark Perryman. London: Lawrence & Wishart, 2009, 68–75.

Williams, Raymond. *Who Speaks for Wales?: Nation, Culture, Identity*. Cardiff: University of Wales Press, 2003.

Wray, Matt. *Not Quite White: White Trash and the Boundaries of Whiteness*. Durham: Duke University Press, 2006.

Zerweck, Bruno. "Historicizing Unreliable Narration: Unreliability and Cultural Discourse in Narrative Fiction." *Style*, vol. 35, no. 1, 2001, 151–178.

Social Sciences and Cultural Studies

Ramón Reichert, Annika Richterich, Pablo Abend, Mathias Fuchs, Karin Wenz (eds.)

Digital Culture & Society (DCS)

Vol. 1, Issue 1 – Digital Material/ism

2015, 242 p., pb.
29,99 € (DE), 978-3-8376-3153-1
E-Book: 29,99 € (DE), ISBN 978-3-8394-3153-5

Ilker Ataç, Gerda Heck, Sabine Hess, Zeynep Kasli, Philipp Ratfisch, Cavidan Soykan, Bediz Yilmaz (eds.)

movements. Journal for Critical Migration and Border Regime Studies

Vol. 3, Issue 2/2017: Turkey's Changing Migration Regime and its Global and Regional Dynamics

November 2017, 230 p., pb.
24,99 € (DE), 978-3-8376-3719-9

Annika Richterich, Karin Wenz, Pablo Abend, Mathias Fuchs, Ramón Reichert (eds.)

Digital Culture & Society (DCS)

Vol. 3, Issue 1/2017 – Making and Hacking

June 2017, 198 p., pb.
29,99 € (DE), 978-3-8376-3820-2
E-Book: 29,99 € (DE), ISBN 978-3-8394-3820-6

All print, e-book and open access versions of the titles in our list are available in our online shop www.transcript-verlag.de/en!